Talcott Parsons and the Capitalist Nation-State
Political Sociology as a Strategic Vocation

Departing from the conventional 'presentist' and 'historicist' interpretations of Parsons's work, this book argues that he can best be viewed
as an activist thinker whose practical concerns derived from his
commitment to the redemptive principles of liberal Calvinism. Confronting the chronic instability of competitive capitalism (the 'Hobbesian problem of order'), Parsons sought to found a practical standpoint
from which the professionalized social sciences could contribute to the
rationalization of the capitalist social order.

In adapting the 'primary' patterns of disinterestedness, universalism,
affective neutrality, and functional specificity from medicine to the
social sciences, he developed a set of categories of intended practical
relevance to the growth and consolidation of the capitalist nation-state.
This set of categories was given social and political specification
through Parsons's engagement with problems of 'national morale' in the
United States during the Second World War and through his efforts to
enhance the credibility of the social sciences during the early years of
the Cold War.

In the 1950s, the same 'primary' patterns became inscribed into the
sub-disciplinary standpoint of political sociology, a convergence between political thought and sociology. Gabriel Almond and Seymour
Lipset generated approaches that were capable not only of producing
knowledge of relevance to the consolidation and spread of the American
socio-political system, but of attracting Ford Foundation funding
earmarked for strategically pertinent 'behavioral' scientific research. In
the wake of increasing turbulence in the 1960s, however, Parsons's
theories were rejected for practical reasons and the union between
political science and sociology was dissolved, each turning to a variant
of 'political engineering.'

The emergence and growth of a practically conceived political
sociology reveals the inadequacies of those models of social-scientific
change derived from Thomas Kuhn's *Structure of Scientific Revolutions*. Suggestions for how social-scientific practice might be redirected
along more critical and emancipatory lines are based on the analysis of
how the social sciences have complemented the growth and consolidation of the capitalist nation-state.

WILLIAM BUXTON teaches sociology at the University of New Brunswick.

WILLIAM BUXTON

Talcott Parsons and the Capitalist Nation-State
Political sociology as a strategic vocation

UNIVERSITY OF TORONTO PRESS

Toronto Buffalo London

© University of Toronto Press 1985
Toronto Buffalo London

Printed in Canada

ISBN 0-8020-5633-4 (cloth)
ISBN 0-8020-6531-7 (paper)

_____

Canadian Cataloguing in Publication Data

Buxton, William, 1947–
  Talcott Parsons and the capitalist nation-state

  Bibliography: p.
  Includes index.
  ISBN 0-8020-5633-4 (bound). – ISBN 0-8020-6531-7 (pbk.)

  1. Parsons, Talcott, 1902–   2. Political
  sociology.   3. Sociology – United States – History.
  I. Title.

  JA76.B89 1985   306'.2'0924   C85-098761-X

_____

Cover photograph courtesy of the Harvard University Archives

This book has been published with the help of a grant from the Social
Science Federation of Canada, using funds provided by the Social
Sciences and Humanities Research Council of Canada, and from the
Publications Fund of the University of Toronto Press.

I dedicate this book to my mother,

Dorothy Lee Buxton,

and to the memory of my father,

Dr Earl W. Buxton

Contents

Preface

This book has its origins in two long-standing interests of mine: political sociology and the sociology of knowledge. My initial attraction to the two fields grew out of my radicalization in the early 1970s while studying at Oxford University, the London School of Economics and Political Science, and Die Freie Universität Berlin. Specifically, I became committed to democratic socialism as the form of political and economic organization most consistent with principles of social justice, equality, and human freedom. Political sociology, as a comparative-historical study of power in its social context, provided insights into how domination has been exercised, anbd how it could be challenged and transformed. My growing conviction that the form of domination practised in capitalist democracies was socially constructed, rather than necessary and inevitable, awakened my interest in the sociology of knowledge. If indeed domination of this kind was constituted through human agency, then its maintenance and reproduction rested in turn upon patterned actions as mediated by ideologies and belief systems. The sociology of knowledge, as the study of how human thought and action are socially contingent, bore the promise of providing political sociology with a self-reflective dimension. In studying how domination in capitalist democracies was constituted through human agency, one was obliged to pay close attention not only to ideas and their consequences, but also to how intellectual activity might be directed in more radically and critically disposed directions.

My interests in the two fields began to coalesce while studying for a master's degree in political sociology at the London School of Economics. It became evident to me that a particular kind of political sociology – i.e., that which concerned itself with the social basis of 'democratic' politics – had attained ascendancy. In my view, the field was questionable not only for its substantive claims, but for the kind of intellectual engagement it implied, namely, generating knowledge about how capitalist democracy could be sustained and cultivated. This concern with the intellectual foundations of political sociology led me to write my required master's essay on how Thomas Kuhn's notions about the history of science could shed light on the emergence, growth, and decline of the field. It was at my next academic port of call – Die Freie Universität Berlin – that the beginnings of the present work crystallized. I decided to write a doctoral dissertation on the relation between political sociology and post-war American society and politics. Discovering that this project could not be properly pursued in Europe, I relocated to Cambridge, Massachusetts, where I continued my research at the Widener Library, Harvard University. Upon a closer examination of the expressions of political sociology in both political science (by Almond) and sociology (by Lipset), it became evident to me that both were drawing upon the thought of Talcott Parsons in their respective efforts to formulate approaches of practical relevance to the cultivation and spread of democracy based on the American prototype. Consequently, I began to work my way through Parsons's copious writings, and soon realized that he was not only acutely aware of the problems of social control faced by capitalist nation-states, but regarded the professionalized social sciences as important contributors to the process of 'rationalization.' The completed dissertation, nevertheless, dealt with Parsons as only one – albeit the most significant – architect of post-war political sociology. In revising the manuscript for publication, I have placed Parsons much more at the centre of the discussion than I had previously. In particular, I have made extensive use of Parsons's pre-1951 unpublished manuscripts (located in his collected papers in the Harvard University Archives) to complement and to provide fresh insights into his more widely known published writings.

The path to the completion of this book, though circuitous and strewn with unforeseen perils, has been royal for the support and sustenance afforded me along the way. Wolf-Dieter Narr, my 'Doktorvater' at Die Freie Universität Berlin, provided me with the unusual combination of acute criticism and warm encouragement while I was writing the dissertation upon which this book is based. The participants in the colloquium 'Philosophy and Social Science,' held at the Inter-University Center for Post-Graduate Studies in Dubrovnik in 1977 and 1978, were a source of stimulation and insight during the initial stages of this work. Our wide-ranging discussions on the nature and assumptions of mainstream social sciences gave inspiration and direction to my thoughts on Talcott Parsons and political sociology.

While doing research at Harvard University for this book – and for the dissertation from which it derived – I have had the generous support of a number of individuals and institutions. Gloria Kibler kindly allowed me the use of her apartment in Cambridge. Jill Brotman skilfully edited and typed the original manuscript. Theda Skocpol, John Bohstedt, Molly Nolan, and Stephen Cornell helped me to gain access to the Harvard library facilities. My participation in a sociology department seminar in 1978–9 deepened my awareness of American politics and history. The following persons read and commented upon drafts of chapters at various stages: Jeff Herf, Gary Gereffi, Bruce Merrill, Gianfranco Poggi, Michael Pollak, David Schulter, and Brad Willis. The Center for European Studies, over the years, has sustained my endeavours materially, intellectually, and in ways that will always remain elusive and intangible. Clark Elliot and the other staff members at Harvard University Archives have been of inestimable assistance to me in my efforts to sort through the labyrinthine Parsons papers. Material from the Parsons papers is published by permission of the Harvard University Archives. I owe a special debt of gratitude to Talcott Parsons, who graciously allowed me to have any items I wished from his personal collection of offprints, and agreed to discuss his life and work with me at a later date. Sadly, his death shortly afterwards prevented us from ever having that conversation.

The more recent stages of writing and preparing this book could not have been completed without the help and generosity of many. I am thankful to Sharon Sutherland for bringing me together with the University of Toronto Press. While revising the original manuscript for publication, I have had the good fortune to work with two exacting, yet patient editors: R.I.K. Davidson and Lydia Burton. I am also grateful to those who made available to me significant new sources of information. Bruce Wearne called my attention to an early article by Parsons (written with Addison Cutler), and Graham Morgan gave me a copy of a letter Parsons had written to him.

The following students, colleagues, and friends at the University of New Brunswick and St Thomas University have assisted me in a variety of ways to see the book through to its completion: Gary Allen, Mireille Content, Randy Kimm, Felix Kofie, Peter McGahan, Tom Murphy, Barbara Pepperdene, David Rehorick, Lois Scott, Susan Scott, Catherine Watson, and David Wilson. I would like to thank in particular Noel Iverson, who gave a close and careful editing to the entire text, and

Nancy Burnham, who patiently initiated me into the art of computer-assisted writing.

Financial support for the study and research leading to the writing of this book has come from the Rhodes Trust, the Deutsches Akademisches Austauschdienst, and the Canada Council. The Arts Faculty Publication Fund at the University of New Brunswick has been a generous source of aid for the preparation of the manuscript. Finally, in the absence of a spouse and children to whom I can convey my domestic indebtedness, I would like to express my deepest gratitude to all those kind souls whose friendship and encouragement have kept the proverbial tunnel ablaze with light from beginning to end.

TALCOTT PARSONS AND THE CAPITALIST NATION-STATE

1

Parsonsian Theory and Its Interpreters

Current Controversies over Parsons's Legacy

Who now reads Talcott Parsons? While the pre-eminent influence of his thought has long been acknowledged,[1] the dismissal of his views has become a staple ingredient of current sociological wisdom.[2] Recently, however, efforts have been made to restore the corpus of Parsons's writings to its place as the fountainhead for sociological theory and investigation. Under the general rubric of 'the theory of action,'[3] this loose movement, while not uncritical of Parsons's work, seeks to develop and draw upon his ideas as the basis for restoring unity and direction to sociological inquiry.[4] Largely treating Parsons's detractors as intemperate and misguided, this group strives either to deflate their criticisms (Loubser 1976, 15–19), or to refashion the direction of Parsons's thought in light of them.[5]

If one accepts the unstated terms of the controversy, more is at stake than simply the acceptance or rejection of Parsons's contributions to sociology; each position also indicates the degree to which one takes seriously Parsons's ideas and seeks to engage oneself with them. The inclination of the critics is to no longer concern themselves with Parsons's thought in any more than a superficial sense. By implication, if one continues to take his thought seriously, with a view to constructing social theory, one is identified with the 'action theory' apologists.[6] My intent in this work is to offer an account that is true to the spirit of those seeking to develop critical alternatives to Parsons's theory, but is at the same time sympathetic to those who contend that his ideas are of continuing importance to sociology.

In a crucial respect, however, the present account differs radically from the assumptions about Parsons that have been shared by critics and sympathizers alike. Both assume, as a matter of course, that Parsons was primarily a descriptive theorist who sought nothing more than to portray reality on a social-scientific canvas. What critics and supporters differ upon is the degree to which Parsons's thought provides the basis for accurate and compelling representations of the social world.

This work challenges the view of Parsons as predominantly a descriptive theorist, thereby recasting the lines of debate and inquiry that follow from it. As a corrective, I argue that Parsonian theory was not so much an attempt to describe an externalized reality, as it was an effort to help constitute this reality in particular ways. To be sure, descriptive and analytical features formed an integral and consistent part of Parsons's evolving framework. But this empirical component, I contend, was itself presupposed by the strategic and purposeful designs of the entire Parsonian project. This perspective can be termed 'activism' in that it views Parsons as an engaged thinker who sought to help change, shape, and transform social and political life through his intellectual efforts. Parsons's 'activistic' orientation, I argue, was presupposed by both an awareness of how particular patterns of knowledge sustained the social order, and how these patterns could be ensured through human effort. His deliberations on the relationship between knowledge and society, however, did not take place in a detached and abstracted manner.[7] Rather, aware of the inherent limitations of capitalism's ability to create the conditions necessary for social stability, his efforts were directed towards elaborating how a more integrated social order – one preserving capitalist social relations, yet providing them with stability – could be constituted. He saw the nation-state as the form of political, social, and economic organization best able to provide the basis for bringing social order to capitalism. The capitalist nation-state was characterized by a state apparatus facing the problems of acting domestically and externally in the interests of the national collectivity, while at the same time providing the symbolic basis for mass loyalty and solidarity. Parsons viewed the emerging capitalist nation-state as the organizational form most conducive to both social order and human freedom. Grasping the importance of the production of knowledge for the problems of intervention and legitimation faced by the state apparatus, he sought to understand and describe how the producers of that knowledge – the professional strata, including the social sciences – could contribute to the success of these ongoing state processes. Parsons was concerned with how the American nation-state could be consolidated, and he eventually came to view it as a prototype for global social transformation.

Historiography and Social-Scientific Practice

There is more to an activist reading of Parsons, however, than simply a reinterpretation of his writings. Viewing his work in this way allows us to grasp the close relation between his ideas and the social reality upon which he reflected. If it is the case that the different variants of capitalist nation-states are indeed constituted – at least in part – by the efforts of social scientists and other professionals, then an analysis of this kind has implications for how the social sciences could reorient their activities in a more radically informed fashion. If the capitalist nation-state is perceived as a source of inequality and oppression rather than of freedom, then an activist account of Parsons can be used as a basis for reorienting the social sciences towards practice on behalf of those who are oppressed rather than those who dominate others.

Viewing Parsons from an activist perspective can cast doubts on the practical implications of both the 'critical' and 'supportive' approaches to Parsons's contributions. Each of these perspectives rests on particular historiographical assumptions about how Parsons's work should be interpreted. While supporters examine him from the standpoint of 'presentism,' critics largely draw on 'historicist' views of his writings. The dispute over the significance of Parsons's thought can be seen as an instance of a much wider argument over how past sociological thought can be most effectively studied.[8]

Until recently, the history of social-scientific thought has been dominated by various forms of 'presentism,' a view in which social-scientific writings of the past are seen in terms of contemporary preoccupations and concerns. The development of social-scientific ideas is thought to proceed incrementally, with the current state of knowledge representing the culmination of this process. In another context, Herbert Butterfield (1931) termed this style of intellectual historiography 'the Whig Interpretation of History,' characterized by the tendency 'to write on the side of Protestants and Whigs rather than Catholics and Tories, to praise revolutions once they were successful, to emphasize "progress" in the past and thus produce a "story" that implicitly ratifies if not glorifies the present' (see Jones summary 1983, 448). Within sociology, this orientation towards the history of the field has received perhaps its firmest expression in the work of Robert Merton ([1949] 1968). According to Merton, the 'systematics' of sociology, in the form of the empirically validated residue of earlier theories, ought to be distinguished from the 'history' of the field, as embodied in 'the false starts, the now archaic doctrines, and both the fruitless and fruitful errors of the past' (3). In true Whiggish fashion, Merton views the history of sociology from the standpoint of the current state of knowledge, with the thoughts and ideas of the past validated against the standards of the present. Merton selectively reads the history of sociology in terms of those theoretical notions that have empirical relevance to contemporary sociological concerns.

Advocates of historicism, in contrast, are not primarily concerned with how past social-scientific thought can contribute analytically and substantively to current research. They seek to understand earlier social-scientific contributions on their own terms, in relation to their historical contexts. Accordingly, they view the presentist inclination to sever the 'context of validation' (systematics) from the 'context of discovery' (history) as arbitrary and misleading. Seeking to overcome the constricting legacy of presentist accounts, such as that of Merton, historicists 'urge the rigorous study of the social and historical context of past sociological thought.' This permits more faithful reconstruction of what was *meant* by a theory, 'the purposes for which it was constructed, and the questions it was meant to answer' (Jones 1974, 355). Applying these precepts to the interpretation of texts such as Durkheim's *Elementary Forms of Religious Life* (see Jones 1977) and to schools of thought such as the utilitarian (see Camic 1979), advocates of historicism have offered a revised statement of 'the process by which ... ideas emerge, are received, grow, change, and are eventually surpassed' (Jones 1977, 311). Taking exception to the presentist inclination 'to understand "the past for the sake of the present,"' historicists seek 'to understand the past for the sake of the past' (Stocking 1965, 211).

The presentist/historicist dispute is not only of significance for interpreting the thought of the past, but also for understanding how the social sciences are practised today. Our orientation towards current issues and problems is inherently related to how we understand earlier social-scientific contributions. This close relationship between social-scientific historiography and social-scientific practice is particularly striking in the case of how Parsons's writings have been interpreted by supporters and critics alike. To a large degree, those who identify with the development of action theory implicitly accept a version of presentism, in that they interpret Parsons's contributions in terms of their own concerns and preoccupations. That is to say, they remove Parsons from his historical context and seek to extract from the body of his thought concepts of use and relevance to the development of action theory. Hence, presentists like Alexander have largely concerned themselves with 'incorporating the important breakthroughs that Parsons achieved' (1979, 175), and with assessing his 'permanent contributions to intellectual tradition' (1978, 177). Muench (1981, 735) seeks to examine 'the substantive and methodological issues in his work in order to reach a just determination of Parsons's contribution to the social sciences.' Thus, 'presentist' commentators view the corpus of Parsons's thought as a rich repository of ideas to be mined for its analytical insights into current issues and concerns.

However, an activist reading of Parsons casts serious doubts on the validity and promise of developing sociology along the lines suggested by his legacy of 'action theory.' In view of the practical embeddedness of Parsonsian categories in wider political and social issues, they can in no sense serve as the basis for neutral, descriptive theory because in using them one is inadvertently representing what amounts to an ideological and practical standpoint in relation to the capitalist nation-state. This, in turn, calls into question the contention of some that the validity of Parsons's analyses can be assessed separately from the moral and political standpoint underlying them (Hamilton 1983, 24; Loubser 1976, 18). In view of the practical nature of Parsons's theory, its validity was contingent upon the ability of the capitalist nation-state to solve its problems of intervention and legitimation. It cannot simply be maintained that Parsons's contributions could equally serve the interests of the dominant and subordinate in society, for his thought was based on a commitment to a particular set of political and social arrangements. It is only by first revealing the practical underpinning of Parsons's theory, therefore, that its empirical basis can be adequately understood. In seeking to understand how Parsons's practical commitments led him to make particular empirical claims about the social world, the inherent relation between his ideas and the contours of the capitalist nation-state must be acknowledged. Through such an analysis, it becomes possible to understand how current patterns of domination are both upheld by knowledge and subject to change through human effort. An examination of the interplay between Parsons's thought and the emerging capitalist nation-state from an activist perspective involves us in a project of reflective criticism. For in examining the interplay between Parsons's thought and the social order upon which he reflected, we are obliged to examine the relation between our own thought and society in a similar fashion.

On the face of it, those who criticize Parsons on ideological grounds share these concerns (Foss 1963; Bottomore [1969] 1975). Acting upon the historicist premise that an understanding of Parsons's political and social standpoint in relation to its context can lead to a better awareness of his theoretical outlook, 'ideological' critics stress how his conservative predilections reflected similar trends in American society.[9] On the basis of these historically informed analyses, the critics then suggest guide-lines for more radically disposed social-scientific orientations. Possibly the most ambitious, notorious, and influential of these forms of criticism has been that of Alvin Gouldner (1971), who sought to reveal the ideological basis of 'Academic Sociology,' as embodied in the work of Parsons, with a view to reconstructing both social theory and society:

My aim, then, is to search out some critical understanding of the social mission of Academic Sociology, and to formulate some tentative ideas about the social mandate with which it operates, the ideologies which it expresses, and the link it has to the larger society. An effort will be made to define the character of Academic Sociology by focusing on its dominant school of thought, Functionalism, and its dominant theorist, Talcott Parsons. While his standpoint is by no means the only one in American sociology today, it is without doubt the leading one. Any effort to understand the changes impending in American sociology today must confront its central intellectual tendencies. And since intellectual tendencies do not develop in a social vacuum, any effort to understand American sociology must relate it to the nature and problems of the society in which it developed. (1971, 26–7)

In Gouldner's view, since 'the old society maintains itself ... through theories and ideologies that establish its hegemony over the minds of men ... it will be impossible either to emancipate men from the old society or to build a humane new one, without beginning ... the construction ... of ... new social theories; and it is impossible to do this without a critique of the social theories dominant today.' (1971, 5). He notes that 'sociology has a dialectical character and contains both repressive and liberative dimensions. The extrication and further development of its liberative potential will depend, in important part, on the penetration of an historically informed critique of sociology as a theory and as a social institution' (12). The liberative potential of academic sociology, in Gouldner's view, can only be extricated through 'action and criticism' and through 'efforts to change the social world and efforts to change social science, both of which are profoundly interconnected' (13).

With his emphasis upon how one can generate radical sociological alternatives based upon critical engagement with Parsons's thought in relation to its context, Gouldner appears to base his analysis on a historicist perspective. Yet because he assumes that Parsons, as 'the grand metaphysician of contemporary sociology' (207), generated models that have no relevance to social reality, it is difficult to see how Gouldner could carry out the task he assigns himself. It is scarcely possible to examine the relation between Parsons's thought and its historical context if it is believed that his 'categories are ... self-sufficient conceptual extrusions that cover rather than reveal the world' (209). Given that he sees Parsons as having developed a 'detached, technically involved sociology' (172), it is not surprising that Gouldner fails to follow through on his promise to examine the formation of Parsons's thought in relation to the development of the United States. Correspondingly, outside of his rather vague discussion of the needs of the welfare state (341–61), Gouldner fails to offer any analysis of how social theory became embedded in American society. This means, in effect, that his advocacy of a 'Reflexive Sociology' in no way follows from an analysis of the interplay between thought and society. In its emphasis upon 'the deepening of the sociologist's own awareness,' and the *transformation* of the sociologist's self' (494–5), it provides no basis for restructuring social theory in relation to the prevailing ideological practices that sustain the social order. In view of its subjective and voluntaristic nature, Gouldner's reflexive sociology can hardly serve as the basis for the kind of 'liberating' sociology he supports.

As a result, because he assumes that Parsons was a detached and metaphysically inclined social thinker, Gouldner is unable either to historicize Parsons's thought adequately or to reveal the ideological nature of his writings. Gouldner has not been alone, however, in failing to reconcile Parsons's alleged conservatism with the view that his detachment rendered his theories irrelevant to the social order. The same tension between ideological and substantive critiques of Parsons has led commentators to make some curious equivocations in their interpretations of his work. The problem of generating an ideological critique of Parsons on the basis of a descriptive interpretation is at its most difficult, perhaps, when commentators attempt to reconcile his theoretical and political-social writings. Daniel Foss attempts to mount an ideological attack on Parsons while retaining the conventional substantive treatment of his views, by arguing that Parsons *abandoned* systems theory when he addressed actual political and social controversies: 'It is to be expected that the intellectual apprehension and conceptualization of such a world [in violent flux] would offer a supreme challenge to an equilibrium theorist, and we indeed find that on these matters Parsons is a good deal less "systematic" than in the rest of this work' (1963, 96).

Faced with explaining the same disparity between the two sets of writings, Andrew Hacker conjectures that 'there are two Parsonses – the political and the sociological, and the two have yet to meet in a consistent way' (1961, 290). The critics thus have been unable to bring the theoretical and empirical components of Parsons's writings simultaneously into focus. Mirroring this inability has been the tendency to draw an arbitrary distinction between Parsons's early and mature phases. Obviously perplexed by his shift of substantive emphasis from 'action' to 'system,' commentators have alleged that Parsons set aside a youthful interest in 'voluntarism' in favour of a more deterministic explanation.[10] Gouldner (1971, 191–5) has gone so far as to compare Parsons's intellectual migration to that of Karl Marx. To account for the apparent contradiction between the 'voluntarism' and 'determinism' in Parsons's thought, the commentators are forced to posit that an epistemological break separated his early and mature writings.

It is my contention that the set of antinomies (theoretical/empirical, ideological/substantive, determinism/voluntarism, youthful/mature) that have characterized interpretations of Parsons's writings is unwarranted, unnecessary, and misleading. However, given the critics' assumptions about the animus of this thought, the fragmentation of Parsons into various personae is understandable. As long as he is implicitly viewed as a detached social scientist, primarily concerned with analysing social reality, a lattice-work of arbitrary barriers must be erected to sustain this position. Parsons's blatantly ideological political and social commentary is considered separately from his abstract and formal theoretical endeavours. His early emphasis upon 'social action' and his later concern with 'systems theory' are taken to be mutually exclusive.

These interpretive difficulties have significant implications for social-scientific practice, for implicit in the critical readings of Parsons is a concern to orient the social sciences in a much more radical fashion towards society. That is to say, the work of Parsons is thought to represent a particular ideological expression on behalf of the status quo.[11] At the same time, however, it is maintained that Parsons was a detached thinker whose ideas were of little relevance to the social order.[12] The critics' imputation of ideology to Parsons is vitiated by their assumption of his theoretical irrelevance. But one can generate an ideological critique of Parsons – at least in the strong sense – only if his ideas are thought to be of historical relevance and consequence to society. As long as it is assumed that his thought was ideological only in the weak sense of espousing particular conservative sentiments,[13] one can neither place Parsons's thought in the context of particular historically defined issues and problems, nor explore the implications of his intellectual efforts for the patterning of knowledge in society. Because of their assumption of the irrelevance of Parsons's thought to social reality, critics not only fail to place it in historical perspective, but also are unable to generate an alternative form of radical social-scientific practice to oppose it. They are limited to suggesting that the social sciences, in opposition to the alleged abstractedness of Parsons's writings, ought to be concerned with real social issues and problems.[14] However, it is disputable whether these descriptive alternatives to Parsons offer an adequate basis for a more radically conceived social-scientific practice. Although the concerns of this approach, namely class, inequality, industrial horror, etc., are more radically disposed than those of Parsons, no guide-lines are offered for reorienting the form and direction of social-scientific practice. If a social science is to be radical in the sense of having a direct bearing upon the way the social order is constituted, then it requires both a theory of how knowledge currently produced serves to reinforce patterns of inequality and oppression and, correspondingly, how a different kind of knowledge could help alleviate these forms of domination. The deployment of 'critical' concepts, with a corresponding empirical content, does not necessarily lead to a more emancipatory social science. As long as the products of the social sciences are validated almost exclusively in terms of their bearing upon academically defined criteria rather than on the basis of their social import and consequences, it is difficult to see how even the most critical of approaches can be radical in any sort of immediate and active sense.[15] We require a notion of how both the form and content of practice could be reoriented in such a way that the tendencies of prevailing social-scientific approaches to both complement and sustain the social order can be counteracted.

A New Assessment

It is with these concerns in mind that this book has been written. I seek to carry out a task similar to the one outlined by Gouldner, namely, to show the relationship between Parsons's thought and advanced capitalist society, with a view towards generating some guide-lines for their mutual reconstruction. Based on the view that Parsons can best be understood as an activist thinker, aware of the central importance of professionalized, social-scientific knowledge for the emergence and growth of the capitalist nation-state, I show how he developed a set of practical categories (the 'primary' patterns) that would permit the social sciences to contribute to the process of national-state formation.

The first part of this book begins by substantiating the view that Parsons was an activist thinker and by examining how he translated his commitment to liberal Calvinist principles into a general orientation toward social-scientific practice. This practical concern derived its purpose and meaning from the reality of competitive capitalism, expressed by Parsons as 'the Hobbesian problem of order.' It was this tension between the redemptive impulse of Parsons's liberal Calvinist commitments and the reality of capitalist society that guided the development of his thought. Parsons's concern to derive a theoretical standpoint of potential practical bearing to the emergent post-capitalist social order was implicit in his treatment of classical social theory. Drawing upon the writings of Marshall, Pareto, Durkheim, and Weber, he fashioned a perspective that overcame the practical deficiencies of utilitarian positivism and idealism, respectively. Parsons encoded the components of this perspective into categories of professional practice – the primary patterns – based on his study of medicine. He gave these categories social and political specification through his engagement with problems of national morale during the Second World War. In the immediate post-war period, the same primary patterns were applied by Parsons to the social sciences, as he sought to provide the basis for their strategic relevance to the problems faced by the American nation-state in the early years of the Cold War. Finally, he came to inscribe the primary patterns into the sub-disciplinary standpoint of 'political sociology,' in response to a number of challenges to the Cold War order that arose during the 1950s. Parsons saw the consolidation of the capitalist nation-state – in its prototypical American form – as interdependent with the development of a strategically oriented political sociology.

The last two parts of the book examine how Parsons's approach came to inform both political science and sociology, resulting in a convergence between the two fields towards political sociology. The leading figures of the two wings of political sociology – Gabriel Almond and Seymour Lipset – drew on Parsons's thought for practical reasons. Not only did Parsons's framework provide a way of producing knowledge of relevance to the cultivation of the American socio-political system on a global basis, but it enabled the two fields to attract Ford Foundation funding earmarked for the support of strategically pertinent social-scientific research. However, this union between political science and sociology, as based upon Parsons's practical precepts, was short-lived. In the mid-to-late 1960s, Parsons's theories were rejected for practical reasons, political science and sociology became decoupled, and each came to embrace a variant of 'political engineering,' a form of social-scientific practice thought to be more appropriate to the changing political and academic circumstances.

Finally, I resume the discussion of how an activist reading of Parsons can provide the basis for a radical reorientation of the social sciences. Based on analysis of how Parsons's thought – and the political sociology derived from it – was strategically related to the growth and mainte-nance of the capitalist nation-state, I offer some suggestions as to how Parsons could be stood on his feet (as it were), providing the foundations for social-scientific practice of emancipatory relevance to our own capitalist social orders.

PART ONE

The Structuring of Social-Scientific Action

2

Parsons as an Activist Thinker

An activist reading of Parsons is not unduly speculative, but closely accords with his conception of the intellectual's mission in advanced capitalist countries. As 'persons concerned with the general definition of the situation, for the human condition as a whole but especially for the meaning and status of social systems' (Parsons and Platt 1973, 279), intellectuals referred to 'the social role category whose incumbents tend to give primacy to cultural considerations over societal in the definition of their expectations and the obligations applying to them' (1970b, 20). For Parsons, the purpose and meaning of intellectual activity was inextricably bound up with 'the cultural tradition,' composed of 'science, common-sense knowledge, religious and philosophical ideas, value patterns, art and other expressional forms which have an important degree of general acceptance and continuity in a social system' ([1942b] 1964, 146).

It was, moreover, through the cultural tradition that the moral imperatives defining 'correct' patterns of action were mediated ([1951] 1964, 11). These 'definitions of the situation,' however, were not generated spontaneously. Rather, they were cultivated by the strata bearing responsibility for the production of knowledge, ideas, and values. Hence, in Parsons's view, the vocation of the intellectuals was inherently an active one. By contributing to the cultural matrix, they could help ensure the regulation of action, the continuation of the social system, and the generation of overall stability.

Since Parsons viewed himself as a member of the intelligentsia, one can conclude that he felt 'a growing sense of concern for the state of society' in which he lived, as expressed in 'a sense of responsibility and in the assertion of "a right to be heard," to exert influence' (1970b, 21).

This suggests not only that Parsons's own contributions flowed from an abiding commitment to a particular set of social and cultural standards, but that he viewed the knowledge he produced as inseparable from its maintenance and reproduction.

Instrumental Activism and American Society

Parsons's activism appears to be closely bound up with his commitment to the liberal Calvinist precepts he saw as providing the dominant pattern for capitalist society in general and for the United States in particular. This is not to say that his personal religious views entered directly into his orientation towards the social sciences. Indeed, even though Parsons's family origins were closely linked to Congregationalism, one searches in vain for any direct reference to his personal religious beliefs in his voluminous writings.[1] Nevertheless, it is arguable that Parsons's activist conception of the social sciences represented a *translation* of religious faith into the secular sphere.[2] What made this possible (or, indeed, provided a justification for it) was his conviction that modern secularized society had its origins in the consolidation of the ascetic Protestant faith. As he noted in his first extended discussion of society (1934a, 228), the Calvinist churches, reacting to the secular authorities' efforts to control them, 'were pushed more in the direction of the radical sects and of the separation of church and state.' Hence, 'the main weight of their ethical sanction [was] thrown ... into the activities of the individual in the sphere of his private relations [and] the concept of the "calling" as a field for proving one's state of grace has served to promote individualism and to emphasize the ethical value of economic activities.' By virtue of its ascetic Protestant origins, modern society, though secular in form, was religious in substance. Indeed, as Parsons would later attest, the United States, as a nation founded on the principles of ascetic Protestantism, represented a form of 'civil religion' (1974, 204–6).[3] Since the way of life in the United States was based on a form of 'ascetic protestantism,' loyalty to the nation implied acting upon liberal Calvinist tenets as part of one's calling. Since Parsons supported the dominant value system, his own orientation – by virtue of his 'calling' as a social scientist – flowed from his commitment to it. This implies as well that his orientation to social-scientific activity embodied the standpoint represented by liberal Calvinism.

According to this pattern, society and its citizens were seen as instrumental to the 'divine will in building a kingdom of God on earth'

(1962, 159). Unlike its Lutheran counterpart, which emphasized 'the more inward, spiritualistic interpretation of emancipation from the institutionally "objective" Catholic Church' (1974, 202), Calvinism was 'thisworldly as distinguished from otherworldly, not in the sense of abandoning the transcendental basis of meaning and legitimation, but in the sense that action in the world, i.e. – in secular society, was the field in which the religious mission of the individual was to be carried out' (1962, 147).

Calvinism, with its 'maintenance of the basic radical dualism between the transcendental and the "world,"' was much more activistically inclined than either Catholicism or Lutheranism. Indeed, 'the Calvinist version of the tensions between the divine mission and the human condition gave a far stronger anchorage to activist orientations than did the Lutheran tendency toward resignation in the face of sin and divine Providence' (1968, 438).

According to the liberal Calvinist teachings, society and its members were to be seen as instruments to the realization of a transcendent social order, namely 'The Kingdom of God on Earth.' According to this vision, human action was not oriented to self-interest, but rather to the collective good. The overall problem was how society and its members could be influenced in such a way as to more closely approximate this transcendental ideal. The active agent in creating this order was the priesthood. Under conditions of the original Calvinism, 'the building of the Kingdom became a direct collective goal under the centralized direction of the putative members of the elect' (1962, 159).

This orientation towards the world, in Parsons's view, had become secularized in the United States. In this sense, the dominant orientation was 'instrumental' in that society was not '"an end in itself" but rather an instrumentality to ends that in some sense are outside or beyond it.' The 'activism' of the society referred to 'an orientation to active mastery of its external situation in an empirical sense of situation.' This 'external situation' included not only 'the physical environment and other societies,' but also 'the motivations and behavior of the human individuals who are members of the society itself.' This involved 'the mobilization of resources, among which the commitments of individuals occupy the key place' (Parsons and White [1961] 1970, 196–7). It is noteworthy that 'instrumental activism' not only defined the 'dominant value pattern' of American society, but also the orientation of sciences in relation to it: 'knowledge ... should be objective, generalized, and detailed in reference. We have seen that both natural and behavioral science are involved. Instrumental activism here means an orientation to "mastery" over the cognitive problems of the empirical world' (1962, 160). The social scientist, through analysing society, would be helping it to realize a set of values transcendent to it. These values centred on the 'achievement of the good life for individuals.' This did not, however, mean that the good society consisted in merely the individuals' 'self-indulgence [and] purely "personal" needs or interest.' Rather, individual fulfilment was to be realized through 'achievement' by making 'some kind of "contribution" to the building (not merely the maintenance) of the good society' (Parsons and White [1961] 1970, 196).

In view of Parsons's support for the value pattern of instrumental activism, one can then give further substance to his conception of intellectual activity. As a form of secularized religion, it would be oriented towards 'constituting' society.[4] This would consist of acting upon the social order instrumentally in order to help realize the creation of a transcendent order on earth. Specifically, following one's calling as a social scientist, one would 'scientifically' assert the presence of consensual values within the secular realm. Through this type of activity, one would help to build a 'Kingdom of God on Earth': by mediating values from the transcendental to the secular sphere, the social scientist would not only be defining and giving credence to them, but ensuring their obedience and sustenance.[5] Parsons's orientation towards the social sciences represented a sublimated version of 'instrumental activism,' given sanctity by his view that American society, though secular in form, was liberal Calvinist in substance. This dominant pattern, in turn, obliged him to obey his calling as a member of the elect to help create a 'Kingdom of God on Earth.' For the social scientist, this involved mediating the transcendent realm of ultimate values to the 'thisworldly realm' of secular society, thereby moving it closer to 'the good life for individuals.'

The Hobbesian Problem of Order and Capitalist Society

Parsons, nevertheless, viewed the real world as potentially problematic to the realization of transcendent values. In particular, he was concerned about how individualistic tendencies within industrial society could lead to social instability. Parsons expressed this state of affairs in terms of the 'Hobbesian problem of order' – the chronic instability inherent in a society composed of individuals egoistically pursuing their interests. In the absence of restraint, there is nothing to prevent them from using the most effective means – namely force and fraud – to realize their ends. The result is what Thomas Hobbes had called 'the war of all against all ... a state where the life of man is "solitary, poor, nasty, brutish and short"' (in [1937] 1968, 89–90). It is evident that the problem, as posed, was more than merely a theoretical one. Rather, it anticipated in graphic and startling fashion what lay in store for a society composed of egoistic individuals, acting on their 'discrete randomly variant ends of action' (90). Accordingly, the solution to the Hobbesian problem was not merely of analytic interest, but had important implications for how social control in society could be ensured.

That the Hobbesian problem of order held more than an abstract interest for Parsons is evident in an early unpublished manuscript (1929–67). What it reveals is that the world described by Hobbes was not simply an analytical artefact for Parsons, but was very much rooted in his concern with the chronic disorder that he perceived during the 1930s. Above all, he noted in this manuscript, unrestrained activities in the economic sphere were disruptive of social order: 'Many symptoms of our present economic situation such as the widespread prevalence of and public equanimity toward fraud, and the ruthless methods of competition, indicate that spontaneous institutional control of our economic activities is not functioning with perfect smoothness.'

Parsons's analysis of the capitalist order embodied Hobbes's conception of a 'war of all against all.' Indeed, his diagnosis of endemic 'fraud' and 'ruthless methods of competition' corresponds to his reading of Hobbes in *The Structure of Social Action*: 'In the absence of any restraining control men will adapt to this immediate end the most efficient available means. These means are found in the last analysis to be *force* and *fraud* [emphasis mine]. Hence a situation where every man is the enemy of every other, endeavoring to destroy or subdue him by force of fraud or both. This is nothing but a state of war' ([1937] 1968, 90).[6] That these practices are prevalent, in Parsons's view, indicated a breakdown in social control. Specifically, as he noted, the two predominant modes of institutional control that historically had characterized Western societies were no longer efficacious in their regulation of economic activities.

In the first, 'harmful forms of the pursuit of self-interest are in general effectively prevented by the closeness of family solidarity.' However, under conditions where family ties have been largely superseded by 'impersonality of relationships,' a different sort of social control is exercised. In this second case, 'certain general norms of conduct in "economic" relations may be spontaneously accepted as moral obligations – as honesty, fair dealing, etc. Social pressure by boycotting the offender of course helps in enforcement, especially so long as common feeling is strong.' In effect, social control under conditions of market exchange is predicated upon informal mechanisms (1929–67, 3).

These two modes of control, based on 'family solidarity' and 'spontaneous enforcement of market exchange,' correspond to the 'positive types of social relationship, that is, modes in which individuals are bound together,' namely *Gemeinschaft* and *Gesellschaft*, elaborated by Parsons in *The Structure of Social Action* ([1937] 1968, 686–94).

As Parsons's comments on social disorder in the 1930s reveal, both these forms of social control had been ineffective. Nevertheless, he gives consideration to a third alternative for restoring social order, namely the extension of state control.

There is still as a last resort the application of sanctions by an external organized agency like the state. The degree to which this can effectively replace the other two kinds of spontaneous discipline is highly dubious, especially since control of the machinery of the state is itself the object of a struggle for power among interested groups and hence cannot be held to be a true and infallible servant of the common values of the community. (1929–67, 3–4)

As Parsons seems to suggest, this mode of control had not been completely successful, in that 'the trend to formal state control is not necessarily an extension of the total area of control, but to a large extent rather the substitution of a more clumsy and less effective for the more effective kind which can be created by deliberate policy' (1929–67, 4).

Parsons's analysis of the shortcomings of state control as a solution to social disorder echoes his reservations about Hobbes's leviathan: 'The difficulty of constraint in the sanction sense as a basis for the enforcement of a system of norms as a whole is that it cannot be generalized. The Hobbesian theory is the classic attempt to do it – and it breaks down, in part under the necessity of organization for applying the coercion, which cannot itself rest on coercion in the same sense' ([1937] 1968, 402). Neither the state nor the institutional framework of a *Gemeinschaft* or a *Gesellschaft* was able to ensure social control. Indeed, in Parsons's view, a 'complicated economic order can only be restored to stability and health by the re-imposition of a ... kind of control which no man knows how to create deliberately. At least in the past [it] has rather been the byproduct of great religious and ethical movements which have generally been mainly concerned with quite other – sometimes otherworldly things.' What Parsons finally suggests is that 'basic reconstruction is only possible on a level much deeper than any tinkering with the external machinery of our economic life.' Stabilizing the economic order 'can only be done by a revivification of values and their effective embodiment in institutions' (1929–67, 5).

The Hobbesian problem of order was thus of very real and immediate interest to Parsons. The increasing incidence of force and fraud served notice that the formerly effective modes of social control were no longer capable of constraining action. The solution to social disorder Parsons proposed was a normative one. Specifically, it would take place through a 'common system of ultimate ends shared by the members of society.' As Parsons emphasizes,

this system would, among other things, define what they all held their relations ought to be, would lay down norms determining these relations and limits on the use of others as means, on the acquisition and use of power in general. In so far, then, as action is determined by ultimate ends, the existence of a system of such ends common to the members of the community seems to be the only alternative to a state of chaos – a necessary factor in social stability. (1935b, 295)

In Parsons's view, 'the common ultimate value-system of the community' operates through 'normative rules' which 'both define what immediate ends should and should not be sought, and limit the choice of means to them in terms other than those of efficiency,' and 'define standards of socially accepted effort.' He defines this 'system of rules, fundamental to any society not in the state of "active religion" ' as 'its institutions' (1935b, 299).

Parsons's discussion of how a system of ultimate ends ensured orderly action represented the direction that modern society must take if it were to overcome its tendencies towards social disorder. Through channelling interests by means of institutions, a mode of social control appropriate to capitalist social relations could be effected.

Activism and European Social Theory

It was this tension between the 'otherworldly,' integrated system of ultimate values, and its realization in the 'thisworldly' Hobbesian disorder, that provided the fulcrum for Parsons's encounter with European social theory. Specifically, he sought to ground a theoretical standpoint that articulated this vision of the emergent social order. Implicit in Parsons's evolving thought was not only an emergent conception of modern society, but also a theoretical framework oriented towards it. In his early writings, culminating in *The Structure of Social Action*, Parsons's analysis proceeded on two interdependent levels, which gradually unfolded and took shape as he came to terms with the developments in social thought that he considered to be most significant. Parsons sought to show that advanced capitalist society, though consisting of discrete individuals pursuing material interests, could still be integrated through 'ultimate ends of action' that 'must ... be regarded as integrated into a harmonious system of ends, governing in various ways all the actions of the members of the group.' These ultimate ends were not 'scientific theories in the positivistic sense,' nor 'mere reflections of external empirical reality,' but rather were 'non-scientific or even metaphysical' (1934a, 230). As metaphysical postulates, the ultimate ends were not scientifically established by the actors themselves, but rather represented transcendental standards of moral action. Nevertheless, they were not imagined, but were 'real' or 'empirical' ([1937] 1968, 256). Given that they were not constituted by the actors themselves, how could their presence be accounted for?

Within Parsons's developing schema, the immediate source of the ultimate values was in the 'voluntaristic theory of action,' as found in the 'analytical sciences.' That is to say, by virtue of using the 'action frame of reference' in analysing society, one could scientifically establish the presence of a system of ultimate values. In view of the accessibility to the public of their ideas, the analytical scientists would perform the role of 'mediating' ultimate values from the transcendental realm to the secular sphere. They would not only be confirming the presence of these values, but ensuring that this set of values had moral force. Because the values were scientifically determined, then obedience to them was obligatory – in the same manner that one was compelled to obey any order of truths having their origins in science. Parsons selected from the social order particular features and trends – which he saw as anticipatory of 'the good society' – and incorporated them into his theoretical system. This system, in turn, was meant to help consolidate and reinforce the developments of which he approved. Since the theoretical framework was derived from a practical analysis of the social order, this implied that the two would stand in an 'isomorphic' relation to one another.[7] From this standpoint, it would be possible for social scientists, like their counterparts in the Calvinist priesthood, to help move society further in the direction of becoming a 'Kingdom of God on Earth' in which a secular religion effectively integrated the actions of individuals.

This concern to ground a theoretical standpoint of practical relevance to the emergent social order directed Parsons's encounter with classical social theory in *The Structure of Social Action* and related works of the same period. Parsons's engagement with classical social theory was practically conceived: through his reading and interpretation of classical social theory he sought to gain insights into how a social theory having strategic relevance to 'modern' society might be established. In this sense, *The Structure of Social Action*, as grounded in his early writings, did not represent a convergence so much as it did a progression. Parsons did not simply demonstrate that a number of major European thinkers came to share the same analytical schema. Rather, based on his concern to ground a theoretical perspective of practical relevance to the emergent social order, he examined four major writers, along with less-central figures and other schools of thought, in a particular order with specific concerns and issues in mind. Such a procedure enabled him to both preserve and transform the insights of each thinker and approach he considered; for by dealing with them serially, he could use each successive set of ideas to draw upon the strengths and correct the weaknesses of the perspectives he had previously considered. Parsons sought to formulate a standpoint that was at once value oriented and scientific. By virtue of this orientation, it would stand in strategic relevance to the emergent social order – characterized by objective and subjective dimensions. This meant that he had to come to terms with the two dominant strands of thought representing the poles of objectivity and subjectivity respectively – namely positivism and idealism. Parsons's early writings represent an effort to incorporate these into a unified perspective of practical relevance to the emergent social order. Closely related to this task was overcoming the domination of orthodox economics, which, with its denial of ultimate values, effectively precluded practical relevance for the social sciences. One of Parsons's main concerns, then, was to establish sociology – with its concern with institutions and ultimate values – as a field of study complementary to a more circumscribed economics. This bifurcation of the two disciplines would in turn provide the basis for a division of labour with the other sciences of action. In sum, Parsons's early explorations of social theory were informed by his concern with how social control could be exercised.[8]

This encounter could be divided into six main phases. In the first, Parsons discusses how variants of utilitarian social theory – in particular, orthodox economics – with their exclusion of ultimate values, lack relevance to the emergent social order. In the second phase –

covering his discussion of Marshall and Pareto – he shows how a theoretical perspective relevant to the emergent social order was immanent within the corpus of conventional economics. Drawing on Pareto's cyclical theory of social change to call into question theories of linear evolutionism, he gives credence to the notion that an emergent social order, based upon consensual values, *could* be established. In the third phase, relying on the thought of Durkheim, he seeks to show that this theoretical conception of the social order was already approximated in reality. Durkheim, however, with his commitment to positivism in both social theory and in the social order, failed to conceptualize either correctly. Parsons then traces how Durkheim abandoned this positivism in favour of idealism, thereby providing the basis for a social theory of value relevance to an emergent consensual social order. This move, however, came at the expense of scientific objectivity in social theory and the social order, implying a relativism in both. This conclusion to his analysis of Durkheim forms the transition to the fourth phase of his investigation – an inquiry into the other great tradition of thought, German idealism. Similar to Durkheim's final position, its value-oriented conception of social theory and the social order came at the expense of objectivity. In phase five, Parsons relies on Weber to show how one could overcome relativism in both social theory and the social order, therby uniting idealism and positivism in social theory and conjoining ultimate ends with rational action in the emergent society. Finally, in phase six, Parsons elaborates a standpoint representing a culmination of his encounter with European social theory. It not only embodied an activist relation to the social order and synthesized the objectivism of positivism with the subjectivism of historicism, but also implied a division of labour for the social sciences. Standing in an isomorphic relation to the emergent social order, such a standpoint would permit the analytical social sciences to help build a 'Kingdom of God on Earth.' Parsons began his exploration of the limits and possibilities of social theory with a discussion of the utilitarian-positivist tradition.

The Limitations of Utilitarian Social Theory

As Parsons emphasized, the body of European social thought centring around utilitarianism neglected the normative dimension in its theoretical frameworks:

The general effect of the individualistic elements of the European cultural tradition ... has been to emphasize the discreteness of the different individuals who make up a society, particularly with regard to their ends. The result has been to inhibit the elaboration of certain of the most important possibilities of the theory of action, those having to do with the integration of ends in systems, especially those involving a plurality of actors. ([1937] 1968, 56)

With its emphasis upon individualism and discrete ends, the utilitarian tradition of thought lacked a normative bearing in relation to contemporary society. Parsons concluded in his 1934 article on 'Service' that

since the eighteenth century various purely secular doctrines of service have arisen to fill the gap left by the fading religious sanctions. Rationalistic humanitarianism and social utilitarianism are perhaps the most widespread. They seem to lack the power of justifying to the individual a real submergence of his self-interest, which the transcendental basis has given to the ideals of service arising out of Christianity. (1934, 674)

In his discussion of how the utilitarian tradition evolved after Hobbes, Parsons sought to show that because of its individualistic and positivistic premises, utilitarianism is incapable of generating a normative theory of action. Rather than solving the Hobbesian problem of order, later utilitarian theory – as developed by John Locke – evaded it by assuming that people, by virtue of Reason, 'subordinate their actions' to certain rules specifying that they should 'respect the natural rights of others, to refrain from injuring them.' Thus, through the postulate of 'the natural identity of interests,' Locke is able to account for social order within an individualistic society. In Parsons's view, 'this is the device by which it has been possible for utilitarian thought, with few exceptions, for two hundred years to evade the Hobbesian problem' ([1937] 1968, 96–7).

The utilitarian system, moreover, because of its assumptions about the randomness of ends, was inherently unstable and tended to break down in one of two 'radical positivistic' directions, each of which fully excluded a normative dimension to human action. On the one hand, 'rationalistic radical positivism,' characteristic of 'the "left" wing of individualistic positivism ... the French rationalists, Godwin ... Owen, and Utopian socialists,' saw ends determined in conformity with the ultimate conditions of action. Hence, ends themselves play no part in human action, which is limited to the rational adaptation to 'the "facts" of our empirical external world.' This means that 'in so far as the "conditions" ultimately form the sole determinants of action the subjective aspect becomes merely a reflection of these "facts"; it is purely epiphenomenal' ([1937] 1968, 120).

On the other hand, 'radical anti-intellectualistic positivism,' characteristic of Malthus, biological determinism, and social Darwinism, views action in terms of non-normative conditions such as heredity and environment, which, in determining the course of history, render human agency superfluous (113–14). Even though the variants of radical positivism differ in terms of the role they ascribe to people's rational activity, according to Parsons, they share the feature of denying ends a place in human action.

Orthodox Economics and Its Limitations

The variant of radical positivism that concerned Parsons most was the pre-eminent social scientific orientation of his day – orthodox economics. This perspective 'assumes the wants as given data which the economist at most simplifies into relatively general types' (1934b, 416). From this standpoint, action is viewed as 'the maximization of want-satisfaction or utility.' Consistent with its utilitarian roots, orthodox economics holds that society consists of atomized individuals seeking to satisfy their wants by selecting the means most appropriate to their ends. Not only was orthodox economics incorrigibly individualistic, rationalistic, and positivistic, but it suffered from a lack of relevance to concrete historical situations. That is, 'Anglo-American economic thought,' as a 'child of the seventeenth and eighteenth centuries,' has been characterized by its 'rather abstract generality; its formulation in terms implying, or at least not denying, universal applicability wherever human economic life is lived.' From this standpoint, it has 'tended to neglect the economic problems connected with the growth and development of types of economic society, and in particular with the working out of the differences between, and the specific characteristics of, the different cultural epochs' (1928, 641).

Orthodox economic theory, with its emphasis upon rationalism, positivism, and the denial of a subjective element, was the object of Parsons's concern in his early period.[9] In this sense, he shared the viewpoint of the so-called American institutionalists like Commons, Veblen, and Mitchell, who criticized orthodox economic theory for its abstractness, formalism, and lack of historical specificity. Indeed, as Parsons would later reminisce, he originally had begun to study the social sciences as a result of his exposure to 'institutional economics': 'As an undergraduate at Amherst, influenced by an older brother who had gone into medicine, I had intended to concentrate in biology with a view either to graduate work in that field or to a medical career. But in 1923, my junior year, I was converted to social science under the influence especially of the unorthodox "institutional economist," Walton Hamilton' (1970a, 826).[10]

However, while sharing the institutionalists' dissatisfaction with orthodox economic theory, Parsons felt that the alternatives they proposed were inadequate. Rejecting 'orthodox theory' as positively wrong, they 'substitute other positivistic elements in its place as explanations of the concrete facts of economic life' (1934b, 435). Veblen, for instance, while stressing the centrality of institutions in the analysis of economic activity, 'has hardly gone beyond methodological discussions and scattered, unsystematized appeals to certain nonrational factors to explain certain concrete phenomena' (440). Institutionalists, then, 'have remained on "positivistic" ground.' Rather than seriously addressing the positivistic basis of orthodox economic theory, they have merely invoked 'such factors as the external "conditions" of action, technology or biological or psychological properties of the human individual' (442). That is to say, 'in the tradition of Anglo-Saxon economics ... unorthodox movements have concentrated their attention on the "conditions" rather than the "ends."' Hence, 'attention is thrown to such factors as the external environment, the ultimate source of natural resources, population and the laws of growth, scientific knowledge and its resultant technology or finally the "social environment" consisting above all of forms of business organization' (422). It could be considered as a variant of 'radical rationalistic positivism.' Lacking an orientation towards ultimate ends, in Parsons's view, institutional economics scarcely offered a reasonable alternative to orthodox economics.

The Historicist Alternative

There was, however, another approach to economics – the adherents of the so-called German historical school who 'have gone farther radically to repudiate the factors formulated in orthodox theory.' Maintaining a 'radical historical relativism,' the German historical school believed that 'the attempt of orthodox theory to build up a general economic

science' was 'foredoomed to failure.' Rather, 'each economic organization must be considered as a reality "sui generis," as a thing by and for
itself, without essential connection with others. Economics cannot
hope to set up a universal system of analytical concepts but must attack
each period as an entirely new problem' (1934b, 445). What provided
order in each epoch, according to the historical school, was 'an
ethico-spiritual factor, the *Volksgeist*, which is an irreducible entity,
above all not a psychological factor in the positivistic sense' (445). While
Parsons was sympathetic with the efforts of the German historical
school to ground a theory of economics based on shared values, he was
concerned about the relativism that this position implied (1934b, 423).
Indeed, he expressed concern that one of the harshest critics of orthodox
economics – R.W. Souter – was developing a position that led to the
'radical historical relativism of the more extreme German "Historisis-
mus" ' and to the standpoint of Sombart that 'there can be no such thing
as a generally applicable economic theory, but only a plurality of
theories each applying to a particular historical economic system'
(1934c, 531). Souter's empiricism, 'if followed through to its logical
conclusion, would altogether eliminate systematic abstraction from the
social sciences' (544). By embracing a version of 'historicism,' the
theorist ran the danger of lapsing into irrationalism.

The respective shortcomings of both the 'positivist' and 'historicist'
schools of economics were more than of analytical concern to Parsons.
They embodied the inadequacy of the contemporary 'analytical sciences' in the face of the Hobbesian problem of order besetting modern
society. Since economics was pre-eminent among the social sciences,
its shortcomings represented a failure on the part of the totality of
social-scientific fields. In this sense, neither wing of economic thought
offered an adequate standpoint for dealing with the Hobbesian problem
of order.

Positivist economics, with its attention confined to individualistic
wants, failed to define and articulate the system of ultimate ends.
Implied by its positivistic-utilitarian assumptions, moreover, was the
belief in linear evolutionism: given that 'the pursuit by each individual
of his own self-interest and private ends would result in the greatest
possible satisfaction of the wants of all,' then progressive development
could be ensured if all obstacles to the 'rational pursuit of self-interest'
were to be removed ([1937] 1968, 4). Accordingly, 'the dynamic factor' in
this 'linear theory of social evolution' is 'the progressive accumulation
of scientific knowledge' (123). This meant that the role of the 'analytical
scientist' in this process of social change would be one of providing a

greater awareness of 'means and conditions,' thereby helping to eliminate 'ignorance and error' from an increasingly rational form of human
action. As noted earlier, Parsons saw contemporary social trends as
belying the linear conception of social development and proposed that
the current disorder could be overcome through the infusion of a system
of ultimate ends. With its emphasis upon linear evolutionism and
rational individualism, however, the dominant variants of utilitarianism – orthodox and institutional economics – were irrelevant to the
recognition and articulation of such a system.

Historicism, with its emphasis on the spiritual *Volksgeist* uniting the
social actors, seemed to offer a promising alternative. However, with its
denial that society could be scientifically apprehended, it implied a
dangerous relativism, because lacking a scientific standpoint, it was
incapable of claiming that the values or ends that it recognized were
objectively determined. For if the system of values currently ascendant
in society was only one among various alternatives, then the perspective embracing it could do little to ensure that conformity to it would
take place. With its inherent relativism, historicist idealism could
contribute little to social control.

The limitations of historicism pointed towards the development of a
standpoint that combined the scientific objectivity of 'positivism' with
the normative orientation of 'idealism.' It would consist of interrelated
analytical sciences, each examining a different aspect of society. Such a
theoretical system would be *relevant* to the post-utilitarian social order
that Parsons envisioned. That order was characterized by a system of
ultimate ends embodied in institutions that would channel action,
thereby ensuring order. Such a normative system, as it were, would
provide the immediate ends, which would then serve as the proximate
goals of human action. Action itself, however, would still proceed in a
rational way, as the actor chose means and adapted to conditions. The
model of man as a calculating scientist would no longer be appropriate,
for he did not simply fit means to given ends, but rather acted on the
basis of ultimate values. This meant, in turn, that society could not be
reduced to economic activities, but instead could be differentiated into
economic, social, and political spheres of action, depending on the level
of the means-end chain that is examined.

This model of society was implicit in Parsons's critique of utilitarian
society and was thought to provide a better approximation of how social
order could be created under conditions of capitalist individualism. If a
practical 'solution' to the Hobbesian problem were to be effected, a
theoretical system isomorphic with the central features of the new

social order had to be developed.[11] Parsons's efforts to synthesize idealism and positivism in *Social Action* can be viewed as an effort to establish an approach of this kind. Given its congruence with the post-utilitarian model of society that Parsons viewed as the most promising and realistic alternative to Hobbesian anarchy, this standpoint would contribute to the consolidation of the new order.

Parsons's treatment of utilitarianism constituted, then, the necessary prelude to his discussion of the four main figures in *Social Action*. Having shown that utilitarian social theory could not provide the basis for scientifically defining a system of norms relevant to integrating social action, he was now in a position not only to elaborate how a post-utilitarian society could be constituted, but also to formulate a theoretical approach of practical relevance to this task. It was this concern that informed Parsons's treatment of Marshall, Pareto, Weber, and Durkheim (and to some degree Sombart and Marx) in *The Structure of Social Action*. Parsons's encounter with classical social theory was practically conceived: through his reading and interpretation of classical social theory, he sought to gain insights into how a social theory having strategic relevance to 'modern' society might be established. This is reflected in his choice of theorists, the order in which they are discussed, the issues selected, and the emphases given. These practical designs account in part for the distortions that critics have detected in Parsons's interpretation of classical social theory (Camic 1979; Cohen et al. 1975; Pope et al. 1975; Giddens 1976a).[12] It is, however, not the purpose of this account to demonstrate that Parsons offered a biased rendering of classical theory. Rather, I seek to show that a particular reading and ordering of classical thought follows from his practical designs, and that an emerging isomorphism between theory and society can be detected in his discussion of classical thought.

3

The Redemption of Positivism

The Sociological Moment in Marshall's Economics

In elaborating upon the movement of European social theory towards a voluntaristic system of action, Parsons begins by discussing the work of the British economist Alfred Marshall. In view of the fact that his main concern was with the sociological writings of Pareto, Durkheim, Weber, Simmel, and Tönnies (1935b, 282–3), this inclusion of Marshall might be considered inconsistent.[1] Yet in terms of his practical designs, Parsons's critique of Marshall was essential, for he was 'overwhelmingly the most eminent representative of his generation of the orthodox school.' Indeed, 'their case may be almost said to stand or fall with his work' (1931, 101). Marshall's work represented to Parsons the embodiment of orthodox economic thought, a perspective that rested on the foundations of utilitarian positivism. As noted in chapter two, neo-classical economics had little practical bearing on the modern social order because of its failure to acknowledge ultimate values in its framework. Through its advocacy of an encyclopaedic sociology, founded on economic thought, it limited the emergence of other disciplines. By working through the implications of Marshall's ideas, then, Parsons sought to come to terms with his doubts about orthodox economic theory.[2]

Yet as a representative of conventional economic thought, Marshall was not altogether typical. For unlike other notable economists such as Lionel Robbins whose systems were thoroughly positivistic,[3] Marshall had broken with orthodoxy, developing a body of economic thought that could be reconciled with a broader framework of social-scientific analysis. He had distanced himself from the view of utility economics that human wants are given, and he 'refuses to take wants as ultimate data without inquiring into their genesis' (1931, 111). Instead, Marshall emphasizes the importance of 'economic activities,' which, 'pursued not for ulterior motives but as ends in themselves, are the principal agents in the formation of the noblest qualities of human character and main fields of their expression' (107). Within such a framework, wants are not accepted as 'given data,' but rather 'an expression of wants, adjusted to or created by activities,' always goes with 'the development of activities' ([1937] 1968, 143).

Embodied in Marshall's theoretical framework, then, was a conception of society representing a significant departure from utilitarian theory. He viewed the social order as consisting of a 'single, relatively well-integrated system of value attitudes' (703). As embodied in the activities, this 'value system becomes to him the primary moving force of social evolution' (703). Given that the activities as shared standards of character development shaped individual wants, it follows that social order could be ensured through the cultivation of these activities throughout society. Such a conception of society was clearly incompatible with the orthodox school of economic theory whose efforts to 'construct an abstract science of economics' led to a body of thought of little relevance to the 'concrete historical individuals' of contemporary capitalism (620).

Marshall's approach, moreover, represented an advance over the critiques of orthodox economic thought developed by the 'institutionalists.' Unlike the proponents of this approach, Marshall did not dismiss the possibility that economics could make use of analytical theory. At the same time, however, with his conception of 'activities,' he went beyond the positivism of institutionalist thought. This meant viewing the value-laden activities as equivalent to a 'calling' or 'ethic,' which in turn guided and shaped the rationally inspired wants. The implication for the social sciences was that economics, as a field of study concerned with 'rational' action, could be complemented with a more sociologically grounded approach dealing with 'systems of values.' Implicit in Marshall's work is a 'position on the broadest questions of social theory so definite that it must be held to constitute a system of sociology' (1932, 345).

Nevertheless, Marshall's efforts were incomplete. Because he shared the 'empiricism' of his 'predecessors and contemporaries,' he failed to work out the theoretical implications of his line of reasoning ([1937] 1968, 169). In accepting the assumptions of laissez-faire thinking as the social basis for human conduct, he assumed that one could explain *all* action on the basis of rational means-end oriented behaviour. Marshall, in this sense, 'dealt with the value factor only in the peculiar form of "activities"' (175). These 'became the basis of a theory of the "progressive development of character" which promotes the concrete realization of an individualistic economy, of free enterprise' (176). This led him to embrace a linear view of social evolution in which the present epoch was seen as characterized by the ineluctable expansion of rational conduct. Consistent with his conception of the social order, he supported a theoretical perspective that incorporated sociological insights into the rational corpus of economic theory. For inasmuch as the inevitable tendency in development was towards the standards of rational conduct supplied by 'activities,' the normative dimension of action was seen as merely an aspect of economic life. Hence, Marshall was committed to 'an "economic imperialism" in the bad sense of suppressing the "rights" of neighbouring sciences to an "independent" existence in the society of the sciences' (1934c, 522). Parsons found this to be far too naive in its implications, for if Marshall had taken into account the great variation in systems of ultimate values as they related to economic activity, he would have perhaps recognized how his theoretical approach differed from that of orthodox economics. While Marshall did indeed go beyond utilitarian thought by introducing the notion of 'activities,' this was 'fitted in in a way to cause remarkably little disturbance of the general outline of the system' ([1937] 1968, 176).

In his subsequent analysis, Parsons seeks to draw out some of the implications of Marshall's theory of activities for developing a social theory of relevance to the capitalist social order. Of particular concern was overcoming the view implicit in Marshall's account that society was evolving in a linear fashion towards capitalist rationality. This conception of society, with its emphasis upon individual rational action and unbroken progress, was greatly at odds with the notion of the modern social order held by Parsons. With its implied inevitability, it offered no scope for possible intervention. If a theoretical approach were committed to this kind of inevitability, it could scarcely have any practical bearing on the chronic problems of disorder that Parsons detected in the society of the period. It was crucial that the rational corpus of economics be complemented by a body of thought – sociology – which would concern itself with the 'irrational' or 'non-rational' aspect of social life. All the same, if sociology were to achieve the status of a fully credible social science, its statements would have to originate in a standpoint of scientific objectivity. The problem facing Parsons, then, was one of demarcating a sphere of inquiry specific to sociology that was both objective and normatively oriented. From such a standpoint, the set of transcendental ultimate values could be defined and articulated. This, in turn, would contribute to the normative ordering of modern society.

However, before a perspective of this kind could be elaborated, a conception of the social order embodying both 'non-rational' and 'rational' components was required. As a more realistic account of contemporary society than that given by positivism, or the linear evolutionism of Marshall, such a view of the social order would serve as the necessary backdrop to the development of a social theory of relevance to problems of social control. Parsons's immediate task was to elaborate a conception of the social order that combined both rational and non-rational features, yet did not fall prey to the linear evolutionism of Marshall. He then could indicate how a systematic sociology of practical relevance to that order might be formulated. It was with this set of concerns that Parsons turned to the writings of Vilfredo Pareto.

Pareto

Parsons emphasized that Pareto's conception of the changing social order differed dramatically from that of Marshall and his utilitarian contemporaries.

Pareto explicitly and emphatically rejected the theory of linear social evolution which plays such an important part in Marshall's thought and that of his generation, above all in England. In its place he puts mainly a theory of cycles according to which social forms pass through a series of stages which are repeated again and again in approximately the same order ... it is certainly legitimate to regard his theory of social change as radically different from that of Marshall and the other evolutionists. ([1937] 1968, 178)

This cyclical theory of history had enormous implications for the way the 'contemporary social situation' was viewed. In particular, there was no certainty that 'the trends of development in the later nineteenth and early twentieth century,' such as 'technological "progress" and increasing economic prosperity,' would continue (178–9). In opposition to this optimistic vision of social change, Pareto offers a much more sobering assessment of what lies in store for modern societies. Rather than the 'individualism, humanitarianism, intellectual freedom, [and] skepticism' of the recent past, 'restrictions on individual freedom, intellectual, economic and political, a revival of faith in place of skepticism and an increase in the use of force' were to be expected in the near future ([1937] 1968, 179). Moreover, unlike Marshall who had an essentially harmonious view of the social order, Pareto emphasized the 'disharmony of class interests' and 'the role of force and fraud in social life.' According to the theory of linear evolution, this set of phenomena disruptive to the social order was thought to be 'permanently outgrown' or 'destined to be superceded with increasing effectiveness, and permanently' (179). However, as Pareto's cyclical theory attested, such things as force, fraud, ideologies, and limitations on freedom were enduring features of a changing social order, occurring with patterned regularity.

It is evident that Pareto's conception of social order, in Parsons's view, offered a much closer approximation to contemporary society than that held by Marshall and those working within the utilitarian tradition. With its emphasis upon tendencies like the use of force and fraud, it accurately captured the kinds of social disorder that could occur at any time.[4] Moreover, Pareto's conception of social change as cyclical had significant implications for how the current situation might be transcended. If such tendencies in the past had given way to periods of stability and integration, then, presumably, the present period would be no exception. Parsons drew on Pareto's cyclical theory of social change to elaborate a perspective that offered a *theoretical* solution to how the current state of social disorder could be overcome.

Pareto's Theory of Social Order

What interested Parsons above all in Pareto's conception of the social order is the distinction he makes between 'logical' and 'non-logical' actions. Action is viewed as logical if it corresponds to the standard of rationality found in logico-experimental science. Correspondingly, non-logical actions are those that depart from the standards of logico-experimental science ([1937] 1968, 192 ff). Parsons gave particular attention to one class in Pareto's schema of non-logical action, namely the residues, 'the relatively constant element, a "manifestation of sentiments" not rationally based or justified' (1933, 577). The residues figure prominently in Pareto's schema, in that they form the basis for his cyclical theory of social change; it is the alternating rise and fall of these forms of non-logical action that provide the dynamism for cyclical social development. On the basis of these non-logical residues, Pareto's theory of the social order could be distinguished from that of the linear evolutionists. Since these forms of non-rational conduct periodically manifest themselves, the social order could scarcely be viewed as inevitably moving towards greater rationality of action.

The residues, however, were not simply of abstract interest to Parsons. They were also valuable analytical devices for apprehending the problems of social disorder that were current. In this sense, Parsons's discussion of the residues is highly informed both by Calvinist sympathies and Hobbesian fears. On the one hand, he continually expresses his approval of the epochs of the past when religious movements were able to provide the basis for social order. On the other hand, he shows great concern for those periods of history when the pursuit of self-interest – akin to the world of Thomas Hobbes – threatened to undermine social stability. Accordingly, what Parsons seeks to realize in his reading of Pareto is insight into how a social order providing the stability of traditional religious societies in an age of self-interests could be realized. It is with this set of concerns, then, that Parsons examines Pareto's conception of how the cyclical alternation of residues forms the basis for social transformation.

In Pareto's cyclical theory of social change, two residues are, according to Parsons, of particular importance, namely the 'instinct of combinations' and the 'persistence of aggregates.' These two classes of residues are in continual struggle for supremacy in the social order, and their rise and fall in relation to one another form the basis for cyclical change. Pareto's cycle begins with the accession to power of the aggregates. Those persons strong in this residue 'value the future above the present, the ideal above the material, and subordinate their personal interests to those of the collectivities to which they belong' ([1937] 1968, 279).

The period when those strong in 'aggregates' – the 'lions' and 'speculators' – dominate society is known as an 'age of faith.' During such a time, 'non-scientific' religious ideas are in ascendancy, ensuring social order through the provision of a value system common to the community. That is to say, when 'residues of persistence' predominate in society, there is widespread '"faith" in the reality of certain nonexperimental entities.' These commonly take the form of 'transcendental' or 'ideal' ends, which 'may be thought of as exercising a discipline over conduct' (284). In this sense, Parsons saw Pareto as restoring 'religion to a vital role in social life, above all to the role of the great stabilizer. It is vital, Pareto says, because it is the only force which can bring about a subordination of mens' individual interests to the larger "utility" of a society' (1932a, 23). Faith can justifiably be enforced by the use of force, if it represents the collective interest. Faith gives the governing classes 'the strength of character and the forthright resolution to act in pursuit of their ends without deviation and above all to use force if necessary' (19–20). Indeed, 'force frequently attends the "creative" process by which a new value system becomes established in a society in part through the accession to power of a new elite' ([1937] 1968, 291).

The ascendancy of 'persistent aggregates,' then, despite their use of force, is thought to be beneficial to the stability of the social order.

Socially considered, the residues of persistence are important largely as agencies of discipline. They are responsible for the individual's subordination of his interests to a higher and wider 'cause' or 'good' and this 'cause' usually works for the 'good' of the whole in the sense of ensuring its meeting the fundamental conditions of its existence such as protection from external enemies and provision for the future of the society, besides making some advance toward realization of a 'higher utility' in terms of the 'end' of the society. (1932a, 21)

Hence, a regime based on faith, using force when necessary, would be an acceptable social arrangement, for it could ensure stability and exert social control.[5]

Nevertheless, the predominance of the residues of persistence, as based on force, is inherently unstable. While force can be used to advantage to gain power, it is not an effective means for maintaining it. There is a tendency to turn to more indirect means, characterized by the use of 'ruse,' to keep power secure. This, however, permits the rise into the governing ranks of those skilful in ruse, namely the class that is strong in 'combinations.' Putting a premium on 'innovation, inventiveness, projecting and scheming,' they seek to attain their goals by 'cleverness and resourcefulness.' As the ruling elite becomes more predominantly composed of the 'foxes,' the use of 'ruse' increases. This practice 'shades all the way from clever strategem and maneuvering, appeal to interest and sentiment, over to outright fraud' ([1937] 1968, 279–80). But 'as the dominance of the residues of combinations becomes more complete,' the 'ruse associated with the foxes ... shades off' into the 'polar extreme' of fraud. In '"getting something out of others," which is the main point of view from which both the concepts are framed, it is no longer mere cleverness in devising ways and means but passes over into deception' (290).

The growing dominance of the 'instinct of combinations' in the elite, however, comes at the expense of the 'persistence of aggregates,' which now become more concentrated in civil society. If they are not somehow given increased access to the governing elite, they could form a 'forceful opposition' who could overthrow the governing elite, whose 'resistance to force' has been weakened by the 'increasing predominance of the men of combinations' (282). The accession to power of the lions would thus initiate a new cycle of change.

In examining the interplay between 'persistent aggregates' and 'combinations,' Parsons, in effect, imposed Hobbes's and Tönnies's vision of society on the writings of Pareto. The ascendancy of the persistent aggregates in society can be likened to the form of social control found in the traditional religious-based *Gemeinschaft*. In this case, order is based on the shared sentiments of common faith. The persistent aggregates, however, have difficulty maintaining social stability under pressure from appetites and interests: 'There would seem to be an inherently difficult problem of control, of keeping the interests in conformity with an ultimate value system. Such a system, above all in the form of a system of institutional norms is subject to a continuous 'bombardment of interests' which, in the absence of especially powerful controls, is likely eventually to break it down to such a degree as seriously to endanger social stability' (285–6).

The combinations appear to embody the egoistic self-interests of Hobbes's state of nature and Tönnies's *Gesellschaft*, for they are characterized by 'a state of the absence of effective control by such ideal ends or value elements over conduct. Here attention centers on the immediate rather than the ultimate, the satisfaction of the appetites, the pursuit of wealth and power. In other words, a high development of this class of residues places a particularly strong premium on interests' (285). As Parsons elsewhere notes, 'It has appeared at several points that there is a close connection between the residues of combinations and the "interests." In a sense we may say the former provided for Pareto the non-rational background above all of economic activity. It is thus noteworthy that he holds economic acquisitiveness does not come into full development until the control of the residues is somewhat relaxed' (1932a, 21).

According to Parsons, then, it is the growing predominance of the residue of combinations that threatens the well-being of society: 'Social life becomes instead of a common pursuit of a common end, a struggle for power and wealth. This struggle is, unless kept within bounds by the common ends of the society by the faith, essentially disintegrating in its effect. Above all, it leads to the unbounded reign of corruption and fraud, of ruse' (22). In this sense, 'fraud ... attends the later stages in the breakdown of the persistence of aggregates ... and may become an important factor in the state of instability which necessitates a reintegration' ([1937] 1968, 291). Overall, 'the cycle is essentially that of the effective control and discipline over action by ... value complexes' alternating with 'the relaxation of that control opening the door to a relatively free play of appetites.' This latter state of affairs, in turn, 'creates conditions of instability which sooner or later put an end to this phase of the cycle' (288).

Parsons thus regarded the social order attendant upon the ascendancy of the persistent aggregates as a standard for subsequent developments. The rise of the combinations represented a trend towards increasing disorder as individuals use fraud to attain their ends. 'These tendencies are ordinarily held in check, not, as Hobbes thought, by the policeman, but by the "persistence of aggregates" or in more common terms by "moral scruples." ' Moreover, 'while force is a symptom of strong faith and devotion to ideal ends, the prevalence of fraud and corruption is a symptom of social disintegration' (1932a, 28). The shift from the use of fraud rather than force signals a corresponding change in the relative presence of 'ideal ends' or 'religion' in society. 'The use of force is the direct result of their living vitality. The prevalence of fraud is one of the surest aftersigns of their decay' (29). Hence, 'in the long run a society given over so exclusively to the pursuit of "interests" of wealth and power as such, cannot even meet the indispensable conditions of its existence, to say nothing of accomplishing any "higher end." ' This form of society, as discussed by Pareto, corresponded closely to Parsons's conception of the contemporary social order. Pareto's cyclical vision of history, then, held the promise that a new form of 'faith' could restore order to society. Parsons remarks that although Pareto does not state 'what the faith should be ... he leaves no doubt that in his opinion the very existence of our society depends on there being one' (34). This suggested, then, that society could be cyclically moving towards a new age of faith – supported by coercive force – serving to reintegrate society.

Pareto's Theoretical Solution to Social Disorder

Parsons goes further than claiming that Pareto holds faith to be an essential element of society. He suggests that Pareto's theoretical conception of contemporary society rests on a feature very much akin to 'faith.' Parsons notes that in opposition to the utilitarian view that society consists solely of rational, self-interested actors, Pareto emphasizes 'the *end* which the society should pursue by means of logico-experimental reasoning' ([1937] 1968, 224). Parsons takes great pains to draw out the implications of this statement in developing his notion that 'the ultimate ends ... must to a significant extent constitute a coherent system' (231). That Parsons accepted this conception of the social order is evident in his views on the 'most modern conception of society.' According to this perspective, the 'non-scientific' or 'metaphysical' ultimate ends must 'be regarded as integrated into a harmonious system of ends, governing in various ways all the actions of the members of the group.' Moreover, 'the system of ultimate ends' not only determines 'what is specifically sought after as wealth and power,' but 'the system of ultimate ends of the community ... may form the basis of a framework of regulatory norms which guide and control action in pursuit of immediate ends, maintaining orderly processes and relationships and keeping the vast complexes of such utilitarian actions in some kind of harmony with the ultimate value system of the community' (1934a, 231).

This ultimate value system integrating the ends of action represents a stabilizing *Aufhebung*[6] of the cyclically alternating ages of faith and scepticism. The system of ultimate ends corresponds to the normative character of society in an 'age of faith.' At the same time, however, the social order preserves the rationality characteristic of an 'age of scepticism.' For within the system of ultimate ends, actors still rationally pursue their interests.

The conception of the social order as based on a system of ultimate ends was central to the theoretical standpoint that Parsons developed from Pareto. Although this standpoint conformed to the tenets of logico-experimental reasoning, it was still guided by the normative standard of a 'system of ultimate ends.' From this perspective, the residual non-logical normative elements could be distinguished and analysed. Implicitly, then, the theoretical framework Parsons derived from Pareto was more than merely a potentially fruitful way to describe the social order. By its very nature, it had practical implications for the exercise of social control. What gave this approach its practical bent was its relation to the non-logical normative residues of society. The theoretical perspective developed by Pareto permitted one to identify the degree to which 'combinations' or 'aggregates' were present in society. As Parsons emphasized, from the standpoint developed by Pareto, the residues do not merely refer to the psychological attributes of particular social groupings but represented 'theories' or 'ideologies' that can permeate society, directing the actions of its members. The ages of 'faith' and 'scepticism' are seen as periods when the 'ideologies' of the 'aggregates' and the 'combinations' exert a hold on the behaviour of social actors. That the ascendancy of the residues can lead either to rampant force or to fraud indicates that neither aggregates nor combinations can provide a satisfactory basis for social order.

However, by using the framework developed from Pareto's work, it becomes possible to contribute to the control of such destabilizing residues. The very process of apprehending these ideological deviations helps undermine their credibility. In demonstrating that these theories make claims not on logical but rather on non-logical grounds, their irrational and partisan character would be exposed.

Implications for control can be detected in both of the two main residues discussed by Parsons. Persistence of aggregates could be revealed as non-scientific, irrational tendencies that resort to force in order to impose their beliefs on the community. The residues of persistence are, in this sense, the social embodiment of idealism. Their irrationality and subjectivism can be threatening to the order when they pursue their ideals by using forceful means to attain their ends. In contrast, combinations could be shown to be pseudo-scientific, claiming to be objective when they represented nothing more than immediate interests. Combinations thus approximate the perspective of positivism, with its rational pursuit of discrete ends. As Parsons approvingly remarks on Pareto's treatment of the various ideologies or 'theories' of this kind, 'his first great service is, by his exhaustive critique of these theories, the revelation of their extremely wide extent. Above all by deflating the pretensions of very many such theories to scientific status he has greatly altered the view held in many circles of the relative importance of the logical and the nonlogical elements of action' ([1937] 1968, 269).

This applies in particular to rationally conceived reform programs, such as 'democracy, humanitarianism, equality, progress [and] evolutionary ethics,' which 'are not and cannot be scientifically justified ... From the point of view of logico-experimental science, these beliefs are in exactly the same status as all other previous beliefs, as Christian theology, as the natural rights theories, as the Homeric tales about the adventures of the gods' (1932a, 6–7). Hence, the theoretical framework derived from the writings of Pareto permitted undermining the credibility of both non-scientific and pseudo-scientific theories. What made this possible was a standpoint that was scientifically objective, yet oriented towards values. Through the very process of identifying residues in this manner, a social order founded on interests pursued within a system of ultimate ends would be affirmed and consolidated.

The standpoint inherent in Pareto's schema, then, could provide the basis for intervening in the social order, moving it in the direction of greater integration through overcoming dissident variations of either 'aggregates' or 'combinations.' Parsons emphasized that a theoretical approach of this kind could not rest on the foundations provided by either orthodox economic theory or social Darwinism. While the former has no place for the 'ultimate ends' that make up the 'distributive order in a social system' ([1937] 1968, 265), the latter reduces these ends to non-normative factors such as heredity and the environment (219–28). By rejecting these positivistic accounts as inadequate, and by indicating how normative non-logical actions might be scientifically studied, Pareto also laid the basis for the formation of sociology as an independent field of inquiry. If 'pure economics' as 'an analytically abstract theoretical system' was 'to be concretely applicable' it 'needed to be supplemented with other, sociological elements' (264). Pareto was 'acutely conscious of the concrete problems his economics could not solve[;] he felt an intense need for a broader science to supplement it and so turned to sociology' (1933, 577). All the same, this did not imply that economics ought to be dispensed with entirely. Within the schema derived from Pareto, it would still concern itself with 'the processes of rational acquisition of scarce means to the actor's ends by production and economic exchange, and of their rational allocation as between alternative uses' ([1937] 1968, 266). Complementing this more circumscribed economic theory, sociology, following Pareto's insights, would concern itself with the 'common system of ultimate ends' that constituted society.

The approach founded on the writings of Pareto was, like that of Marshall, incomplete. Most notably, while it provided a critical standpoint in relation to the changing social order and prevailing theories of social development, it did not elaborate a detailed alternative to either. Pareto was, in Parsons's view, 'a "knocker" not a "booster." He is pointing out what he believes to be elements of instability which are dangerous from the point of view of the maintenance of the regime and its further development' (1932a, 33). Nevertheless, with 'the general distinction between the normative and the non-normative nonlogical elements,' and through 'the differentiation of the normative side of the structure,' Pareto's work, according to Parsons, makes important breakthroughs towards 'a new theoretical reconstruction' ([1937] 1968, 300).[7] Indeed, argued Parsons, Pareto's theoretical conception of the social order 'opens the way to an interpretation of the basis of order in a society which is in a sense "immanent," founded in the character of the society itself. Whether this element is to have empirical importance is essentially a question of fact and cannot be answered in terms of the present abstract analysis alone' (238). If this approach were to be fully developed it would be necessary to specify how this 'immanence' was not merely a theoretical artefact, but could be revealed empirically in social reality. This would involve an examination of 'the structure of social systems as such' (300), observing how the system of ultimate ends as embodied in institutions is able to successfully constrain actions. Such an investigation, in turn, would permit one to better determine the subject matter and content specific to sociology. To build on and elaborate the insights derived from Pareto, Parsons gave consideration to the writings of Emile Durkheim.[8]

Emile Durkheim

Having derived a theoretical conception of modern society from his examination of Pareto, Parsons shows how an *empirical* account of that social order could be found in the writings of Emile Durkheim. In his view, Durkheim stresses the 'empirical fact' that the 'vast complex of action in the pursuit of individual interests takes place within the framework of a body of rules, independent of the immediate individual motives of the contracting parties.' This, in Parsons's view, 'is the central empirical insight from which Durkheim's theoretical development starts, and which he never lost' ([1937] 1968, 314).

In effect, Parsons's treatment of Durkheim's 'empirical insight' into the nature of society is guided by his preoccupation with the Hobbesian problem of order and the shortcomings of utilitarianism. 'It is clear that what Durkheim does here is to reraise in a peculiarly trenchant form the whole Hobbesian problem. There are features of the existing "individualistic" order which cannot be accounted for in terms of the elements formulated in utilitarian theory' (314). Reiterating the same argument that had been advanced on behalf of Marshall and Pareto, Parsons claims that the empirical social order as described by Durkheim cannot be accounted for by utilitarian theory. In this case, Herbert Spencer's 'contractual relation,' with its emphasis upon mutual exchange as the basis for social order, fails to acknowledge that 'the rules regulating relations of contract – has not been agreed to by the parties but exists prior to and independently by any such agreement' (311). With his emphasis upon the 'common value element,' Durkheim provides an account of the social order superior to that of Spencerian individualism. As a variant of utilitarianism, then, Spencer's contractual theory is lacking in relevance to society.

However, Parsons emphasizes that the theoretical perspective initially developed by Durkheim is not without its weaknesses. Commenting on Durkheim's writings, Parsons notes that in 'the earlier period his empirical insights were a good deal nearer his final position than was the theoretical scheme.' Indeed, 'the attempt to bridge this gap was doubtless an important driving force in the process of theoretical development' (315). As an extension of his treatment of Marshall and Pareto, Parsons distinguishes between Durkheim's conception of the social order ('empirical insights') and the social theory ('theoretical scheme') that he used to analyse society. Regarding Durkheim's early writings, Parsons suggests that the two were at odds with each other. While Durkheim's 'empirical insight' of 'the importance of a system of regulatory, normative rules' was essentially accurate, the 'conceptual scheme' he used did not permit him to provide a correct account of how these rules formed the basis for social order (314). Specifically, in his early phase, Durkheim was still very much attached to the positivistic approach as inherited from his 'acknowledged master,' Auguste Comte. Indeed, as 'the spiritual heir of Comte ... every element in his thinking is rooted deeply in the system of thought of which Comte was so eminent an exponent' (307).

Positivism, as the term is used by Parsons, is not confined to describing the orientation of the social scientist towards his subject matter – the conventional understanding of the term.[9] Rather, it refers simultaneously to the stance of the individual actor in relation to the social order. In both instances of actor and observer, 'positivism' means that one treats the social order as an objective or natural one, consisting of 'facts' exterior to the actor, and exerting a constraint upon him. In this sense, according to Parsons, 'social facts,' to Durkheim, 'were thus *choses*, to both the observer and the actor, characterized by exteriority to and constraint of the actor' (352). They were 'social facts ... not only to the sociological observer, but also the actor himself' (359).

Parsons emphasizes that 'positivism' as it pertains to both actor and observer had significant implications for the way social control was understood by Durkheim. In Parsons's view, Durkheim's early commitment to positivism led him to misrepresent the nature of social control as exercised through regulatory rules.

Durkheim seems to think of a rule and its sanctions as morally or emotionally neutral to the actor. The actor is thought of as if he were a dispassionate and objective scientist. Just as the conditions of biological existence are unalterable facts of the external world which

*it would be foolish either to approve or resent, so are the rules of
conduct of one's society and the things that will happen to one if one
violates them just facts.* ([1937] 1968, 380)

In this sense, 'the attitude of the actor' is one of calculation. Indeed, 'this
calculating "individual" is to Durkheim still the concrete individual at
least so far as his subjective aspect is concerned' (380). Given this stance
towards the order on the part of the actor, 'there is no other possible
motive of obedience to the rule than avoidance of sanctions' (381).

With his early commitment to positivism, then, Durkheim shared
the utilitarian conception of the ' "individual" ... as pursuing his own
private ends under a given set of conditions.' This in turn led him to
view constraint in terms of the actor rationally choosing to avoid
sanctions. However, such a position, in Parsons's view, is inherently
unstable. Durkheim could only with difficulty emphasize the 'social
factor' as the basis for constraint, while at the same time retain
essentially individualistic and rationalistic assumptions about social
action. The view of the actor as a 'calculating individual' assumed as
well that wants were individually given, a state of affairs incompatible
with the primacy of the social factor in society. Parsons suggests that
Durkheim overcame this contradiction in his schema when he sought
to come to terms with the occurrence of 'anomie.'

Specifically, anomie refers to the 'state of disorganization where the
hold of norms over individual conduct has broken down.' Hence, 'when
this controlling normative structure is upset and disorganized, individual conduct is equally disorganized and chaotic – the individual loses
himself in a void of meaningless activities' ([1937] 1968, 377).

The occurrence of anomie represented, then, a momentary breakdown of 'socially given moral norms by which ends of action are
defined.' In this sense, 'if anything happens to break down the discipline
of these norms the result is personal disequilibrium, which results in
various forms of personal breakdown, in extreme instances, suicide'
(336). Anomie represents a state of disorganization in the social order,
the extension of which 'is dangerous to physical life itself' (392).

The concept of anomie, however, was more than merely a theoretical
possibility within Durkheim's analytical framework. It was based on a
'body of empirical fact' of relevance to the 'problem of control.' This
implies that anomie, as the momentary release of 'appetites and
interests' from social discipline, posed a real threat to social integration
and stability. Parsons interprets the concept of anomie in terms of his
concerns about the increasing trend toward social disorganization in the

contemporary social situation. The fact that anomie occurs indicates that the normative order is no longer capable of exerting control over appetites and interests. As a state of normlessness, the widespread presence of anomie, in Parsons's view, corresponds to the 'fraud of the foxes,' the 'individualization' and 'the dissolution of community ties,' attendant upon the 'combinations' phase of cyclical social development described by Pareto.[10] With this breakdown of the normative system – analogous to the decline of aggregates – society begins to approximate more closely 'the state of "pure individualism" which is for Durkheim as it was for Hobbes the war of all against all' ([1937] 1968, 377; see also 407).

Anomie was for Parsons yet another way of diagnosing the tendencies towards breakdown he detected in the social order. Indeed, with its emphasis upon the release of appetites and interests, normless conduct, and personal disorganization, it embodied in a stark and concise form various elements from Pareto's 'age of scepticism,' Tönnies's 'Gesellschaft,' and Hobbes's 'war of all against all.' Anomie, then, represented an effective way of comprehending a rather disturbing trend in the course of social development.

Parsons, however, did not confine his concern to the manner by which Durkheim and the other theorists diagnosed the tendencies in Western civilization. He was also concerned with the kinds of solutions to the problem of growing disorder they suggested. Consistent with these concerns, his discussion of anomie shows a practical interest in how it could be overcome. Specifically, in Parsons's view, Durkheim's concern with the regulation of anomic tendencies leads him to completely abandon positivist assumptions about social action. With its neglect of the normative system, positivism can neither explain adequately how action in the social order occurs, nor show how anomie is subject to controlling norms. The concept of anomie presupposes a normative system, and its appearance means that the normative system is not working satisfactorily. Nevertheless, that anomie can be discussed at all in this manner suggests that a system of norms is an inherent feature of society. Thus, with his conceptualization of anomie, Durkheim takes the position 'that the body of normative elements governing conduct in a community forms a consistent system and that its control over the individual is actually effective – that it gets itself obeyed' ([1937] 1968, 377). This suggests that the normative system is immanent within society – although it may not always be manifest. Parsons argues that Durkheim came to this realization when confronted with the phenomenon of anomie.

The fact that anomie could arise means that Durkheim's notion of constraint as external could not be sustained. Given that anomie reveals that 'wants are in principle unlimited, it is an essential condition of both social stability and individual happiness that they should be regulated in terms of norms.' The norms, however, do not 'merely regulate "externally" ... they enter directly into the constitution of the actors' ends themselves' ([1937] 1968, 382).

This way of viewing social action has important implications for the maintenance of social control. No longer does the actor rationally choose a course of action so as to avoid constraints externally imposed on him by an objective social order. Instead, he voluntarily complies with symbolic norms that exert a *moral* force on his actions. In this sense, 'adherence is binding on the individual ... not from physical necessity but from moral obligation' (384). This means that the attitude of the actor towards the order is not one of moral neutrality or expediency but rather of respect. He obeys the normative rule because 'obedience to it is held to be desirable ... the individual's happiness and self-fulfillment are bound up with it' (387). 'That men have this attitude of respect, is, if true, an explanation of the existence of order' (386). Thus, social control is not confined to external constraints but takes on an *internal* dimension: 'In so far as the actor maintains an attitude of moral obligation toward it, the norm to which his action is oriented is no longer exterior in the same sense. It becomes, in the Freudian term, "introjected" to form a constitutive element of the individual personality itself' (388).

Social control, then, is ensured through the process of *internalization*. What makes for control is the subject's incorporation of the normative rules into his personality, using them as a standard for his subsequent activities. This means that constraints can no longer be viewed as exclusively external. Each member of society voluntarily chooses to obey the set of normative rules that reinforce their effectiveness in regulating social action. This implies an interpenetration between the individual and society. Through the set of normative rules internalized by each person, 'the social,' in effect, 'becomes a constitutive element in the individual's own concrete personality' (399), providing the guide-lines for his or her actions. This form of control rested upon *social institutions*, the 'body of rules governing action in pursuit of immediate ends in so far as they exercise moral authority derivable from a common value system' (407). This body of rules, in turn, acting through the ends pursued by subjects is the 'embodiment of ultimate common values' (404). The institutions of society serve as the point of mediation between the ultimate values and the ends and actions of social members.

Indeed, in Parsons's view, social institutions in their operations were equivalent to religious practices. Taking Durkheim's discussion in *Elementary Forms of Religious Life* as a commentary on social control in contemporary society, he draws the conclusion that 'every "society" is characterized to a certain degree by the possession of a common "religion." For without a system of common values, of which a religion is in part a manifestation, a system adhered to in a significant degree, there can be no such thing as a society' (434). In this sense, 'every community, if it is more than a mere "balance of power" between individuals and groups, constitutes ... a moral community in a significant degree, and as such may be said to have a common religion' (434).

Parsons stresses that this moral community does not come about through the passive acceptance of norms, but is actively constituted through *ritual*. 'Ritual brings the attitudes into a heightened state of self-consciousness which greatly strengthens them, and through them strengthens, in turn, the moral community. Thus religious ritual effects a reassertion and fortification of the sentiments on which social solidarity depends. As Durkheim sometimes puts it, it recreates the society itself' (435). It is through the active pursuit of ends, through rituals, that institutions are able to ensure the realization of ultimate common values in society. This points towards a 'voluntaristic conception of action – a process in which the concrete human being plays an active, not merely an adaptive role' (439). Durkheim, according to Parsons, maintains that society undergoes fluctuations between 'quiescent and effervescent periods.' The latter are characterized by 'great common rituals' in which 'not only are old values created, but new ones are born.' Parsons suggests that Durkheim's thought reveals 'the germ of a theory of social change, perhaps of the cyclical type' (450). In his reading of Durkheim's theory of social order, Parsons reiterates the same conclusions he had reached in his discussion of Pareto. Although recent trends in society may be towards social disorganization in the form of the 'ascent of the combinations' or 'anomie,' the reimposition of social control was still a real possibility. If society develops cyclically – alternating between periods of order and anarchy – there is good reason to believe that the current tendencies towards social disruption could give way to a revitalized social order founded on shared values. Specifically, social stability could be restored through the embodiment of a system of ultimate values in institutions and rituals. The imposition of such an order, however, would be in no sense automatic. Its establishment would require an active agency – analogous to the religious movements that had unified societies in the past.

These practical considerations guided Parsons's discussion of Durkheim's social theory as well. He demonstrated that Durkheim developed an approach to the study of society relevant to its formation and maintenance. 'Sociology should,' according to Durkheim, 'be thought of as a science of action – of the ultimate common value element *in its relations* to the other elements of action' (440). More specifically, 'Durkheim ... defined sociology as the science of institutions' (408): sociology would articulate transcendental ultimate values by affirming their presence in institutions. This would make sociology akin, therefore, to a modern priesthood. By providing authoritative judgments on how values were embodied in institutions, sociology would help ensure the viability and effectiveness of both. If sociology were to exert this influence on the social order, however, it would have to be oriented towards the normative and symbolic dimensions of society. The subject matter of sociology would have to be congruent with the value contours of society. Parsons indicated how Durkheim turned to idealism – in his conception both of the social order and of his social theory. Previously, with his 'positivistic position ... no status whatever could be allowed to elements of reality not susceptible of empirical treatment from the points of view both of the observer and of the actor' (426). Nevertheless, Durkheim 'in escaping from the toils of positivism has overshot the mark and gone clean over to idealism' (445). According to this contrary perspective, 'society has become the thing the idealist philosophers are talking about' (444). Specifically, this implies that the actor relates to society in a manner differing markedly from the 'analogy of the scientist' who stands 'primarily in a cognitive relation to the conditions in which he acts' (438). Rather than passively adapting himself to the 'facts of the external world,' the member of an idealistically conceived society orients his actions on the basis of symbolic meanings having moral force. Given his 'attitude of respect' to norms, the actor will in fact be obligated to obey them.

Along similar lines, social theory as it relates to the social order would also have an idealistic orientation. 'The aim of sociology' is 'that of studying the systems of value ideas in themselves' (446). Through this kind of enterprise, the sociologist could contribute to the process of social control. For the very acceptance of a common system of ultimate values that ought to be obeyed would enhance their status as the standards of social action. Implicitly, by virtue of this orientation, sociology could help strengthen the system of ultimate values that served to guide and regulate actions. Parsons noted that 'far from being automatic, the realization of ultimate values is a matter of active energy, of will, of effort, hence a very important part may be played empirically by agencies which stimulate this will' (440). Hence, it was the orientation of sociology towards idealistically conceived institutions that would permit it to serve as an agency of social control. In affirming common ultimate values it would, in effect, be conjoined in an intersubjective sphere in common with social actors, allowing it to exert influence over their actions.

Nevertheless, the idealist turn traced in Durkheim implied a debilitating relativism – in terms both of social theory and of the social order to which it was to be congruent. As Parsons describes Durkheim's later approach to the study of society, 'one of his leading empirical theories is that of the relativity of social types. The different ultimate-value systems which constitute the defining elements of different concrete societies are so radically different as to be incommensurable. For this reason he was forced to define normality with reference to the social type alone, thus ending in a complete ethical relativism' (447). That is to say, with its acceptance of various ultimate value systems as descriptively valid, Durkheim's theory implied a stance of relativism. Since all 'social types' or 'concrete societies' were equally admissible in terms of the values they embodied, no one standard of normality could be offered and no particular ultimate value system or set of institutions could be affirmed as valid. This meant that the possible relevance of social theory to social control would be jeopardized. As long as it lacked an objective basis for affirming specific values and institutions, it could scarcely contribute to the latter's strength and efficacy. What the social theory of Durkheim lacked, then, was scientific, universalistic standards that would permit it to objectively affirm the presence of a particular subjective system of values. Hence, if it were to lend authority to a specific set of values and institutions, it required a more authoritative standpoint from which its evaluative judgments were to be made.

This relativism was also evident in Durkheim's conception of social order in that 'his epistemology has brought the basis of human reason itself into the same relativistic circle' for 'the relativism of social types is itself a product of a system of categories which are valid only for the particular social type' (447). The relativism of the various social types was rooted in Durkheim's alleged move from a positivistic to an idealistic conception of social action. In terms of the latter, members of society were thought to act on the basis of moral ends rather than of rational calculation. By internalizing the moral dictums of ultimate value standards, they would then voluntarily constrain their own actions. What gave the values this moral force, in turn, was the actors' imputation of sacredness upon them. However, given that the value standards stemmed from the subjective views of social actors, there was nothing in these standards themselves that provided them with moral force. Each system of values ascribed to could in principle be equally acceptable because there is no basis for adjudicating between the value preferences of different sets of social actors. This relativism of value standards, in Durkheim's idealistically conceived social order, threatened to undermine the form of social control upon which it was based. For if a set of values embodied in institutions lacked a basis of validity apart from the actors' beliefs in it, the values could scarcely serve as an overall standard within society. Hence, if the relativism inherent in Durkheim's later conception of the social order was to be overcome, a basis for validity independent of subjectively conceived moral standards would have to be discovered.

The problem Parsons faced, then, was in overcoming the relativism inherent in Durkheim's turn towards idealism both in his social theory and in his description of the social order. As long as values were merely creations of either the actor or the scientist, respectively, a unitary system of ultimate ends, as embodied in a specific set of institutions, could not be upheld. The implementation of social control, as founded in authoritative symbolic standards of action, would be jeopardized. Parsons's detection of the idealistic turn in Durkheim capped his efforts to trace an emergent theory of normative social control within the utilitarian-positivistic tradition. Yet this idealistic breakthrough – foreshadowed in both Marshall and Pareto – had come at the expense of threatening the objective foundations of social science and the rationality of social action. If Durkheim's idealistically conceived insights into social control were to be incorporated into the social order and made a part of a congruent social theory, they would have to be coupled somehow with the objectivity of the positivistic-utilitarian tradition. To effect this reconciliation, Parsons began from the opposite direction to show how Max Weber – working within the German idealist tradition – was able to overcome the relativist tendencies inherent in this perspective by developing a theory that was at once objectively valid, yet subjectively informed.

4

Idealism and Science

Marx, Sombart, and the Development of Capitalism

As a prelude to examining the thought of Max Weber, Parsons shifts his attention from positivism to the 'other great tradition of thought,' namely, German idealism. He stresses that 'against mechanism, individualism [and] atomism [idealism] has placed organicism, the subordination of the unit, including the human individual, to the whole.' Rather than seeking to uncover 'intrinsic causal relationships in the phenomena,' it concerns itself with 'the discovery of relations of meaning, of *Sinnzusammenhang*' ([1937] 1968, 485). Because of its interest in the subjective basis of human action and the organic nature of societies, idealism has spawned 'detailed, concrete history on the one hand, the philosophy of history on the other,' both of which 'have undoubtedly been the main lines of social thinking and research in Germany since the great days of idealistic philosophy' (475).

The idealist tradition was of great promise as a source of insights in regard to Parsons's concerns about the problems of order and social control. In emphasizing the intersubjective, symbolic foundation of social action, it provided a basis for understanding how individuals could be integrated into a social order. And by stressing the historical uniqueness of cultural totalities, it was, by its nature, of relevance to present-day societies. Parsons was initially drawn to the German idealist tradition because of its culturally and historically enlightened approach to the study of society.[1] In particular, he chose to study in detail the thought of two thinkers – Werner Sombart and Max Weber – whose work exemplified a concern with 'the idea of capitalism as an epoch of history.' By explicating their contributions, Parsons could come to terms with his doubts about Anglo-American economic thought and the positivist tradition as a whole. Yet lurking behind these two exponents of idealism was a 'special forerunner' – Karl Marx. While Parsons does not include Marx or any of his followers in the convergence he imputes to European social theory, his concern with Marx's thought and its implications are obvious. Indeed, the manner in which Parsons deals with Marxist theory – both explicitly and implicitly – is instructive for what it reveals about his own practical designs.

As Parsons acknowledges, Marx, like Sombart and Weber, was concerned with 'capitalism as a great epoch in social and economic development' (1928, 642). The approach he developed to capitalism 'forms an important bridge between the positivistic and idealistic traditions of thought' ([1937] 1968, 110). In this respect, Marx's perspective was similar to his own emerging 'voluntaristic theory of action,' which 'provides a bridge between the apparently irreconcilable differences of the two traditions [idealist and positivist]' (486). Yet Parsons not only refuses to include Marx among the major contributors to European social thought, but chooses to deal with him largely indirectly, through the writings of Sombart and Weber. The explanation for this exclusion can undoubtedly be found in the value premises that underpinned Marx's historical explanation – a set of assumptions with which Parsons did not agree. Specifically, Marx's analysis, flowing from a particular perspective on the necessity of historical development, implied the transcendance of capitalism and the formation of a society organized along socialist lines. This prognosis of the path of historical development was, according to Parsons, inherent in Marx's conception of the capitalist order. Marx maintained that 'the fault of capitalistic exploitation lay, not with the capitalist as an individual, but with the system to which he as well as everyone else was forced to conform.' It was only by 'changes in the fundamental basis of class interests within the system' that the abuses could be remedied. Hence, according to Marx's philosophy of history, the 'causal effect' is attributed 'to an immanent law of the material conditions of production' (1928, 659).

However, unlike the 'positivist evolutionists,' Marx did not conceive of the historical process as 'a continuous single line.' Drawing on Hegelian thought, he viewed human development as proceeding dialectically, with discrete stages of social organization succeeding one another in a continuous, yet patterned, manner. What provides the 'propulsive dynamic force' in this dialectical process of change is class conflict, as embodied in 'the organized concerted action of the proletariat to overthrow the existing order and establish socialism' ([1937]

1968, 494). That is, immanent within the compulsively organized system of capitalism was its eventual overthrow through the process of escalating class conflict. Hence, by virtue of his theory of the relation between action and social structure, a particular dynamic of social change is implied. In Parsons's view, Marx holds that 'the interests people pursue are determined by the particular social situation in which they find themselves' (491). These situations are generated by the 'compulsive discipline' inherent in the conditions of production of capitalism. It is this rational pursuit of interests, then, within the compulsive 'total structure of the system' that provides capitalism with its historical dynamism. 'The system itself would be thought of as self-acting. Once the individuals involved in it are placed in the situations that are given, their actions are "determined" so as to maintain the system as a whole, or rather to drive it forward on the evolutionary course, to end at last in its self-destruction' ([1937] 1968, 492).

Marx's account of the social order, as a 'version of utilitarian individualism' (110), emphasized that 'men ... acted rationally within a given concrete situation,' thereby following 'their "interests" as defined for them by the situations in which they are placed' (491). Thus, the capitalist system 'creates for each acting individual a specific situation which compels him to act in certain ways if he is not to go contrary to his interest' (492). Marx is viewed by Parsons, then, as a 'social determinist' in that, according to Marx's conception of the social order, a particular course of social action must follow from the 'originally deterministic set of conditions of production out of which the whole thing flows' (493).

Consequently, Marx's social order, with its emphasis upon the rational pursuit of interests, coincided with that of Hobbes and the utilitarian thinkers. To be sure, action was determined socially rather than individually. But the overall implications for social order were the same: chronic conflict eventuating in an unsatisfactory solution to the problem of order. The socialism advocated by Marx and others suffered from the same limitations as that of Hobbes's leviathan. Indeed, Parsons agrees with Durkheim's verdict that socialism, as premised on 'the economic view of society,' shows a lack of concern 'for controlling the economic element in the interest of something higher.' Given its economism, 'socialist economics failed to meet the issues raised by the theory of laissez-faire individualism.' Mirroring the point of view held by both Pareto and Weber, Durkheim, according to Parsons, maintains that 'socialism and laissez-faire individualism are of the same piece – they both leave out of account certain basic social factors with which all three are concerned' (341). Following from its individualistic premises, Marx's socialism, like Hobbes's leviathan, advocates a solution to the problem of order that did not truly address the question of how social control can be maintained in a society consisting of individuals pursuing their self-interests.

Parsons not only rejects Marx's conception of the social order, but also calls into question Marx's view of social theory. He stresses that Marx is an 'ethical absolutist' because 'his whole system of thought' focused on 'the conditions for the realization of his own ideal' (495). According to Marx's view, social action had meaning by virtue of its striving for the ideals of socialism and its negation of the existing capitalist order. Socialism constituted a set of 'ultimate values' that provided meaning and purpose to social action. A theory of society based on Marxist thought would both affirm these 'ultimate values' and define social action in relation to them. With its vision of historical change, Marx's theory was of great relevance to contemporary capitalism. Yet its relevance came by virtue of a set of values to which Parsons could not suscribe; hence he was compelled by his own value commitments to dismiss Marxism as a mode of analysis.

In rejecting the empirical analysis of Marx, Parsons was also rejecting the value commitments accompanying socialism. At the same time, however, he could not abide by the tenets of laissez-faire liberalism. Even though it supported the principles of capitalist rationality, its lack of historical relevance meant that it could have little bearing on the contemporary social order. The inadequacies of Marxism and liberalism could only be overcome by an approach that dealt with capitalism in a historically instructive manner without implying the chronic disorder of Hobbes or the historical determinism of Marx.

It is in the spirit of the suggested inadequacies of Marx as an 'economic determinist' and 'evolutionist' that Parsons approaches the contributions of Werner Sombart. Parsons suggests that Marx was a forerunner of Sombart (1928, 658), whose polemic about 'historical materialism' resulted in a perspective that drew on some of the insights of Marxism, but incorporated them into an approach of greater relevance and validity.[2] Sombart takes 'over the Marxian description of the [economic] system ... but he differs profoundly in his interpretation of the relations of its elements' ([1937] 1968, 496). Specifically, in giving priority to the 'spirit of capitalism [he] may be said in a sense to have assimilated the main content of Marx into the framework of orthodox historicoidealistic thought' (495). Rather than emphasizing the material conditions of production, Sombart discusses capitalism in terms of a

'*Geist* ... a common value element,' which manifests itself in 'the total concrete phenomenon of capitalism' (499). Through this denial of the 'economic interpretation of history,' then, Sombart radically recasts the Marxian theory of history. While he 'takes over the system as a historical epoch ... the dialectic evolutionary connection between systems' is discarded, 'leaving them in principle quite discrete' (1928, 659). The emergence of capitalism 'as an internal necessity imposed by the conditions of production' is denied. And by extension, the necessity of socialism emerging from capitalism could not be sustained. According to Sombart, each economic system is separate and distinct, representing the manifestation of a particular spirit, and is 'a thoroughly unique phenomenon, occurring only once in history.' Since 'there is no line of development leading from spirit to spirit, and thus from system to system' (644), each of these must be separately considered. Reacting to the 'optimistic social philosophy of the enlightenment and its heirs,' who contend that 'there is one single line of progressive cultural evolution,' Sombart maintains that, rather than progress, there is 'only a succession of mutually independent cultures, which are born, grow to maturity, and die' (652). In Parsons's view, 'Sombart's method is radically opposed to the hypothesis of continuous evolution as held by most Western sociologists' (653).

In line with his discussion of Pareto and Durkheim, Parsons sees Sombart's approach as offering a much more realistic account of modern capitalism than that of Marx and the other proponents of rationalist, evolutionary thinking. Parsons's analysis of 'the internal difficulties of the utilitarian tradition,' as exemplified in Marx's approach, leads him to accept 'a position empirically favorable to Sombart's criticism' ([1937] 1968, 499). As he elsewhere notes, 'Sombart has presented a view of capitalist society which is a formidable alternative to the orthodox liberal one' (1928, 654).

Despite its overall validity, Sombart's conception of capitalism, with its polemical tendency to overstatement, represents a perspective as one-sided in its own way as that of progressive evolution. By substituting an 'equally metaphysical entity, the "spirit," for that of progress,' Sombart, in Parsons's view, mistakenly includes 'all of social life' within his closed system. Moreover, the origins of the 'spirit of economic life [and] why it should produce a given economic system at a given time and place remains as much a mystery as why we should be so obviously progressing toward a millenium' (652). Hence, 'like Marx in the opposite sense – he overshoots the mark and attributes an undue rigidity to the system' (653). 'His view results in fully as rigid a determinism as that of Marx. All that the individual can do is to "express" this spirit in his thoughts and actions. He is powerless to change it' (660).

While Sombart's account of the social order indicates how social actions can be controlled and disciplined, it suffers from both irrationality and relativism since there is no way of knowing how the spirit would manifest itself in a particular epoch. Sombart's conception of capitalism's appearance made it seem both capricious and mysterious. In principle, it could appear at any time in any form, and there is no way of guaranteeing that actions following its precepts would be rational ones. By implication, it could be assumed neither that history progressed rationally, nor that the present epoch was any more rational than the one preceding it. Given that the spirit was not rationally grounded, there was no way of affirming it against other systems of values that might appear. As it stood, Sombart's conception of the spirit underpinning a common value system could scarcely serve as the basis for social control.

Sombart's social theory, though of historical relevance to the social order, could have little bearing on problems of social control because of its anti-rationalist foundations. By virtue of its attack on rational progress, Sombart's approach tended towards the irrational, providing no objective basis for the apprehension of the 'ultimate values' specific to contemporary capitalism. With his anti-rational biases, Sombart reveals his affinities with 'the "conservative" wing of the romantic movement.' In common with this perspective, he views 'capitalism ... as a destructive force tearing down the social ties of an older and more "organic" civilization (651). Sombart's 'work is not oriented "forward" to the emergence of the successors of capitalism, but is concentrated rather in the system itself; ethically he looks backward, if anything' ([1937] 1968, 498). As opposed to the forward-looking rational views of progressive cultural evolution, then, Sombart's approach takes as its evaluative standpoint the 'state of nature' corresponding to 'the precapitalist era, by which to measure the shortcomings of capitalism' (1928, 651–2). Given this implicit values standpoint, the social theory of Sombart was lacking in scientific credibility.

What Parsons's analysis of Marx and Sombart pointed towards was a perspective that could draw on the latter's insights into the spiritual underpinnings of the capitalist order without sacrificing the rationality of the utilitarian-positivistic tradition. 'In the transition from capitalism to a different social system,' Parsons suggests, 'surely many elements of the present would be built into the new order' (1928, 653).

The emerging social order would somehow combine the normative dimensions of Sombart's 'spirit of capitalism' with the 'rational pursuit of interests' central to Marx and the positivistic-utilitarian school of thought. What was needed was an approach that could build on Sombart's historically specific spirit of capitalism, without succumbing to the relativism that his position implied for both the social order and the social theory apprehending it. It was with this set of reconciliations in mind that Parsons turned to the writings of Max Weber.

Max Weber

Parsons stresses that Weber, as 'a thinker steeped ... in the idealistic tradition of thought' ([1937] 1968, 499), sought to overcome the difficulties inherent in this perspective. In Parsons's view, Weber took as his starting-point an outlook equivalent to Durkheim's later orientation, namely, an idealistic conception of both the social order and social theory. The social order was viewed as 'a particular *Geist*, a specific cultural totality clearly distinct from and incommensurable with all others' (478). Idealistic social theory implied a 'repudiation of the type of analytical theory inherent in the conceptual structures of the positivistic tradition' (480). In Parsons's view, this idealist tradition made for a pervasive relativism in Weber's immediate political and intellectual surroundings. 'In both these contexts,' Parsons maintains, 'Weber faced a *milieu* in which the dominant note was relativism, a relativism which threatened to issue in an attitude of general scepticism. The trend of the historical schools of German social thought had been to lay increasing stress on the relativity of social arrangements and institutions and the underlying value-systems which were employed to understand them.' Correspondingly, 'on the practical side he was faced with a warring plurality of conflicting political viewpoints.' Faced with the spectre of both political and intellectual relativism, Weber, according to Parsons, 'sought to determine the logical conditions and criteria of valid objective knowledge [as a] reliable landmark ... in a relativistic world, where values and historical interpretations were in flux.' Parsons argues that it was Weber's intent to develop a perspective that would ensure 'valid objective knowledge [for both] science [and] rational action' (1936, 675–6). Predisposed by his 'neo-Kantian "subjectivism,"' Weber wished to preserve the 'orientation to values' of both social and scientific action. Hence, in Parsons's view, one of Weber's overriding concerns was to overcome the relativism inherent in idealism, while retaining its subjective dimension. This would involve showing how a rational standpoint could be made compatible with more subjective concerns. Yet, as Parsons emphasizes, Weber at the same time sought to avoid the kind of objectivist approach that would deny the presence of value orientations in both social order and social theory.

Parsons's discussion of Weber reflects a concern about showing how he overcame the problem of relativism in the two spheres. Such a demonstration would both redress the difficulties he had traced in Durkheim's move from positivism to idealism, and provide evidence for the convergence he imputes to the two traditions. But most important, in reconciling idealism and positivism in both the social order and in social theory, he could establish the congruence between the two realms, ensuring the empirical, normative, and practical relevance of the social sciences to the emergent social order. Of central concern to Parsons, therefore, was Weber's conception of the modern capitalist order.

In Parsons's view, Weber was quite familiar with the 'particular empirical problems' that were of concern to Marx and Sombart. He also sought to understand the nature of 'a particular historical-social phenomenon – "modern capitalism."' In certain respects, his analysis of capitalism coincided with that of Marx and Sombart. In a manner similar to that of the two theorists, he saw the capitalist system as consisting of enterprises, each of which 'was primarily oriented to the attainment of profit, to the exploitation of opportunities of acquisition in a system of market relationships' ([1937] 1968, 504). Weber viewed the system not only as acquisitive, but as 'compulsive and "objective" in much the same sense that it was for both Marx and Sombart.' However, Weber's account of modern capitalism differs from that of Marx and Sombart in a fundamental way. According to Parsons, Weber sees 'the principal characteristic [of] "rational bourgeois capitalism" [as] "bureaucratic organization" in the service of pecuniary profit in a system of market relations.' The rationality of modern calism is embodied in bureaucratic organization, which 'Wrs to be the principal distinguishing feature of thnomic order' (508). Parsons stresses that eber a special case of the 'professional secific attribute required for the efficienthat special case where the impersonaical devotion is directed, contains the s a basic component' (515). Seen in thisrn capitalism takes on a distinct meansuit of gain' takes place in a 'continuous, ted enterprise,' there is 'a high degree of disciplining and tempering of the acquisitive impulse' (505). Indeed, the participant in the 'modern capitalist bureaucracy' is thought to take the role determined by an office. By virtue of this 'profession or calling' (*Beruf*), the incumbent is obligated to 'a certain impersonal devotion to the tasks of the office.' Modern bureaucratic capitalism, with its rationally conceived structure, is distinguished by its discipline and 'its fitting of individual actions into a complicated pattern in such a way that the character of each and its relations to the rest can be accurately controlled in the interest of the end to which the whole is devoted' (507). With its capacity to enjoin 'systematic, continuous rational honest work in the service of economic acquisition' (515), modern capitalism can be distinguished from 'adventurers' capitalism' characterized by an 'amoral undisciplined greed for gain' (516). The latter form of capitalism was analogous to the 'combinations phase' of Pareto, the 'anomie' of Durkheim, the 'state of war' of Hobbes, or the *Gesellschaft* of Tönnies. In contrast, in modern capitalism, 'such work is necessarily subjected to a strict discipline which is incompatible with giving free rein to impulse' (515).

Parsons suggests that through the process of bureaucratization, the unrestrained impulses of the earlier form of capitalism could be controlled. Hence, bureaucracy could be understood as an essential feature of social change. In Parsons's view, 'for Weber, bureaucracy plays the part that the class struggle played for Marx and competition for Sombart.' Yet, despite this rational bureaucratic structure, as Parsons observes, the system is still imbued with normative concerns in that the 'explanation of the system lay in a system of ultimate values and value attitudes, in part anchored and in part dependent upon a metaphysical system of ideas' (510). Parsons stresses that, according to Weber, this value orientation of capitalism had its origins in the ascetic Protestant faith.

Capitalism, in this sense, embodies the ultimate values of the transcendental realm. It is through the faith and commitment of believers, mediating God's concerns, that ultimate values become approximated in the organization of society. Specifically, 'service [to God] cannot be in the direction of indulgence in the things of the flesh, or of adaptation to it; it must lie in that of *control* over the flesh, in its subjection to a discipline for the glory of God.' Along the same lines, 'ascetic activity in the service of God's will is diverted away from ritual channels of expression into active control over the intrinsic relations of the world' (523). Thus, ritual action was linked to ultimate values in the sense that through 'rational, systematic labour' one could take part in 'the building of the Kingdom of God on Earth' (526–7).

The control exercised by bureaucracy came by virtue of its embodiment of 'ultimate values.' According to Parsons, modern capitalism, as founded on ascetic Protestantism, was by its very nature capable of exerting control over its members. The ethos of Calvinism, stressing sober labour for impersonal ends, ensured that action taking place within bureaucratic capitalism and its institutional counterparts would not occur in a fully self-interested, and therefore destructive, way. Rather, with its devotion to transcendent, impersonal ends, it would serve to support the collective interests of society. According to Parsons, Weber has found 'a system of ultimate-value ideas "adequate" to the spirit of capitalism [whose] leading traits find their counterpart in the Protestant attitude properly interpreted.' Weber shows how the '"irrational" element' in capitalism, 'so incomprehensible from any hedonistic point of view,' can be given meaning' (528).

The bureaucratic outlook, as elaborated by Weber, bore the same relationship to utilitarian society as Calvinism did to pre-Christian society. With the Calvinist faith came 'the suspicion of all things merely human and worldly, the abhorrence of "idolatry"' ([1937] 1968, 526). According to Calvinism, 'activity in the world should be directed toward rational mastery of the flesh in the interest of the glory of God, not use of the things of this world for self-indulgence and hedonistic gratification. The Calvinist works *in* the world, but neither *of* nor *for* the world' (534–5). The 'idolatry' to which the Calvinists were opposed was analogous to the rational, calculating actors of utilitarianism who hedonistically pursue their wants, calculating the most efficacious way of realizing them. By implication, the utilitarian social order, like its pagan counterpart, was idolatrous if not sinful. However, in the same way that Calvinist society promised salvation to its members through 'service of impersonal ends,' the emergent bureaucratic social order would allow the social actors within it to achieve a state of moral grace through their submission to the system of ultimate ends.

Weber's analysis of the Protestant ethic provided a way of fusing the idealist and positivist conceptions of how the social order was constituted. In this sense, one could still think of the actor as rationally pursuing empirical ends, *pace* positivism. However, given that these ends corresponded to 'the ultimate ends of intrinsic means-ends chains' (256), forming an integrated system, then society could be viewed as 'the thing the idealist philosophers are talking about' (444).

Through this conception of the social order, Weber, according to Parsons, was able to overcome the problem of political relativism. The issue arose in tracing an idealistic turn in the thought of Durkheim. According to Parsons, Durkheim began to see the actors as obeying rules because they ascribed moral value to them. Thus, Durkheim abandoned his former position that the actors obeyed rules on the basis of rational calculation. The rules held moral sway because social actors saw them as sacred. Nevertheless, a problem of relativism was implied, because there was nothing in the order itself to ensure that obedience ought to be forthcoming. In view of the lack of an independent standpoint for establishing society's moral validity, the implication is, of course, that there will be a chronic instability.

In seeking to overcome the spectre of political relativism, Parsons's modus operandum is to show how the source of an order's legitimacy could be removed from the subjective ascription of the actor. Relying heavily on Weber's writings in political sociology, he argues that Durkheim's insights into people's moral respect for the order are not at all incompatible with a criterion of obligation that is not dependent upon the state of public consciousness. What enables Parsons to proceed in this manner is the consonance he detects between Weber's concept of legitimacy and Durkheim's notion of sacredness. According to Parsons, legitimacy is a quality imputed to the order 'by those acting in relation to it.' This involves an attitude of 'disinterested acceptance,' in that 'for one who holds an order to be legitimate, living up to its rules becomes ... a matter of moral obligation.' In Parsons's view, with his development of the theory of legitimacy, 'Weber has arrived at the same point Durkheim reached when he interpreted constraint as moral authority,' and indeed 'has approached the question from the same point of view, that of an individual thought of as acting in relation to a system of roles that constitute conditions of his action' ([1937] 1968, 661). In Parsons's view, legitimacy is directly akin to 'a specific attitude of respect ... owed to a recognized duty' (662) implied by charisma. 'Charisma is directly linked with legitimacy, is indeed the name in Weber's system for the source of legitimacy in general' (663).

Parsons now shows how the basis of charisma, ergo legitimacy, shifts from the orientation of the actor to the order itself, accompanying the transition from charismatic to legal-rational authority. 'Charisma becomes inherent only in the office of the objective system of rules' (664). However, it is emphatically stressed that the charismatic quality of the order is still retained under conditions of rational legality: 'What changes ... is not the quality charisma as such but its concrete modes of embodiment and its relations to other elements of the particular concrete complex ... in a rational bureaucratic structure there must always be a source of the legality of the order which is in the last analysis, charismatic' (665).

The persistence of the charismatic element in the social actor's orientation ensures that the social order would be treated as 'sacred' or as 'an end in itself'; the rational nature of the order ensures that this orientation would be obligatory. Drawing on his analysis of how Calvinism has become embodied in the emergent social order, Parsons argues that ultimate values have attained objective status. Collapsing reason and morality in the same order implies, moreover, that rational action consists in obeying the prevailing norms that are themselves rationally constituted. As a consequence, the possibility of political relativism has been averted, because the basis of legitimation has come to inhere in the legal-rational system of rules, rather than in personal subjectivity. Any alternative orientations developed by the actor can only be irrational/illegitimate/immoral and hence subject to rational/legal/moral constraints.

In terms of the social theory congruent with the social order, Parsons develops a similar line of argument. Just as the problem of political relativism is solved by removing the basis of legitimacy to the legal-rational order, the problem of scientific relativism is addressed by removing the grounds for scientific validity to an abstract logical system. To establish an ' "island" of scientific objectivity in the shifting ocean of conflicting values and policies,' Parsons argues that Weber falls back on a form of neo-Kantian subjectivism: 'the facts ... are determined by his [the scientist's] direction of interest, which is in turn a function of the values motivating his action.' Here again the line of argument for 'scientific validity' continues to run parallel to that of 'political legitimacy.' As noted previously, the charisma/sacredness of an order, solely based on subjective ascriptions, implies a chronic political relativism. Now in the same way, the notion of a *Wertbeziehung*, the 'relevance to value' determined by the scientist himself, suggests an equally debilitating scientific relativism. The problem for the scientist is to 'escape being drawn into a closed relativistic circle so that "knowledge" becomes a function only of the subjective values of the scientist, an expression of his valuations (*Wertungen*).' In his political sociology, Weber is seen as having salvaged the legitimacy claims of the order by removing the grounds for legitimacy from the actor's orientation to the legal-rational order. Similarly, in his methodology, Parsons sees Weber as ensuring the objectivity of scientific methodology by removing the grounds for validity to 'a formal schema of proof which is universal.' In the same way that the grounds for legitimacy become independent of particular actors, any empirical proposition is '*logically* independent of any value-system and hence outside the relativistic circle' (1936, 676). Just as bureaucratic-legal rationality forms a bulwark against competing legitimacy claims, the formal schema could be seen as the 'foundation of the solid island of empirical knowledge – on the solidity of which the possibility both of scientific objectivity and of rational action depend' (677). While the solution to the problem of legitimacy enables the social actor to act rationally in relation to a normative order, the solution to the problem of validity enables the social scientist to retain his *Wertbeziehung* 'not merely to "know about" phenomena but to find solutions to *problems* ... set by relation to his motivating values. Scientific investigation is itself a process of action, not of passive contemplation of the panorama of "given" reality' (676).

It is Weber's alleged incorporation of idealism into a scientific methodology that permits Parsons to overcome the 'relativism' lurking in his analysis of Pareto and Durkheim. Paralleling his contention that Pareto and Durkheim take a subjectivist turn, Parsons argues that Weber's idealism is correspondingly transformed:

But until recently the positivistic-idealistic dualism of modern social thought has created, both methodologically and theoretically, a hiatus which has prevented its integration with the other elements into the description of a single comprehensive general system of action. Only the corresponding breakdown of the idealistic methodology which has been traced in the study of Weber has made possible the bridging of this hiatus and the convergence of the two developments. ([1937] 1968, 719)

This took the form of *Verstehen*, whereby 'the scientist is able to impute motives to men, to "interpret" their actions and words as expressions of these motives. That is, we have access to the subjective aspect of action.' Parsons suggests that this process of *Verstehen* gave the scientist access to the system of ultimate values.

The religious ideas Weber is primarily concerned with are not as such exclusively value ideas, or ends of action. They are rather rationalized interpretations of the meaning of the world, including a complete metaphysical system. Out of these fundamental metaphysical postulates, then, is to be derived what meaning the world can have for man, and, from this, in turn, what his ultimate values can 'meaningfully' be. ([1937] 1968, 668; see also 583)

Parsons, however, did not hold to this interpretation without some equivocation. In order to support his contention that the two traditions had been reconciled in Weberian thought, he had to come to terms with Weber's persistent neo-Kantianism and his claim that the social sciences characteristically seek to understand unique historical individuals:

Weber, following Rickert, tried to maintain an untenable distinction between the relative roles of generalizing concepts in the natural and social sciences respectively. The position is that in the natural sciences the end of scientific endeavor is the building up of systems of general theoretical concepts, while in the social such concepts can serve only as means to the understanding of unique historical individuals. (1936, 678)

As a corrective to Weber, Parsons insists that the 'individual' versus 'general' distinction is a specious one, and that both the natural and the social sciences form divisions that are generalizing (theoretical physics and theoretical economics). In both forms of inquiry, Parsons argues, one finds generalizing and individualizing concepts in a means-end relationship to one another: 'In the one case general concepts constitute an end in themselves, in the other a means' (1936, 678).

Imbued as they are with 'general theory,' both forms of inquiry can express a 'relevance to value' without falling prey to relativism. For even though the form given the facts is 'relative to the conceptual schema in terms of which they are formulated,' the content itself is 'capable of restatement in terms of any other schema which also meets the same criteria' (679). Even though the facts are in some sense structured by values, this does not at all detract from their objective status. Parsons expresses doubts, none the less, that a 'general theory of action' fits readily into the Weberian scheme of things: 'It has been possible to elicit by analysis a definite scheme of the structure of a generalized system of action which appears at the most strategic points of Weber's work and, though he did not clearly recognize its logical nature, this scheme was absolutely essential to Weber's specific results both empirical and theoretical' ([1937] 1968, 716). He is even more explicit in his introduction to a collection of Weber's essays, which he later edited: 'The basic source of difficulty lies in Weber's failure to carry through a systematic functional analysis of a generalized system of action ... One of the sources of Weber's failure to think explicitly in terms of a theoretically generalized social system lies in certain features of the biological thought of his time' ([1947d] 1964, 18–19).

Parsons's discontent with the Weberian distinctions between the natural and social sciences reveals itself in a more overtly practical form. Weber, according to Parsons, quite mistakenly holds that the natural and social sciences differ fundamentally in their capacity to exercise control:

In Weber's view, as far as it seems clear on this point, there is a common human basis for the interest in natural phenomena, that is, control. It is through the aspects formulable in terms of abstract general concepts that this is possible ... But this is just where the difference lies between natural phenomena and the social case. Human beings, their actions and cultural achievements are the embodiments of value toward which we must, in some degree, take a value attitude. ([1937] 1968, 592)

By holding to this distinction between the natural and the social sciences, Weber is affirming once again a sharp fact-value distinction, and an incommensurability between science and ethics. The question of exercising control itself is dependent upon whether we relate to phenomena in a 'general' or a 'specific' fashion. In accepting the social world in its historical specificity, we must also forgo an interest in exercising control over it. The very possibility of exercising control implies that we must perceive phenomena in general, objectified terms, capable of manipulation.

Weber's line of reasoning, if not overturned, had of course grave consequences for the Parsonsian project. By perpetuating the division between values and reason, Weber's neo-Kantianism effectively precludes the establishment of a normative order that is scientifically grounded. In terms of the social order, the possibility of legal-rational means compelling charismatic attachment to the order could never be grounded. Similarly, the social theorist would be prevented from defining a particular set of values scientifically. It is crucial, therefore, that Parsons show that the notion of control is as central to the social as it is to the natural sciences: 'There seems to be no reason to doubt the importance of the motive of control with reference to the phenomena of nature. But it is possible to doubt ... that it is as unimportant as Weber maintains by implication in the sociocultural field' ([1937] 1968, 595).

Just as natural phenomena could serve as either means or conditions of action, so could social phenomena, for 'surely in rational action generally the social environment looms at least as large as does the natural. Particularly in the field Weber had primarily in mind, that of political action, this seems to be the case.' Thus, 'general theoretical knowledge' is equally applicable to 'any concrete situations that might arise' in the 'context in which social studies are considered' ([1937] 1968, 595).

Toward a Strategic Standpoint

With his synthesis of idealism and positivism, Weber, according to Parsons, overcame relativism in both the emergent social order and the social theory apprehending it. Nevertheless, the perspective derived from Weber's writings cannot be understood apart from the other thinkers and approaches Parsons had previously considered. *The Structure of Social Action* ([1937] 1968) – as the culmination of his early writings – can be understood as a dialectical progression through the traditions and tendencies in social thought germane to Parsons's activist concerns. Through his examination of the classical social thinkers, he sought to preserve their strengths, while overcoming their deficiencies, thereby transforming and unifying them into a perspective of strategic relevance to the emergent social order.

Parsons's study of classical social thought reflects his commitment to the activist principles inherent in liberal Calvinism: to follow one's calling of working within and acting upon 'thisworldly' secular society with the purpose of moving it closer towards an 'otherworldly' transcendent state embodying ultimate ends. He was also committed to the development and furtherance of science as a progressive and rationalizing force. These twin commitments undoubtedly account for Parsons's concern with the legacies of idealism and positivism, seeking to define a perspective drawing on both. Idealist and positivist precepts provided the basis for both an 'immanent' or potentially transcendent order, and a social theory of relevance to it. From this emergent perspective, Parsons evaluated contemporary social theory and social order with a view to how they might be concurrently transcended. His empirical point of departure was the current state of Hobbesian disorder he detected in society. This concern was evidenced in some of his unpublished manuscripts and in his observations on Pareto (combinations), Durkheim (anomie), Tönnies (*Gesellschaft*), and Weber (adventurers' capitalism). In terms of Parsons's designs, this state of disorder could be overcome through a 'system of ultimate ends' gaining ascendance in society as articulated by the scientifically elect. However, variants of the utilitarian-positivistic tradition, with their emphases upon individualism and randomized ends, were incapable of defining and articulating the presence of a normative system that could ensure stability of the social order. Particularly remiss in this respect was neo-classical economics, which with its empiricist bias, emphasis upon discrete, individual wants, and domination over the 'analytical sciences' represented a barrier to the emergence of more normatively based perspectives. It was with these concerns in mind that Parsons studied the work of Marshall. He sought to show that implicit in Marshall's economic 'organon' was a concern with ultimate values in the form of 'activities.' Since this orientation was inherent within the body of orthodox economic thought, it could serve as the basis for a perspective – the sociological – which could concern itself with ultimate values and their embodiment in society. At the same time, however, this approach could be elaborated without changing the corpus of conventional economics, whose objective and rational basis would not be jeopardized. The emerging sociological standpoint would both complement and supplement it. Such a perspective, then, could articulate the ultimate values immanent within the social order, thereby contributing to their consolidation.

Nevertheless, another aspect of Marshall's thought – his faith in linear evolutionism – stood in the way of a perspective oriented towards the emergent social order developing. With its view that society was teleologically progressing towards greater rationality, it left no room for value elements in society's future, and by virtue of its determinism, did not allow for an actively oriented social theory grounded in transcendent normative values. Building on this analysis of Marshall, Parsons turned to another economist – Pareto – and showed that his cyclical theory, with its emphasis upon epochs succeeding each other in patterned progression, affirmed the possibility that the current state of social disorder could be transcended. To this end, he also indicates how Pareto – in a manner similar to Marshall but going beyond him – developed a theoretical system based on shared ends that anticipated how the emergent social order might be conceived. Lacking in Pareto's theory, however, was any firm account of how this immanent society was approximated in reality. It is in Durkheim's writings that Parsons discovered the empirical basis for such an order in the form of shared rules embodied in institutions. Yet Durkheim, because of his commitment to positivism, is initially unable to adequately conceive of either the social order or the social theory standing in relation to it. However, in coming to terms with anomie, Durkheim, according to Parsons, not only comes to view the social order as consisting of normative ideals introjected by the social actor, but also advocates an idealistically grounded social theory.

At this stage, Parsons had shown how a social theory of relevance to the emergent social order could be generated. However, the idealism that made this congruence possible also implied a state of relativism in both spheres. This he attempts to overcome by demonstrating how one could incorporate the scientific standpoint of positivism into the idealist tradition. To effect this synthesis, he first indicates how the perspectives of two of the main contributors to the German historical tradition – Marx and Sombart – were inadequate to the task of generating a standpoint that was at once objective, subjective, and of relevance to the historical development of modern capitalism. While Sombart's account was overly idealistic and lacked a scientific basis, that of Marx – as a variant of the positivistic-utilitarian tradition – was far too deterministic. He then shows how Max Weber was able to combine the historical specificity of German idealism with the scientific outlook of positivism. According to Parsons, by unifying idealism and positivism in this manner, Weber not only overcame the problem of relativism in both the emergent social order and social theory, but also generated a standpoint that would permit the dialectical interplay between the two realms. From this perspective isomorphic with the main contours of the emergent social order, the social sciences could theoretically grasp empirical changes occurring in that order. At the same time, because of their congruence with modern society, the social sciences could generate knowledge of practical relevance to society's course of development. In this sense, the social sciences not only would be in a position to undermine dissenting intellectual positions, but they could defeat ideologies that threatened the stability and progressive institutionalization of the social order.

Common to the social order and the evolving social theory of Parsons were four components. The first was a general relational one – defining the link between theory and society. The other three were specific dimensions – what one may call the objective, subjective, and the federational – shared in common by the social order and social theory. Sometimes explicit, but more often implied, they guided Parsons's encounter with European social theory.

The Relational Component

This category provided the general basis for the interplay between social theory and action within the social order. In terms of social theory it took the form of 'disinterestedness.' The social scientist, fulfilling the duty of his office to be of service, would not align himself with the worldly interests of secular society, but would be devoted to values transcending it. Fulfilment of his mission to help build a 'Kingdom of God on Earth' would involve the mediation of ultimate ends into secular society. 'Disinterestedness,' then, embodied the 'instrumental activism' of Calvinist inner-worldly asceticism.[3] That is, social scientists shared the responsibility to be of 'service' to society, as carried out through 'an office held on behalf of the larger impersonal whole' (1934, 673). Correspondingly, the relational category of disinterestedness implied that the social order was emergent, and therefore capable of being constituted through actions of the elect – including the social sciences. In effect, society did not develop in the manner proposed by linear evolutionists. Its development was a cyclical one, as different theories and belief systems successively were able to gain ascendancy in the social order. The modern era, in Parsons's view, was to be characterized by social disorder giving way to consensus and shared values, as a system of ultimate ends gradually became institutionalized into secular society.[4]

Sustaining and supporting this emergent order was the 'disinterestedness' of the social actor in the form of the 'ascetic devotion to impersonal tasks for their own sake' ([1937] 1968, 532). This orientation was linked to the 'quality of an order ... of a system of norms governing conduct' in the form of 'legitimacy.' That is, legitimacy is imputed when 'a given type of attitude toward the norms involved' is taken 'which may be characterized as one of disinterested acceptance.' In Parsons's view, both Weber and Durkheim make 'the same distinction of attitude elements toward the rules of such an order, the interested and the disinterested. In both cases, a legitimate order is contrasted with a situation of the uncontrolled play of interests' ([1937] 1968, 661).

This implied that the legitimation of the order hinged upon a value orientation of this kind. It was only if the actors disinterestedly accepted the norms as morally valid that social control could be forthcoming. A society characterized by rampant self-interest in which norms were only obeyed out of expedience would be lacking both in legitimacy and in any capacity to generate social control. The development of a legitimated social order, capable of restraining individual impulses, was thus contingent upon both its disinterested articulation by the social-scientific elect and its disinterested acceptance by the social actor.

The Subjective Component

It has been widely acknowledged that the subjective component – in the form of voluntarism – figured prominently in Parsons's early writings.

Gouldner (1971, 185) attests, for instance, that 'it is a central point of Parsons's "voluntarism" that men's efforts always make a difference in what happens.' Commentators, however, have failed to examine how Parsons dealt simultaneously with subjectivity in terms of the social order and with social theory standing in relation to it. Once this simultaneity is revealed, however, the particular status of the subjective component in Parsons's schema becomes evident. In terms of the social order, Parsons's entrée into subjectivity came via a system of ultimate ends. The presence of this overarching normative system served to integrate the actors into society through their individual subjectivities. The subjective dimension enters into Parsons's schema only in so far as it ensures the operability of the system of ultimate ends. It is a mistake, therefore, to hold the view that Parsons stressed 'voluntarism' in his early writings in the sense of emphasizing the creative and purposeful behaviour of the social actor. His main concern was to articulate scientifically the existence of a system of ultimate ends whose very presence *compelled* the obedience of all members of society,[5] a process that required access to subjectivity if it were to be effective.[6] Parsons thus argued for the presence of a 'normative order ... relative to a given system of norms or normative elements, whether ends, rules or other norms. Order in this sense means that process takes place in conformity with the paths laid down in the normative system' ([1937] 1968, 91).

Similarly, for the 'sciences of action,' both the 'subject aspect' and 'the method of *Verstehen*' were indispensable (764–5). By virtue of the 'voluntaristic theory of action,' characteristic of the sciences of action, 'ends ... become integral with the system itself, positively interdependent with the other elements in specifically determinate ways' (82). Hence, 'ideas may be said to be constant data for the theory of action in the same methodological sense as are physical data' (758). Parsons maintained that the 'voluntaristic theory of action' permitted the social analyst to apprehend the 'ultimate values' forming the basis of the normative order in society. He emphasized, nevertheless, that the social order and social theory both had a significant objective aspect to them. This characteristic accounts for the 'conditional' nature of the third component.

The Objective Component

Complementing the normative dimension of the social order, Parsons maintained, one could detect 'the objective non-normative influence of the conditions of action, usually of heredity and environment' ([1937]

1968, 114). While Parsons emphasized that these 'non-normative' elements were an essential feature of society, he none the less repeatedly stressed that society could not be *reduced* to these features, as had been the case with different variants of positivism (64). Instead, these conditional factors would take their place as a permanently valid precipitate within the emergent social order. While action within this system would still involve rational matching of objective means to ends, the ends themselves would be independently conceived as constituent elements of the normative system. In effect, by virtue of this interplay between objective and subjective factors, social action could be rational and yet morally guided by the dictates of the normative system.[7]

Similarly, the objective orientation was integral to the 'voluntaristic theory of action,' which like other 'analytical sciences,' sought to 'develop logically coherent systems of general analytical theory.' What distinguished the voluntaristic theory of action from the others was its concern with 'normative elements in human action.' Hence, in the same way that the society was simultaneously a normative order and a factual order (91–2), the voluntaristic theory of action combined the objective 'logical system' of the 'analytical sciences' with an orientation towards the normative component of action systems. By scientifically affirming the presence of these ultimate ends, it could contribute to their articulation and credibility within the social order.

The Federational Component

Finally, in view of his analysis of how subjective and objective elements were constituent features of both social order and social theory, Parsons was able to show how each could be separated into various interdependent realms. In terms of the social order – given that action involved means, conditions, and ends – discrete spheres of action could be differentiated. As he noted, 'it is possible to speak of three classes of immediate or proximate ends falling within the intermediate sector – the achievement of technological efficiency, of control over wealth and over coercive power.'

By virtue of the kinds of intermediate ends related to means, the social order could be differentiated into its economic, political, and techno-logical components. Economic action was concerned with 'the alloca-tion of scarce means as between their various potential uses' ([1937] 1968, 233). Similarly, 'political action elements' were concerned with the 'normative regulation of the power aspect of the relations of

individuals within the system' (768). The technological element referred to the degree of efficiency of particular means for achieving ends.
Parsons also distinguished a higher order of ends, namely 'ultimate ends
of individual action systems [which] are integrated to form a single
common system of ultimate ends' (249). This provided the basis for the
'sociologistic theorem that society is a reality *sui generis.'* Finally,
Parsons distinguished the psychological level of society by its individual, subjective dimension interacting with hereditary features (85–6).
Such a society, based on social action and divided into various spheres,
was to be distinguished from the utilitarian version which saw society
as being reducible to conditions.

In terms of social theory, Parsons developed a division of labour
among the 'analytical sciences' of relevance to these sectors of the social
order. Specifically, he put forward 'the view of the proper abstraction for
the social sciences [as] abstract analytical systems each of which
assumes as data the main outline of fundamental structure of concrete
systems of action including the elements other than those immediately
dealt with by the science in question' (466). In line with this thinking,
sociology was viewed by Parsons as 'the science which attempts to
develop an analytical theory of social action systems in so far as these
systems can be understood in terms of the property of common-value
integration' (768). Sociology, as based on a scientific system oriented
towards values, shared the standpoint of the social order, consisting of a
set of ultimate values within an objectively conceived system. Economics, according to Parsons, was concerned with action at lower levels of
the means-ends chain. He defined it as 'the science which studies the
processes of rational acquisition of scarce means to the actor's ends by
production and economic exchange, and of their rational allocation as
between alternative uses' (266). Economics, in effect, was to concern
itself exclusively with means-ends action *within* a system of ultimate
values. 'The political discipline,' in his view, 'is primarily the social-
relationship schema in the special form of power relationships.' At the
individual level, Parsons maintained that psychology, as a 'science of
action,' had categories that 'refer to properties of action systems with
special reference to the subschema of personality' (770). It was,
moreover, 'concerned with those elements of human nature through
which man's biological heritage is related to his purposes, ends,
sentiments' (86). Finally, Parsons distinguished a residual set of disciplines – the technologies – that were concerned with 'classes of concrete
ends.' Although 'important concretely,' in his view 'they add relatively
little to the systematic theory of action' (770). Taken together, the

division of labour among the 'analytical sciences of action' was to supersede the 'encyclopaedic' view centred on economics. In terms of Parsons's practical designs, these sciences, by dealing with discrete spheres in a manner guided by relational, objective, and subjective categories, could contribute to the constitution of the emergent social order. This would involve a complementary course of action in which all the analytical sciences would participate.[8]

Parsons was particularly concerned to establish firmly sociology's credentials as a recognized form of social-scientific inquiry. As evidenced by commentaries like those of Crane Brinton and L.J. Henderson, sociology was not taken seriously – at least in the inner circles of Harvard – as a valid approach to the study of society.[9] Clarifying its subject matter, method, and relations with the other social sciences would thus overcome the criticisms of its detractors. Parsons's concern to establish sociology had its impetus in his immediate professional circumstances. The Department of Sociology at Harvard was formed in 1930 and needed to define itself in relation to social ethics (which it had in effect replaced) and to the powerful and prestigious Department of Economics.[10]

Despite his stated intentions of supplementing rather than supplanting economics with a sociological frame of reference – oriented towards the embodiment of ultimate values in institutions – Parsons in the end was just as guilty of 'social scientific imperialism' as had been orthodox economics. Within the sciences of action, sociology was to concern itself with the overall orientation towards ultimate values. The remaining branches of the social sciences were to concern themselves with various internal dimensions of the action frame of reference. This socio-centric vision of the sciences of action was to supersede the encyclopaedic view centred on economics.

Through his sustained practical encounter with classical social theory, Parsons had forged a theoretical perspective of strategic relevance to the emergent social order. From this standpoint, the 'analytical social sciences' would be in a position to mediate the system of ultimate ends into the institutions of secular society, thereby ensuring social control. In the same manner that the early Calvinists had overcome the idolatrous and hedonistic practices of non-believers, the 'positivistic-utilitarian tradition ... is the victim of the jealous god, Evolution, in this case the evolution of scientific theory' ([1937] 1968, 3). The standpoint that Parsons had derived from his study of the main traditions in social theory represented the restoration of God's word – albeit in a scientific form – to the social order. From such a perspective, combining an activistic orientation towards the social order with objectivity, subjectivity, and specialization, it would be possible to help create a 'Kingdom of God on Earth.' For sociology, in particular, a field of investigation was established – the scientific study of how ultimate values became embodied in institutions. By generating knowledge of this kind, it would be possible for the discipline to both define and articulate the normative order, thereby contributing to the process of social control. Fully consistent and continuous with the conclusions reached in his first full-scale work, Parsons now sought to specify and account for how the institutions of the emergent social order were actively cultivated through professional practice.

PART TWO

The Patterning of Social-Scientific Growth

5

Medical Practice and Social Control

Institutionalization and the Professions

Upon the completion of *The Structure of Social Action*, Parsons turned his attention to some of the issues and problems that arose out of his examination of classical social theory. As he noted in an application for a Social Science Research Council (ssrc) grant, 'I am just now in process of carrying out a major shift in the direction of my scientific work in the field of sociology ... I am now turning to a program of empirical research in the broad field of social institutions, a field in which my theoretical work has awakened great interest for me' (1923–40a).

In Parsons's view, the 'institutional aspect of sociology' was of importance because it dealt with the relation between human actions and normative rules, 'including not only the extent to which they are actually complied with, but also the conditions leading to evasion and direct disobedience of them.' The rules, as embodied in institutions, 'may be of direct intrinsic significance in maintaining the functional efficiency of the activities they regulate.'

Given the practical interests that underlay his 'series of studies in the field of sociological theory' (1923–40a), the shift of interest was, however, not an abrupt one. It was fully continuous with his concerns about how social control could be brought to bear in a capitalist society because the institutions of society – as embodiments of ultimate values – served to control and pattern social action. 'There is in every society a more or less coherent underlying system of common ultimate values ... institutions are primarily an expression of these attitudes in certain particular relations to action. It follows that the institutions themselves will constitute a *system* that is a system of regulative norms' (1935c, 28).

In terms of the standpoint Parsons had reached in *Social Action*, institutions – as expressions of ultimate values – represented the point of mediation between social-scientific practice and the emergent social order. By elaborating upon the nature and significance of institutions, then, Parsons could specify how the practice of social sciences could help to constitute the emergent social order. If this were to be explored, however, he would need to examine the prevailing social order and the degree to which social control was operable within it. Consistent with his diagnoses of 'Hobbesian disorder,' Parsons detected a failure of the business class 'to consolidate its position as a national elite in a sense closely approaching that of a "governing class"' ([1951] 1964, 319). Parsons stressed that 'one of the important reasons why the business class failed ... is that its primary role has been defined in "self-oriented" terms, thus exposing it too readily to the charge that power would not be exercised as "responsibility" but as exploitation' (319). In other words, the self-interested 'definition of the situation' provided by the business class was incompatible with the cultivation of a consensual order based on the common values and the *identity* of interests. This meant the 'public confidence necessary to facilitate a "therapeutic" function' (319) would not be forthcoming. The business point of view could scarcely serve as the dominant definition of the situation, for ideological challenges against this ethic could be easily mounted. 'A deviant movement which opposes the "profit system" on moral grounds has relatively easy going if there is nothing to counteract the profit symbol' ([1951] 1964, 319). In effect, the business class represented the social embodiment of utilitarian-positivist theory. In the same manner that this body of thought could not provide the basis for overcoming Hobbesian disorder, the inherently self-interested concerns of the business class ran at cross-purposes with the institutional stability of capitalism. If the crisis of belief in the capitalist order were to be overcome, a stratum capable of 'defining the situation' to the public more in consensual terms had to become ascendant in the social order.

The Professions and Modern Society

This 'new class,' in Parsons's view, was the professional class, a group whose orientation could not be described as one of economic self-interest. Indeed, according to Parsons, professionals themselves denied that economic self-interest was characteristic of their outlook (1964a, 327). More generally, the professional bore responsibility for 'society's cultural tradition [and] for its perpetuation *and* ... further development'

(1959a, 547). By virtue of professional activity, social institutions were able to function (1923–40b, 3). For within the 'institutional frame work' of 'the professional type' are carried on 'many of our most important social functions ... notably the pursuit of science and liberal learning and its practical application in medicine, technology, law and teaching' ([1939] 1964, 48). Such 'highly professionalized groups' are 'the primary institutionalized bearers of [modern Western society's] main cultural traditions and leaders of its thought' ([1942b] 1964, 165–6). Without their role, 'the distinctive characteristics of cultural traditions would be very greatly altered' (165–6).

As 'the most important single component in the structure of modern societies,' the professional complex is the 'crucial structural development in twentieth-century society' (1968a, 545). It was, according to Parsons, a much more fundamental development than 'capitalist or socialist modes of organization.' Indeed, the emergence of the professions made this distinction specious: 'they provide a central focus for the differences of opinion between capitalists and socialists and among the theorists who have concerned themselves with the impact of the industrial revolution' (1970a, 834). The presence of the collectivistically inclined professions posed serious difficulties for 'ideologists' who have 'overlooked the presence and strategic significance in our society of a set of occupational groups which are not either in their own opinion or by and large in the public estimation, devoted mainly to the goal of their own profit, but rather in some sense to "service" ' ([1952] 1964, 370–1). It was evident to Parsons that 'many of the most important features of our society are ... dependent on the smooth functioning of the professions. Both the pursuit and the application of science and liberal learning are predominantly carried out in a professional context. Their results have become so closely interwoven in the fabric of modern society that it is difficult to imagine how it could get along if they were seriously impaired' ([1939] 1964, 34).

As bearers of our 'cultural tradition' with a responsibility for 'its maintenance, development and implementation,' the professions formed the practical point of mediation '*between* two major aspects of our social structure' ([1952] 1964, 381), namely, society on the one hand and groups or individuals on the other. They could then 'be regarded as what we call "mechanisms of social control"' (382).

The exercise of social control was in Parsons's view inherent in the practice of professions. In terms of the conclusions he had reached in *The Structure of Social Action*, the professions as a social stratum were the carriers of 'instrumental activism,' as originating in liberal Calvinism. By virtue of their 'calling' to disinterestedly pursue ultimate ends in service to society, they could help bring the Kingdom of God to secular society. Through 'the application of science to practical affairs,' the professions were the bearers of rationality. 'The importance of rationality in the modern professions generally, but particularly in those important ones concerned with the development and application of science serves to emphasize its role in the society at large' ([1939] 1964, 37). In more general terms,

the progress of science and related elements of rational thought is the core and fundamental prototype of the process [which Max Weber has called the 'process of rationalization'] ... Through this dynamic factor, a continuing process of change is introduced, both into the primary symbolic systems which help to integrate the life of a society, and into the structure of the situations in which a large part of the population must carry on their activities. ([1947] 1964, 315)

Through the consolidation of the scientifically imbued professions, rationalization would be forthcoming and social integration would be effected. In short, the growth of the professions represented to Parsons the long-term solution to the Hobbesian disorder he saw as endemic. It was consistent with his conclusions from *The Structure of Social Action*, then, that he began to study the professions in earnest: 'In deciding what to do in the personally critical phase following the completion of *The Structure of Social Action*, I made a major bet on the fruitfulness of investigating the professional sector of modern social systems (1972, 251). More specifically, Parsons undertook an intensive examination of the medical profession, which he saw as 'a kind of prototype of the possibilities of generating useful knowledge and applying it to the solution of critical human problems' (1970a, 836).

Medical Practice and the Pattern Variables

According to Parsons, medicine embodied in its most highly developed form the elements of professional practice so critical for the mainte-nance and reproduction of advanced capitalism. Not only was medicine rigorously scientific and capable of generating empirical knowledge, but it offered a means whereby the practitioner could intervene symbolic-ally in a system of values. With its treatment of illness as both a normative and objective affliction, the medical profession embodied the standpoint for social control that he had derived in *The Structure of*

Social Action. 'Illness [was] more than an objective "condition" which came about independently of the motivational balances of the social system' and was not 'merely "acted upon" by a "technology" in the therapeutic process.' Rather, 'it was itself integrally involved in the motivational balance and hence institutionally defined.' Sickness did not simply refer to a biological illness, but was 'a type of deviant behaviour which was socially categorized in a kind of role' ([1964a] 1970, 332).

By 'institutionally defining' illness as a 'social role' at the outset, Parsons conjoined the physician and the patient in a common symbolic sphere. Accordingly, the physician did not merely 'cure' the patient by technically manipulating objective conditions; the patient became motivated to get well as a consequence of accepting the physician's definition of his unhealthy situation. It was by virtue of placing the physician and patient within the same 'action framework' that Parsons came to terms with how illness was socially controlled by medical practice.

Parsons's analysis of medicine can perhaps best be thought of as an elaboration and a social specification of the standpoint he had arrived at in *The Structure of Social Action.* Analogous to the social theorist and the social order, he conceived of the medical practitioner as acting in relation to the 'sick role' in society. In *Social Action* Parsons had developed a standpoint in which the social order was congruent with social theory. It was on the basis of this congruence that ultimate values could be mediated through institutions, thereby ensuring social control. However, what was lacking in *The Structure of Social Action* was both an analysis of how this congruence was to be socially embodied or a theory of how it could be established. In Parsons's analysis of the medical profession, both of these questions were addressed.[1] On the one hand, he demonstrated the patterns within society that *mediated* between the practitioner and the social actor, thereby permitting social control. On the other hand, by specifying these patterns in terms of the practice of medicine, he showed how they could be actually put into practice. Through the analysis of what made this 'social control of illness' possible, he was able to isolate a set of elements crucial to successful medical practice – the notorious 'pattern variables.' Scientific medicine, Parsons noted, 'was the context in which the beginnings of what later took shape as the scheme of "pattern variables" were worked out' (328).

'The "pattern-variable" scheme ... originated as an attempt to formulate a theoretical approach to the interpretation of the professions' (1970a, 842). This framework of analysis took the form of paired polarities: disinterest/self-interest, universalism/particularism, affective neutrality/affectivity, and functional specificity/diffuseness.[2] Given this manner of construction, commentators have commonly viewed these pairs as an abstract schema describing historical contrasts or as a set of choices available to social actors (Menzies 1975). However, in view of their origins in professional practice, this conception of the pattern variables is inadequate. From the outset, the pattern variables were not only abstract descriptions of value orientations, but also *practically* conceived categories, describing what features of medical practice permitted doctors to exercise social control over patients. They provided insights into how the activities of the professional elites served to ensure effective and thoroughgoing social control. The pattern variables, then, were by their very conception *asymmetrical*. One-half of the patterns – disinterestedness, universalism, affective neutrality, and functional specificity – defined the practical orientation of the pro-fessional. In contrast, self-interest, particularism, affectivity, and diffuseness referred to a residual non-professional practice. Since professionalization was intrinsically related to the process of rationalization, the presence of what one can call the primary half of the pattern variables was to ensure modernity and progress.

The primary patterns represented the basis upon which social control in the emerging post-capitalist society was to be founded. As mechanisms for the regulation and ordering of social action, they formed a point of institutional mediation between the professional elites and the general public. This implied that they not only served to control the actions of members of civil society, but also regulated the practice of the professionals. As Parsons noted in relation to medical practice, in controlling the patient, the doctor 'must himself be controlled, he must adhere ... to an institutionalized definition of his role, and to a situation which is enforced overwhelmingly by automatic informal mechanisms' ([1942b] 1964, 159–60).

What gave rise to Parsons's derivation of the primary patterns through his study of the medical profession was his motivation 'to understand a high-level occupational role which deviated from that of the businessman who, according to certain theorists, represented the one strategically crucial type of such role in modern "capitalistic" society' ([1951] 1964, 463). Such theories, by unquestioningly accepting the dominance of the business orientation in society, would contribute to this definition of the situation, thereby affecting the state of social order itself. Accordingly, Parsons sought to provide a different outlook in relation to the social order that would capture the distinction between the business and professional points of view. This contrast was embodied in the distinction between the paired concepts of 'disinterestedness' and 'self-interest.'[3]

Disinterestedness

According to Parsons, as opposed to the self-interest of the businessman, the medical professional was oriented towards serving the interests of society as a whole: 'by contrast with business ... the professions are marked by "disinterestedness." The professional man is not thought of as engaged in the pursuit of his personal profit, but in performing services to his patients or client, or to impersonal values like the advancement of science' ([1939] 1964, 35).

The notion of disinterestedness as a general orientation towards action had been foreshadowed in Parsons's earlier writings. It embodied the general relational orientation obtaining between social theory and social order. In terms of social theory, 'disinterestedness' corresponded to 'the central ethical element' of the 'ascetic devotion to impersonal tasks for their own sake' ([1937] 1968, 532). This primary pattern embodied the general 'calling' of the elite to place ultimate ends over self-interest, thereby bringing transcendent values to secular society. The order constituted in this manner was accepted in a disinterested manner by the social actor, who ascribed legitimacy to it. This implied that the legitimation of the order hinged upon a value orientation of this kind. It was only if the actors disinterestedly accepted the norms as morally valid that social control could be forthcoming. A society characterized by rampant self-interest in which norms were only obeyed out of expedience would be lacking both in legitimacy and in the capacity to generate social control. The development of a legitimated social order capable of restraining individual impulses was, therefore, contingent upon the cultivation of a general orientation of disinterestedness. Correspondingly, the sciences of action, as concerned with society as a whole, disinterestedly accepted the 'ultimate values' as having moral validity. This was perhaps most noticeable in the case of sociology, which was defined as 'the science which attempts to develop an analytical theory of social action systems in so far as these systems can be understood in terms of the property of common-value integration' (668). That is, in the same way that the social actor accepted the norms of society in a disinterested manner, the scientist of action would unquestioningly confer moral validity on the same normative system.

In *The Structure of Social Action* the impetus behind the generation of this outlook was as yet unspecified. It was through his analysis of the medical profession that Parsons was able to give social specificity to the theoretical standpoint he had developed in his first major work. The primary pattern of 'disinterestedness' represented, then, the *general* orientation mediating between professional practitioners and civil society. As aspects of this overall outlook, Parsons distinguished three other primary patterns – universalism, affective neutrality, and functional specificity – all of which provided particular guide-lines for how the general orientation was to be operable. As with 'disinterestedness,' each of these was consistent with patterns of orientation towards the social order delineated in *The Structure of Social Action*. In their new guise, however, they were much more specifically related to social control as exercised by the medical professional over the social role of the patient.

Universalism

The first of these primary patterns, 'universalism,' involved 'a generalized "impartiality" ... treating a sick person as a problem for applied science' ([1964a] 1970, 329). This orientation was continuous with Parsons's discussion of the 'conditional component' in *The Structure of Social Action*. The scientific approach was viewed not only as a theoretical standpoint, but also as a constitutive feature of the social order itself. 'Since science and rationality of action are indissolubly bound up together' ([1937] 1968, 715), a scientific orientation was common to both the social actor and the social theorist. In terms of the social order, Parsons viewed rational actions as inherently linked up with a scientific orientation. Indeed, 'the ultimate justification of the starting point of this whole study,' he noted, was the 'basic solidarity of science and action [and] the role in action of the norm of rationality in the sense of a scientifically verifiable intrinsic means-end relationship' (683). Within Parsons's emerging conception of the social order, action was rational and scientifically based in so far as it involved determining the most efficient way of choosing means to realize particular ends. These ends themselves, as noted, formed a normative system independent of the individual actors. Those non-normative features of action – encompassing such things as heredity, environment, and biological make-up – were considered to be the 'conditions' of action. In Parsons's view, 'action must always be thought of as involving a state of tension between two different orders of elements, the normative and the conditional,' and consists of 'the process of alteration of the conditional elements in the direction of conformity with norms' (732). If action was considered solely in terms of its purely rational or scientific aspects, it would then be viewed as part of a *factual* order. The ability of a 'scientific theory' to apprehend the 'factual order' of 'empirical reality' which was 'of a character ... congruent with the order of human logic' (753) is one of its distinguishing features. 'The general concepts of science ... "grasp" aspects of the objective external world' (730). Parsons maintains that scientific theory, with its emphasis on the logical relations of rational action, is *congruent* with the conditional elements making up the 'factual order' of society.

The primary pattern of 'universalism' incorporates the theoretical and social aspects of the scientific orientation into a single concept. By virtue of combining a constitutive feature of society with a theoretical orientation, it is also a *practical* category. It not only provides an orientation to the order for the practitioner, but also implies a particular outlook on the part of members of civil society. Through the primary pattern of 'universalism,' the medical practitioner relates in a scientifically objective fashion to the factual order of illness. This means 'abstracting from considerations of personal relationship or group belongingness in favor of diagnosis and treatment as a "case" of whatever the disease category happened to be.' The eligibility for treatment is not based on status, but rather on the 'objective condition' and the 'state of illness' of the patient. Hence, the medical practitioner makes decisions about treatment not on the basis of '*who* the patient is but ... *what* is the matter with him' ([1939] 1964, 41). This 'universalistic' orientation, based on standards 'independent of the particular social relationship to a particular person,' is contrasted to particularistic standards and criteria, 'which apply by virtue of such a relationship' to a particular person (42). This constitutes the pattern variable of universalism/particularism. Through the spread of universalistic practices, particularistic orientations in the social order were to be supplanted. By virtue of practice upheld by objective, scientific standards, the medical profession gained authority over decisions affecting the physical well-being of the patient. Medical practice treated the '"conditional" components of the state of illness,' through the utilization of 'a complex technology' ([1964a] 1970, 335). Thus, control over the 'factual order' corresponding to the conditional components of illness was made possible by the primary pattern of 'universalism.'

Affective Neutrality

Parsons stressed that 'the conception of medical practice' merely as '"applied biological science"' in no way captures the social character of this profession – what one can call '"the art of medicine"' ([1942b] 1964, 152–3). Fundamental to medicine was a decidedly human element, the 'psychic factor of disease,' which gave testimony to the notion that '"health" is not simply a state of the biological organism, but is a matter of a person's total adjustment to his life situation.' This was particularly evident in the case of conscious or unconscious psychotherapy, in which 'the way ... doctors have in fact handled patients has had an important effect on their states of health through their mental and emotional states as well as acting directly on the physiological systems of their bodies' (153–4). These considerations gave rise to a primary pattern – affective neutrality – that corresponded to 'the "art" as distinguished from the "science" of medicine' ([1964a] 1970, 330). This required the physician to have a '"neutral" attitude' toward the patient, inhibiting 'what would otherwise be "normal" emotional reactions' (330). Although the medical practitioner has 'access to the body of his patient for physical examination and various treatment purposes,' there is a clear 'discrimination between attitudes appropriate to personal intimacies of various sorts and the "professional" attitude' (330). Hence, the orientation of 'affective neutrality' served to insulate the physician from the 'affectivity' or emotional involvement with the patient that might arise. Affectivity, as the opposing concept in the paired dyad, refers to an involvement that 'would be altogether appropriate in a relationship within the family' (334). Through the development of the primary pattern of affective neutrality, then, a value orientation towards the collectivity could supersede the many and disparate affective loyalties rooted in familial and other personal associations.

Affective neutrality emerged from the orientation to values that Parsons had derived from the idealist tradition in *The Structure of Social Action*. This normative standpoint was found in both the modern social order and the social theory congruent with it. In the social order, it referred to the system of 'ultimate ends.' The system could thus be viewed as the 'normative order [which] is always relative to a given system of norms or normative elements, whether ends, rules or other norms' ([1937] 1968, 91). Correspondingly, if a theoretical approach were to be capable of apprehending the normative order, it would require an orientation to values. In this manner, it would incorporate the Weberian insight of *Verstehen*, in the sense of the scientist being 'able to impute motives to men, to "interpret" their actions and words as expressions of these motives. That is, we have access to be subjective aspect of action' ([1937] 1968, 583).[4]

The primary pattern of 'affective neutrality' embodied the social and theoretical aspects of the normative orientation into a single concept. It thus had practical implications for social control because it indicated how theory could direct patterns of action. For example, in medicine, by orienting towards the 'normative order' while treating patients, a stance of 'affective neutrality' in relation to particular 'motivational states' could be maintained. In view of its interplay with the emotions of the patient, 'it seemed likely that the attitude of affective neutrality then had something to do with important processes of social control' ([1964a] 1970, 330).

The orientation of affective neutrality enabled the medical doctor to successfully practise psychoanalysis. In acknowledging that illness has a psychic factor and is motivated, the physician relates to the patient on an intersubjective basis, much akin to the idealistic perspective inherent in *Verstehen*. What makes this standpoint possible is a commitment to the overarching values of the collectivity. Through this commitment the medical practitioner can relate to the patient in an 'affectively neutral' manner, and resist being seduced into 'a community of defense of the sick position.' In this manner, 'the pattern of affective neutrality can ... be seen to be part of a mechanism which protects the physician against this seductive pressure (including his own unconscious motives) and enables him to maintain his position of "leverage" against the motivated elements of illness' ([1964a] 1970, 335). Given the patient's trust in the doctor, attendant upon the latter's affective neutrality, he is quite willing to treat him as 'a "neutral screen" on which the patient projects his affects and definitions of situations in human relations' ([1942b] 1964, 157).

Correspondingly, the doctor-patient relationship allows for the breakdown and eventual overcoming of rationalizations, concealed motives, and other forms of cognitive distortion. In normal interaction, when people take each other at face value, this obligation and the mutual expectations that it generates can lead to 'the operation of the vicious circles which may eventuate in neuroses' (157). In other words, given the nature of interaction, by putting up an acceptable, though distorted 'front,' others are induced to carry out a particular course of action, which in turn distorts the front even further, and so on. However, in the doctor-patient relationship, characterized by authority and dependency stemming from the patient's 'trust' in the practitioner's competence, this vicious circle can be overcome. In this sort of milieu, in which the normal obligations, roles, and expectations are suspended, the patient puts '"himself in the hands" of a physician ... accepts the latter's authority,' and most significantly, 'accepts the obligations to re-examine his own rationalizations and underlying motives again and again' (158). In this way, deviance can be effectively controlled, almost without recourse to 'a system of formal controls and sanctions. Neither the law of the state nor the disciplinary machinery ... plays a major role' (156). Instead, through the interaction of doctor and patient within a patterned relationship, rationalizations, hidden motives, and the lack of adaptability could be overcome. Seen in this way, medical practice 'is a particularly striking case of the existence of relatively unconscious automatic control mechanisms in society which tend to counteract the vicious-circle mechanisms of at least one broad class of deviant tendencies on the behavioral level' (159). The particular case of psychoanalysis decisively demonstrates that 'the institutionalized role of the physician provides a particularly strategic vantage point from which to apply deliberate psychotherapeutic techniques' (159).

Functional Specificity

A fourth primary pattern – functional specificity – captured the division of labour inherent in professionalization. This orientation to action had previously appeared in Parsons's discussion of the growth of bureaucracy in *The Structure of Social Action*. As Parsons described it there, 'one of the fundamental requirements of modern bureaucratic structure is specialization of function and, with it, specialized technical knowledge, legal or scientific' ([1937] 1968, 549–50). This specialization had its roots in the orientation of the Puritan, whose 'highest self-fulfillment lay in playing his part, even though it be a highly specialized part, in a calling' (550). In terms of social theory, this was reflected in the various sciences of action that were to bear a particular relation to the social order. 'The systems of scientific theory under consideration are obviously not ... external reality itself, nor are they a direct and literal representation of it, such that one and only one such representation is in any sense valid. They stand, rather, in a functional relation to it, such that for certain scientific purposes they are adequate representations of it' (753).

Each of the psychology sciences of action, namely economics, sociology, and political science, was to bear a functional relation to the apposite sub-system in society. Each 'theoretical system' was to deal in a specialized manner with one aspect of empirical reality. The primary variable of 'functional specificity' thus combined both aspects of the orientation detected in *The Structure of Social Action*. Hence, this pattern referred simultaneously to the standpoint of the medical practitioner and to the social situation as defined to the patient.

The 'functional specificity' of medical practice described the delimitation of 'the scope of mutual concern' between physician and patient 'to matters relevant to the health of the patient.' The specificity of function enabled the medical practitioner to exercise professional authority even 'over people who are, or are reputed to be, his superiors in social status, in intellectual attainments or in moral character. This is limited to a particular technically defined sphere'. Functional specificity 'is to be contrasted with the diffuseness of relations and kinship,' which are found in such institutions as marriage. Whereas the physician, for instance, has 'no claim to information about the patient's financial affairs if they are not relevant to his state of health ... a husband must positively justify refusal to answer his wife's questions about his financial affairs; he cannot just say "this has nothing to do with our marriage"' ([1964a] 1970, 329). As a key aspect of the process of bureaucratic rationalization, the differentiation inherent in the growth of 'functional specificity' would permit professionals to contribute to the process of social control in modern society.

Medical practice, as founded upon the primary patterns of disinterestedness, universalism, affective neutrality, and functional specificity served as a prototype for understanding how the modern social order could be constituted. Through action patterned by this set of value guide-lines, social control, as mediated by institutions, could be ensured.

When ... a pattern is institutionalized, conformity with it is part of the legitimate expectations of the society, and of the individual himself ... Institutional patterns in this sense are part of the social structure in that, so far as the patterns are effectively institutionalized, action in social relationships is not random, but is guided and canalized by the requirements of the institutional patterns. So far as they are mandatory, they in a sense directly 'determined' action, otherwise they set limits beyond which variation is not permissable and sets up corrective forces. ([1940b] 1964, 54)

'From the point of view of the social system, the institutional patterns are, in one principal respect, agencies of the "control" of the behavior of its members, in that they keep it in line with the established structure and functional requirements of the social system' ([1942b] 1964, 144). The patterns constituted a structural relation mediating between the medical professions and the sick role. As Parsons took pains to emphasize, 'the role of the physician is not confined to what in the ordinary sense the doctor "does" to or for his patient' that made this therapy successful, but rather 'involves the specific structure of the kind of social relations in which the latter [the patient] is placed when he turns to medical aid in his difficulties' (154).

The Pattern Variables and Social Control

The set of primary patterns, as structural mechanisms mediating between professional practitioners and civil society, provided the basis for the exercise of social control in the emergent social order. With their emphasis upon orientations to action that were at once rational, yet not self-interested, these patterns, in Parsons' view, were the defining feature of a social order alternative to both capitalism and socialism. By combining collective integrity with rational individualism, the primary patterns represented a synthesis of the positive features found in both the other forms of social organization. At the same time, the primary-pattern schema represented the transcendence of another constricting dualism, namely the *Gemeinschaft-Gesellschaft* schema developed by Ferdinand Tönnies. Within Parsons's frame of reference, as we noted, the two societies are distinguished by the way that particular orientations to action – scientific rationalism and commitment to common values – provided cohesion in the social order. In his view, however, neither the contractual relations of the *Gesellschaft* nor the moral solidarity of the *Gemeinschaft* was in itself adequate as a basis for social control in an emerging, post-capitalist society. What was needed was an analytic scheme that somehow combined rational action with moral solidarity. In terms of the pattern variables, this concern was reflected in the problem 'of how to bring the universalism especially characteristic of cognitive rationality, and ... the status of nonrational emotion or affect, into the *same* analytical scheme.' In response to this problem, 'quite early a dichotomous variable which I called "affectivity-affective neutrality" was formulated and incorporated in the same system which also included "universalism-particularism"' (1970a, 843). By incorporating universalism and affective neutrality into the same framework, Parsons, to his satisfaction, had indicated how the dilemmas of capitalism/socialism and *Gemeinschaft/Gesellschaft* could be overcome. Moreover, by linking these value patterns to the process of professionalization, he had provided a concrete social basis for their realization.

However, if the overall practice of professionals were to be oriented in this manner, the insights derived from the medical profession had to be shown as applicable to professional practice in general. What Parsons had to show, then, was a common link between medicine and the other professions. This he found in the institution of science. In his view, the 'institutionalized status' and 'therapeutic effectiveness' of the medical profession came by virtue of 'its integration with one fundamentally important part of the cultural tradition, namely certain branches of science ... Medical science is a part of the whole tradition of scientific culture, and of the associated fields of rational-liberal learning which is characteristic of Western society as a whole' ([1942b] 1964, 163).

In so placing medical science within the 'associated fields of rational-liberal learning,' Parsons could indicate how medicine was linked to the liberal tradition through institutions of higher education.

It is of very great importance that medical training is placed under the auspices of the universities ... It ... articulates the medical sciences with ... other fields of learning, such as humanities, which are not ordinarily thought of as scientific. The universities, in short, are the primary formal carriers of the great Western rational-liberal cultural tradition. Direct affiliation of the medical profession with them – which is true of the other principal professions as well – integrates it directly with this cultural tradition. (163–4)

It was then possible to argue that 'medical practice represents one particular type of a much larger class of roles which is specialized in the direction of exerting a particular kind of influence upon persons' (170–1). One could, in turn, raise the question of

whether for mass tendencies to deviance, rather than individual pathology, there is any analogous vantage point or set of them which can be used for deliberate propagandistic control. It is, furthermore, reasonable to suppose that systematic recognition of the mechanisms by which unconscious control operates on the social level might contribute significantly to the formulation of propaganda policies. (159)

Parsons's response to the growing American involvement in the Second

World War fuelled his interest in 'strengthening attachment to the basic institutional patterns and cultural traditions of the society and deliberately and systematically counteracting the very important existing deviant tendencies' (171–2).

6

Wartime: Fascism, Militarism, and National Morale

Parsons's Wartime Activism

With the onset of the Second World War, Parsons's practical concerns became more specifically oriented towards the rise of national socialism and the threat that it posed to 'the rationalized liberal culture of the Western world' (1942a, 168). He became increasingly preoccupied with how the United States could best contribute to the fight against fascism, and in turn, how public support for increased American involvement in the cause of the allies could be developed. In addition to lobbying on behalf of lend-lease to the United Kingdom (1941a) and responding to various newspaper articles (1941, 1941b), he became involved 'in the work of the [Harvard] Faculty Defense Group, holding the titular position of vice-chairman of the committee on morale' (1940c).[1] This group, as Parsons recounted in a letter to a friend in the United Kingdom, 'is trying to do what it can to promote the greatest possible aid to Britain and the realization among our own public of the critical character of the situation.' One of its activities was to 'give a digest to American opinion by radio to Britain over station WRUL four times a week (1940d, 4).

Underlying his various activities was a particular concern: how the necessary public support for an increased level of American involvement in world affairs could be developed. In Parsons's view, if 'the "sense of national destiny"' and the 'mission and great responsibilities on the world stage' of the United States were to be realized, the 'national morale problem' would have to be solved (1940, 36). By 'promoting attachment [to] a basic desirable common orientation' it would be possible 'to foster solidarity at a group level.' This would in turn permit the development of a 'national defense program ... the necessary foundation for the accomplishment of our historical mission as a nation' (36–7). An issue of concern to Parsons related to the problem of national morale was the susceptibility of the United States to propagandistic appeals. He contributed 'a rather extended memorandum' for the Council for Democracy[2] 'on some of the sociological background of "minority group phenomena" which might be capable of exploitation by Nazi propaganda' (1940c).[3]

American Society and Its Susceptibility to Propaganda

Parsons's memorandum to the Council on Democracy based itself implicitly upon his prior analysis of how the process of institutionalization made social control possible. Yet his account of the American social structure given in the memorandum represented a departure from his earlier writings. The emergent social order, as based on the institutionalization of ultimate values through the mediating activities of the professions, he now saw as in the process of formation. This development, however, brought in its wake 'social disorganization and the attendant personal disorientation and conflict [which] are particularly widespread in this country at the present time.' In Parsons's view, 'one of the most important and deepest-lying sources' of these tendencies 'lies in the "rationalistic" character of our culture ... in which science, rational technology and critical thought occupy a place of very unusual prominence.' The overall changes occurring also led to destabilization, for the process of rationalization was bound to meet with resistance from various strata in society whose orientations and beliefs were disrupted by the transformation taking place.

This tension between the emergence of an increasingly rationalized social order and social strata resistant to it was diagnosed by Parsons as a 'strain.' The growth of an increasingly 'rationalistic culture' is not only 'largely responsible for the great achievements of our civilization, but ... is also responsible for a good many strains' (1940, 13). Rationalization induced strains because of 'the presence of a relatively self-consistent social tradition to which the great majority of individuals in the social system are strongly attached' (10–11). As composed of 'ideals,' 'goals,' and 'symbols,' this tendency provides the basis for stable and integrated orientations to action. Parsons argued that some manifestations of social and personal disorganization were attributable to shortcomings in the social tradition. 'Certain kinds of "pathology" in the action of individuals who fail to conform with social standards of expectation [such as] neurotic and psychotic behavior, suicide, some kinds of crime, [and] even a good deal of "organic" illness ... are typically understandable as modes of reaction of individuals to the strains involved in conflict situations and the "disorientation" which results from being confronted with a confused and inadequate social tradition.' Social disorganization could also take the form of 'certain types of movement on a mass scale ... which center about what is generally in some respect a new symbolic orientation.' These include 'explicitly religious cults [and] other groupings of a "semi-religious" or "pseudo-religious" character [such as] movements of a political character' (12). The degree and strength of these deviant phenomena could be seen as a 'quantitative question of the balance between disorganizing processes and reintegrating processes' (13). Using the 'social tradition' and the 'rationalistic culture' as integrative standards, Parsons proceeds to diagnose the nature and extent of various phenomena that pose a real or potential threat to 'the absence of too much overt internal conflict between different groups' (10–11).

Of particular concern was how the process of rationalization worked itself out through the occupational system. Using his analysis of professionalization, Parsons maintained that the system of stratification – as based upon rationally oriented occupations – was the fundamental structural feature of American society (1–5). By the gradual institutionalization of this occupational structure through the consolidation of a rational culture and the development of science and technology, a new form of social order was to be ensured. Yet, in Parsons's view, this process also generated tensions that made for social instability. Of particular concern to him was the dissent resulting from the egalitarian ideal in American society. He noted that 'there is a good deal of evidence that the egalitarian elements of our democratic tradition serve on balance to increase rather than to mitigate the strains.' This was the case because the American cultural tradition cultivates 'the highest ambitions among the young of virtually all classes of the population [yet] only a very small number can ever reach the top, as there are only a few places up there.' This leads to a 'widespread frustrated ambition ... in the lower middle class [which] is undoubtedly one of the most important sources of explosive material in our society' (3–4). The occupational system led to strains in other ways as well. Social mobility from rural to urban settings resulted in 'the strain of adjustment.' 'The large amount of rapid technological change ... particularly ... in industry ... tends to disrupt the social structure of working groups,' resulting in ' "irrational" reactions which often involve defensive formation of solidary groupings' (10).[4]

Closely related to the occupational structure as a source of strain was the family, 'the most important repository of all those elements of tradition and cultural pattern which are not readily capable of reduction to universalistic terms and terms of efficiency.' The family, with its emphasis upon 'sentiments' and 'solidarity,' was in tension with the values of 'occupational success and achievement.' By virtue of familial support and connections, one could commonly gain 'advantages in competition,' thereby overriding standards of achievement. Hence, in Parsons's view, 'this relation of family and occupational hierarchy is one of the central points of strain in our social system' (5–6).

Parsons also examined how strains were induced by religious commitment. This subject was closely linked to his interest in the 'extent to which ... devotion to ... institutional fundamentals is backed up by solid sentiments which are relatively immune to "subversive" influences under the kind of strains to which many people are subjected.' Not surprisingly, in his view, 'in general the Anglo-Saxon Protestant traditions supply the solidest foundations for this kind of loyalty' (7). Other religions, such as Catholicism and Lutheranism, however, predisposed their members towards disloyalty. Because of the 'authoritarian element in the basic structure of the Catholic Church ... individual self-reliance and valuation of freedom' might be weakened. Similarly, those with 'a Lutheran background ... are apt to be partial to a political authoritarianism and old-fashioned legitimist conservatism' (8).[5]

Parsons examined more generally the degree to which various immigrant groups had been able to assimilate themselves to the dominant Anglo-Saxon pattern. Those lacking 'the strong Anglo-Saxon tradition of responsibility in the affairs of the community ... are ... apt to be particularly pliable material in the hands of any strong leadership which is able to exploit their characteristics and position.' In contrast, certain 'population groups' who were able to experience 'prestige and success' would be 'relatively free of exploitable resentments and senses of inferiority,' depending upon the degree to which they assimilated into 'the Anglo-Saxon traditions' (9). On balance, in Parsons's view, the United States had 'failed to develop a culturally homogeneous community in the sense in which for example the British do.' For when immigration takes place, 'people are subjected to certain sorts of strain which involve frustration and security [and] there is a strong tendency to resort to what appear to be strong anchorages.' Hence, the resistance of 'national traditions [to] assimilation ... has been one of the most important kinds of reaction to these strains' (10). In general, despite its overall capacity to resist the appeals of national socialism, Parsons still maintained that 'the American nation constitutes, as a result of various strains and circumstances of its past, a relatively badly integrated social system with an unstable orientation on the part of large numbers of individuals, and many internal differences and conflicts. Many of the sentiments associated with these strains are capable of exploitation by the great movements of the present which are attacking our institutions' (24).

Social Disorganization and the Redirection of National Policy

In Parsons's view, the lack of stability and integration of its social structure not only made the United States vulnerable to enemy propaganda, but threatened to undermine the increasing American involvement in world affairs. Given the effect of its political and social arrangements on the ability of the United States to intervene in the world order, Parsons was concerned with how these arrangements might be restructured to permit the redirection of national policy. The expansion of state activities along more internationalist lines could only take place if sufficient consensus in the form of a high level of 'national morale' could be developed. Parsons's line of thinking on the interplay between political and social concerns was influenced by his commitment to the precepts of liberal Calvinism as they pertained to politics. He noted that according to Calvin, 'the state is co-ordinate with the church in promoting God's kingdom on earth; the two have a common purpose but different spheres of influence.' Moreover, 'Calvin's own system ... was an authoritarian Christian socialism strictly subordinating individuals to the one great aim of increasing the glory of God' (1930a, 152). The Calvinist state sought to use its powers to promote transcendent values in secular society. This Calvinist conception revealed itself in Parsons's advocacy of an 'instrumental conception of the role of the state ... [It] becomes not so much a contractual instrument for promoting individual interests as an organ of the entire community for the promotion of certain of its common ends.' Thus, 'the coercion of a sovereign authority has come to be seen as only one means of enforcing on the individual the supremacy of common ideals and attitudes.' Parsons maintained that the state had a 'triple role':

First, it is the principal organ of common action in the community. Secondly, it is the main guardian of its institutions, especially in so far as their automatic and informal functioning through custom breaks

*down and the need of deliberate and sometimes coercive enforce-
ment arises ... Thirdly, the state constitutes one but only one of the
principal focuses of the common sentiment and thus plays an important symbolic role.* (1934a, 231)

Reflecting his view that the 'coercion of a sovereign authority' was
necessary, he maintained that in view of the 'dangerous character of the
world in which we live [and] of the extent to which our interests are
bound up with Great Britain,' the United States was in 'truly an
emergency situation which calls for emergency powers in the hands of
the executive.' Parsons stressed 'the extreme importance of being able
to act quickly' (1941, 1).

In indicating what the expansion of powers would entail, Parsons
implicitly drew upon the Calvinist prototype for the relation between
state and civil society.[6] Rather than simply reflecting the '"popular
will" ... government ... must take a positive responsibility for maintaining the basic democratic patterns.' Such a necessity 'is greatly accentu-
ated by the presence of anomie and hence the instability of orientation
on the part of large elements in the population and their liability to
"distorted" definitions of the situation.' Thus, 'relative immunity to
dangerous propaganda appeals cannot be simply left to the "common
sense" of people.' The government not only must maintain 'a plane of
public discussion and "agitation" which ... puts a premium on rationality and responsibility,' but also must use its 'strategic position and
prestige ... to affirm the main tradition and to create or back symbols
adequate to it' (1941c, 2). In his view, this realignment and extension of
governmental powers would be possible only if certain aspects of
American democratic practices were recast. Reflecting his Calvinist
commitments, his view entailed the subsumption of individually
defined goals to those in the collective interest. In terms of congressional behaviour, he suggested in a letter to representative Edith Nourse
Rogers (1941a) that 'on matters ... which touch the most vital questions
of the national welfare at this time, opposition for the sake of opposition
seems to be both politically unwise and morally reprehensible.' The
exigencies of the day required the re-examination of the notions of
democracy and civil liberties. Given the importance of 'technical
competence' for the development of leadership, according to Parsons,
the 'question of democracy' ought to give way to 'the most efficient means
to secure an end [and] the selection of the most competent persons for
a position.' Indeed, 'the term democracy was not adequate as a slogan to
state the issue raised by the national socialist movement.' National

socialism 'presents a challenge not merely to democratic authority, but to the broader type of rational-legal authority (1929–67a, 17). Accordingly, consistent with his commitment to rationalization associated with the spread of ascetic Protestantism, he maintained that rational-legal authority, rather than democracy, ought to be strengthened. Parsons suggested that 'some modification of traditional conceptions of civil liberties ... seem to be needed [for] they have often been formulated in such a way as to suggest absolute inalienability regardless of the ethical quality of action under their protection.' According to Parsons, this conception of civil liberties has resulted in various forms of abuse, including 'subversive actions' and the 'refusal to accept responsibility.'

What is most needed seems to be a more positively functional conception of rights and liberties. If authority is to be conditioned by performance of function on behalf of communal goals it is difficult to see why liberties should not equally be conditional on performance of a functionally important role – or at least pulling one's own weight in the boat ... Society should not be a mere collection of individuals each pursuing an independent self-interest seeking only to minimize restrictions on his liberty to do so, but a company engaged in the pursuit of common goals – which include *and do not interfere with the self-fulfillment of individual personality.* (1940, 28–9)

Parsons's notion about the performance of a functionally specific role sprang from his views on service as rooted in the ascetic Protestant calling. That is, individuals, by virtue of their membership in society, were morally bound to serve its collective interest, rather than their own goals. Correspondingly, the state had a mandate to act on behalf of the collectivity.

Mirroring this limitation on democracy and civil liberties, Parsons maintained that 'one of the most important points for the focus of national solidarity lies in the character of the elite in our society and its relation to the rest of the social structure.' In his view, 'it is of the greatest importance for the stability of the society that this elite group should be able to maintain its privilege solidly and thus the basis of its claim and second should be broadly in harmony with the more general value system of the community' (43–4).

If the United States were to assume a more active role in world affairs, a significant realignment of the social structure was necessary. This meant that a new definition of the situation – consonant with the extension of state powers – would have to take place. In Parsons's view, the government itself was not completely adequate to this task in that 'since an administration holds office by the electoral victory of a party, its acts are inherently "partisan" and hence "prejudiced"' (1941c, 2).

Parsons's analysis of American society during the Second World War reflected both his fears of Hobbesian disorder and his commitment to a political and social order founded on Calvinist principles. Reacting to what he regarded as widespread anomie and strains in the social order, he advocated both the expansion of state powers and the strengthening of the rational-legal order on which it was founded. Correspondingly, he called for disinterested acceptance of this order on the part of all members of society. Nevertheless, the coercive state, because of its partisanship, could not on its own provide the basis for commitment of this kind. It was crucial, then, that a source for generating loyalty and sustaining national morale be defined and elaborated. To this end, Parsons suggested that 'there is an opportunity to use sociological analysis in such a way as to redefine the situation in terms of a more realistic and less distorted version of the liberal democratic view.' As Parsons noted to Hartshorne, what 'we can "do" about it [is] with the backing of the Defense group, to state our views and contribute our bit to getting across an acceptable definition of the situation' (1941c, 2).

Parsons suggested that the sociologist could play an active role in helping to build national morale and curb dissonant tendencies. This concern was implicit in his discussion of how propaganda, as 'an extension of the general use of the power of government,' could best be defined and implemented ([1942b] 1964, 172).

The Social Analogues of Medical Practice: Propaganda and Social Control

In his discussion of how propaganda policy should be formulated and implemented, Parsons used medical practice – in particular psychiatry – as a prototype 'for controlling action ... through appeal to the "subjective" non-situational aspects of action' ([1942b] 1964, 149). Just as 'conscious psychotherapy takes advantage of the patterning of the physician's role' to control the patient, Parsons argued, 'influence on the social structure might be exerted by deliberately working "along with" existing control mechanisms' (171). More basically,

the structure of Western society in its relation to the functions of social control provides an extraordinary opening for the deliberate propaganda of reinforcement as an agency of control. Just as

deliberate psychotherapy in the medical relationship is in a sense
simply an extension of functional elements inherent in the structure
of the role of the physician, so, on the social level, the propaganda of
reinforcement would be simply an extension of many of the
automatic but latent functions of existing institutional patterns. (173)

The medical analogue suggested, then, a set of criteria, both for the
'health' of the system and for the well-adjusted character structure of
the individual. 'The reality principle,' 'strong ego development,' and
'affective reciprocity' – all indicative of successful adjustment in
psychoanalytic terms – could be effectively used to describe emotional
maturity for social behaviour in general. Similarly, the role of the
physician was taken to be the appropriate model for the application of
propaganda because 'to treat propaganda policy as a kind of "social
psychotherapy" is to act directly in accordance with the essential nature
of the social system' (174).

Parsons maintained that medical practice was in no sense unique in
its ability to ensure social control. Rather, it was a reflection of broader
patterns of institutionalization taking place in society. It was able to
exert influence on the social structure by virtue of 'automatic, informal
mechanisms ... peculiar to the modern Western world.' Hence, 'it would
be surprising if the fundamental structural and functional aspects of it
should be confined to the one relatively narrow functional sphere of
medical practice' (160). Parsons contended that the institutionalization
of these informal social-control mechanisms was not confined to
medicine, but also governed the practice of the clergy and academics.
In his view, there were 'similarities in the ways in which the medical,
the academic, and the clerical roles exert a steady discipline on the
people to whom they are subjected.' He noted that 'in his role as
personal adviser and spiritual guide to the parishioner the clergyman
has long been known to perform functions which have ... an element of
unconscious psychotherapy.' And in a manner somewhat similar to the
medical man, 'the clergyman ... is directly seeking to bring – or keep –
his parishioner in conformity with a normative tradition' (166–7). For
the academic role, the same relation to the control problems of the
social order obtained:

Included in the subjects of professional competence of academic men
are precisely those fields of the cultural tradition which, in Western
society, have been most central to the definitions of the situation
which have, on the one hand, been institutionalized in the social
structure, and which are, on the other hand, the necessary starting

*points for any deviant definitions which could conceivably help
to crystallize important processes of structural change.* (166)

In terms of social control, the academic structure was particularly
significant 'in relation to definitions of the situation rather than to the
direct control of attitudes.' Among the academic professions, Parsons
emphasized that 'the social sciences ... have been particularly important
in the diagnosis of the situation of society, the meanings of various
phases of its history and of tendencies to change' (165–6). Given that
academic, clerical, and medical professions were able to exert influence
on the social order by virtue of their structurally based practices, 'it is ...
reasonable to suppose that systematic recognition of the mechanisms
by which unconscious control operates on the social level might
contribute significantly to the formulation of propaganda policies' (159).

In his suggestions for establishing a propaganda agency, these
social-control mechanisms were specified. They did not, however,
signify a new departure in Parsons's thought and analysis but represented an elaboration of themes and concepts developed in his discussions of classical social theory and the professions. Indeed, in no small
measure the main characteristics of a propaganda agency embodied
the 'primary patterns' he had derived from his study of medicine. It
was by virtue of this set of orientations that medicine was able to exert
social control over the behaviour of patients and contribute to the
process of rationalization.

Above all, Parsons stressed the pattern of 'disinterestedness' as
providing the general basis for the success of medical practice.[7] In the
same manner, 'closely parallel to the impersonal components of the role
of the physician on which "confidence" in him is focused ... the
academic and clerical roles [are] "representative" of an objectively
impersonal cultural tradition' (170). This pattern was to govern the
activities of a propaganda agency as well, in the sense that 'it is essential
to establish a position of impersonal authority' (174). Within this overall
orientation of 'impersonal disinterestedness,' the patterns of universalism, affective neutrality, and functional specificity were also to guide
the activities of a propaganda agency. Universalism, as embodied in
medical practice, meant that 'the patient is ... significant in a technical
context rather as a "case" than as a "person."' In this sense, all cases
of illnesses 'should be treated alike, subject to technically founded
variations, regardless of "who" they are.' Without the scientific
objectivity inherent in universalism, 'a high development of medicine
as applied science would not be possible' (161). Since a 'technical

competence in "social psychiatry,"' comparable to the medical case, cannot be found in any professional group, 'the next best thing seems to be the deliberate cultivation of a reputation for scrupulously reporting of information, the sources of which the public cannot have direct access to' (174). Because the agency had technical competence in a particular area – namely in providing information about public issues – it would also be conforming to the pattern of functional specificity 'in that it defines the role with reference to a specific content of function and segregates this "area," that of the professional relations, from any other of potential relation between the parties' (160). Given 'the authority of the propaganda agency,' as based on its expertise in matters specific to public information, there would be 'a disposition to turn to it for "help" in matters where a person is necessarily incompetent' (174–5).

Finally, Parsons showed that 'affective neutrality' – avoiding emotional involvements with a client or patient – could be applied to wider social issues. Parsons argued that 'one primary source' of a physician's 'ability to "get at" his patient' was by avoiding the expression of 'moral judgement of much of his patient's conduct' ([1951] 1964, 160). This is not, however, to say that the physician was to 'assume a morally nihilistic attitude.' Rather, 'this pattern implicitly assumes agreement on certain moral fundamentals of our institutionalized patterns, especially those involved in the acceptance of "mature adjustment" as a goal of therapy' ([1942b] 1964, 175). In a like manner, a propaganda agency must concern itself with 'moral fundamentals about its own role, its fiduciary position on behalf of the national welfare, and its moral integrity in fulfilling its obligations. Implicitly this would carry with it acceptance of the fundamental orientation of national policy toward the war, above all, and acceptance of the principal fundamentals of the historic institutionalized values and cultural tradition' (175).

By so obliging itself morally 'on behalf of the national welfare,' the propaganda agency would thereby avoid an effective involvement with members of the public and permit 'mature adjustment' to the moral dictates of the order.

In dealing with particular tendencies to deviance which arise, the agency or agencies should assume a role as closely analogous to that of physician as is possible in the circumstances. Specifically, it should so far as possible identify itself with those elements of the institutional patterning of government and other structures in the society which are symbolic of the integration of the society as a

*whole. In relation to government this means above all that it should
avoid involvement in any of the internal struggles for power in
partisan groups.* (174)

Parsons did not elaborate upon the exact manner in which the
national propaganda agency was to be implemented. He had, none the
less, provided the broad guide-lines for 'a very complicated technical
subject' (175). He had demonstrated how insights drawn from medicine
and psychiatry were of relevance to the maintenance of order during a
national crisis. By indicating that the physician-patient relationship
could be generalized to society's institutions of social control, Parsons
could further explore how the *professional strata* could cultivate such
mechanisms. This line of reasoning is evident in his discussion of how
we could both understand the social orders of America's main wartime
enemies – Japan and Germany – and, in turn, also restructure these
societies along the lines of Western liberal democracies.

Controlled Institutional Change in Germany and Japan

As an outgrowth of his involvement in the Committee on National
Morale and in American Defense – Harvard Group, Parsons turned
his attention to the study of the social structures of Germany and
Japan, with particular attention given to questions of national morale,
social control, and the possibilities of exercising 'controlled institutional change.'[8]

Of particular concern to Parsons was German national socialism and
the threat that it posed to Western liberal democracies.[9] Mirroring his
analysis of social disorder in the United States, he argued that fascism
represented a strain engendered by the extension of '"rational" patterns
of Modern Western Society' into Germany: 'These patterns have
been able to develop as far as they have only by virtue of undermining
many of the values which have played an important part in our past
history, especially in the informal, traditionalized social structures'
(1942a, 159–60). With their established system of values threatened,
members of the traditional sectors vent their aggression by attacking
symbolized versions of the rationalizing and modernizing interests.
Correspondingly, they profess an exaggerated loyalty to the traditional
values that are allegedly being eroded. This reactive pattern varies, of
course, according to historical and political circumstances. Quite often
the fundamentalism assumed a nationalistic guise, as real or potential
enemies in the international power alignment came to serve as a

rallying point for support. Those rational interests that favoured internationalism could conveniently be condemned for undermining national solidarity. Perhaps of greatest significance for the differential success of these movements was 'the symbols of the rationalized patterns of Western culture' ([1942c] 1964, 138). In the case of Germany, where the symbols of liberalism were associated with Versailles, national sentiments could be easily mobilized against the political conditions implied by this settlement.

In Parsons's view, fascism represented a societal strain induced by the rationalization process and concentrated in the more traditionalistic elements of society. 'The probable consequences of the permanent consolidation' of National Socialist power (158) would, according to Parsons, be the development of 'a system of ideas which overwhelmingly favored a traditionalistic type of institutionalization, and which undermined the ideological foundation of the rational-legal system of authority in favor of a traditional [one]' (1942a, 162). In contrast to the universalistic standards such as 'rational knowledge,' 'personal rights,' and 'technical competence,' national socialism placed membership in the ' "mystical body" of the German people' above all other considerations, emphasized 'racial and party particularism,' 'unlimited loyalty to the *Fuhrer*,' and in general advocated 'patterns that are much more appropriate to a traditionalistic organization of authority than a rational-legal one' (159).

Parsons analysed Japan's path into modernity in a similar manner. Even though Japan 'has been a society in transition from a "feudal" preindustrial organization ... to a modern urbanized industrial society' ([1946] 1964, 275), this development did not occur without widespread disruptions. The 'rapid and drastic internal social transformation' generated tensions that were 'expressed in heightened nationalistic feeling and thus formed the popular basis of Japanese expansionism.' In Parsons's view, 'the special insecurity introduced by the consequences of Westernization,' as in the case of Germany, took the form of social strains that jeopardized the modernizing process (283).

Reiterating his contentions about the strategic centrality of the spread of science and technology, Parsons argued that the most effective way to transcend both German national socialism and Japanese militarism was through a continuation of rationalization. In Germany, one could 'displace the conservative pattern and ... reduce the tension by systematically fostering those elements of the pattern of modern Germany, especially of industrialism, which are closest to their counterparts in the democratic countries' ([1945a] 1964, 251). 'As a lever of institutional change,' in Parsons's view, 'the most promising is the economic-occupational structure.' Since a good proportion of the population 'spend nearly half their waking hours' at their place of work, the occupational system constituted a 'highly strategic point in the total structure' (263). It was, moreover, interdependent with 'kinship and the class structure,' which meant that 'an important change there would have major repercussions in these neighboring areas' (263).

The aim of policy should then be one of

fostering a highly productive, full-employment, expanding economy for Germany. The inherent tendencies of the modern industrial economy are such that if this is achieved its influence on institutional change will be automatically in the right direction. Conversely, tendencies to particularism, the breakdown of functional specialization [and] overemphasis on group solidarity are overwhelmingly defensive reactions to the insecurity attendant on a contracting field of opportunity. It is not modern industrialism as such, but its pathology and the incompleteness of its development which fosters those phenomena. (265)

Along similar lines, Parsons suggested that in order to 'bring Japanese society closer to the model of the Western democratic nations ... it is indispensable that conditions should favor the continual extension of "individualism" in the fundamental sense.' What is needed, then, is 'a situation ·where the individual can become emancipated from the pressure of the particularistic group solidarities which have been so prominent in traditional Japanese society.' Paralleling his recommendations for 'controlled institutional change' in Germany, Parsons argued that in Japan 'the most favorable conditions' for the spread of the value of individualism 'are those of the Westernized type of urban society with occupational roles of the type best exemplified in modern industry. Therefore a situation is essential that places large masses of the population in a position where their fundamental interests and security are bound up with further extension of this type of pattern. If such a development is to be realized, 'opportunity for reasonable economic expansion along peaceful lines is an essential prerequisite' ([1946] 1964, 295).

With his emphasis upon situations as the basis for attitudes and actions, Parsons contended, for both Japan and Germany, that one could not simply induce desired social transformations by changing the character structures of the individual members of the two societies.[10]

Consistent with his views on how the emergent social order would develop, he suggested that the most effective way to transcend national socialism was through a 'dynamic change in institutions' – 'those patterns which define the essentials of the legitimately expected behavior of persons insofar as they perform structurally important roles in the social system' ([1945a] 1964, 239). A stable institutional structure would in turn ensure 'the interlocking of so many motivational elements in support of the same goals and standards' (240). The implied interdependence between character structure and institutions meant that 'any permanent and far-reaching change in the orientation of the German people probably cannot rest on a change of character structure alone, but must also involve institutional change; otherwise, institutional conditions would continue to breed the same type of character structure in new generations' (238).

In both Germany and Japan, the impetus for this transformation was to come from the professional strata. For Germany, Parsons suggested 'that the first major steps in the reintegration ... into the Western community should be the admission of the professional representatives of these values into the community of their Allied "opposite numbers." This should be true of technologists, trade groups, scientific societies, professional groups [and] university exchange' (265). To ensure the transformation of Japanese society, 'conditions should aim at building up into a progressively stronger position those persons who have an important stake in a liberal system: professional and technical people, individuals with substantial administrative positions either public or private, small and moderate businessmen, trade union leaders and the like' ([1946] 1964, 296).

Parsons's recommendations for German and Japanese reconstruction underscored his commitment to the professional strata as the source of stability and cohesion in advanced capitalist societies. Through a form of practice consonant with the guide-lines offered by the primary patterns, mechanisms of social control would be operable. The emergence of the professional strata acting in this manner heralded a new phase in the process of rationalization. The earlier period, marked by increasing rational-legal administration, the ascendancy of the business class, and an untrammelled market economy, led to 'strains' in the social order and to the development of fascism and militarism. The most effective way of controlling this pathological outbreak, in Parsons's view, was through the selective introduction of rationalizing patterns into points of influence 'of strategic significance to the entire system.' In so diffusing 'disinterestedness,' 'universalism,' 'affective neutrality,' and 'functional specificity,' throughout the occupational system in particular and the social order in general, the professions, in effect, would help along a new phase of rationalization. While the specific locus of this 'strong movement of positive institutional change' was to be Germany and Japan, in principle it was of relevance to all societies undergoing the same sort of transformation. The development of widespread professional practice along the lines suggested by the pattern variables indicated a means of overcoming the anomie and atomism of the market economy, while still preserving capitalist social relations.

From Classical Social Theory to Professionalization

Parsons's suggestions for the reconstruction of German and Japanese societies represented more than a set of policy guide-lines. They had enormous implications for recasting ideologies and intellectual orientations in modern societies. In his view, it was only through the transformation of the belief systems underpinning national socialism and militarism that a transition toward liberal democracy would be possible in Japan and Germany. This tension between the patterns of 'traditionalism' and 'modernism' was particularly evident in his analysis of German society. According to Parsons, any possible success that the national socialists could have in consolidating their position would come about through the establishment of their 'patterns' on a widespread basis. Only by replacing the dominant value schema of 'rational-legality' with their traditionally oriented version would they have a sufficient basis for political power. What was at stake, then, was the whole grounding of legitimation and the core structure of values and symbols that gave meaning and direction to action at all levels. The battleground between national socialism and 'rational-legal authority' thus lay in the realm of ideas or, more concretely, in the cultural sphere that mediated between the public and the social system.

The conflict between rational liberalism and national socialism was only an aspect of a broader struggle between competing 'definitions of the situation.' Indeed, the tension that Parsons detected between the two patterns was connected to the conflict between different theoretical outlooks he had traced in his earlier analysis of classical social theory. The 'radicalism of the right,' in the form of fascism, with its indictment of 'the whole penumbra of scientific and philosophical rationalism' ([1942c] 1964, 135), bore an affinity to 'neo-Kantian idealism,' which professed 'opposition to positivistic trends of thought [and] to anything in the nature of a "reduction" of the facts of human life and destiny to terms of the physical world or to biological terms' ([1937] 1968, 475). Such a criticism of 'the "enlightenment" ideas of utilitarianism, positivism [and] rationalism' issued in 'an "organic" social theory all through the nineteenth century and up to the present' (481). Along the same lines, he argued that the radical right was rooted in the German romantic tradition:

At least one critically important aspect of the National Socialist movement lies in the fact that it constitutes a mobilization of the extremely deep-seated romantic tendencies of German society in the service of a violently aggressive political movement, incorporating a 'fundamentalist' revolt against the whole tendency of rationalization in the Western world, and at the same time against its deepest institutionalized foundations. ([1942] 1964, 123)

The ideology of national socialism represented an extremist political embodiment of the idealist and romantic traditions in German social theory. Correspondingly, Parsons maintained that left-wing radicalism, in the form of Marxism, was an extension of utilitarian thought. Utilitarianism appeared in the guise of 'naive rationalistic utopianism,' which held that 'if only certain symbolic sources of evil, superstition, or privilege or capitalism were removed, "everything would be all right" automatically and for all time.' In his view, 'this type of insecurity has had much to do with the cognitive biases and inadequacies of utilitarian thought ... It has contributed largely to the currency of a definition of the situation which contains conspicuous elements of utopianism and of distorted caricature' ([1942c] 1964, 137). 'What in terms of the recent situation is "leftist" social thought is overwhelmingly "positivistic" as well as utilitarian' (134). As Parsons pointed out, there was a close connection between the general intellectual orientations of a nation and the political ideologies that held sway within it.[11] For instance, with 'the conspicuously greater tendency of German social thought to repudiate the primary rationalistic and emancipated ideological structures which have dominated the intellectual traditions of France and England,' Parsons argued, 'there has been conspicuously less intellectual "liberalism" in Germany – the obverse of the predominant "conservative" tendencies being the extreme of rationalistic radicalism found in Marxism' ([1942] 1964, 119). Parsons's implicit practical concerns guiding his treatment of classical social theory thus illuminated his discussion of the two 'ideological' tendencies that he saw as posing a threat to Western societies. The 'rational radical utopianism' that

Parsons attributed to left-wing thought was foreshadowed by his earlier treatment of Marx, while the 'romanticism' he detected in the radical right was anticipated by his earlier analysis of Sombart. The epistemological positions of utilitarianism and idealism, as embodied in the perspectives of Marx and Sombart, created the dilemma of having to choose either rational utopian determinism or irrational reactionary voluntarism as a standpoint for comprehending the social order.

In Parsons's discussion of how post-war German society might be restructured along liberal democratic lines, the Marx/Sombart dilemma recurs in the form of 'naive rationalistic utopianism' and the 'idealist romanticism' of national socialism. Both perspectives, in Parsons's view, posed a threat to the stability and welfare of post-war Germany. The 'rationalistic scheme of thought,' as he stressed,

has not been adequate to provide a stably institutionalized diagnosis of even a 'modern' social system as a whole, nor has it been adequate to formulate all of the important values of our society, nor its cognitive orientation to the world. It has been guilty of the fallacy of misplaced concreteness in neglecting or underestimating the role of what Pareto has called the 'non-logical' aspects of human behavior in society, of the sentiments and traditions of family and informal social relationships, of the refinements of social stratification, of the peculiarities of regional, ethnic or national culture – perhaps above all of religion. On this level it has indeed helped to provoke a most important 'anti-intellectualist' reaction. ([1942c] 1964, 134)

By the same token, national socialism, as influenced by 'idealist romanticism,' according to Parsons, 'would strongly favor a traditionalistic rather than a rational-legal outcome of the process of routinization' (1942a, 162). The consequence of national socialist predominance, he conjectured, would be the transformation of society increasingly in a 'traditionalistic' direction, undermining the prevailing 'rational-legal' institutions.

Other elements of the social system which in the Western world have been relatively independent of the political organization as such, such as the dominant forms of private property and economic enterprise, market relationships, education and cultural activities, could hardly avoid being drawn into the same basic course of change. That the most distinctive cultural features of our civilization could not long survive such a change, would scarcely seem to need to be pointed out. (166)

Parsons found his way out of the Marx/Sombart dilemma by drawing on the thought of Weber. Through the Weberian conception of a personal calling – as rooted in the bureaucracy – he incorporated idealism and utilitarianism into a unified standpoint. This formed the basis for his subsequent analysis of how the emergent social order was constituted through the primary patterns of professional practice.

It was through his engagement with the intersecting domestic and international problems faced by the United States in the Second World War that Parsons was able to refine and elaborate the possible practical relevance of the primary patterns. From his analysis of how a national propaganda agency could contribute to national morale by overcoming tendencies towards dissent, he had indicated how the psychiatrist-patient relationship could serve as a prototype for the exercise of social control. Through an orientation using the primary patterns, a propaganda agency could help ensure consensus around national values.

Similarly, Parsons saw the strengthening of the professional strata as a way of overcoming competing ideological perspectives and inducing 'controlled institutional change' in post-war Germany. 'These groups have a key influence in defining crucially important patterns in democratic society. Genuine integration of the German counterparts would do much to set a right tone for the corresponding development in Germany. It would also help to avoid defining the situation in terms of corrupting German "idealism" with Western commercialism and "materialism," since science, technology and the professions are relatively immune to this charge' ([1945a] 1964, 266). By virtue of the growth and spread of professionalization, according to Parsons, the potentially disruptive tendencies of idealism and materialism could be overcome. Within modern societies as a whole, then, the increasing ascendancy of the professions was to ensure social control. What made this possible was a form of practice governed by the primary patterns. Disinterestedness, universalism, affective neutrality, and functional specificity served as social-control mechanisms that regulated both the actions of professional practitioners and members of civil society. The primary patterns mediated between the normative system and the everyday beliefs and actions of the general public and the professional elites. Given that the patterns were unconscious mechanisms, their tacit acceptance by members of society would ensure that social action proceeded in a manner consonant with prescriptions of the normative system. Nevertheless, in specifying and articulating the primary patterns and showing how they could be operable in practice, Parsons had indicated how they could be intentionally cultivated. The very fact that the patterns could be made explicit implied, as well, that an orientation towards action could be consciously established along the lines that they suggested. Once they were in place, however, and taken for granted, they could serve the dual role of regulating professional practice and public action, thereby ensuring social control and a stable order.

During the Second World War, when Parsons perceived the United States as facing problems of internal dissent and external aggression, he was able to work through some of the practical implications of the primary patterns for developing social-control mechanisms. With the return to peacetime, however, he directed his attention away from immediate practical problems towards issues surrounding the theory, practice, and orientation of the social sciences. This shift of concern, however, represented a continuity in both interest and purpose. In accordance with the political and social context accompanying the onset of the Cold War, Parsons thought that much of the burden of supporting the national purpose had devolved upon the social sciences. In his efforts to orient the social sciences in a manner of strategic use and relevance to the Cold War order, he drew on the insights provided by his analysis of how medical practice could serve as a prototype for ensuring social control.

7

Mid Century: The Social Sciences and Cold War America

The National Science Foundation Controversy

After the Second World War, Parsons became closely involved in the controversy about whether social-scientific research ought to be supported by the newly formed National Science Foundation (NSF). In the initial National Science Foundation bill (as amended by Thomas C. Hart), passed in the Senate on 3 July 1946,[1] the social sciences were not directly included. Senator Hart justified the omission of the social sciences on the grounds that 'no agreement has been reached with reference to what social science really means.' It could include 'philosophy, anthropology, all the racial questions, all kinds of economics, including political economics, literature, perhaps religion, and various kinds of ideology.' He maintained that an ill-defined field of this sort would burden the new foundation unduly and that there was 'no connection between the social sciences, a very abstract field, and the concrete field which constitutes the other subjects to be dealt with by the proposed science foundation.' In the debate that followed, Senator Kilgore announced that in a committee discussion with 'scientific leaders' it had been agreed that 'the natural sciences and the social sciences were linked together,' but that the foundation would not extend support to the social sciences 'until social scientists were able to draw up a program acceptable to the foundation staff on its "scientific merits"' (U.S. Senate 1946, in Lyons 1969, 127).

The response of social scientists to their exclusion from the bill was undoubtedly a reflection of their own weakness. Rather than lobbying for their own interests, they banded together with other scientists to form the Inter-Society Committee for a National Science Foundation.[2]

Its purpose was to press for legislation that would give control of the foundation to a board selected by the scientific community. Apparently discouraged by the vote in the Senate, and resigned to the 'permissive, but not mandatory,' status of the social sciences within the pending legislation, they chose not to act in a partisan and directly political manner. Instead, 'they made efforts to promote a better understanding of the social sciences among their colleagues in the natural sciences, in Congress, and in the general public' (135). In particular, through such works as Stuart Chase's *The Proper Study of Mankind* ([1948] 1956) and the assessment (Merton and Lazarsfeld 1950) of Samuel Stouffer's *American Soldier* (1949) sponsored by the Social Science Research Council (SSRC) and the Carnegie Foundation, an effort was made to consolidate the contributions of the social sciences and to draw attention to their accomplishments. As a leading advocate of the social sciences, Talcott Parsons took an active part in the deliberations on their status within the NSF. This was reflected in a number of articles and reports that he wrote immediately subsequent to the passage of the initial National Science Foundation bill in 1946 (1946a, 1947b, 1948). Judging by their style and content, these writings were intended as a contribution to the post-war discussion of the relevance of the social sciences to American life. At the same time, however, they played an important role in the consolidation of a number of long-standing themes in Parsons's thought, for the distrust, misunderstanding, and rejection of the social sciences revealed by the debates on the NSF forced Parsons to give more serious consideration to the relation of social-scientific research to American society. In reflecting upon the strengths of the social sciences, the conditions for their success, and the problems they faced in gaining acceptance, he elaborated and refined some of his most central concerns about social-scientific practice.

In the post-war controversy that divided the scientific community over the nature and make-up of the proposed National Science Foundation, Parsons stood in opposition to the position held by the Committee to Support the Bush Report, representing 'an inner group which had played the leading role in the work of the Office of Scientific Research and Development during the war.' In his view, this group sought to 'preserve the control of the Foundation in the hands of highly qualified scientists who had proved their capacities in the field of war research.' Indeed, they felt that this model of research should serve as a precedent for the post-war program. They placed emphasis on 'technical research,' and a concern with 'devising ... specific means to attain specific ends, using fundamental scientific knowledge ... but not primarily concerned with adding to it.' As centred in 'the applied and engineering fields,' with less concern for 'fundamental science,' this approach to research issued in a 'close liaison between industry and physical science.' It was not surprising, then, that the industrial elites supported the Bush position, for it advocated the direct control of science policy by private citizens with no direct constraints imposed by the government. In keeping with its partisanship, the Bush position, as supported by elite scientists and big business, had little concern for issues of national politics, national defence, and the general welfare. In view of its general pro-business sympathies, it tended to identify with political conservatism and to support the exclusion of the more liberally inclined social sciences from the NSF (1946a, 657).

As an opponent of the Bush position, Parsons's support lay with the Committee for a National Science Foundation, composed of 'a much broader group of scientists all over the country.' This group argued that the base for the new foundation should be broadly conceived – both geographically and institutionally – with a direct responsibility to the president and Congress as embodiments of the national interest. In Parsons's view, the various scientific groups who supported the position of the Committee for a National Science Foundation felt 'that the fundamental orientation of their fields of knowledge, and its potential significance to the welfare of the nation, are altogether above and beyond the immediate political issues of the day' (657).

Parsons's interpretation of the controversy over the NSF followed directly from his evolving perspective on knowledge and society. The Bush position, with its partisanship and narrowly applied view of rational action, was both particularistic and utilitarian. By advocating a form of science based on the interests of a limited sector of American society, it went against Parsons's notion of rational progress. Moreover, with its purely technical criteria of scientific knowledge, it not only neglected fundamental scientific research, but denied the validity of the social sciences.

Parsons's appraisal of the social sciences, offered in various of his post-war writings, can be understood as an effort to advance the cause of the Committee for a National Science Foundation – a position that corresponded more or less to his own views on the relation between science and the national interest. He reaffirmed his view that science represented a progressive, rationalizing force in society. 'Science,' as he put it, 'is unquestionably one of the most fundamental elements of the culture of the Western world. There must be healthy and full cultivation of science and its potentialities unless the culture and society we have known is to stagnate, if not go up in flames' (662). Since 'science is inherently dynamic,' efforts to stop its advance would lead to 'profound alterations in our whole society which would not be acceptable to most of its advocates.' Science was not, however, confined to the study of the natural world: 'It should and must be extended wherever its methods are intrinsically applicable [which] ... includes man's social life and behavior ... It is impossible to draw any distinct line between the natural and the social sciences [for] they shade imperceptibly into one another' (660). He noted that 'strictly military defense and enemy and domestic morale are most intimately interconnected. Where health is defined to include mental health [then] organic medicine, psychiatry and the social sciences are increasingly bound up together.' If the groups of disciplines were included in the same foundation, 'the divisions of National Defense or of Health would not be confined to applied natural science but ... would certainly include very important contributions from the social sciences.' Finally, Parsons stressed that 'it is impossible to draw any rigid line between science as the pursuit of knowledge as such and its practical applications to the rational management of human interests and affairs' (662).

With this line of argument, Parsons had not only provided a rationale for the support of 'fundamental science,' but had offered a justification for the encouragement of social science as well. He maintained that 'in proportion as sound "pure" scientific knowledge is developed in *any* field it will have applications, though applicability will also prove uneven relative to the development of knowledge itself' (663). Because 'social science is in a rapidly evolving and formative state [with] much that is solid to work from, and much promise for future development,' it is, 'with due care, in a position fruitfully to make use of considerably increased resources' (663). Parsons stressed that the social sciences must 'as rapidly as possible ... be brought as nearly to a level of co-ordinate achievement and prestige with their sister disciplines as can be achieved' (655–6). Excluding them from 'federal financial support ... while it is tendered to the natural sciences would impose a grave handicap on the social sciences which could hardly fail to be detrimental to the larger interests of the nation.' Parsons believed that the social sciences ought to be accorded the same degree of support as the natural sciences. Such support, in turn, was contingent upon the social sciences being *institutionalized* in the same manner as their natural-science counterparts. This meant that like other forms of '"professional" scientific investigation' the social sciences 'can exist only through the tolerance and positive support of other elements in the social system.

There must be a complex system of interlocking of sentiments and interests to account for this' (1950a, 225). In this sense,

Any *professionalized science must, in order to function, be integrated in the social system in terms of a set of complex dependencies on other, non-scientific elements. Moreover, the 'gap' which separates the professional scientist from the laity and raises the problem of what motivates the latter to tolerate and support him, cannot be fully bridged by rational understanding on the layman's part of what the scientist is doing and why it is important to him and to society. It involves a whole series of the subtler aspects of social control, including the non-utilitarian prestige of knowledge and learning ... the reasons why empirical knowledge has a special place ... the role of education as a prestige criterion ... and the semi-magical respect for the 'miracle men' of science.* (229)

In his efforts to define the constitutive elements for the institutionalization of the social sciences, Parsons based his thinking on the prototype provided by medical practice.[3]

The Medical Prototype: Towards the Control of Ideological Deviance

Through his examination of medicine, Parsons derived the 'primary patterns' of disinterestedness, universalism, affective neutrality, and functional specificity. Guided by the orientation suggested by these patterns, the medical profession was able to control illness as defined by the sick role. The latter was 'a mechanism which in the first instance channels deviance so that the most dangerous potentialities, namely, group formation and successful establishment of the claim to legitimacy, are avoided ... The sick thus become a statistical status class and are deprived of the possibility of forming a solidary collectivity' ([1951] 1964, 477).

Control in this sense was not the outcome of personal volition by either the doctor or the patient, but rather was exercised unconsciously through a set of patterned mechanisms. 'Indeed ... the very effectiveness of the control mechanisms seems to be dependent on their latent functions remaining unrecognized' ([1942b], 1964, 159). In other words, the success of physicians in controlling the ill was not a result of individual initiative, but rested upon the 'institutionalization' of the physician's role along the lines suggested by the primary patterns. That pattern variables were in principle 'not confined to the one relatively functional sphere of medical practice,' Parsons sought to establish through his discussion of a national propaganda agency. Just as the medical profession controlled *illness*, the agency, according to Parsons, would have the task of controlling *deviance*. Parsons was able to extend the analogy from illness to deviance by arguing that both represented *motivated* forms of actions. Thus, illness could be overcome only if patients were motivated to get well and only if they accepted the physician's definition of their pathological situation. Now similarly, dissidents could become loyal citizens only if they were motivated to believe in the worth of the political order. This state of affairs could be ensured if they accepted and internalized the definition of the political situation provided by the propaganda agency. For Parsons, this discussion of propaganda provided the transitional step to this examination of the social sciences. He could now, in principle, apply his insights from the medical profession to the social sciences and their relation to social pathology, as embodied in *ideology*.

To do so, he drew close parallels between medicine and academia. It is noteworthy that within the professional matrix, Parsons singled out these two branches for more extensive study: 'For the medical and academic professions I have attempted a close approximation to a standard empirical study, more so than in other aspects of my work. But in both cases I have wanted to understand the professional groups in question in the context of the wider system of which they have come to constitute particularly important parts' (1970a, 862). What lay behind this dual interest was a concern with how medical and academic practice contributed to the functioning of the order. The medical profession was for Parsons prototypical for 'the possibilities of generating useful knowledge and applying it to the solution of critical human problems.' Now, similarly, he made the case that 'even in the pragmatic, "tough-minded" United States the groups with intellectual training ... have either actually become, or are rapidly approaching the position of being, strategically the most important in American society, possibly for its day-to-day functioning, certainly for its longer-run future' (1970b, 20).

Parsons's analysis of the academic profession derived from his previous study of medicine; he sought to understand how the categories of medical practice were potentially *generalizable* to academic life as a whole. Of particular interest to him was how *scientific investigation* in general corresponded to the medical prototype. 'Medical practice must be part of the general institutionalization of scientific investigation and of the application of science to practical problems, which is a characteristic feature of modern Western society' ([1951] 1964, 474).

It was in the field of social-scientific practice that Parsons sought to apply the medical analogue with the greatest rigour and detail. We can detect a striking correspondence between Parsons's account of how medicine controlled illness and his discussion of how the social sciences controlled ideological deviance. Medical practice, Parsons argued, could successfully control illness by proceeding along the lines suggested by the primary patterns. This meant that the exercise of social control was an *unconscious* process. Doctors did not actually seek to control patients. Rather, just by carrying out the role of a professional, social control over illness would invariably follow. The actual personal dynamics of the doctor-patient relationship were, then, not of primary importance; they were secondary to the *control mechanisms*, i.e. the primary patterns that made this relationship possible. Illness, according to Parsons, 'was itself integrally involved in the motivational balance and hence *institutionally* defined. To be "sick" was not only to be in a biological state which suggested remedial measures, but required exemptions from obligations, conditional legitimation, and motivation to accept therapeutic help. It could thus, in part at least, be classed as a type of deviant behavior which was socially categorized in a kind of role' ([1964a] 1970, 332). It was largely through contact with the definition of the situation as provided by the medical profession that those who were ill could become aware of their deviant state, accept it as an undesirable condition, and become motivated to get well.

For Parsons, an identical bond obtained between the social-scientific practitioner and the 'ideological deviant.' In the same way that the overall well-being of a society hinged upon the motivation of its members to reject illness and seek health, 'the social system ... must ... have a sufficient proportion of its component actors adequately motivated to act in accordance with the requirements of its role system, positively in the fulfillment of expectations, and negatively in abstention from too much disruptive, i.e., deviant behavior' ([1951] 1964, 27). In this case, the expectations were not to be provided by the medical profession, but by the social-scientific practitioners:

It becomes clear that the social sciences have a particularly crucial, and in certain respects precarious position relative to the ideological balance of the social system. On the one hand the more important social ideologies cannot avoid concern with the subject matter of the social sciences, nor can the latter simply avoid problems which touch on ideological interests. But on the other hand, the circumstances in which ideologies are developed and operate are such, that it seems practically impossible to avoid the presence of an important area of conflict between the two major types of cognitive interest. (358)

The implications of this congruence between social-scientific and medical practice were far reaching. Through their professional activities, social scientists could contribute to the social control of ideological deviance. This need not involve actual personal contact with deviants. In so far as social control was exercised both unconsciously and through mechanisms, it would suffice that social science be practised in a 'professional' manner. Its 'scientific' views on the nature of the social order would, as it were, come to constitute part of the cultural definition of reality. Potential deviants, bowing to the authority of science, would recognize their own aberrations, internalize this interpretation, and acquire the necessary motivation to obey the dictates of the system.

Just as the medical profession and the sick role share in common a perspective on the 'health' of the system, the social scientist and the ideological deviant intersected in their respective fields of concern. 'The *cognitive* standards of ideological legitimation of value-orientations must be the same as the canons of scientific validity' (354). It is significant that Parsons defined ideology as both the belief system of a society and a partisan perspective (349).

Given that both social scientists and ideological deviants shared the same cognitive and evaluative interests, it was in Parsons's view 'likely, then, that ideologies will become the symbolic battleground of the principal elements of tension and conflict within a social system.' This would lead to a process of 'ideological polarization' eventuating in the exercise of 'social control [which] operates through the linking of ideologies with the institutionalized pursuits of the intellectual disciplines dealing with their subject matter' (358).

What made this process of social control possible, Parsons emphasized, was the institutionalization of social-scientific practice. 'The definite establishment of results of social science is bound to have complex further repercussions on the social system in other respects.' Of primary importance is 'the effect on the structure of the belief systems of the society as such, particularly through "taking the wind out of the sails" of an important part of the ideological pseudo-science which is inevitably current' ([1951] 1964, 519). Thus social science 'is both needed and demanded as an inevitable extension of an established cognitive orientation pattern' (518).

If social science were to be successfully institutionalized along the same lines as its medical counterpart, the orientation suggested by the pattern variables had to guide social-scientific practice as well. The categories of practice for the social sciences advocated by Parsons implicitly drew on the prototype provided by the medical profession. Because Parsons sought to help orient the social sciences towards a practice that would be of use and relevance to the Cold War political order (as I will argue), these categories were congruent with the contours of the American nation-state as they had emerged in the post-war period.

The Pattern Variables and Social-Scientific Practice

Disinterestedness and Relative Autonomy

Parsons described the overall orientation of the medical professional to the social order as one of disinterestedness. That is, unlike the business man who pursues personal profit, the medical practitioner, as a professional, is 'engaged in performing services to his patients or clients, or to impersonal values like the advancement of science.' Parsons, however, did not mean to imply that the physician was lacking in social concern, as the term disinterestedness might suggest. Rather, the concept was meant to convey the opposite of self-interest, in the sense of the physician placing wider ends before personal gain. Perhaps recognizing the misleading implications of the term, Parsons later reformulated it as 'collectivity-orientation.' By this latter designation, 'the important characteristics of the physician's role could be taken account of by considering him as performing a function as a member of a collectivity.' In this way, 'the classic "doctor-patient relationship"' could be viewed as 'the minimal relevant collectivity' whose solidarity 'constitutes the basis of mutual "trust"' between the physician and patient' ([1964a] 1970, 338). Through the orientation provided by disinterestedness or collectivity-orientation, then, the physician contributed to the solidarity of the order. By implication, that solidarity could not be taken for granted, but rather was inherently based upon the overall relation of the professional practitioner to the social order. In Parsons's post-war writings, this orientation to action received further specification in his discussion of the social sciences. He noted that for 'fully specialized "occupational" roles' such as that of scientific investigation, the specialist 'can no longer have a direct and immediate personal interest in the consequences of his work.' Rather, 'the connection between what a particular scientist does and the basis of his own interest in its ultimate "use" may become very remote, involving a large number of steps' (1950a, 222–3). Just as the professions in general were to eschew the pursuit of self-interest, in Parsons's view, 'science has ... become autonomous relative to the system of practical interests in society' (235). In the same manner that the physician disinterestedly orients himself towards the impartial canons of medical science, the social scientist was 'not to try directly to solve the immediate practical problems, but to let the ramifications of scientific problems lead where they may, realizing that eventually the consequences will come back to practical applicability, often in ways which could not have been foreseen' (236–7).

However, because the social sciences were grounded in a system of ultimate values common to practical interests, this autonomy could never be more than relative. In practice, this meant that empirical research would be guided by a circumscribed cluster of values and ends, predetermining the nature of the encounter with empirical reality. Thus, it was possible to admit to a certain 'value-relatedness' in the act of investigation, and yet still claim complete scientific objectivity for any discoveries made. This entailed that values be internalized by the social scientist, in the sense that the 'institutionalization of his privileges ... be combined with ... a high level of responsibility.' 'His knowledge,' like that of the medical profession, would thus 'be used for socially legitimate purposes' (244). Through the overall orientation of 'relative autonomy,' then, the social scientist, like his medical counterpart, would be able to contribute to the well-being of the collectivity.

It was through such an overall orientation that the social sciences could be of optimal service to the state, since relative autonomy implied a particular institutional locus in relation to the state and to the practical interests of civil society. While Parsons believed that the social sciences ought to be federally supported, he also maintained that they should be centred in universities, where they could preserve their independence. Noting that neither universities, foundations, nor businesses were capable of providing resources adequate for 'the type of detailed empirical work that social sciences ought to be undertaking,' Parsons suggested that 'an essential source for the kind of support needed for many new developments of social science lies in the government.' However, because the social sciences were concerned with issues of moral and political sensitivity, the danger existed that controls upon research would be put into place. Parsons advocated that the 'first prerequisite of support ... must be that it does not destroy ... independence, or unduly limit it [for] the independence of the learned professions, and particularly of the profession which is the trustee of the intellectual basis of all the professions, that of research and the higher levels of teaching, is one of the most fundamental bases of our social structure' (1946a, 664). Organizationally, this meant that 'leading university scientists would serve in advisory capacities, and the bulk of the work would not be undertaken by agencies of government itself, but especially by university groups with careful safeguards of their independence' (664–5).

It was by placing the social sciences solidly within the universities, Parsons argued, that knowledge relevant to the national interest could be produced. At the same time, the universities would serve to protect the social sciences from the encroachment of practical interests.

Institutionalization ... of the social sciences ... centers in the universities in the modern world. Status in the organization of universities provides the social scientist with a professional role which makes his work an integral part of the social structure ... He shares in the protection which the prestige and recognized status of universities gives against interference with his functions by the many elements in the community who for one reason or another might be disposed to interfere. (1950a, 242)

With the protection and security afforded by the universities, then, social science could overcome the obstacles to its growth and begin to develop the solid theoretical base that would permit it to make a practical contribution to national welfare. The barriers to its development were not only provided by partisan practical interests; the social sciences also had to contend with 'naive, popular misunderstandings ... such as, that it is nothing but a haven for crack-brained reformers ... a glorified form of social work, or ... that it is primarily concerned with promoting sexual libertarianism' (1946a, 661–2).

By virtue of the prestige and professional status offered by the universities, coupled with increased financial support, it would be possible, in Parsons's view, to change the conception of the social sciences held by both governmental officials and the public. And in so generating increased support and acceptance for social-scientific research, a more closely integrated relationship with the social structure could be accomplished. From such a strategic standpoint, in turn, greater influence upon society could be exercised. By adapting the primary pattern of disinterestedness to the social sciences in the form of what one can call relative autonomy, Parsons not only provided an overall guide-line for how the social sciences might be practically oriented, but indicated how this could be embodied in a particular kind of institutionalization in relation to the state and practical interests. This meant that the social sciences could effectively mediate between civil society and the state from their position of relative autonomy within the universities.

Universalism and General Theory

The primary pattern of universalism referred to a profession's commitment to maintain *scientific* standards of truth. As Parsons described it in relation to medicine, 'the imperative of scientific objectivity required abstracting from considerations of personal relationship or group belongingness in favor of diagnosis and treatment as a "case" of whatever the disease category happened to be' ([1964a] 1970, 329). Treatment of cases would then add to the existing stock of knowledge about pathology that could be drawn upon later. It was this universalistic quality of medicine that gave it both its capacity to produce technically useful knowledge and its scientific credibility.

If the social sciences were to approximate the scientific level attained by medicine, in Parsons's view, an equivalent orientation to *social phenomena* through *general theory* had to be developed. Better theory, he emphasized, was indispensable 'for progress beyond certain levels.' This was the case, in part, because 'social scientists are plagued by the problems of objectivity in the face of tendencies to value-bias to a much higher degree than is true of natural scientists' ([1950b] 1964, 348). Just as universalism permitted the medical practitioner to avoid partisanship, general theory for the social scientist would keep him from espousing particular values. This would be achieved through a '*generality of implications* by which it is possible to relate findings, interpretations, and hypotheses on different levels and in different specific empirical fields to each other' (352). However, theory was much more than merely a means of bringing disparate findings together under an overarching framework. It offered a way of achieving consensus, coherence, and unity among its practitioners, providing a 'general theoretical tradition of some sophistication, really *the* tradition of a working professional group.' Such a working tradition would be 'bred into the "bones" of empirical researchers themselves' (350). This in turn would necessitate 'a common conceptual scheme that makes the work of different investigators in a specific sub-field and those in different sub-fields commensurable' (352). These investigators would share in common 'a set of general categories of orientation to observation and problem choice in the field which defines its major problem areas and the directions in which to look for concealed factors and variables in explanation' (353).

The 'working tradition,' 'generality,' and the 'common conceptual scheme,' when treated institutionally, all presupposed a consensus or agreement on the part of investigators as to what constituted the concepts and categories of the framework of discovery. Generality, as opposed to particularism, by its very nature was only operable if a scientific community had some kind of agreed-upon set of categories, conceptual framework, and method of validation. Social science and its general theory thus bore the same relationship to society as medicine and medical knowledge did to the 'health' of the system. In the same way that the medical practitioner 'treated' a particular case as a problem for applied science, social science would examine discrete phenomena only as related to overall general theory. Through research undertaken within this framework, a body of scientific knowledge of possible application could be gradually accumulated. In establishing such a body of knowledge by virtue of a general theory, the social sciences could thus ascend to the level of their natural-scientific counterparts.

Parsons's advocacy of general theory in the social sciences represented a response to the dismissal of the social sciences by scientists and government officials during the deliberations on the National Science Foundation. According to Parsons, the social sciences were viewed by many as not only theoretically immature, but incapable of producing 'significant practical results ... which could make important contributions ... to national defense, health, prosperity or welfare.' Parsons admitted that in terms of ' "social technology" ' nothing existed that is 'comparable in importance, scope and productivity to that of applied natural science.' This did not mean, however, that the social sciences were inherently incapable of achieving a comparatively high level of practical application. Rather, one had 'to act in terms of future promise rather than of past record alone,' for within the social sciences 'highly significant beginnings do exist' (1946a, 662). Although the social sciences had largely been ineffectual in comparison with the 'matter-of-fact competence of the natural sciences,' Parsons felt that 'there is ground for considerable, though modest confidence [for] in a limited number of fields ... social research is ... in a position to deliver results of first-rate practical importance [such as] the diagnosis of friction and inefficiency within organizations, the analysis of opinion and attitudes, the analysis of population movements and migration trends, and certain aspects of the control of the business cycle' (663). Elsewhere, he noted at length the practical contributions that the social sciences had made to the war effort. Research in areas such as aviation psychology, army psychiatry, and Japanese morale, in his view, provided examples of the 'important practical functions of social science research' (1948, 55).

However, it was in relation to the 'new social problems' created by 'technological advance' that the social sciences could make their most notable contribution. According to Parsons, 'it does not seem sensible to pour resources into the acceleration of technological change and at the same time ignore any possible means of coping with the social problems which are directly produced or aggravated by such changes' (1946a, 662). 'The urgency of the social problems of our time, and their close connection at so many points with technological development means that someone is inevitably going to undertake action to solve them.' Parsons felt that natural scientists themselves were not equipped to address these problems, and that the responsibility had fallen to social science because ' "scientific" competence in the field of social problems can only be the result of a professional level of training and experience in the specific subject-matter. If ... science is to help solve its social problems, it must be social science which does so' (665).

What made practical contributions of this kind possible, Parsons maintained, was the 'development of a broad integrating conceptual scheme which serves to orient the major statements of problems and directions of analytic thinking.' While it is still in 'a highly primitive and unsatisfactory state ... there has been notable growth and there seems to be ample evidence of an accelerating tempo in advance ... we can feel confident that we have sufficiently solid foundations to justify every effort to push further' (1948, 25). Through the development of a general theory, comparable to universalism within medicine and the natural sciences, the social sciences would be able to produce knowledge of relevance to the instrumental problems faced by state managers. That is to say, information of this kind could provide the basis for more effective interventions into the social order by those in power. In attaining greater technical competence and practical relevance by virtue of theoretical development, the various branches of the social sciences could begin to close the gap between themselves and their natural-scientific counterparts.

Affective Neutrality and Cultural Commitment

Universalism provided medicine with a capacity to generate empirical scientific knowledge. Through a third primary pattern, affective neutrality, Parsons showed how medicine could retain its scientific status, yet control the patient by affirming and communicating a particular definition of the situation. This implied that medicine had two components, for 'in addition to the "science of medicine" which may be taken to include the practical application of exact biological and biochemical knowledge, there has always been, in a position of great importance, something called the "art of medicine" ... those "intangibles" in the function of the doctor which were most important to the "human" problems of practice' ([1942b] 1964, 153). Correspondingly, he held that illness had both 'motivated' and 'conditional' components as well, in the sense that ' "health" is not simply a state of the biological organism, but is a matter of a person's total adjustment to his life situation' (154).

To treat the 'conditional component,' Parsons argued that 'medical practice utilizes a complex technology.' However, for the 'motivated' component, treatment 'involves processes of *social control, i.e.*, acting upon the "intentions" of patients, as Freud above others has taught us, at unconscious levels' ([1964a] 1970, 335). In practice, this involves an orientation of 'affective neutrality' towards the patient. In other words, the physician does not relate to the patient emotionally on a personal basis, but rather acts as a neutral screen 'on which the patient projects his affects and definitions of situations in human relations. The very discrepancy between the attitudes the patient manifests toward his analyst, and what the analyst actually is to him, is a major factor in forcing the patient to analyze his own reactions and investigate the deeper sources of his own failures to adapt to reality more generally' ([1942b] 1964, 157). Strictly speaking, then, the physician's orientation is not really neutral, but rather embodies the mainstream values of the Western rational tradition. Successful treatment entails that the patient 'internalizes' this definition of reality, and becomes 'motivated' to conform to its dictates.

For the social sciences, Parsons suggested an analogous stance of neutrality in the form of a commitment to the 'moral values and ethical standards' of society. In his view, 'the values which govern the scientist in his most technical procedures of scientific investigation are not isolated, but are part of a total system of values which govern his [the scientist's] action as a whole.' These values must, moreover, 'be well integrated with the larger value system which governs the action of all the principal elements in the society; of farmers, industrial workers, businessmen.'

Since science has been so tightly embedded in 'modern western civilization ... if we are true to the great tradition of western science we will have to use the discoveries of science in terms of a system of ends which has deep roots in the broader cultural tradition of the western world' (1947c, 215). More particularly,

while science itself cannot from its own resources determine the ends
for which it will be used, where science is an integral part of a great
cultural tradition in a major civilization it is in fact integrated with a
... value system in such a way that many of the basic values with
which it is associated, and which will determine these ends, are not
arbitrary but are inherent in the cultural tradition itself. Abandon-
ment of them could almost certainly lead to radical changes
in the society and culture as a whole, and in all probability to a major
diminution in the role of science itself. (216–17)

Parsons later characterized this aspect of society as 'the cultural standards of the value-science integrate' (1959b, 39). In defining the cultural tradition, this complex combines 'a conceptual framework for interpreting the empirical state of society, with a set of premises from which this state is evaluated positively or negatively.' He stressed that the value-science integrate is at once objective in its orientation, while still supportive of societal values: 'We can ... legitimately think in terms of an ideal type of objective scientific knowledge about a society, which is subject to all the fundamental canons of science, but which in selectivity ... of content, and in the basis of its meaning within the society, is relative to the values of that society at a given time' (36).

Just as the health of the system from the standpoint of medicine was composed of motivated and instrumental components, and just as the physician complemented the technical treatment of disease with communicative action, the social scientist combines scientific technique with the affirmation of values, for 'no social science integrated with the value system of society can give answers to *all* the possible significant problems of societies, but only to those which have meaning within this integrate.' To complete the analogy, the social equivalent to the patient is the ideologue, who professes a viewpoint that is both 'selective' and 'distorted.' An ideology is selective 'in that among the problems and phenomena known to be significant for the social sciences of the time, they [ideologists] select some for emphasis, and neglect or play down others' (37). In a similar vein, 'the criterion of distortion is that statements are made about the society which by social-scientific methods can be shown to be positively in error' (38).

In the same manner that the physician defines the patient's pathological or deviant state, the social scientist identifies an ideology through its 'secondary selection and distortion [that] can only be demonstrated by reference to their deviation from the cultural standards of the value-science integrate' (39). If social science is to defuse ideology in this manner, 'what is required is not a standard of absolute correctness, but of relative validity, since the problem of ideology arises where there is a *discrepancy* between what is believed and what can be scientifically correct ... The range over which such discrepancies can be demonstrated is a function of the advancement of social science' (38).

The social scientist embodies that 'neutral screen' upon which the selectivity and distortions of the ideologue are projected. The process of eventual adaptation of the ideologue to the order closely corresponds to the patient's overcoming his illness through interaction with the physician: 'The cognitive distortions which are always present in ideologies, often compulsively motivated, will tend to be uncovered and challenged by the social scientist. Some of the results may be accepted, but only painfully and with allowance for a process of assimilation and adjustment over time' ([1951] 1964, 358). By subscribing to the tenets of the value-science integrate, then, and projecting these to the public, the social scientist could contribute to the social control of ideology in a manner analogous to the physician's control of the patient exercised through affective neutrality.

The cultural commitment of the social sciences had a great bearing on the immediate post-war period. It was through the variant of affective neutrality that the social sciences could help to legitimate the political and social order emerging in the United States in the early years of the Cold War. That Parsons was aware of this new cultural milieu and its inherent relationship to the expanded global commitments of the United States is evident from his reflections on the Cold War:

The Cold War's impact on American society operates primarily on two levels. One is by its effect on national security – primarily a political problem. Since the United States can no longer rely on a stable European power system for its security, as it did through the nineteenth century, the Cold War is the immediate cause for maintaining a large military establishment and attempting to foster the rapid development of military technology – with all the repercussions that this essentially new peacetime situation has throughout the society. The Cold War also has an important impact at the level of commitments to values and the most generalized

*level of norms. Without this 'challenge of communism' – not just
the challenge of a strong military power, but a challenge to the
legitimacy of the 'American way' – the current situation would be
far less disturbing.* (Parsons, et al. 1961, 73)

He argued that the conjunction of the two realms made for a destabilizing of the social order.

*These two components are empirically associated. But they are
analytically distinguishable, and their proportionate importance
may vary, in the same case over time as well as in different cases.
A comparably serious military threat to national security,
unaccompanied by the ideological factor, would be much less
disturbing at present to the United States, because internal changes
in American society have produced factors of instability at
integrative levels that were not previously so acute.* (73)

Parsons suggested that 'given the main system of values, there has been
in the cold-war period a major problem of motivating large sectors of the
population to the level of national effort required to sustain a position of
world leadership in a very unstable and rapidly changing situation' (39).
The growth of America 'to an enormous potential of power [and] the
changed relation to the rest of the world [required] a change ... in the
development of the attitudes and institutional machinery required to
implement a greatly enhanced level of national political responsibility'
([1954] 1963, 209).
  'The successful accomplishment of the social changes to which we
are called by our position in the world and by our own domestic
requirements' demanded, according to Parsons, a 'close alliance' between a strengthened political elite and 'predominantly "cultural"
elements, not only perhaps in the universities, but also in the churches'
(229). By defining the situation in a manner consonant with the Cold
War order, the expanded activities of the state would be supported and
legitimated. What made this possible for the social sciences, in
Parsons's view, was a commitment to what can be called cultural
commitment. In the same way that the physician affirmed the mainstream cultural values in opposition to the patient's definition, the
social sciences would present an authoritative interpretation of what
was good and proper to the potentially dissident. As with other
professions, the social sciences, in Parsons's view, 'exercised a trustee-
ship [of the] cultural tradition.' And in so far as institutional patterns,

through 'their involvement in the cultural tradition,' are interwoven with the 'primary orientation system [and the] non-empirical "beliefs"' (1942b, 147) of the members of society, the commitment of the social sciences to the culture of the Cold War order would have a great potential bearing on the state of public consciousness.

Functional Specificity and Disciplinary Specialization

The first three primary patterns provided guide-lines for the orientation of the professional to the social order. A fourth pattern – functional specificity – defined the boundaries of professional expertise. That is, the 'technical competence' of the profession that it exemplified had to be 'limited to a particular field of competence.'

In medical practice, as indicated, this pattern took the form of the delimitation of 'the scope of mutual concern' between physician and patient 'to matters relevant to the health of the patient' ([1964a] 1970, 329). Only if the physician confined his expertise to issues concerning health could the medical profession successfully control illness. The equivalent within the social sciences was a disciplinary specialization. While all the social sciences would address themselves to the social world, each would have a delimited sphere of expertise. As Parsons described their specialization in relation to economics, 'the proper theoretical subject matter, not only of economics, but of the other principal social science disciplines that are primarily theoretically oriented, should be the analytically defined functional subsystems of the larger systems involved' (1969, 311–12). Just as the competence of medicine derived from its concern only with matters pertaining to health, the various branches of the social sciences could ensure their professional credibility by specializing in particular, limited areas.

The Division of Labour within the Social Sciences

Parsons's concern to delineate a division of labour among the analytical sciences of action was already evident in his early writings where he sought to develop sociology as a field of study distinct from economics. Within the configuration he established, sociology was to concern itself with common value integration, while economics was limited to the study of how actors rationally choose material means and match them to ends. Both disciplines were to orient themselves to different levels of the means-end chain in society – sociology to the highest level of ultimate values, and economics to lower-level means as they related to the higher ends. Parsons also briefly distinguished two other analytical sciences of action – politics and psychology – which were to concern themselves with particular intermediate sectors of the means-end chain. Sociology, with its orientation towards the ultimate values that defined action in the other realms, integrated the activities of the sciences of action as well. Moreover, because of the inherently practical nature of sociological inquiry, this meant that the other sciences of action, by implication, would also be practically informed. Sociology was to scientifically affirm the presence of 'the common ultimate value element,' thereby mediating ultimate ends to the social order. This meant that sociology was to play a considerable part in helping to constitute the normative order of society. By defining and articulating a system of common ends, it would contribute to the control and regulation of social action. Correspondingly, working in conjunction with the overall orientation provided by sociology, the other sciences of action could contribute to the consolidation of particular levels of action.

In his subsequent writings, Parsons's preoccupation with the division of labour among the social sciences continued. Indeed, *The Social System*, in a manner similar to *The Structure of Social Action*, concluded with an account of the nature and orientation of the various sciences of action as they related to specific aspects of the social order. However, in Parsons's discussion of the division of labour among the sciences of action after *The Structure of Social Action*, he began to stress how the interdependence and interpenetration of the action systems in turn defined the boundaries and orientation of the sciences of action oriented towards them. He focused on how the process of institutionalization at a social level intersected with a complementary development of a motivation to conform at an individual level. This shift towards a more dynamic and interactive account of the process of social integration could be explained by Parsons's adaptation of psychoanalysis to sociology. In his early writings, culminating in *The Structure of Social Action*, sociology was limited to scientifically affirming the presence of ultimate values in society. While such an orientation served to articulate the normative order it could not fully ensure widespread commitment to it. Parsons saw as necessary a much more elaborated account of how motivation to follow norms could be ensured through more direct interaction between the scientific elect and the social actor. This led him to explore psychoanalytical medicine and adapt its insights to the social sciences. The interpenetration and interdependence he detected in the realms of action presupposed the psychoanalytic stance on the part of the scientist of action. Projecting a 'definition of the situation' based upon mainstream values into the public sphere could overcome the 'selectiveness' and 'distortions' of ideologies and could inculcate widespread motivation to conform to the normative order. The process of institutionalization intersecting with the integration of individuals, via their motivations, was inherently related to a social-scientific practice guided by psychoanalytic concerns. In Parsons's revised account of the division of labour among the 'sciences of action,' his concern with the interplay between institutionalization and individual integration resulted in a shift of emphasis towards how sociology intersected with the converging fields of psychology and social anthropology.[4] In conjunction with the 'culture and personality' field, sociology as the science of institutionalization was to provide the matrix for the remaining sciences of action.[5]

Sociology

As a leading sociologist, Parsons had a particular concern with the role and status of his discipline in the post-war period. In comparison with 'lawyers, economists, and the psychologists,' Parsons noted, 'sociologists as a professional group were not in a favorable position to make a major contribution to the war,' largely because they lacked a 'clearly recognized sphere of technical competence which would have made it a matter of course for those in authority to call upon their service' (Parsons and Barber 1948, 247). In that it lacked 'unity and definiteness of orientation or security of status' (245) Parsons was worried that sociology might become 'a pragmatically justified bit of intellectual scaffolding which has served a useful purpose for a limited period [rather than] one of the major basic divisions of human knowledge.' In order for sociology to realize its potential as an integral part of academic life, Parsons advocated not only 'the development of research techniques,' but more important, the move towards a 'theoretical synthesis, of the production of a sufficiently integrated yet diversified and flexible scheme which can do justice to the extreme complexity of our problems, and yet produce the kind of ordered and generalized analysis without which science worthy of the name cannot exist' (256–7).

Such an orientation would provide the 'general theory' for sociology necessary for its credibility as a real science. At the same time, however, the problems of the sociologist 'concern the balance of motivational forces involved in the maintenance of, and alteration in, the structure of a social system' ([1950] 1964, 340). 'The sociologist is, in the first instance, concerned with behavior and attitudes which are of strategic significance to the social system ... this means tendencies which either support the structure of an existing social system or tend to alter it in specific ways' (339). That is to say, 'the sociologist must face the problems of human motivation whether he wants to or not' (347). When combined with general theory, this meant that '*differentiations* of motivational orientation ... crucial to the understanding of socially structured behavior' would *theoretically* be connected up in a 'systematically generalized way' (361).

This account of sociology represented a clear departure from his earlier concern with the scientific study of 'ultimate value elements.' In the new version, sociology was to concern itself with the degree to which institutions successfully elicited motivated support. This suggested an emphasis upon the 'crucial role of institutional definitions of the situation and the ways in which they channel many different components of a total motivation system into the path of conformity with institutionalized expectations' (355). Sociology was treated, then, 'as the science of institutions ... or more specifically of institutional structure' ([1945] 1964, 235). Such an orientation, by authoritatively providing a definition of the necessary pattern of motivation, could effectively undercut the evaluative and cognitive claims made by ideologies. The institutional and integrative perspective inherent in a sociology of this kind, in Parsons's view, was to underpin the orientations of the other social sciences.[6] While each would retain a specific focus, all would have an institutionalized view of human action. This changed emphasis was perhaps most evident in the complementary field of psychology.

Psychology and Personality Theory

Consistent with his concern about how motivation to conform to the normative could be elicited, Parsons argued that conventional psychology was inadequate because of its tendency to reduce the 'structuring of motivational forces [to] particular personality structures' ([1950] 1964, 338–9). 'The early tendency of psychology was to consider "personality" as largely an expression of genetic constitution or of unique idiosyncracy' ([1945] 1964, 233). This meant that 'it has not been possible ... to derive an adequate theory of the motivation of socially structured mass phenomena through the simple "application" of psychological generalizations' (233). In Parsons's view, questions relating to motivation had to 'be couched in terms of the frame of reference of the social system, not of personality, though of course they must be compatible with established knowledge of personality' ([1950] 1964, 340). He viewed psychology, then, 'as the science concerned with the elementary processes of action and their organization in personalities as systems' ([1951] 1964, 547). He saw great hope for social psychology as 'an interstitial mediating field between sociology and psychology in a sense directly analogous to that of biochemistry or of psychobiology or physiological psychology ... the social psychologist is not directly concerned with analysis of the structure of social systems, but with motivational processes and personalities in their specific relations to and interdependence with the structure of social systems' (552–3). Overall, Parsons sought a greater rapprochement between sociology and psychology, for 'the problem of the motivation of socially structured behavior' meant that sociologists' 'relations to psychology become peculiarly crucial and intimate' ([1950b] 1964, 362).

Anthropology

Along similar lines, Parsons maintained that 'in systematizing the structural variable of social systems, our relations to anthropology are correspondingly crucial' ([1950b] 1964, 362).[7] Thus, sociology could draw on anthropology to gain insights into 'the ways in which the basic cultural orientations underlie and interpenetrate the structuring of social systems on the action level' (362). However, anthropological theory, in his view, had been disappointing. Commenting on the prevailing approaches, he noted that there had been far too much emphasis upon a 'biological model of thought – an organism and its environment, an actor and his situations. We have not *really* treated culture as independent, or if this has been done, as by some anthropologists, the tendency has been for them in turn to absorb either personality or social structure *into* culture, especially the latter, to the great discomfort of many sociologists' (357). The theory of culture, in Parsons's view, 'must be the theory concerned not only with the properties of culture as such but with the interdependence of patterns of culture with the other components of systems of action ... The focus, however, is always on the culture pattern system as such, and neither on the social system in which it is involved, nor on the personalities as systems' ([1951] 1964, 553). 'Only by some such definition,' Parsons argued, 'can anthropology become an analytical empirical science which is independent both of sociology and of psychology' (554).

The scope of inquiry that Parsons proposed for anthropology turned on the firm distinction he made between the cultural and social systems. Distancing himself from the American anthropological tradition, Parsons wished to restrict the reference of anthropology 'to transmitted and created content and patterns of values, ideas, and other symbolic-meaningful systems as factors in the shaping of human behavior and the artifacts produced through behavior.' Culture, then, was to be distinguished from 'the term *society* – or more generally *social system*,' which he felt should 'be used to designate the specifically relational system of interaction among individuals and collectivities' (Parsons and Kroeber 1958, 583). Parsons's desire to distinguish the field of concern of anthropology from that of sociology, while elaborating the interdependence between the two disciplines, derived from his interest in showing 'the complete continuity theoretically between the analysis of the institutional structure of literate and nonliterate societies.' The new 'theoretical focus' of sociology would allow it to 'extend its treatment of the role of culture (as distinct from social structure) to a level of literate societies' (1948, 30). The conjunction of sociology with anthropology not only permitted exploration of the interplay between social structure and culture, but allowed for these new insights to be universalized as standards of behaviour.

Economics

In his early writings, Parsons had taken issue with conventional economics for its individualism, positivism, and lack of concern with ultimate values. While his dissatisfaction with its theoretical suppositions after *The Structure of Social Action* continued, the reasons for his discontent underwent a shift. Consistent with his concern about how commitment to conform to the normative order could be elicited, he began to question orthodox economics for its inability to adequately deal with motivation. In his view, 'economic theory and other versions of the conceptual schemes which give predominance to rational instrumental goal-orientation cannot provide an adequate model for the dynamic analysis of the social system in general terms. It has been repeatedly shown that reduction of motivational dynamics to rational instrumental terms leads straight to the Hobbesian thesis' ([1951] 1964, 42–3). With its inability to link motivation to wider social ends, economics, as it stood, could not serve as an integrative basis for the sciences of action. Rather, it would have to take its place *within* the matrix defined by sociology, psychology, and anthropology. 'Within a given institutional role-structure,' Parsons maintained, 'it concerns the processes of allocation of resources, i.e., "labor power" and facilities within the system' (74). And in terms of motivation, 'it concerns ... the processes of balancing advantages and cost within a given role-structure' (75).

The role structure itself, however, was a 'specifically sociological problem [concerning] the kinds of value-orientations which are institutionalized in it, and the degrees to which and ways in which they are institutionalized to define the roles of the component actors. It concerns the mechanisms of learning of these patterns and of social control where tendencies to deviance from them exist' (74).

The field of economics was thus *redefined* within the institutional framework appropriate to sociological analysis. Accordingly, Parsons maintained that the traditional object of economic analysis, '"rational action" is a type which presupposes a certain mode of the *organization* of all the elements of action. It is something which is possible within the limits imposed by value-orientation patterns and by the situation, and by a certain mode of integration of motivational elements' (549). This implied, moreover, that '"economic action" cannot be conceived as taking place in a social vacuum, but that since it involves the exclusion of certain highly useful (from the point of view of the actor) means to acquisition, there must at the very least be some system of control over activities which eliminates or keeps within bounds the use of such means as force, fraud, and strategic position (e.g., monopoly)' (1934c, 532). As he emphasized, then, 'economic activity takes place within the "institutional" framework of society; economic behavior is concretely a phase of institutional behavior.'

In the same manner that the egoistical business ethic could never serve as an effective basis for social integration, an economics founded on principles of individualism could not contribute to social control. What was required, then, was a sociologically informed economics that viewed phenomena such as exchange, production, and rational action in institutional terms. Above all, economic motivation would be viewed not as 'a result of a corresponding uniformity in "human nature" such as egoism or hedonism, but of certain features of the structure of social systems of action which, however, are not entirely constant but subject to institutional variation' ([1940b] 1964, 53).

Political Science

In Parsons's early writings, politics, as one of the 'analytical social sciences of organized action systems,' was to concern itself with political action, in the form of the 'struggle for power' ([1937] 1968, 767–8). This conception of politics was rooted in his preoccupation with the Hobbesian problem of order, and the 'solution' he had provided in the form of 'the system of ultimate ends of the community [which] determines what is specifically sought after as wealth and power ... [and] may form the basis of a framework of regulatory norms which guide and control action in the pursuit of immediate ends, maintaining orderly processes and relationships and keeping the vast complex of such utilitarian actions in some kind of harmony with the ultimate value system of the community' (1934a, 231). Given this 'normative regulation of the power aspect of the relations of individuals within the system,' politics, as an analytical science of action, would direct its attention to the 'emergent property [of] political action elements' ([1937] 1968, 768).

As Parsons began to show how institutionalization in tandem with the elicitation of motivations could ensure social control, his notions of power and politics shifted as well. Building on a Calvinist notion of the polity, he became increasingly concerned with how the modern state played the dual role of providing the focal point for national symbolic integration, while acting instrumentally in the interest of the collectivity. In discussing 'the institutionalization of government with reference to the problem of attitudes,' he notes that 'on the one hand, it is the primary focus of the integration of the national social system as a whole, and is hence of key importance to any consideration of the state of the system. On the other hand ... it provides the most single strategic vantage point for implementing any deliberate policy of control' ([1942b] 1964, 168). Correspondingly, Parsons now defined power as 'the realistic capacity of a system-unit to actualize its "interests" (attain goals, prevent undesired interference, command respect, control possessions, etc.) within the context of system-interaction and in this sense to exert influence on processes in the system' ([1953] 1964, 391). This implied that 'the problem of control of political power is above all the problem of *integration*, of building the power of individuals and sub-collectivities into a coherent system of legitimized authority where power is fused with collective responsibility' ([1951] 1964, 127). Thus, 'the problem of *power*' was seen as the 'basically relational problem of order [that] concerns the problem of the allocation of facilities' (121). Given that power, as directed toward the problem of integration, was inherently diffuse, this meant that 'a theory of political power must in the nature of the case take into account *as variables*, most of the variables of the social system.' Accordingly, it was appropriate that political science be designated as a 'synthetic science in the social system field' (551), concerning itself with how the generation of power is linked to social integration.

The task that Parsons assigned to political science reflected his general concern with the process of institutionalization and what is implied for the division of labour among the sciences of action. Within the new matrix defined by how motivation to conform to institutionalized patterns could be elicited, political science was to concern itself with the problem of how a system of legitimated authority intersected with the coercive activities of the state.

The specialization of the disciplines into various spheres was not simply of analytical interest to Parsons. The division of labour of the 'analytical sciences' anchored by sociology was practically oriented towards constituting the social order along particular lines. 'Science in general' in his view 'is not only technical knowledge of phenomena but also part of our outlook on life. In technical terms I should call it an "ideology"; or rather it is a component of an ideology.' Not only is scientific knowledge of importance per se, but also 'it is of very great importance to the society and to the ways in which society is organized and human action in that society is oriented.' 'The sciences which have embarked on the path of scientific thinking about human behavior have now come to occupy a strategic place in our social tradition' (1949, 52–3). In terms of Parsons's embryonic division of labour among the analytic sciences of action, this implied a constitutive relation between their fields of concern and the emergent social order. Through a practice given direction by the primary patterns, the analytic sciences collectively could help constitute the emergent social order as based on interpenetrating and interdependent systems of action. In the early 1950s, Parsons began to conceive of these in terms of discrete subsystems, each oriented towards a particular 'functional problem of systems of action.' These were,

(1) 'adaptation,' i.e. to objects in the situation outside the system,
(2) 'goal-attainment,' i.e., establishment of 'consummatory' relations to situational objects – by 'instrumental' processes, (3) 'integrative,' the maintenance of a state of internal 'harmony' or absence of conflict among the units of the system and (4) 'latent pattern-maintenance and tension-management,' the maintenance both of the structure of the internalized-institutionalized normative or cultural patterns, and motivation to conformity with their requirements. (1953a, 624–5)

These discrete yet interdependent sub-systems, in turn, provided the theoretical basis for the sciences of action, in the sense that 'the proper theoretical subject matter ... of the ... principal social science disciplines that are primarily theoretically oriented, should be the analytically defined functional subsystems of the larger systems involved' (1969, 312). This implied that economics, political science, and sociology were to concern themselves with the system problems of 'adaptation,' 'goal-attainment,' and 'integration,' respectively. The fourth functional location – 'pattern maintenance' – did not correspond to a particular discipline. Parsons suggested, however, that anthropology 'may be said to have moved halfway in,' with its recent concern with 'the status of values and their position in cultural systems' (312–13). The focus on individual motivation by pattern maintenance would suggest the relevance of the field of psychology. In sum, 'the theory of action,' as oriented towards the functional sub-systems, represented 'an emerging and as yet very incomplete, single body of theory comprising the whole range of the sciences of action, or to use the Ford Foundation's phrase, the "behavioral sciences"' (1953a, 619–20).

Parsons's account of the sub-systems isomorphic with particular 'sciences of action' was continuous with the relations between the emergent social order and the social-scientific elect of his early writings. Anchored by a sociology articulating ultimate values to secular society, the analytical sciences of action were to define and make explicit 'the emergent properties of action systems.' Through an activity given form and direction by an implicit commitment to ultimate ends, the analytical sciences would contribute to the 'building of a Kingdom of God on Earth.' Within Parsons's revised schema, the same practical relation obtained. The 'functional problems' facing each of the sub-systems represented a differentiation of the transcendent ultimate values into particular spheres and levels of action. It was through the 'solution' of these problems, then, that the social order could more closely approximate a transcendent state.[8]

Correspondingly, given the implicit commitment of each science of action to the 'problem' of its apposite sub-system, the knowledge it produced would be of practical relevance to that problem being solved. Through the production of knowledge based on the 'primary patterns,' social scientists could contribute to the consolidation of a particular sub-system and to the process of enhanced social control.

The sub-systems, in Parsons's view, were not simply analytical artefacts, but rather had an empirical basis: they were meant to refer to social life in the real world (1969, xvi–xvii, 1). Given Parsons's practical concerns to see the world transcended, it is possible to understand these sub-systems in relation both to historical events and to social-scientific practice. Parsons assumed the standpoint of the modern nation-state as embodied in America and transformed its tensions and problems into metaphysical imperatives. The government or state apparatus was assumed to be acting on behalf of the collectivity to realize higher ends. Similarly, the economic system, over which the state presided, was placed in the role of trying to produce wealth. Finally, the other two systems were given the task of producing integration and loyalty, respectively. While all of these processes, i.e. state intervention, legitimation, and the production of wealth, can be seen as having real historical reference, they appear in an ideological guise in Parsons's framework. Moreover, commitment to them implies a particular form of activity for the social sciences.

What this meant was that changes or threats in the empirical world would find their way into Parsons's schema in terms of problems, implying a change in the orientation of the sciences of action. The following chapter will show how Parsons, in responding to some of the tensions of the Cold War order, expanded and elaborated the hitherto neglected political aspect of his schema, laying the basis for the full-scale emergence of political sociology as a field based on his practical concerns.

8

The Politicization of Parsons

Social Theory

As Parsons reflected on the development of his thought in the introduction to his collected political essays, politics was one of his long-standing, yet never fully articulated concerns. His most notable early interest was the 'problem of the status of economic theory [as] documented in *The Structure of Social Action'* (1969, xv). The growth of governmental activity and responsibility that accompanied the New Deal in the 1930s, however, drove home to Parsons the significance of the political: 'The whole tenor of the New Deal ... made coping with the Great Depression and its consequences as much a political as an economic problem' (474). In the period after *The Structure of Social Action* (1937), 'the problem ... of the "political aspect" of the social system, in its relations both to the economic and the sociological aspect, was very much on my mind ... I made a serious attempt to deal with it as late as *The Social System* (1951), which I now recognize to have been quite unsatisfactory' (xv). Just as the inherent instability of liberal market society (the Hobbesian problem of order) led Parsons to a critique of classical economic theory, his new concern with political issues represented a direct reaction to the changing circumstances in the post-war domestic and international order: 'The political aspect of a variety of *empirical*-theoretical problems with which I became engaged, such as McCarthyism, the concentration of power, the patterns of voting behavior, the role of mass media, the inclusion of the Negro American, and the bases of international order, not only continued to be unmistakably prominent, but increasingly cried for a better theoretical solution' (xv–xvi).

In terms of Parsons's practical interests, his 'empirical' concerns were mediated by his commitment to the transformation of the social order along particular lines. By extension, the theory generated by this encounter was practically linked to seeing this transformation take place. In particular, given his concern with the generation of power, he held the view that the primary 'substratum' of politics 'was more "social" than economic. In this often relatively vague reference of the term social lay the opportunity for a discipline which was not altogether new, but which was necessary at least to supplement economic preoccupations, though by no means necessarily to supplant them' (xiv–xv). This distinctly 'political sociological' perspective became increasingly more explicit in Parsons's schema as he responded theoretically to the various forms of dissent in Cold War America. His analyses of these tendencies, and the alternative to them he developed, were meant to both defuse and overcome them, while affirming and consolidating the pattern of political integration Parsons saw taking place. Providing the initial impetus to this changing orientation was the McCarthyist hysteria.

McCarthyism

The rise of McCarthyism both rekindled Parsons's interests in political questions and pushed him to consider political issues more completely in his writings. Indeed, Parsons's encounter with McCarthyist excesses at Harvard, and his later problems in gaining governmental clearance, appear to have been the catalyst in the spontaneous generation of an article he wrote on the subject (1969, 157–8).

However, almost of equal concern to Parsons as McCarthyism itself were the intellectual interpretations of it, which depicted that movement as an incipient form of fascism. Such analyses, in Parsons's view, represented an imposition of the European experience upon the American case – a perspective fully at odds with the United States' burgeoning primacy and leadership in the capitalist world order.[1] In emphasizing the strength and autonomy of McCarthyism as a right-wing social movement, these accounts by implication would call into question the viability of the United States as a modern and progressive society, capable of rebuilding the world in its image. Accordingly, it was critical that an explanation of the McCarthyist outbreak be squared with the view that the United States was undergoing a process of rationalization. Consistent with his earlier engagement with wartime dissent, national socialism, and militarism, Parsons now maintained that the emergence of McCarthyism resulted from the expansion of responsibilities and activities undertaken by the American state in the world order ([1954] 1963, 209). The increased power of the American state – as evidenced by its expanded capacities – had come to embody the locus of 'rationalization' in Parsons's thinking. That is to say, it was only by virtue of this augmented power of the American state apparatus in the global arena that progressive development in the world could take place.

McCarthyism, in Parsons's view, embodied a vestigial and irrational reaction to these external and internal developments by certain elements of the social structure threatened by the rationalizing dynamic. In terms of Parsons's wider vision of rationalization, the McCarthyist outbreak was 'an ideology' – a claim on reality that was at once cognitive, evaluative, and expressive, yet selective and distorted. Specifically, it was characterized by 'high levels of anxiety and aggression, focused on what rightly or wrongly are felt to be the sources of strain and difficulty [and] wishful patterns of belief with a strong "regressive" flavor.' Despite its ideological nature, Parsons maintained that McCarthyism was understandable in terms of the exigencies of the Cold War. Indeed, it was inherent in the need 'to mobilize American society to cope with a dangerous and threatening situation which is also intrinsically difficult' ([1954] 1963, 218). This required 'loyalty' – the 'readiness to make commitments to a collective interest.' Accompanying this effort to generate loyalty, however, was 'a grossly irrational set of anxieties about the prevalence of disloyalty, and a readiness to vent the accompanying aggression on innocent scapegoats' (218–19). The particular *object* of the McCarthyist outbreak could be understood as a reaction to the overall changes in national concern. According to Parsons, 'internally it is felt that Communists and their "sympathizers" constitute the primary focus of actual or potential disloyalty' (220). Certain elements in the social structure used communism in an irrational manner to impugn those in positions of power and influence – those 'associated with political liberalism [and] the Eastern upper-class groups who have tended to be relatively internationalist in their outlook' (223).

Parsons emphasized that McCarthyism was rooted in the internal changes resulting from the assumption of greater responsibilities by the United States in the world. As the American state apparatus expanded its sphere of activities, requiring a change in its mode of legitimation, an irrational backlash (embodied in McCarthyism) to these changes took place. Accordingly, it was through further strengthening of the state, in conjunction with other social strata, according to Parsons, that McCarthyism could be held in check. 'The solution of the problem of McCarthyism,' according to Parsons, called for 'the successful accomplishment of the social changes to which we are called by our position in the world and by our own domestic requirements.' Through co-operation of political, economic, and cultural elites, he emphasized, 'notable progress toward this objective' could be made. 'The current flare-up of stress in the form of McCarthyism can be taken simply as evidence that the process is not complete' (229). The appropriate counterfoil to such a disturbance was the 'definition of the situation' provided by the cultural elite – in particular the social sciences that shared the same subject matter with the ideological tendencies. By defining the situation in a manner consistent with the dictates of the 'value-science integrate,' the selectivity and distortions of such perspectives as McCarthyism could be overcome.

The *content* of the social science in question, then, had to be congruent with the depiction of reality appropriate to the process of rationalization. Hence, Parsons's *own* theoretical account, given his commitment to the legitimacy and necessity of this pattern of change, would approximate its standpoint. Through the very act of defining and studying outbreaks such as McCarthyism along the lines suggested, the social scientist could participate in helping implement 'a greatly enhanced level of national political responsibility.' Not only could one affirm the necessity of enhanced power and greater loyalty, but one could also produce empirical information about how social strains become channelled into threatening political movements. The corollary to the latter diagnoses was, of course, understanding which institutions served to integrate disparate social factions and ensure political power. An empirically based and value-relevant analysis such as this could also defuse the criticism of intellectual detractors who viewed movements like McCarthyism as indicative of massification and potential totalitarianism. Pointedly opposing such analyses, Parsons concluded that 'while many of the ingredients which had gone into the Fascist movements in Europe in the previous period were present in the United States, the total balance of forces made it unlikely that the main trend here would be the ascendancy of such elements and the consolidation of that ascendancy' (1969, 158). His next task was to demonstrate the ideological basis of the intellectual criticism itself by promulgating an alternative conception of American society based on the tenets of political sociology. Appropriately, he confronted a work, 'which, almost immediately on its publication, had a substantial impact on intellectual opinion, ranging from high social science expertise to more diffuse intellectual circles' (158), *The Power Elite* by C. Wright Mills.

C. Wright Mills

Parsons's review article of Mills's *The Power Elite* ([1956] 1959), as he described it, 'discussed one major position in the diagnosis of the relation to state and society in America, a conceptualization that attempted to specify certain conditions which seemed to imply a chronic susceptibility to Fascism' (1969, 158).

Mills's theory, with its conception of 'the monolithic character of the "power structure" ... the primary cognitive basis of the claim that there is an essentially evil "system" which must, by ethical imperative, be combated,' was similarly threatening. Parsons's response to Mills was not merely to point out that his 'emphases were highly selective,' but also to undertake 'a revised version of a defense, not specifically of "capitalism," but of pluralistic-democratic society. It is in this context that the evaluative aspect of the critique of Mills was to be understood' (159).

It was insufficient, none the less, simply to counter the Millsian thesis with another evaluation. It had to be demonstrated that *The Power Elite* interpretation was both cognitively distorted and normatively biased, and, correspondingly, that the prescriptive virtue of the pluralist position was rationally conceived. In undermining the ideological challenge of the Millsian definition of reality, the efficacy of democratic-pluralist society could be affirmed. 'The issue,' emphasized Parsons, 'was not the simple counter-assertion to Mills's assertion that democratic pluralism was a good thing, but of the actual empirical importance, and probable future viability of this type of sociopolitical organization' (159). Both Parsons's critique of Mills and the empirical alternative he offered were supported by his commitment to the consolidation of a democratic-pluralist system.

Most disturbing to Parsons was Mills's 'uncriticized assumption that power was inherently a zero-sum phenomenon' (159), the view that 'power ... is power *over* others' ([1957] 1969, 199). Hence 'there is ... the tendency to think of power as presumptively illegitimate; if people exercise considerable power, it must be because they have somehow usurped it where they had no right and they intend to use it to the detriment of others' (200). Mills maintained that 'the power of the very rich and the corporate rich *within* the economy is inordinately great' (192). By pointing to an overall pattern of domination in the political and economic spheres, Mills not only indicted the United States but also called into question the legitimacy of its key institutions. Given that his analysis was based on empirical data, it could conceivably lead to widespread disaffection with the social order if it were taken at face value.

Parsons's response to Mills was to theoretically elaborate the view that the development of the United States was one of rational progression. Through an overall process of specialization and differentiation, according to Parsons, the United States had developed institutions that allowed it to cope with the problems it faced. For example, the 'pace-setting units' of the business system 'have become both large and specialized. Their development has been part of a general process of structural differentiation in the society which has led to a greater specialization in many fields.' Indeed, 'we can ... regard the emergence of the large firm with operations on a nation-wide basis as a "normal" outcome of growth and differentiation of the economy.' Mirroring this development, 'the rise to prominence within the firm of specialized executive functions is also a normal outcome of a process of growth in size and in structural differentiation' (191); 'given the nature of an industrial society, a relatively well-defined elite or leadership group *should be expected to develop* in the business world' (193). It is through this process of differentiation and specialization, Parsons argued, that the economic system is able to produce wealth, involving 'the "cooperation" or integration of a variety of different agencies – what economists call the "factors of production" ' (200).

To defuse Mills's critique of economic institutions in America, Parsons argued that personal criteria had given way to rational criteria in the selection and evolution of executive personnel. He maintained that there has been an overall tendency 'to link executive responsibility with competence in such a way that the ascriptive rights of property ownership have tended to give way to the occupation functions of "professionals" ' (192). Consistent with his commitment to the view that the capitalist entrepreneur disinterestedly followed his calling, thereby rationalizing the order, Parsons now maintained that economic power was both functionally necessary and historically inevitable. In this manner, to his satisfaction, he was able to deflect Mills's attack on the American business system.

The same line of argument was then generalized to include the redefinition of the emergence of power as well, for in Parsons's view, 'leadership is an essential function in all social systems which, with their increase of scale and their functional differentiation, tend to

become more specialized' (191). In the case of the United States, he argued that 'the development of the American political system ... has lagged behind that of the economy' (194–5) and, indeed, 'the United States has been an almost specifically non-political society' (190). This lag in political development could be traced to 'the economic emphasis inherent in our system of values, and the relative lack of urgency of certain political problems because of our especially protected and favored national position' (195). However, ultimately 'the dynamic of a maturing industrial society [and] the altered position of the United States in world society ... *both* work in the direction of increasing the relative importance of government in our society, and, with it, of political power' (190). The emergence of power, then, represented a response to 'both internal exigencies and the exigencies of our international position.' In terms of America's internal changes, 'the main focus of the development of our political system has been *control* of economic organization and processes, and coping with some of the social consequences of economic growth and industrialization' (195).

By maintaining that the expansion of power represented an overall tendency towards differentiation and specialization, Parsons sought to offer a theoretical alternative to the one offered by Mills. Parsons admitted that Mills's claims were supported with empirical data but held that the credibility of the Millsian thesis was vitiated by its inadequate theoretical scheme, i.e. by 'the zero-sum notion of power.' In order to reduce 'the element of arbitrariness in such judgments' and to protect 'them against at least the grosser sorts of ideological distortions,' Parsons proposed 'the use of a relatively well-integrated and technical theoretical scheme' (186). This took the form of an alternative conception of power that stressed its inevitability, functionality, and system-maintaining virtues.

Power is a generalized facility or resource in the society. It has to be divided or allocated, but it also has to be produced and it has collective as well as distributive functions. It is the capacity to mobilize the resources of the society for the attainment of goals for which a general 'public' commitment has been made, or may be made. It is mobilization, above all, of the action of persons and groups, which is binding on them by virtue of their position in the society. (200)

As opposed to Mills's exclusive concentration 'on the distributive aspect of power' and his interest in '*who* has power and what *sectoral* interests he is serving,' this alternative conception examines 'how power comes to be generated [and] what communal rather than sectoral interests are served' (200).

None the less, Parsons stressed that 'American society has not developed a well-integrated political-government elite, in the sense that it has developed a relatively well-integrated business-executive group.' Hence, 'the non-political stress in American social structure and values generally, and the recency and intensity of the pressures to build up this aspect of our structure' (197), put pressure on other groups, particularly on the professional strata, to take on more responsibility. 'It is true that the people rooted in these areas of the social structure are not prominent in the power elite, and are even subject to some conflicts with it; but they would not be expected to be prominent in this way – their functions in the society are different. Nonetheless, they must be taken very seriously into account in a diagnosis of what has been happening to the society as a whole' (198).

'The services of technical professional groups,' Parsons emphasized, 'have come to penetrate the structure of business and of government, a circumstance which over a period of time has greatly enhanced the role of the universities as custodians of learning and sources of trained personnel.' 'The enormous development, over a century, of science and learning and the professions resting upon them,' Parsons remarked, 'Mills either treats cavalierly or ignores ... completely' (198).

The 'building of the political structure,' then, involved the active co-operation of political, economic, and professional elites. By specializing in the production of power and wealth, politicians and entrepreneurs, respectively, would contribute to the continuing rationalization of the order. Correspondingly, the professional stratum, through the production of technical knowledge, and by its definition of the situation, could aid and abet the process of rational development. As a social scientist identifying with the goals of the professions, Parsons's own theoretical endeavours followed from these overall considerations.[2] It was not surprising, then, that he reacted with such dispatch to the ideological threat posed by The Power Elite. The Millsian thesis with its combination of cognitive and moral claims (i.e. 'empirical one-sidedness and distortion, and moral indictment and sarcasm') was potentially deleterious to the stability of the order, particularly if its influence were diffused over ever-widening circles. Accepting Mills's empirical analysis of the concentration and abuse of economic and political power meant being bound to his evaluation and thus predisposed to carry out some form of political dissent. Parsons thought it of the greatest urgency to discredit Mills's empirical analysis by presenting an alternative, empirically relevant perspective that made power by *definition* a functional resource of the social system. This functionality embodied the earlier metaphysical or transcendent impulse of the system of ultimate ends. The functions, by implication, corresponded to the gradual approximation of a higher state, whose form and direction were not immediately understood to the actors of society. In presenting a functional view of the social order, the social scientist would be mediating this definition of the situation to civil society, thereby contributing to the acceptance of the prevailing social order. So long as power was rationally viewed in this way, the social actor would be compelled to evaluate it as legitimate, and inclined to act so as to support it. Parsons's reconceptualization of power, as it related to American political, economic, and cultural development, thus provided the categorical foundations for his emerging conception of political sociology.

McCarthyism had impressed upon Parsons the importance of developing an approach to the study of politics that stressed the intersection between political institutions and social integration. Now through his analysis and critique of Mills, he formulated a conception of power that could provide an integrating framework for codifying previous data and generating future political and social research. By conducting empirical inquiry along the guide-lines suggested by this conception of power, the social scientist could not only produce relevant empirical knowledge, but counter the 'pseudo-rational' and ideologically founded claims made by both political and intellectual dissenters. Such a venture was part of the overall task of taking 'serious stock of the ideological assumptions underlying the bulk of American political discussions of such problems as power' (1969, 203).

It was entirely appropriate, therefore, that Parsons's next undertaking was 'to attempt an empirical-theoretical assessment of the spate of studies of voting behavior in the American system which had appeared over a period of years.' By showing the relevance of empirical studies of voting to his overall notions of how social integration made for the generation of power, he could elaborate further the methodological framework and content of political sociology. This would serve, moreover, to offer a more refined and empirically founded depiction of American politics and society to set against those views that were prominent among dissidents. In wedding the empirical analysis of voting with his normative framework, he chose to concentrate on one study, 'that by Berelson, Lazarsfeld, and McPhee, on the 1948 presidential election ... in Elmira, New York' (1969, 160).

Voting and Political Equilibrium

Parsons's analyses of McCarthyism and *The Power Elite* offered a theoretical defence for American pluralist democracy, with a view towards defusing the challenge to it that they posed. He was concerned with pointing out how the accounts of the United States offered by Mills and the interpreters of McCarthyism were misguided, distorted, and at odds with reality; he took exception to their conceptions of power and how it was exercised. Accordingly, as a corrective to these 'erroneous' perspectives, Parsons began to elaborate an alternative version of power, focusing on its role as a rationalizing and stabilizing force. This theoretical framework, in his view, was to serve as a basis for furthering empirical inquiry into the nature of American pluralist democracy.

In his discussion of *Voting* (Berelson, Lazarsfeld, and McPhee [1954] 1968; Parsons 1969) Parsons further refined this approach, with particular attention given to how the United States was able to maintain a stable system of power during a period of rapid social change. The fact that both political and intellectual dissent (as represented by McCarthyism and Mills, respectively) had been successfully resisted signified that the American socio-political order possessed particular attributes that ensured its functioning. Accordingly, his analysis of *Voting* could be understood as a stock-taking of the various characteristics of American pluralist democracy that permitted it to both absorb dissent and operate as a smoothly functioning system of power. In doing so, he could thus contribute to the development of a social-scientific approach that would be capable of producing knowledge of this kind on a sustained basis.

Parsons was particularly intrigued by the 1948 election, which indicated to him how the two-party system was able to ensure the smooth transition from the Roosevelt era to the Eisenhower era with little disturbance. Parsons was concerned with how the American political system was able to cope with McCarthyism, whose peak 'came in the early years of the Eisenhower administration, and was considerably foreshadowed in the Truman era' (1969, 160). Such an occurrence was an example of 'the major type of "pathology" of our system and, if not controlled, may have highly disruptive consequences' ([1959] 1969, 225).

Nevertheless, McCarthyism's eventual demise convincingly demonstrated the overall capacity of the political system to contain dissent. 'There is a great deal of sociopolitical dynamite in the political process in a rapidly changing society. That it breaks over into charismatic "radicalism" – of right or left – so seldom, and that these "fires" have usually been so relatively and quickly extinguished, is testimony to the power of the mechanisms of social control that operate in this area' (233). The mechanisms of the political system also provided a ready answer to *The Power Elite* critique by demonstrating that the concentration of power was not monolithic and that the electoral process made for democratic participation (233).

Parsons's discussion of *Voting* built upon his conception of power and integration, formulated to diffuse the attack of McCarthyites and Mills. Parsons sought to refine his model of politics and society by adapting the data of *Voting*, whose 'findings and interpretations ... fit very well with a generalized analysis in terms of the theory of social systems.' He turned his attention to 'how the voting process functions as part of the *social system* in which it operates.' In particular, continuous with his earlier views, he sought to better understand the 'generation and distribution of power,' which 'involves a special problem of the *integration* of the system, including the binding of its units, individual and collective, to the necessary commitments' (204–5).

As directed by these goals, power is generated in a sub-system parallel to the economy that Parsons called the 'polity.' He then sought to show how in the same way that the economy produced wealth through combining the factors of production, the polity generated power by successfully mobilizing *support*, utilizing *facilities*, and illiciting *legitimation* and *unconditional loyalties*. His main concern was to indicate how support for leadership was mobilized through a 'set of processes by which control of the federal government is decided, its major politics ... worked out, and public attitudes toward them ... influenced and brought to bear' (209). Of particular importance, in Parsons's view, was the voting process as it articulated with the two-party system. Together, they served to stabilize American political life through 'the firm institutionalization of "the rules of the game" [and] the control of ... divisive potentialities' (214).

Within this general institutionalization provided by 'supraparty consensus,' Parsons specified three additional features that ensured political stability, adapted from similar conclusions in *Voting*. All were premised on the assumption that social welfare was optimized by the stable workings of the two-party system; the problem then became one of grasping which social mechanisms made the functioning of this system possible. First, he noted the significance of 'traditionalism' and 'cross-pressure voting' in ensuring political stability (215–19). Second, he argued that the lack of 'correspondence between political polarization and other bases of differentiation' ensured a balance between consensus and cleavage (215). Because most groupings in society 'contain considerable portions of adherents of *both* parties' (223), the effects of political cleavage will be compensated for by ties of solidarity to 'nonpolitical bases [that] cut across their political allegiances.' As a consequence, 'the activation of essentially nonpolitical sentiments of solidarity acts as a break on processes leading to divisive cleavage' (224). Finally, Parsons stressed that 'American society is not static, but dynamically evolving.' Thus, 'the political system ... must include mechanisms of adjustment to social change.' Most notably, these serve to 'mediate the balance between right and left without running the risk that either set of elements will be oppressively overwhelmed by the other' (216). In this way, Parsons used the findings of *Voting* to demonstrate how the two-party system served as a mechanism for controlling conflicts and ensuring structural change (233).

None the less, as Parsons admitted, this set of mechanisms could not be completely relied upon. In particular, the secondary defence of 'supraparty consensus' had to be evoked, when the mechanism of 'cleavage-consensus' got out of order. Such a consensus, in the form of the 'cultural tradition,' as he emphasized, was also the repository of the values affirmed by the professional strata, including the social sciences. Hence, Parsons's own deliberations on the political system and its stabilizing mechanisms can be viewed as an intended contribution to the cultivation of supraparty consensus. By affirming the viability of the political system in the face of dissenting threats, Parsons could help subvert the extremist impulse of such political tendencies as McCarthyism. There was, however, more to his analysis than his response to right-wing dissent. He also established some important guide-lines for the implementation of future research in political sociology. His analysis of the structural mechanisms that permitted the stability of the political system lent itself to further elaboration and specification through empirical inquiry. With his conjunction of the empirical study of voting within the integrative framework of the political system, Parsons had demonstrated how researchers could combine objectivity with the value components of American democracy. In carrying out inquiries of this kind, the investigator would not only be providing empirical knowledge of possible technical use, but would also be offering an integrative definition of reality to the public.

Parsons's refinement of his conception of power through an extended analysis of the political system further substantiated his contention that the theories of the 'power elite' and 'mass society' were cognitively incorrect. In his next topical essay (Parsons and White [1960] 1969), he continued his counter-attack on intellectual dissent by applying some of his analytic insights to Raymond and Alice Bauer's (1960) discussion of the then current disputes about mass society and the mass media.

Mass Media and the Structure of Society

Parsons's treatment of the Bauers' article (1960) represented a further attempt to refine, elaborate, and give empirical content to his emerging redefinition of American society and politics. What made the Bauers' discussion particularly appropriate for a reformulation of this sort was its attack on mass-society/mass-culture critics[3] through a summary and synthesis of empirical research supportive of a more sanguine vision of American life. The adaptation of the Bauers' findings complemented Parsons's critique of *The Power Elite*, and the subsequent 'discovery' of the 'primary group' in his analysis of *Voting*. This line of continuity, Parsons adduced, succeeded in demonstrating the fundamental mistakenness of intellectual critics.

There seemed to be an important continuity between the critique ... of Mills's use of the concept of mass, the theme of the pluralistic solidary groups in the determination of voting behavior ... and the corresponding features of pluralistic social structure as impinging on the role of mass media. Though there is much about mass media which we do not know, it seems highly unlikely that the 'mass culture' interpretation, as that prevailed in the late 1950's, will prove to be adequate. (1969, 161)

The Bauers, Parsons noted, concluded 'that in general the proponents of the theory of mass society operate both as commentators on the empirical state of the society and as evaluative critics of it.' By distinguishing between these two problems, it became possible for them 'to see the theory of mass society as an ideological position congenial to *certain groups* of intellectuals.' This standpoint, as the Bauers pointed out, revealed that 'these intellectuals place one of several possible interpretations on items of evidence – in ideological fashion – that does not support their evaluative strictures' (Parsons and White [1960] 1969, 241–2). The Bauers referred to the intellectuals' contention that 'cultural standards have deteriorated and that social structure has tended to become an aggregate of mass men, alienated from the meaningful ties that would uphold standards' (242). This, according to the intellectuals, has made the 'mass men' vulnerable to exploitation and subject to the lure of cultural mediocrity.

Parsons agreed completely with this assessment, and indeed saw a congruence between these intellectuals and more political critics: 'It seems legitimate to consider the theorists of 'late monopoly capitalism' and those of the 'power elite' as exponents of an ideology in the same sense in which we have attributed this to the theorists of mass culture' (248). Accordingly, Parsons met the challenge of the 'theorists of mass culture' in the same way that he had sought to counter the Millsian critique – with an empirically based and normatively informed depiction of American life.

As an alternative to the position of the intellectuals, we wish to suggest a line of theoretical analysis that attempts to fit the evidence on the mass media (and on 'mass culture') with that available on other aspects of the society, and that interprets this evidence in the larger context of some of the major features of American social structure and trends of its change. It is only through such a consideration of a wider range of evidence and of the larger social system, we feel, that steps can be taken to reduce the admittedly serious dangers of ideological selectivity and distortion. (242)

In keeping with his previous analysis, Parsons suggested that communications, like economics and politics, was characterized by the process of 'extension, differentiation and upgrading' (250). Parsons believed that the system of mass communications offered a combination of individual choice and institutionalized control similar to the political and economic systems. 'Such a system,' he maintained, 'could be expected to produce degrees of freedom for the typical recipient analogous to those of the economic consumer or the member of the political public.' According to Parsons, the mass communications system of the United States offered 'a wide range of choice with respect to content [and] freedoms with respect to both "time" and "cost"' (249).

This freedom was ensured in all these spheres by the 'same order of specialization of function between "producing" and "consuming" units, and – most importantly – between different kinds of communication output.' Just as concentrations of wealth and power were necessary and inevitable in politics and economics, the system of mass communications 'involves relative concentration of resources in the hands of larger producers.' And in the same way that the voter is separated from politics, and the worker from the product of his labour, 'the mass communications system' involves ' "alienation" of the recipient from control over the sources of communications' (248).

This alternative account, stressing the place of mass media and culture within a rationally evolving society, was intended to help consolidate the Bauers' analysis of mass society theory. Contrary to 'the assumption that this is an "atomized" mass society where the relations of one individual to another have become increasingly amorphous,' Parsons gave further support to the notion that 'American society is one of the preeminent examples of a *pluralistic* society in which – through the course of structural differentiation – an increasingly ramified network of criss-crossing solidarities has been developing.' Although he admitted that 'American society has – in terms of our high expectations for it – many inadequacies ... we believe, they cannot be "explained," much less confronted with any degree of sophistication, by the currently prominent theory of mass society' (251). He concluded with the hope that

the combination of our treatment of the ideological problem with the parallel we have drawn between the selectivity of the mass-culture theorists and certain critics of the American economy and political system will serve to broaden the problem raised by the Bauers. By placing the mass-culture issue in a larger perspective, one can perhaps see that it is a special case of more general processes and that there is the same kind of problem in interpretation – not only of mass culture but of American society as a total system. (251)

Parsonsian Theory, Political Sociology, and the State

At the analytical level, Parsons's response to the dissent of the 1950s led him to develop the political sub-system (goal-attainment) of his evolving fourfold schema ([1959] 1969, 237). In terms of the overall Parsonsian project, the polity corresponded at once to a depiction of reality and to a theoretical framework that gave form to the content of political inquiry. That the political sub-system served this dual purpose is evident in the following analogue he drew between economic and political theory in relation to their respective subject matters. 'Economic theory,' he argued, 'can be shown to be a special case of the general theory of social systems; it is the case defined as applicable to certain processes in the economy conceived as a social system, i.e., as a differentiated subsystem of a total society' (1958, 297). He suggested that 'a great deal of current political theory could be codified and systematized, and better articulated with economics and sociology, if an analogous conception of its scope were worked out and placed within the general theory of social systems as another special case' (298).[4]

The duality of purpose that Parsons assigned to the sub-systems – including the polity – was inherently related to his practical designs. The polity as an empirical entity assumed the standpoint of the integrative problems faced by the capitalist nation-state, and vested them with a divine purpose or functionality. That is, implicit in the empirical account of the polity was a transcendent form of socio-political order towards which the nation-state was moving. This movement, however, was not necessary or inevitable but was contingent upon social-scientific activity. What made this practical relevance possible was the correspondence between the political sub-system as empirical reality and as theoretical framework. By producing knowledge in terms of the 'problems' as defined by the theoretical framework, the researcher, in effect, could contribute to solving the 'problems' in the empirical world, thereby moving the nation-state closer to the transcendent ideal. This duality between the theoretical framework and empirical reality ensured the relevance of social-scientific knowledge to society. The correspondence between theory and reality would permit social scientists to engage themselves with the ideological tendencies threatening the integration of the social order.

As a theoretical system having practical relevance to the formation of the modern nation-state, the polity affirmed the tendencies that made for its stabilization while countering movements that jeopardized its development. Parsons's conception of power, defined as a positive resource or capacity of the system, inherently rested upon the successful mobilization of support – the interplay between 'the polity' and the 'public' and the processes through which consensus was cultivated and dissent overcome. This involved a specification of the social-control mechanisms, 'tradition-flexibility, consensus-cleavage, progress-conservation,' which, as articulated by the 'American two-party system,' ensured that a 'relative equilibrating balance in a pluralistic society is maintained, so that conflicts and tendencies are more or less resolved.' In view of Parsons's conception of power, the task of social scientists was to show how the political system was able to strike the appropriate balance between tradition and flexibility, consensus and cleavage, as well as progress and conservation. This would suggest

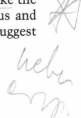

analyses of voting patterns oriented towards understanding how social interests and movements were integrated into the political system. Implied by this perspective was a form of political sociology that would examine how certain social conditions made for particular kinds of political development. Practising a political sociology of this kind would not only contribute to the affirmation and consolidation of these trends, but also undermine tendencies that threatened this pattern of development. As we have indicated, Parsons was particularly concerned with intellectual dissent in the form of interpretations of McCarthyism as a form of fascism, the 'power elite' thesis, and mass-society/mass-culture theory. As Parsons elsewhere noted more generally, the subject matter of sociology intersects with outside groups who 'have special relations to selected portions of the scientific community because of their common "interests" in a particular subject matter.' Such considerations apply to 'the relations between political science and the political elements of society' and to sociology which, 'with values as a central part of its subject matter, stands in a relation of strain to those elements in the society that are particularly concerned with the guardianship of its values' (1959b, 44).

Political sociology, it followed, shared a subject matter with those groups that made claims pertaining to political power and social integration. Given that the general task of the social sciences was to undermine the ideological thrust of outside groups by demonstrating the selectivity and distortions inherent in their perspectives, the specific task of political sociology was to defuse those ideologies making claims of a *political sociological* nature. This implied the elaboration of an alternative definition of the situation, which, Parsons argued, would empirically demonstrate the moral worth of American politics and society. Political sociology, with its conception of power as a functional and inevitable resource providing the basis for social order, presented a picture of society that was essentially stable and harmonious. Moreover, with its linking of a normative framework to empirical voting studies, it lent itself to further refinement and elaboration. Parsons's nascent conception of political sociology, then, embodied his general intention to orient the social sciences towards the practical problems faced by the American state in the Cold War order.

A political sociology of this kind could potentially generate knowledge of *instrumental* value to the elites of the state. The intrinsic congruence between the problems of the state and the orientation of the social sciences was precisely rendered in Parsons's comparison the Great Depression and the McCarthyist era:

Thus we may ask: Was not the Great Depression an 'economic'
phenomenon? And was not McCarthyism a 'political' phenomenon?
The whole tenor of the New Deal, however, made coping with the
Great Depression and its consequences as much a political as an
economic problem. I have suggested, further, that the primary roots of
McCarthyism lay in strains in the societal community, not in the
polity as that concept has here been defined with analytic strictness.
Yet certainly it deeply involved the processes of government. My
general view is that the depression presented problems of political
economy par excellence, and McCarthyism, of political sociology.
(1969, 474)

In specifying the problems characteristic of the New Deal and the McCarthyist era, Parsons implicitly assumed the standpoint of the state apparatus. The social-scientific approach appropriate to each era – political economy and political sociology – bore the promise of generating instrumental knowledge pertinent to the adaptive problems faced by the state apparatus in each instance. In the Great Depression, of course, the state faced the enormous task of somehow inducing economic recovery. Correspondingly, as Parsons inferred, in the postwar period the major difficulty faced by the state was one of overcoming the internal strains attendant upon its assumption of new global responsibilities. Political sociology was to help overcome such dissent, through diagnosing its origins and suggesting appropriate mechanisms for its control. Hence, the knowledge that political sociology could offer was of an instrumental kind, with its treatment of phenomena on objective terms implying technical solutions.

Parsons's concern with the integrative problems of the American nation-state in the Cold War era led him to develop the foundations of a field having potential practical relevance to the problems it faced. Within secular society it was to serve as a point of mediation between the 'state' and the 'nation,' generating knowledge of relevance to stabilizing the relations between them. This meant that political sociology was to produce knowledge useful to the instrumentally defined problems facing the state apparatus, and to the legitimation of state structures and processes to civil society. The primary patterns made the generation of this knowledge possible. In relation to the state, the scientific or universalistic quality of such knowledge would make it instrumentally valuable. By virtue of its 'affective neutrality,' this knowledge would be of normative relevance to the set of integrative problems faced by the state. In relation to civil society, the same cultural component would allow for an intersubjective 'definition of the situation' consistent with the goals and priorities of the state apparatus. The universalistic quality of the definition offered would provide it with authoritative force. In this manner, the selectivity and distortion of potentially divisive ideologies could be overcome. The specialization of political sociology in problems of integration, and its location in disinterested, relatively autonomous institutions,[5] would give it credibility to both state elites and members of civil society.

Although Parsons was deeply concerned with the practical and empirical implications of his theory, he himself rarely went beyond the codification of the empirical work done by others. Nevertheless, the political sociology he developed in the domestic heat of the Cold War was not to be stillborn. As an articulation of the concerns, aspirations, and practical interests of mainstream social scientists, the framework of analysis he had evolved found almost immediate resonance in the academic community. As embodied in the 'sociology of politics' and 'comparative politics,' guided by the leadership of Seymour Lipset and Gabriel Almond, respectively, Parsons's approach to political sociology underpinned sustained programs of research that set the standard in both disciplines for the better part of the 1960s.

PART THREE

The Making and Undoing of Political Sociology

9

Cornucopia of the Intellectuals

The Ford Foundation and the Behavioural-Sciences Program

Despite their virtual exclusion from the National Science Foundation (see chapter 7), the social sciences were not destined to be without extensive external financial support in the post-war period. With the announcement by the Ford Foundation in 1950 of its intention to support research in human behaviour, the immediate prospects of the social sciences were greatly enhanced. The Ford Foundation's program for the development of the behavioural sciences was based on a report submitted by a study committee to the trustees the previous year (Ford Foundation 1949). The task of the study committee 'was to make recommendations based upon the best available thought concerning the ways in which the Ford Foundation can most effectively and intelligently put its resources to work for human welfare' (13). Given that 'human welfare ... though the keystone of the Foundation's charter [was] not defined or elaborated there,' a major concern of the committee was to 'arrive at a clearer understanding' of the term (13). The conception of human welfare arrived at by the committee was 'in large measure synonymous with a declaration of democratic ideals.' It concluded not only that 'the real hope for the advancement of human welfare lies in the reaffirmation in practice of democratic principles,' but that 'today's most critical problems are those which are *social* rather than *physical* in character – those which rise in man's relation to man rather than in his relation to nature. Here ... is the realm where the greatest problems exist, where the least progress is being made, and where the gravest threat to democracy and human welfare lies' (emphasis mine) (14). As a way of contributing 'to the increased realization of democratic goals, and thus to the advance of human welfare,' the committee recommended that the Ford Foundation 'should concentrate strategically upon those areas showing maximum promise of progress, including the relief or elimination of significant factors which tend to block it.' Specifically, in view of 'the exigencies of the world crisis and of present political and economic problems,' the committee arrived at five program areas that they felt should set the priorities for Ford Foundation support. The first three program areas, 'the establishment of peace, the strengthening of democracy, and the strengthening of the domestic and world economy,' were to address the problems that the committee considered to be of greatest urgency. Program areas four and five – dealing with education and research – were designated as the primary ways in which the problems guiding the first three program areas could be solved. Of the five program areas, two and five were of particular relevance to social-scientific research. Area two was concerned with clarifying the meaning of democracy and discovering what features made it possible. The committee noted that 'to a vast number of sincere and loyal Americans the principles of democracy are merely a collection of clichés, serving chiefly as reminders of historical events and social conditions of the past.' This widespread confusion made it imperative that 'a meaningful, contemporary, and usable definition of democracy' be developed (64). Moreover, supplying 'our friends and allies abroad ... with examples of democratic philosophy at work may in the long run prove to be the most important part of our logistics in the ideological war. This can be accomplished only if we ourselves understand the basic principles of freedom and democracy and interpret them through sustained, consistent demonstration' (65).

Program area five was 'to increase knowledge of factors which influence or determine human conduct, and to extend such knowledge for the maximum benefit of individuals and of society' (90). This involved 'strengthening the bases of research in the social sciences' and developing 'scientific inquiry by the most competent investigation following the most promising theory and utilizing the methods of greatest proven or potential effectiveness' (in Herring 1950, 25).

In light of the state of the social sciences at the time, it was fitting that certain disciplines were singled out for emphasis: 'The focus of attention in this program is the study of individual behaviour and human relationships. Thus individual and social psychology, social anthropology, and sociology are most directly concerned. However, there are aspects of economics, political science, and history that will be relevant' (25).

The committee, however, did not suggest that the Ford Foundation should support the study of human behaviour for its own sake. Rather, 'greater knowledge of human behavior and techniques for acquiring and utilizing such knowledge, would be exceedingly useful in the fields of government, business, and community affairs ... The Ford Foundation would make a valuable contribution to human welfare by sponsoring immediate studies of the current application of human behavior and of the feasible means for extending such application' (Ford Foundation 1949, 93). The committee argued, then, that the Ford Foundation could contribute to the eventual solution of problems by supporting long-term research programs producing cumulative empirical results. Among the areas for research the committee suggested were public opinion, political behaviour, and communication. Through the strengthening of the behavioural sciences in these fields, a contribution to the building of democratic institutions was to be made. Along similarly practical lines, the area-five concerns also included 'the scientific study of group organization ... the causes of personal maladjustment ... the develop-ment of reliable measures of the effectiveness of professional practices [and] increasing the use of the knowledge of human behavior in medicine ... and other professions' (1949, 90–1). The proposal of the committee that the Ford Foundation ought to support the growth and development of the behavioural sciences, as outlined in area five of the 1950 report, was thus inherently related to the consolidation of democracy and the solution of social problems. The committee's report was well received by Ford Foundation trustees. It's 'recommendations were accepted unanimously by the Trustees and are believed to represent the best thinking in the United States today' (11). The program that the Ford Foundation inaugurated in 1950 thus rested firmly upon the recommendations of the 1949 study report.[1]

The Ford Foundation's priorities as outlined in area five considered sociology to be in a relatively advantaged position compared to the other 'non-economic' social sciences. With the advances it had made in methodological techniques, it was in a strong position to orient itself towards the foundation's designated concerns. The Second World War had given impetus to this deve-lopment, as sociologists and social psychologists increasingly turned their attention to an unprecedented set of practical problems. 'Prior to the war,' as Dorwin Cartwright notes, 'men of practical affairs relied very little upon the services or advice of social psy-chologists. During the war, in a period of extreme crisis, social scientists were called upon to apply their special knowledge and skills to urgent social problems' (Cartwright 1947, 348). Out of the war experience 'emerged new and useful techniques, a tremendous mass of information, and a group of social psychologists who now view their field and their place in society in new and radically different terms ... the second World War ... brought to maturity social psychology' (333). In general, 'the wartime developments' had led to a 'blurring of the boundaries between traditionally defined academic disciplines within the social sciences' (335). The particular subject matter of social psychology – a concern with how civilian and military morale could be cultivated, enemy propaganda defused, and psychological warfare successfully undertaken – was a *product* of wartime exigencies, and resulted in a convergence on the part of psychology and sociology towards a common practical terrain (337–47).

Notable in this regard was the voluminous study by Samuel Stouffer, *The American Soldier* (1949),[2] the industrial studies at Harvard (Roethlisberger and Dickson [1939] 1961), and the pioneering studies employing survey and market-research techniques (Lazarsfeld and Stanton 1949; Lazarsfeld et al. [1944] 1968).[3] Given this orientation of sociology, it can be understood why the Ford Foundation included the discipline of sociology as a vital part of its behavioural sciences program.[4] The foundation developed a close connection with the group within the social sciences known for its production of objective, potentially useful information – the Bureau of Applied Social Research at Columbia University under the direction of Paul Lazarsfeld. Indeed, Lazarsfeld himself was chosen to establish replicas of his research institutes in Europe under the auspices of the Ford Foundation (Pollak 1979, 57). The fact that Bernard Berelson, a member of the bureau and a collaborator with Lazarsfeld on a number of projects, was chosen to direct the Behavioral Sciences Division is indicative of the close ties between the bureau and the Ford Foundation in the early fifties. Under the leadership of Berelson, the Behavioral Sciences Division concerned itself in its first two years of operation with improving the personnel, content, and methods of the behavioural sciences. Not only was support given for the development of research programs and the training of personnel, but the Center for Advanced Study in the Behavioral Sciences was established in Palo Alto 'to advance the scientific study of man ... by encouraging research and scholarship' (Ford Foundation 1952). Given the close involvement of Berelson and the Bureau of Applied Social Research in the early deliberations of the Ford Foundation, the survey-research branch of sociology could be well assured of support and encouragement by the Behavioral Sciences Division.

Political Science in the Post-War Period

However, unlike sociology, political science was ill prepared for the behavioural revolution that swept through the social sciences in the post-war period. Despite the urgings for greater scientific rigour by such leading figures as Charles Merriam ([1925] 1970) and Harold Lasswell ([1936] 1958), 'the subject matter' of the discipline, as Gabriel Almond wrote, was 'still limited to the traditional conceptions of political science [and] the methods were historical and descriptive' ([1950] 1960, 155). Almond was only one of a number of commentators who decried the state of political science in the years following the Second World War (Easton 1953; Griffith 1948; Hawley and Dexter 1952). This general sense of irrelevance and scientific inadequacy had gained force as a result of political scientists' involvement in the war effort. According to Somit and Tanenhaus ([1967] 1982, 141) the wartime experience impressed upon political scientists not only their inability to adequately describe reality, but the lack of marketability for the services that they offered.

Robert Dahl similarly noted that for those political scientists who served the government during wartime, 'the confrontation of theory and reality provoked ... a strong sense of the inadequacies of the conventional approaches of political science for describing reality, much less for predicting in any given situation what was likely to happen' (1961, 764). Through increased contact with other social scientists during the war, political scientists came to realize the extent of their methodological and scientific backwardness compared to sociology, psychology, social psychology, and economics. It was widely acknowledged that the other disciplines had begun to make serious inroads into what had traditionally been the bailiwick of political scientists (Friedrich 1947).

With its rigorous and methodologically innovative treatment of voting, social psychology was of particular concern and interest to political scientists, for the new discipline's sophisticated handling of voting data threatened their own authority in the areas of political behaviour and international politics. Almond noted, for instance, that the work of social psychologists and anthropologists 'reflects a development of increasing significance for future research in international relations. Perhaps the most promising research in the field of political behavior has been carried on by these "younger brothers" of the social science disciplines' (1950a, 281–2). According to Dahl, 'political scientists found their presumed monopoly of skills in the scholarly interpretation of voting and elections rudely destroyed by sociologists and social psychologists' (1961, 765). This assessment of the methodological backwardness of political science was shared by government funding agencies and corporate philanthropists as well. The National Science Foundation from the outset was consistently reluctant to support research in political science. As Evon Kirkpatrick summarized his 'conversations with and letters from officers of the National Science Foundation' on behalf of the American Political Science Association, 'it is sometimes said that there is no basic research, ... ; at other times it is said that political science research is too closely related to controversial issues of public policy for the Foundation to support it; at still other times ... it is said that political science does not meet the Foundation's standards of scientific objectivity, quantitative measurement and the like' (quoted in Somit and Tanenhaus [1967] 1982, 154).

While the Ford Foundation was not as adamantly dismissive of research in political studies as the NSF was, it still accorded political science only secondary emphasis in its 1950 program on funding for the behavioural sciences. In a survey of 'recent sociological trends' in the United States, Becker noted that 'the numerous foundations – Ford, Russell Sage, etc. – had much to do with the fluctuations, notably the stress on "behavioral sciences". These comprising sociology, social anthropology and social psychology received much attention. Social sciences not of "behavioral" type, such as political science, human geography and history were not so directly favored – although by no means neglected' (in Senn 1966, 114).

Given the extent of the Ford Foundation largesse earmarked for bona fide behavioural sciences and the precarious financial and methodological situation of political science, it is entirely understandable why prominent political scientists began to embrace behaviouralism with such ardour. As Dahl observed, 'in spite of obvious defects, the voting studies seemed to provide ground for the hope that if political scientists could only master the tools employed in the other social sciences – survey methods and statistical analysis, for example – they might be able to go beyond plausible generalities and proceed to test hypotheses about how people in fact do behave in making political choices' (Dahl 1961, 765).

In the late 1940s and early 1950s, the SSRC and the Committee on Political Behavior sought to orient political science towards a more systematic, empirical study of its subject matter, largely through the infusion of methodology from the newer social sciences.[5] That the behavioural revolution had a significant impact upon political science in the early 1950s was acknowledged by a number of commentators. 'Political science,' noted David Riesman, 'now finds it subject matter, the state as a subject to be studied in isolation, withering away.' With the spread of state activities and the discovery of power relations throughout society, 'the once firm boundaries of clientele between political science and the newer social sciences break down, and the once lordly field is invaded by new men, nurtured within it, called students of political behavior. These men take their topic from the parent body but their methods from psychology and sociology' (Riesman 1956, 333). Berelson similarly pointed out that the field of public opinion 'helped to stimulate the growth of a "new" interest ... in "political behavior" – and the banding together of an *avant-garde* who sought to take the gospel of empirical, behavioral studies of political matters to their document-oriented brethren' (1956, 313).

By virtue of its adaptation of the techniques of social psychology, the political-behaviour movement developed within political science and converged with survey-research tendencies in sociology. Both fields were proving themselves capable of producing empirical knowledge about attitudes, beliefs, and political behaviour. Their reorientation was consistent with the Ford Foundation's priorities as outlined in area five of its 1949 report. Nevertheless, little concern was given to how the knowledge accruing from this methodological advancement was to be of relevance to the strengthening of democracy, as outlined in area two of the report. With the Ford Foundation's increased emphasis upon the relevance of empirical knowledge to the consolidation and spread of American democracy as a result of external pressures, there was a corresponding change in both wings of the behavioural-science movement.

The Congressional Investigations

Despite its interest in helping to build democracy and to solve social problems in the United States, the Ford Foundation was subject to 'violent criticisms' from ultra-conservative forces 'from the very start of its full-scale operations in 1951' (Reeves 1969, 15). This attack reached its most virulent expression in two congressional investigations into 'tax exempt foundations and comparable organizations' by the Cox committee and the Reece committee (u.s. Congress 1953; 1954). Even though the Cox committee, in its report issued in January 1953, concluded that the '"international activities"' of the foundations '"are motivated chiefly by consideration of the welfare of the American people and as such are entirely praise-worthy"' (U.S. Congress 1953 in Macdonald 1956, 29). One member, Brazilla Carrol Reece, voiced his dissent. 'While signing the report,' noted Macdonald, Reece 'appended an ominous postscript proposing "a more comprehensive study" because "the Committee has had insufficient time for the magnitude of its task."' Specifically, he felt that the Cox committee had failed to '"get" the Fords' and the Rockefellers' foundations,' and in the summer of 1953 he called for another congressional investigation, principally to scrutinize the activities of the Ford Foundation. According to Reece, the Ford Foundation was using its fortunes, '"amassed in a competitive free market place in the last fifty years ... to undermine and subvert our institutions ... The Ford Foundation – which is the wealthiest and most influential of all foundations – was not actually investigated by the Cox Committee"' (29–30). In relation to the social sciences, the Reece committee concluded that the foundations often support forces that weaken American society, thereby providing opportunities for communist activity (U.S. Congress 1954, 201). In the view of the committee, by virtue of their leftist orientation, the social sciences undermined the fundamental institutions and principles of American life. The committee saw this trend as particularly noticeable in the arena of international politics, in which they concluded that the foundations supported propaganda on behalf of a particular viewpoint, namely that of 'empiricism.' It was the opinion of the committee that this kind of approach to research attempted to reach conclusions solely on the basis of observation, while ignoring moral principles and behavioural norms (194).

'The so-called empirical findings,' testified Professor Hobbs at the committee hearings, 'must be fitted into a framework of the legal precepts, the traditions, the history, the moral codes, [and] the military principles of the area in which they are applied' (60). The committee closed its account by recommending that 'the substantial weight of foundation effort must operate to strengthen, improve and promote the economic, political and moral pillars upon which society rests' (206).

In effect, the committee impugned the Ford Foundation for its emphasis upon empiricist research, to the neglect of the core values of American society. This allegation had some basis in fact. In the years prior to the congressional investigations, the foundation had been primarily concerned with training personnel in empirical methodology and with funding research programs and institutes. In terms of the program for the behavioural sciences, the development of methodology had taken precedence over the need to strengthen democracy.

In the midst of the two congressional investigations into tax-exempt foundations, the Ford Foundation began to redirect its concerns in line with the criticisms made against it. As Roland Gaither noted in 'The President's Review' of foundation activities during 1953, more emphasis had been placed upon the 'promotion of international understanding [and] the strengthening of democratic institutions and processes' (Ford Foundation 1953, 12), as part of the foundation's commitment to fight world communism. And in its international projects, 'the Foundation sought to support institutions and activities which might help strengthen the economic, social, and political fabric of nations whose welfare is of unusual significance to the Free World. The Foundation supports undertakings only in those nations whose political philosophy and objectives, if sustained or achieved, are incompatible with Communism' (14). The foundation trustees, Gaither reported, decided 'to invest most of the funds to be spent overseas in Western Europe, the Near East, and South and Southeast Asia, even though this prevents substantial investment in other areas of need' (22).

As Dwight Macdonald suggested, the overseas activities of the Ford Foundation, premised on the solution of 'problems,' complemented the global anti-communist concerns of the United States. 'From 1951 through 1954, the Ford Foundation put $54,000,000, or almost a third of its total outlay for the period, into its international programs.' The Ford Foundation, 'being problem-oriented – the problem here is how to win allies and influence neutrals – is less interested in research per se than in promoting sympathy and understanding between us and the rest of the non-Communist world' (1956, 60–1).

This shift was mirrored in developments within the behavioural sciences themselves. As Oliver Garceau, a leading political scientist, observed, the new scientific orientation came into conflict with the traditional normative commitments of political science. He expressed the concern that 'political science, in a fresh enthusiasm for empirical research, may become so engrossed with uniformities and determinants that it will obscure or abandon the normative commitments of a democratic polity.' Garceau suggested that a 'conceptual scheme that will place data in meaningful context' – namely, that of the democratic system – had to be developed (1951, 69). The 'dilemma for political behavior research,' observed Garceau, 'is the apparent and oft-berated contrast between observable behavior patterns and the heritage of democratic belief.' Traditional political thought, in his view, 'has particularly beclouded research in democratic politics because in very large part it antedated the effort to practice democracy in nation states of the industrial era.' Such 'early stereotypes [have] colored with negative valuations the perceptions of operating behavior that did penetrate the barriers of dogma. Associated with the lag in observation has been the delay in reworking the conceptual scheme of the democratic polity' (70). The implication was that political research attuned to the realities of democracy could lay the basis for an empirically grounded normative theory of politics.

Garceau had pointed to an unresolved tension in the behavioural tendency within political science. So long as the sheer production of data was not attuned to the wider values of democracy, political science would become increasingly irrelevant to the national purpose. This implied as well that the behavioral persuasion in political science alone would not assure the discipline of extensive foundation support. For the problem-oriented approach to philanthropy by such funding behemoths as the Ford Foundation demanded not only social research of scientific rigour, but also of normative relevance to the cultivation of democracy. Apparently, it was the congressional investigations into the foundations and the research they supported that brought this tension to a head. This was most evident in the creation by the ssrc of a new Committee on Research in Comparative Politics as an outgrowth of the Committee on Political Behavior. The transition to the new committee from its predecessor, it may be argued, marked both a subsumption of behavioural methodology to strategic dictates and an adaptation of the ssrc and political science to the global priorities of the Ford Foundation. While both the ssrc and the political science profession had previously taken preliminary initiatives to upgrade research in comparative politics (Loewenstein 1944), the immediate impetus to the formation of a separate ssrc committee to pursue and consolidate the approach appears to have come from Pendleton Herring's address to the American Political Science Association (APSA) in September 1953 (Herring 1953). After Gabriel Almond had been invited to become a member of the Committee on Political Behavior, he noted that 'Herring ... in his presidential address ... raised questions about the condition of the study of comparative and foreign governments and politics. Not long after this the Committee on Political Behavior initiated steps which led to the formation of a separate Committee on Comparative Politics' (1970, 11).

Herring's speech came in the midst of the congressional investigations into tax-exempt foundations (u.s. Congress 1953; 1954). Whether these allegations directly influenced the research priorities of the Ford Foundation and the ssrc, one can only speculate. Nevertheless, Herring's presidential address evinced a new resolve to align political science with private foundations in a common effort to solve the problems faced by the United States in the new world order. Political science, in Herring's view, required 'support from official agencies and from private foundations.' Support of this kind 'will often be granted when specific plans are drawn up and concrete projects offered for consideration.' Moreover, 'the problems of present-day government call for more systematic, better-supported, and larger-scale fact-gathering if political scientists are to do their jobs effectively and if citizens are to understand the nature of their political institutions' (Herring 1953, 966). Herring envisioned a close working relationship between the foundations, funding agencies, and political science in the pursuit of America's national interest. As 'part of our national strength,' the political science profession, maintained Herring, 'is the core of that broad and continuing study of government and thoughtful concern with politics vital to the successful operation of free institutions' (961). In Herring's view, with the changing global circumstances, political science must of necessity consider domestic issues in their international context.

Today, basic questions of national destiny and of world stability are bound up with phenomena quite beyond the day-to-day experience of most citizens. A rational response and a responsible attitude in such a situation can best come as the consequence of thought applied to knowledge. As government extends to matters far beyond the familiarity gained through participation, or direct observation, the conscious effort at understanding – that is to say, the study – of government becomes vitally important. (962)

By implication, one of the tasks of political science was to help in the process of adjusting national will to the international exigencies of the day and to cultivate 'effective political behavior' (962). At 'a time when world responsibilities demand courageous and constructive action,' Herring averred, 'we cannot as citizens permit faith diminished in our capacity as a free nation to direct public policies to the enhancement of justice and liberty at home and abroad' (974). To these ends, suggested Herring, political science had a good deal of responsibility for discovering how political behaviour intersected with democratic government and for affirming the values that made this form of politics possible. 'The study of government must proceed from the values that make the Republic secure and free. Teaching enlightened by these values has never been more meaningful. Because the constant study of government is integral to the successful operation of our institutions, the teaching of political science is a high calling and one that remains squarely within the tradition of liberal education' (964). At the same time, in Herring's view, the support of democratic values must work in tandem with empirical research, for 'big democracy needs to know itself. Big business, big labor, and big agriculture all find large-scale, systematic data-collection and analysis too useful to do without. The conduct of large-scale operations calls for large-scale fact-gathering and fact-analysis' (965). Such empirical research was to be directed internationally as well: 'Hard training, sober judgment, and systematic effort is required to disclose and analyze adequately the designs of Soviet Imperialism. The exposure of these maneuverings is a job for specialists, and requires high intelligence' (972).

Herring cautioned that the sheer accretion of empirical data does not guarantee professional progress, for 'research, as unbridled empiricism, offers little beyond the practical utility that specific findings may have for an immediate purpose' (967). Only if political analysis is informed by 'theoretical work' can the significance of research and the cumulativeness of its findings be assured. The most crucial task of a comparative approach, then, is to develop its theory, in the sense of 'a conceptual scheme for the analysis and ordering of empirical data on political behavior' (968). Herring, however, did not separate the scientific development of politics from the problems of democracy. A refurbished political science would, as it were, protect democracy from demagoguery by offering a realistic definition of the situation to the public (973).

The development of theory in political science would not only ensure greater rigour and the cumulativeness of results, but would also contribute to the workings of democratic politics. 'As we clarify and develop political science as a discipline,' Herring argued, 'we both serve our professional needs and perform the vital function of helping our democracy to know itself better' (971). To this end, Herring felt that the most promising direction for political science lay in the comparative field.

I think a strong case can be made for greater attention to a comparative approach across the wide range of political science – comparative public law, comparative political philosopy, comparative political institutions and governmental systems, comparative political behavior whether of individuals or societies. We have found, in trying to explain our political institutions to peoples in other countries, that there is not nearly enough in the literature of American government and democracy that is suitable for export. Can it be that, in the past,

*we have been so much concerned with piecemeal reports, or frag-
mented studies of our own system that we have missed analyzing as
fully as we should the larger picture – the factors that have made this
country so relatively strong, productive, and free? (966)*

In Herring's view, the comparative study of politics was the approach
most appropriate to political science's study of the intersecting domestic and international problems faced by the United States. Such a
theoretical consolidation of the comparative approach would enable
political scientists to take advantage of the Ford Foundation's growing
beneficence, since the foundation had begun (in the midst of the
congressional investigations into tax-exempt foundations) to place
greater funding priority on research that contributed to promoting the
cause of the free world against communism. In light of the Ford
Foundation's shifting concerns, the development of a behavioural
orientation by political science did not by itself hold out the promise of
attracting long-run material support. What was needed in addition to a
concern for understanding the realities of behaviour was a conceptual
framework that permitted comparisons between American democracy
and other political systems. Only by grasping what forces, conditions,
and attitudes made for democratic as opposed to totalitarian politics
could desired political change be brought about. The theoretical
framework that was to guide research in comparative politics had to
serve the purpose not only of integrating empirical data, but also of
providing a normatively referential basis for comparing political
development abroad with the American prototype. These concerns
were implicit in the early deliberations of the Committee on Research
on Comparative Politics, which quickly took shape after Herring's
presidential address.

Democratic Practice and Democratic Theory

In line with the reorientation of political behaviour research outlined in
Herring's speech, the study *Voting* (Berelson, Lazarsfeld, McPhee [1954]
1968) represented a reconciliation between empirical research and a
normative defence of politics. This new direction was most evident in
the concluding chapter of *Voting* written by Bernard Berelson, who had
come to play an important role in acting as a mediator between survey
research and the concerns of the Ford Foundation. Echoing the remarks
of the Reece committee, he noted that 'with respect to politics,
empirical-analytic theory and normative theory have only recently

become truly separated – and often to their mutual disadvantage and impoverishment' (305). It was through the results of survey research, he argued, that political theory could be revitalized.

The voting studies seemed to indicate that the average voter was less motivated, less knowledgeable, and less rational than classical theories would suggest. Rather than taking these indications as a sign that the system was awry, Berelson concluded that the conception of democracy itself had to be reconstructed to fit the empirical data: 'Classic theory is defective ... in its concentration on the *individual citizen*. What are undervalued are certain collective properties that reside in the electorate as a whole and in the political and social system in which it functions' (312). Berelson went beyond the empiricist limitations of survey-research data by placing their results within a *normative framework* corresponding to the institutions of American democracy. The apathy, irrationality, and ignorance the data uncovered were not thought to be morally questionable, but rather were viewed as the *functional* requirements making for systemic stability. The shortcomings of the voters had to be evaluated on a *systemic* basis. Such personal qualities as indifference and apathy actually contributed to the heterogeneity and stability of the political order (314–15).

Explaining empirical findings in terms of normative theory, Berelson was able to parry the critical thrust of classical political theory. For if the realignment of political theory meant that 'its categories are the categories in which political life really occurs,' then an independent normative critique was no longer credible. In so affirming democratic values through empirical research, it would be possible 'to clarify the standards and correct the empirical presuppositions of normative theory.' This meant that such research would be 'more realistic and more pertinent to the problems of policy' (306).

In terms of future empirical research, the framework of Berelson and his associates raised questions of how elite politics could be combined with mass electoral activity, permitting a balance between stability/ flexibility, involvement/indifference, progress/conservation, and consensus/cleavage. *Voting*, by linking politics and society and fusing prescriptive and descriptive elements, provided sociology with the same basis for reorientation that Herring's APSA speech gave to political science. In their respective efforts to integrate research into political behaviour with a normative defence of democracy, the two disciplines converged towards a common political sociological approach. The path to this convergence was led by Gabriel Almond, focusing on comparative politics and by Seymour Martin Lipset, focusing on the sociology of politics. In seeking to develop and consolidate the theoretical basis for cumulative research of empirical and normative relevance to the growth and spread of American democracy, Almond and Lipset adapted and elaborated the framework for social-scientific activity developed by Talcott Parsons.

10

Gabriel Almond and Comparative Politics

Almond's Political Development

As the self-confessed 'exhorter' and 'lead hound' of the Committee on Comparative Politics from 1954 to 1963, Almond brought to political studies an activist commitment strikingly comparable to that of Talcott Parsons (Almond 1970, 11–13). In the same manner that Parsons's social-scientific concerns could be understood as a translation of liberal Calvinist faith into secular activities, Almond's efforts on behalf of political science appear to be derived from his Judaic upbringing. As he noted in an autobiographical statement:

As a child I spent each Sabbath confronted by four texts – the Bible in Hebrew, a version of the King James translation, the six volumes of Graetz's History of the Jews *and* The Jewish Wars *by Flavius Josephus ... moving from one to the other with the expectation of being examined by my father on their contents ... Repeating this experience year after year I recapitulated in my own theological development the centuries-long history of Israel's search for deity and for national identity. The issues and the models of this history acquired a vividness and a contemporaneity for me which they have never lost.* (1970, 5)

Almond reveals that his faith took the form of a search for redemption: 'In adult life I have never thought of myself as a man of religious faith, but I believe this search for some form of grace and redemption, without being able to specify their contents, or the most appropriate ways of cultivating them, has remained with me as a powerful theme in both personal and professional life' (1970, 6).

Almond's personal quest for redemption was linked to his identification with the plight of the Jewish nation 'in the Diaspora after the fall of Jerusalem.' Almond, however, could accept neither of the two ways of 'coping with Jewishness' provided by historical example. On the one hand, the actions of Simon bar Giora, in Almond's view, represented a form of 'fanaticism' (7).[1] On the other hand, he could not abide by the 'opportunism of Josephus.'[2] In searching 'for this elusive form of redemption,' without falling prey to either 'ritual and liturgy' or 'mysticism,' Almond was compelled to choose 'means and approach to problem-solving' which combined 'continuity' and 'adaptation' (7). In Almond's view, his 'pre-professional background' accounted for 'the particular manner in which [he] responded to the tensions between opportunities for theorizing, for carrying on empirical research, and for contributing to public policy' (7–8). In particular, this search for redemption left him 'with skepticism and irreverence for two other professional modalities – the Pharisaic identification of "knowing" with method, with instruments and procedures on one hand; and with the naive and direct "knowing" of the prophet-like humanists, on the other.' In the same manner that Parsons sought a reconciliation between rationalist utopianism and idealist traditionalism, Almond sought to steer a middle course between instrumentalism and intuitionism. And similar to Parsons's sublimation of Calvinist activism into his calling as a social scientist, Almond's orientation to the study of politics was influenced by his redemptive concerns. Almond's activist inclinations appear to have been strengthened during the period he spent as an undergraduate and graduate student at the University of Chicago (1928–38). Charles Merriam – as one who had a 'direct and lasting effect' on his work – Almond saw as having a 'style and manner which reminded [him] of the Old Testament and [his] father.' Merriam, in Almond's view, 'was an exhorter, a mover, a prophet,' who not only encouraged 'innovation and experiment,' but also ridiculed the younger members of the department 'for losing contact with real problems' (8–9). He described his intellectual debt:

Merriam bridged my childhood into my professional socialization. He stood for continuity with the past, but looked toward a future of the social sciences as the ultimate stage of the enlightenment which would bring man's capacity for reason to bear on the ugly and intractable problems of the human situation – exploitation, manipulation and war. He consolidated my own impulses against formalism and reductionism. (1970, 9)

While Almond's writings indicated little concern for alleviating the miseries that supposedly moved Merriam, he none the less viewed the mission of the social scientist as an inherently moral and active one. His view of social-scientific practice as an ethical pursuit is evident from his contribution to a symposium on politics and ethics conducted in the pages of the *American Political Science Review* during and shortly after the Second World War (1946). The preceding two articles (Whyte 1943; Hallowell 1944) had consisted of a challenge to political scientists from William F. Whyte, 'in the spirit of "scientific detachment" from man's aspiration and strivings,' followed by an attack by John H. Hallowell on 'the logical fallacies on Whyte's argument' (Almond 1946, 283). Much of the debate turned on Whyte's contention that political scientists should ' "leave ethics to the philosophers and concern themselves with the description and analysis of political behavior" ' (in Almond 1946, 284). Almond's response was to join Hallowell in dissenting from this view and to offer an elaboration of why Whyte's argument was untenable. 'Whyte's position with regard to the relation between science and ethics,' argued Almond, 'is a product of that "scientificism" which has exercised an unfortunate influence upon the social sciences, particularly since the last war.' Agreeing with Hallowell's judgment that such a perspective constitutes 'an evasion of the scientist's responsibility as a man,' (285) Almond contended that the social scientist should not leave ethics to the philosopher, but rather ought to take the responsibility of exercising 'practical judgment of "good and evil" in the area of public policy.'

If a political scientist concludes that 'a particular public policy may have dangerous consequences,' Almond advocated he should 'make himself articulate on the subject.' Indeed, 'if his feelings are strong, there is no reason why he should not become a warm advocate. And there is no reason why warm advocacy and cool objectivity cannot commingle in the same lecture, article, or book.' Because the political scientist 'is a man and partakes of the fate of men,' Almond maintained that he 'should be concerned with the consequences of public policy, and particularly with whether the consequences are "good or bad." ' Almond suggested, then, that science and morality are fully reconcilable. Sympathy for others, as he saw it, 'is in no way in conflict with the capacity for scientific objectivity.' Indeed, 'if his reactions are "healthy," he will be concerned with just these problems which are the matters of social controversy. He will be concerned with the most rational (and therefore the most ethical) solutions of these problems' (292). Correspondingly, in Almond's view, the work of the social scientist 'must be of some use to his community. It must be related to the community's interests or needs' rather than 'to the service of particular "interests." ' For the political scientist in particular, Almond concluded, this implied that 'his function is an essentially ethical one [emphasis mine]. For it is his task to discover the pathway to "good" ends. And desiring and influencing so that the "right path" to the "good end" is taken, far from being in conflict with his duty as a scientist, is the very essence of his responsibility as a scientist and a man' (293).

Almond's personal concerns about redemption were reflected in the orientation he advocated for the social sciences. In his view, the social scientist was to actively participate in the process of policy formation, thereby helping society move towards an idealized state. His contention that the social sciences were inherently of ethical relevance thus coincided with Parsons's views about how the social scientist could articulate ultimate values to secular society.

Like Parsons, Almond felt obliged to recite the Weberian litany in order to justify his blend of science and ethics. He expressed his conception of the 'scientific calling' in the conclusion to his study of communism's appeals:

It is one of the obligations of the scientific calling that, while ethical impulses may affect the selection of a problem and the purposes for which the findings are used, they may not enter into the scientific process – that is, affect the methods of research of the findings themselves. Persons who are unfamiliar with the scientific discipline or who find its requirements uncongenial often assume that this ethical neutrality of the scientific process reflects a general ethical neutrality in those who carry on the work of science. Certainly, for the social sciences nothing could be further from the truth. Indeed, a kind of moral fatigue results from the sustained investigation of a problem such as the present one, which is full of human meaning and significance, and in which ethical and political digressions have, so to speak, been prohibited. (1954, 370)

How one could separate 'ethical impulses' from 'methods of research or the findings' in practice is difficult to understand. Given that both methods and conclusions are premised on values, their alleged objectivity is vitiated by their underlying moral basis. Indeed, The Appeals of Communism (with methods, categories, and content chosen for their relevance to diagnosing and suppressing 'communist' views) could attain scientific objectivity only though the definitional sleight of hand provided by the fact/value dichotomy. More at issue for Almond than the validity of social-scientific research per se was its public meaning and social consequences. By invoking the distinction between facts and values, he could both give free rein to his moral and political preferences, and claim the authority of science for his pronouncements. By virtue of their scientific stature, his statements about political and social life could prescribe particular beliefs and actions for members of civil society, and contribute to the formation of public policy through the clarification of ends and the specification of means.

Almond's practical concerns led him to advocate an orientation for the social sciences strikingly similar to that of Parsons's primary patterns. Like Parsons, Almond saw his theoretical constructs as reflecting empirical reality.[3] Since these theoretical artefacts were of intended moral consequence for the social order, their empirical content was also informed by his redemptive concerns. This meant that empirical reality found its way into Almond's theoretical framework in selective and refracted ways. In reflecting upon the same social reality as did Parsons – American state and society in their Cold War setting – his theoretical approach bore an isomorphic relationship to the constituent features of that order.

Almond, Parsons, and Social-Scientific Practice

The Professional Social Sciences and the Cold War

Like Parsons, Almond believed that the professional strata had a mission to be of service to society. And in a manner similar to that of Parsons, Almond believed that this responsibility was of particular significance given the interdependence between America's post-war position in the world and her domestic political environment. As Almond attested, 'America's capacity for wise foreign policy decisions' in its 'position of world leadership' required both 'military and economic calculations' along with 'an estimate of "psychological potential"' ([1950] 1960, 3). Just as Parsons was concerned with the strains attendant upon America's assumption of world leadership, Almond attacked the 'deviational foreign policy positions,' which stood in disagreement with the 'main themes of contemporary foreign policy,' namely, 'resistance to Communist expansion by economic, diplomatic, propaganda, and, if necessary, military means, and the establishment of a peaceful and legal international order in which American material and security interests would be protected' (159).

Both theorists held the view that much of the responsibility for overcoming internal dissent and cultivating a Cold War consensus devolved upon the cultural elites. In the same way that Parsons called for a close alliance between a strengthened political elite and 'predominantly "cultural" elements' (Parsons [1954] 1963, 229) Almond argued that a foreign-policy consensus was dependent upon the activities of 'the policy and opinion elites,' which he saw as 'the articulate policy-bearing stratum of the population which gives structure to the public, and which provides the effective means of access to the various groupings' (Almond [1950] 1960, 138). According to Almond, effective foreign policy turned on the interplay between the political elites and the attentive public, mediated by the activities of the 'policy and opinion elites.' Echoing Parsons, Almond stressed that 'the hallmark of a mature democratic elite' bearing the responsibility for giving 'structure to the public' was its *professionalism* (236). In defining the constituent features of the professionalized policy and opinion elites, in general, and of the social sciences, in particular, Almond's account bore a close resemblance to Parsons's discussion of the primary patterns.

Disinterestedness and the Public-Opinion Elites

According to Almond, professionalism was founded on 'certain standards of performance [and] the constant evaluation of performance according to the criteria set by the calling itself.' The professionalism of 'the various foreign policy elites ... involves a constant search for the most adequate policy means to realize the values of their clienteles regardless of the causes, interests or goals they happen to serve' (Almond [1950] 1960, 237–8). Ultimately, argued Almond, if the various professional groups disinterestedly pursued their value preferences, 'there comes a point where the values of humanity, nation, and class begin to converge, where common values begin to take their place beside the special ones. This is the "end of the rainbow" of the great rational consensus aspirations of Western man; it is to be sought in the modern era not by democratic spontaneity, but by democratic professionalism' (238).

Closely paralleling Parsons's line of thought, then, Almond held that through the activities and efforts of professionals in various segments of society, a rational consensus could be cultivated.[4] In the same way that Parsons saw the professions as the bearers of objectively conceived ultimate values, Almond thus viewed the professionalized policy and opinion elites as the redemptive force in post-war America. Like Parsons, Almond placed particular stress upon the universities as integral to the building of a national foreign-policy consensus. As he noted in an address to the Army War College on 3 January 1956, 'the forces which can limit the impact of special interest, can contain and overcome indifference and panic, are the attentive public, the universities and colleges which train it, and the quality media which inform it' (1956a, 377). He placed particular stress upon the 'social scientist in institutions of higher learning' as playing a vital role in constituting a consensus. In his view, the social scientist possessed impressive powers because 'practically the whole of the younger elite generation is subject to his influence – future politicians, diplomats, journalists, columnists, clergymen, teachers, trade-union and interest association leaders.' And 'in his capacity as scholar and expert he has a direct channel to public opinion and policy-making' ([1950a] 1960, 153). The social scientist's impact upon the public sphere was ineluctable, maintained Almond, for 'the social sciences in the modern university constitute a kind of throat through which the future elite generations pass' (156). This affords the social sciences an 'enormous opportunity. For they receive the elite cadres at points in their development when there is still a certain flexibility and openness, a receptivity to challenging ideals and images' (157).

Since the 'attentive public ... is largely a college-educated public, and the political, interest, and communications elites are also largely college trained,' Almond concluded that 'it is in the social sciences in the universities that a democratic ideological consensus can be fostered and a democratic elite discipline encouraged' (157). In a manner akin to that of Parsons, Almond maintained that an important locus of disinterested professional activity was in the social science departments of relatively autonomous universities. In specifying the nature of professionalized practice as it pertained to policy formation and consensus, Almond's account bore a close resemblance to that of Parsons.

Universalism and Instrumental Knowledge

Paralleling Parsons's emphasis upon universalism as embodied in general theory, Almond was preoccupied with the production of social-scientific knowledge with the potential for application by the policy elites. In the face of the 'Soviet-Communist threat' that 'has become more explicit and immediate' ([1950] 1960, 107), Almond despaired of political science's lack of preparedness for providing instrumental knowledge pertinent to the policy problems of the state apparatus. 'Since the end of the war,' concluded Almond, 'the political scientist has primarily played the role of providing the historical and descriptive background on foreign governments and politics, foreign and international legal institutions, and foreign ideologies' (155). In Almond's view, such research was of marginal relevance to the formation of effective policy, for it largely ignored the 'basic social, psychological, and economic factors as they apply to policy problems' (156). Accordingly, argued Almond, 'a scientifically adequate approach to the problems of public opinion and public policy must begin with knowledge of psychic, social, and political structure and processes. This is the beginning of realism in the analysis of a democratic policy-making process' (4–5).

Almond considered the prediction and control of public opinion to be a major problem confronting the policy elites. Attitudes held by the public, in Almond's view, were scientifically knowable phenomena that could be technically manipulated by the correct application of *means*. The social scientist could contribute to the choice of the appropriate means by providing empirical knowledge about the psychological, social, and economic conditions making for particular sorts of political behaviour.

Affective Neutrality and Foreign-Policy Consensus

At the same time, however, comparable to Parsons's emphasis upon affective neutrality and cultural commitment, Almond believed that the social scientist could play a vital role in the cultivation of a foreign-policy consensus, which in his view, 'derives from an ideological consensus, a basic acceptance of the importance of reconciling individual freedom with mass welfare. The essential spirit of our foreign policy consensus derives from the will to maintain and foster this value compromise against the threat of Communist expansion.'

Such a consensus involved, as well, 'an agreement on means,' in the sense of giving normative approval to 'the use of any of the instrumentalities of foreign policy [or] some degree of flexibility in considering the threat of coercion implied in security diplomacy' ([1950] 1960, 192). Almond sought to elaborate the most suitable 'tactics of a public information program in the sphere of foreign affairs.' He saw the generation of an agreement on the means and ends of foreign policy as an active process, demanding the dedicated co-operation of the opinion and policy elites. As noted, he put particular emphasis upon the 'social sciences in the universities' for fostering 'democratic ideological consensus' and encouraging 'elite discipline' (235). It was Almond's view that the social scientist did not communicate directly with the general public but rather shaped the view of the elites and the attentive public. These strata, in turn, set the standards of foreign-policy awareness and understanding for the mass public. 'Through a disciplined democratic elite and a broad attentive public,' argued Almond, 'foreign policy moods may be contained, and gross fluctuations in attitude checked [for] the general public looks for *cues* for *mood responses* in public discussion of foreign policy' (232). Accordingly, the social sciences would largely direct their efforts towards clarifying 'the value premises and conflicts of the politically significant cultures and social groupings of our time.' In 'the absence of a coherent theory of society and politics,' the democratic elites, maintained Almond, were both undisciplined and ideologically confused. If the social sciences could 'achieve a measure of theoretical clarity,' he conjectured, 'a type of discussion of public policy issues in which premises would be explicit and consequences of alternative policies comparatively clear' could be facilitated. He concluded that 'A democratic discipline and a democratic consensus do not call for full and continuous agreement. What they require are a rational statement of the alternatives and a consensus as to the mode of selection among them. A homogeneous training in this kind of policy analysis might contribute to the development of a common language among the various elite sectors, a common method of problem-setting and problem-solving' (235).

The social sciences as a profession would contribute to the cultivation of a foreign-policy consensus. This was fully in keeping with 'the dignity of the social-scientific calling [which] rests on the clarification of value premises, the analysis of the adequacy of means, and the consequences of social action.' Indeed, given the importance of training 'character and intellect ... a special responsibility attaches to those who have the task of interpreting man and his institutions to the new elite generation' (238). Almond's contention that the social scientist ought to 'clarify the value premises' of society, thereby contributing to foreign-policy consensus, thus coincided with Parsons's emphasis upon the professionalized social sciences' 'fiduciary responsibility' to 'define the situation' for the general public.

Functional Specificity and Social-Scientific Co-operation

Paralleling Parsons's interest in encouraging a division of labour among the social sciences, Almond advocated that the various branches of social-scientific inquiry co-operate in an effort to provide knowledge of strategic relevance to the post-war problems of policy. And, like Parsons, Almond felt that the social sciences could develop their strategic relevance for policy formation and the building of consensus by giving greater emphasis to the psycho-cultural approach to the understanding of human behaviour. In particular, he maintained that 'there is urgent need for the introduction of psycho-cultural insights in the analysis of the policy-making process itself, a need which cannot be adequately served by political scientists familiar with comparative government and politics but untrained or half-trained in anthropology and psychology' (1950a, 281). It was through incorporation of the insights provided by 'these "younger brothers" of the social sciences' (282) that political science could go beyond its traditional descriptive and historical concerns to develop an approach of relevance to the urgent problems confronting the United States in the post-war period.

Nevertheless, Almond did not maintain that political science ought to be supplanted by 'the newer social science approaches, such as social psychology and anthropology.' Even though, in his view, 'they have developed methods of the first importance and have been enormously productive of insights and hypotheses,' their proposals for foreign policy were often amateurish and pretentious. He maintained, then, that 'if these newer disciplines wish to deliver on their claims to policy relevance, they have to recognize that they have but a piece of the picture and that they cannot fully grasp the potentialities and limitations of their own contributions until they become aware of the contributions and methods of their neighboring disciplines' ([1950] 1960, 156). While Almond offered 'wholehearted support to the efforts on the part of anthropologists to reach policy-makers and the public with these basic insights,' and gave his 'support to ... their efforts to apply their hypotheses and methods in the analysis of the social-psychological factors which affect policy-making in modern nations' (1950a, 279), he none the less admonished them for their overzealousness.

Things will really begin to click when the students in these disciplines turn from an excessive preoccupation with the virtues and skills of the self, and direct attention at what they have to learn from the world. They will discover when they turn to the sober task of analysis of modern society and international relations that there are other workers in the vineland of the Lord who, though lacking in modern tools, have nevertheless developed certain rude formulae about when to come in out of the rain. (281)

In the same way that Parsons advocated a division of labour anchored by sociology, Almond wished to see greater co-operation between political science and other disciplines in the production of knowledge relevant to public policy (see Lerner and Lasswell 1951). It was through this reorientation that the 'policy-sciences' – anchored in political science but heavily informed by the socio-cultural approach – were to be of strategic relevance to the American nation-state in the period after the Second World War.

The Committee on Research in Comparative Politics

The new SSRC Committee on Research in Comparative Politics was formed at a conference held in Princeton on 11–12 December 1953. During the first few years, according to Almond, questions of research strategy dominated the committee's activities. In particular, it concerned itself with 'introducing theoretical sophistication and methodological rigor into the study of non-Western political systems; and ... overcoming the formal and institutional bias of Western European studies' (1970, 14).

These considerations figured prominently in two memoranda that guided the discussions of the committee in the early years (Kahin, Pauker, and Pye 1955; Almond, Cole, and Macridis 1955). Dealing with strategies for researching political development in non-Western countries and Western Europe, the two influential papers helped to make the new committee 'a channel through which [the] theories and research methodologies' of behaviouralism 'began to be applied in European and non-Western contexts' (Almond 1970, 14). As the memoranda reveal, however, the committee members were motivated by more than mere scholarly curiosity. 'With respect to most non-Western countries,' attested Kahin, Pauker, and Pye in their paper, 'it remains difficult to foresee whether the consequences of social change are to be stable, viable political practices or endemic instabilities in government. In many cases, it is still an open question whether the future will bring them a liberal democratic form of politics or some type of authoritarian rule such as communism' (1022). The authors concluded by expressing their vital concern 'with the patterns of political development in societies that have set as their goal the liberal democratic model of politics. Thus both a scientific and a moral-political purpose may be served by the development of a systematic comparative politics' (1041).

In their paper outlining a possible strategy for researching Western

European politics, Almond, Cole, and Macridis enunciated a similar set of practical assumptions:

The impulse for this memorandum arises from ... urgent and practical considerations. The survival of parliamentary and democratic institutions on the European continent is by no means to be taken for granted. The political communities of the major Western European countries – France, Germany, and Italy – are fragmented into exclusive ideological movements. Large bodies of opinion appear to be alienated from the West, politically apathetic, or actively recruited to communism. (1955, 1043)

In developing a research strategy to deal effectively with the foreign cultures in question, both sets of authors turned away from the legal/historical/philosophical approach. This kind of analysis, which 'characterizes the scholarship dealing with these [Western European countries],' argued Almond et al., 'is not by itself adequate to discover how serious these cleavages and alienations are, for by admission the basic problems of civic loyalty and political cohesion lie in large part outside of the formal governmental framework.' This pointed towards the development of 'other methods and approaches ... if we are to have a proper understanding of the causes of the persistent evils of continental European government and politics – instability, stalemate, and the alienation of large elements of the population from the political community' (1043).

In a like manner, Kahin, Pauker, and Pye indicated a scepticism about understanding the politics of non-Western countries through formal institutional analysis because, in their view, structures adopted from the West could conceivably perform functions other than those for which they were intended (1027). By viewing politics in terms of functions and behaviour, the researcher would be better attuned to understanding dysfunctions and extremist behaviour. This was of particular importance because of the 'high rate of recruitment of new elements into political activity' (1024), which made for much volatility. 'In non-Western countries,' argued the authors, 'all the potential political elements do not usually manifest themselves in a continuous manner.' There was, rather, 'an element of latency in the politics of such countries, with many aspirant elites able to enter the political arena only in a sudden, erratic, and often violent way.' This made for a 'potentially explosive' form of politics, as the 'unorganized and generally inarticulate segments of the society' suddenly found expression.

This pattern stood in contrast to the West, where 'regardless of how weak they may be, most potential interests are manifest in the political process and thus a continuous form of adjustment of relative power is possible' (1026).

This preoccupation with potentially disruptive political movements was evident in the research interests of the members of the Committee on Comparative Politics. Shortly after the onset of the European Recovery Program, Almond wrote a lengthy memorandum (1948) whose purpose was to analyse the strength, composition, and influence of Western European movements, and discuss 'the problem of strengthening and stabilizing the moderate, democratic trends in the crisis areas of Western Europe' (2). Guiding Almond's analysis was his concern to understand how the ' "moderate center" ' holding to 'moderate aims and democratic methods' could be cultivated in the face of the two main 'extremes,' namely, 'Communist infiltration and subversion' and 'right-wing authoritarianism.' To this end, argued Almond, 'the assumption that we can keep Western Europe out of the Soviet orbit by measures of economic aid' (35) was questionable. 'It is imperative,' he maintained, 'that we avoid placing all our hopes on the effectiveness of *economic* aid as a means of re-establishing political stability.' Almond instead advocated that greater stress be placed upon politico-military force to counteract the activities of the Soviets (38). It was fitting, then, that Almond's next major study was of 'the appeals of Communism,' an investigation intending to 'throw light on the kinds of social situations and attitudes which contribute to susceptibility to Communism.' Such an analysis, in Almond's view, would serve to 'increase our understanding of the vulnerability of the free world to Communist penetration.' He suggested that 'if we can discover those aspects of the Communist experience which create dissatisfaction among party members and contribute to defection, we may be in a position to suggest the kinds of weaknesses and vulnerabilities which are to be found within the Communist movement.' These contributions would, he hoped, 'provide useful leads in appraising the various policy approaches to the Communist problem' (1954, ix).

On the basis of his analysis of communist tendencies in various countries, Almond was able to propose potentially fruitful policy guide-lines. He was particularly concerned about the fate of France and Italy, where the Communists 'still can mount serious electoral threats [as] the strongest and most effectively organized political movements in these countries' (385). As a means of countering these tendencies, Almond advocated the formation of 'a broad non-Communist movement on the left,' serving as an alternative to communism (388). It is evident that Almond's own research was intended to complement an offensive of this sort. For if 'Western resources' were to be 'adequately engaged' in the 'field of political warfare,' a more detailed understanding of why particular groups were 'disaffected and susceptible to Communism' was necessary (398).

It was also a concern with the potential influence of 'left-wing political theories' in developing countries that gave rise to Lucian Pye's study of communism in Malaya (1956). Given the prevailing 'inarticulateness and ambiguity' of societies in transition, argued Pye, 'it is not surprising that the most coherent political theories and philosophies are those which are imported.' Fittingly, the doctrines that were almost inevitably chosen, he maintained, were 'those which appear the most explicit, the most formal, and the most embracing,' which comprised 'at this stage in the history of Western political thought,' in his view, 'the ideas of the political left rather than the more eclectic and possibly more subtle ideas of the political center' (347). The attractiveness of such theories was enhanced, Pye surmised, by the particular set of circumstances obtaining in transitional societies. Rejecting 'the simple belief' that attainment of self-government made it possible 'for the country to muddle through in its resistance to Communism,' Pye advanced the thesis 'that the real basis of the Communist appeal in underdeveloped countries is the sense of rootlessness of people separated from their traditional ways and unable to realize their ambitions according to new ones.' This in turn implies that 'the post-colonial period may prove to be the time when the appeals of Communism are the greatest. Possibly the real struggle against Communism is still to occur in countries like India, Burma, and Indonesia' (354).

The propensity of traditional societies to embrace communism, Pye emphasized, underscored the importance of advancing a coherent and pervasive political theory *alternative* to that of communism. Such a theory, in his view, would be 'relevant to the actual condition,' and imply a certain set of 'institutional or organizational arrangements that can provide a basis for furthering such ideas.' Political theories, as 'patterns of political thought and behavior which are appropriate to the social problems common to a people in the process of sharp cultural change,' must provide 'a basis for group action that can enable the individual to see that his own efforts have effect and that he can realize personal status and security ... The simple existence of such alternative opportunities for political action can in itself be a powerful factor in destroying much of the attraction of Communism' (355). Pye suggested that an alternative political theory must be aligned with new organizational forms if communism were to be effectively combated. 'For us to try to engage the Communists in a struggle of ideas in the underdeveloped areas of the world without contributing to the organizational basis of democratic ideas and beliefs is to court failure' (356).

It is evident from these analyses that the shortcomings of the legal/historical/traditional approach were as much practical as they were theoretical. If the conditions making for certain forms of political behaviour were to be empirically understood, it was necessary to go beyond formal structures and constitutional arrangements. Given its stated practical intentions of contributing to the spread of democracy, comparative politics required a theoretical orientation that affirmed democratic values. By communicating this standard of political development into the public spheres of foreign nations, it was hoped that the actions and beliefs of the citizenry could be reoriented. While members of the committee were aware of the importance of such a theory for the future of comparative politics, the initial exploratory papers failed to produce a conceptual framework around which the new approach could consolidate. Such a theoretical breakthrough, however, was not long in coming. Through his conjunction of the political culture with the political system, Almond indicated how empirical studies of political behaviourism could be combined with the affirmation of democratic values. This innovative move drew extensively on the schema previously developed by Talcott Parsons.

A Theoretical Framework for Comparative Politics

Consistent with his commitment to the incorporation of insights from other fields into political science, Almond's paper on comparative political systems for the 1956 conference held by the committee on the Comparative Method in the Study of Politics sought to show how 'certain sociological and anthropological concepts' could be of use in comparing the world's major political systems. Reiterating his earlier assessment of how the new social sciences could best be adapted to the study of politics, Almond contended that social theory was in no sense 'a conceptual cure-all for the ailments of the discipline,' for 'there are many ways of laboring in the vineyard of the Lord, and I am quite prepared to concede that there are more musical forms of psalmody than sociological jargon' ([1956] 1970, 29). Given Almond's preoccupation with the redemptive implications of an individual's calling, the biblical metaphor had more than allegorical significance. By adapting the insights from anthropology and sociology, comparative politics was to become strategically relevant to the growth and development of the modern nation-state. Indeed, in applying insights from 'the Parsons-Weber tradition in social theory' (32) to the field of politics, Almond had inadvertently derived a practically relevant political system akin to that of Parsons. And similar to the political system of Parsons, Almond's perspective represented at once a depiction of reality and a basis for the organization of research – a duality that would ensure its redemptive potential. The empirical model of the political system assumed the standpoint of the modern nation-state faced with the complementary problems of acting in its domestic and external environments, while ensuring these lines of action were legitimated.

Almond's conception of the political system fused the 'state' and 'nation' into a unitary concept. From Weber he borrowed the notion of 'a specialized apparatus' that possesses 'the legitimate monopoly of physical coercion over a given territory and population' (33). Almond then combined Weber's conception of the state apparatus with Parsons's perspective on social structure to produce the notion of the political system. He saw a political system as 'a system of *action.*' This perspective, with its emphasis upon how behaviour is systematically regulated by norms and institutions, in his view, permitted one to go beyond legal and ethical descriptions. In particular, he found the concept of *system* helpful, because it 'satisfies the need for an inclusive concept which covers all of the patterned actions relevant to the making of political decisions.' Drawing directly on Parsons and Shils, Almond maintained that 'the unit of the political system is the role "that organizational sector of an actor's orientation which constitutes and defines his participation in an interactive process"' (Parsons and Shils 1951 in Almond [1956] 1970, 32). 'It involves a set of complementary expectations concerning his own actions and those of others with whom he interacts.' Hence, in Almond's view, 'a political system may be defined as a set of interacting rôles, or as a structure of rôles, if we understand by *structure* a patterning of interactions' (32). In applying the Parsonsian concepts of 'system,' 'action,' and 'role' to politics, and combining them with Weber's conception of a state apparatus, Almond had thus come to define 'the political system as the patterned inter-action of rôles affecting decisions backed up by the threat of physical compulsion' (34).

Again, following the lead of Parsons, Almond argued that 'every political system is embedded in a set of meanings and purposes' which constitute 'a particular pattern of orientations to political action.' He referred to this as 'the *political culture,*' whose components, 'the modes of orientation of action,' in the form of the 'pattern variables,' he adapted from Parsons and Shils (35). At a descriptive level, the political system was based on the tension between the actions of the state and their legitimation to the public. At the same time, however, the notion of a political system imbedded in a political culture provided a basis for carrying out empirical research. As Pye described it, the concept of political culture served to 'bridge a growing gap in the behavioral approach in political science between the level of microanalysis based on psychological interpretations of the individual's political behavior and the level of macroanalysis based on the variables common to political sociology' (Pye and Verba 1965, 8). Pye elsewhere noted, 'the concept of political culture sought to reduce the gap between macro- and micro-analysis by suggesting that the linkages lie in the complex processes of political socialization by which political systems maintain their continuity and individuals learn to perform appropriate political roles' (1972, 290). In pursuing research guided by the precepts of political culture, the political scientist would be in a position to exert an influence upon the beliefs and actions of the public. For political culture, as 'an ordered subjective realm of politics,' also implied membership for the *social scientist.* Hence, in communicating particular behavioural standards, he could help give 'meaning to the polity, discipline to institutions, and social relevance to individual acts' (Pye and Verba 1965, 7). In this manner, 'the set of attitudes, beliefs, and sentiments which ... provide the underlying assumptions and rules that govern behaviour in the political system' (Pye 1968 and 1972, 288) could be influenced. At the same time, however, the framework provided by the political system permitted the researcher to generate empirical data on political beliefs, values, and attitudes of relevance to policy. What gave this empirical knowledge its relevance was its inherent connection to political culture.

In terms of the strategic designs of comparative politics, political culture thus ensured a practice that was at once empirically based and normatively relevant. This meant that the political theory it projected was not merely evaluative, but 'significantly' oriented. Correspondingly, the data it generated on the conditions making for democratic politics were not discrete and unrelated, but were pertinent to a particular set of values. What provided the *content* to the theoretical framework was the *comparative* dimension. The comparison in question, however, was presupposed by the overriding concern to influence global political development along the lines compatible with the American experience. Almond noted that 'as American interests have broadened to include literally the whole world, our course offerings have expanded to include the many areas outside of Western Europe – Asia, the Middle East, Africa, and Latin America.' This meant, in turn, that 'our requirements in knowledge have become more exacting. We can no longer view political crises in France with detached curiosity or view countries such as Indo-China and Indonesia as interesting political pathologies. We are led to extend our discipline and intensify it simultaneously' (Almond [1956] 1970, 30). The 'baseline' for comparison was the combination of political culture and political system that corresponded to Almond's view of political practices in Great Britain and the United States. By enunciating a political theory that indicated the disparity between the Anglo-American political system and other forms of political organizations, the researcher could provide the policy elites of these countries with a developmental model alternative to communism that could be projected to the public. Empirical information about the conditions making for different kinds of political behaviour could be of use to the elites in controlling 'extremism.' These practical concerns were evident in the 'fourfold classification [of] empirical political systems' Almond saw as 'operative in the world today.' In addition to the Anglo-American, the schema included the Continental European, the pre-industrial, and the totalitarian political systems.

Almond noted that the terms used 'in discriminating the essential properties [of the classes] and bringing out the essential differences between these political systems have emerged out of the Weber-Parsons tradition in social theory' (31–2). By virtue of the categories derived from Parsons, the comparisons made would be vested with practical relevance. By specifying the conditions and orientations making for political stability in the United Kingdom and the United States, this form of organization could be cultivated in other parts of the world. Consistent with these practical aims, Almond based his comparative typology upon a study of the political system found in Great Britain and the United States.

According to Almond, the Anglo-American political system was characterized by a political culture that was both homogeneous and secular. It was homogeneous in that 'there is a sharing of political ends and means' with widespread acceptance of 'some combination of the values of freedom, mass welfare and security [as] the ultimate goals of the political system.' By secular, Almond meant that the political culture was 'rational-calculating, bargaining, and experimental.'

Almond portrayed action in the political culture as at once rationally directed and normatively oriented, akin to Parsons's 'voluntaristic theory of action.' In conjunction with a similarly secular political system, this made for a political process that could be likened to a laboratory. The holders of office and the electors – as occupants of individuated and autonomous roles – bargained with one another at arm's length, with the candidates offering 'hypotheses' in the form of policies. This meant that political outcomes would not only be rationally optimal but consensually based. Providing overall stability to the political system was its role structure, which Almond saw as highly differentiated, with its various units pursuing 'specialized purposes' and performing 'specialized functions in the system.' In keeping with his commitment to the form of politics in Great Britain and the United States, Almond had vested their political institutions with redemptive power. Each of these units, in carrying out its purpose, would contribute to the realization of a stable and functioning political system. From the redemptive standpoint provided by the Anglo-American political system, Almond could then assess other systems in terms of the degree to which they deviated from this prototype (35–8).[5] This concern was particularly evident in Almond's assessment of 'pre-industrial – or partially industrialized and Westernized – political systems.'

The main distinguishing features of these societies, in Almond's view, were 'mixed political cultures and mixed political systems.' The mixture at issue was between the 'Western system with its parliament, its electoral system, its bureaucracy, and the like, and the pre-Western system or systems.' As the different political cultures impinge, various amalgams emerge, depending on the way in which westernization intersects with the traditional cultures. A common by-product of this 'impingement' is a 'charismatic political culture' resulting from political modernization and the breakdown of traditional practices and customs it occasions. This process leads to the release of 'powerful forces' in the form of feelings of anxiety, rootlessness, and directionlessness, all brought about by the disruption of traditional routines, thereby creating 'a large potential for violence' (40–1). As a response to rationalization, tendencies toward charismatic nationalism develop taking one of two forms: either a new set of political norms or an affirmation of more traditional ones. This leads to 'instability and unpredictability,' as the groups having widely differing views of politics come into contact with one another. 'The most serious problems of communication and coordination' that result are exacerbated by the 'political role structure,' characteristic of these societies. Since there typically is 'a low degree of structural differentiation' in pre-industrial political systems, the emergence of the hitherto latent political interest often takes a form that is both 'spontaneous' and 'violent' (34). And since a 'stable and explicit role structure' is lacking, there is both a 'high degree of substitutability of roles' and an unstable 'division of political labor' (41–2).

Finally, and most important, argued Almond, political role structures in pre-industrial political systems tend to be mixed. For example, a formally rational parliament may be at the behest of more traditional elements such as 'a powerful family, a religious sect, a group of tribal chieftains, or some combination of these.' The concepts of 'mixed political culture or mixed political role structures,' Almond concluded, would permit the field researcher 'to grapple more quickly and more adequately with political phenomena which he might otherwise over-look or treat as pathologies' (42).

In line with Parsons's views on rationalization, Almond had offered a diagnostic framework for bringing more effective Western influence to bear on pre-industrial political systems. The 'secular, homogeneous' political system provided the implicit standard by which the 'mixed political cultures and mixed political role structures' could be evalua-ted. By projecting this alternative political theory to the elites of 'pre-industrial' political systems, then, the comparative politics move-ment could inculcate a greater awareness of and appreciation for Western values. At the same time, analyses of the social, psychological, and cultural tendencies making for movements of charismatic nationalism or traditionalism would permit policy-makers to map out strategies for broadening the 'moderate center' tendencies in their countries, bringing them closer to the standards set by the 'homogeneous and secular political cultures.'

This concern to understand the degree of deviation from the Anglo-American model was equally evident in Almond's treatment of the continental European political systems, referring 'primarily to France, Germany, and Italy [with] the Scandinavian and Low Countries ... somewhere in between the Continental pattern and the Anglo-American.' The most striking characteristic of these political systems, Almond argued, 'is the fragmentation of political culture,' as a result of an incomplete process of rationalization. The survival of a 'pre-industrial sub-culture' in a number of these countries, he maintained, 'is characterized by a failure on the part of the middle classes in the nineteenth century to carry through a thorough-going secularization of the political culture' (45–6). The members of these subcultures are characterized by their 'alienation from the political market' resulting in a general lack of fit between the pattern of political culture and the political system. 'The political actors come to the market not to exchange, compromise, and adapt, but to preach, exhort, convert, and transform the political system into something other than a bargaining agency.' This type of actor is a '*militant* who remains within the confines of his political sub-culture, continually reaffirms his special norms, and scolds his parliamentarians.' Given that 'the center of gravity in these political systems is not in the formal legal rôle structure but in the political sub-cultures,' an 'immobilism' of the formally political organs results. This can lead not only to 'a predominance of the bureaucracy in policy-making,' but also to a situation in which 'movements of charismatic nationalism ... break through the boundaries of the political subcultures and overcome immobilism through coercive action and organization' (47–8).

In effect, the potential of such a 'Caesaristic breakthrough' was closely linked to Almond's diagnosis of the forces that stood in the way of creating 'moderate-center coalitions' in Western Europe. Of particular concern were France and Italy, which, in his view, 'have been held in a state of political siege by the Communist movement' (1954, 399). Germany, in contrast, was not threatened by an impending 'Caesaristic breakthrough,' but rather by 'a strong hierarchical spirit ... so that political responsibility and communication tend to be confined to the very heights of these institutions' (1955, 103–4).

The Anglo-American political system was thus in Almond's view inherently related to possible policy programs in Europe. For Germany – with its weak middle classes and hierarchical institutions – the model suggested that the growth of the professional strata ought to be encouraged. They in turn could transmit 'secular, rational values' to the attentive and mass publics. Along different lines, in France and Italy, the development of a more 'secular-homogeneous' political culture would involve 'a campaign of organization at the grass-roots level.' Such an effort, 'adequately financed and courageously and intelligently directed, may succeed in shaking the hold of the Communist movement in these areas' (1954, 388). In the same way that the 'mix' between Western, traditional, and charismatic tendencies within 'pre-industrial societies' could be shifted, the endemic 'fragmented sub-cultures' of continental European systems might be transformed into a closer approximation of the secular-homogeneous model.

The other political system in Almond's typology, the totalitarian, served as the polar opposite to the Anglo-American variant, and represented the possible fate of the pre-industrial and continental political systems if firm measures were not taken. In contrast to the other political cultures, the totalitarian variant, according to Almond, was lacking in homogeneity, and therefore was *non-consensual*, with 'the characteristic orientation to authority ... some combination of conformity and apathy' (43). The totalitarian political system, with its atomization and centralized state apparatus exacting obedience through coercive force and a refined system of communication, represented for Almond the antithesis of the Anglo-American system. Yet unless a combination of ideology, organization, and military force was brought to bear on the nations falling into the other two classes of political system, in Almond's view, movements of 'charismatic nationalism' could possibly lead to the ascendency of totalitarian politics.

Almond's comparative typology was grounded in his concern to further the spread of Western democracy throughout the world in the face of possible totalitarian expansion. He noted in the introduction to the second edition of *The American People and Foreign Policy* ([1950] 1960) that 'it has now become clear that the outcome of the so-called "East-West" struggle will be determined not so much by the military competition between the U.S. and the U.S.S.R. ... but by the way in which the new states and the newly emerging states of the non-Western world organize themselves economically and politically in their efforts to modernize themselves and gain the benefits of an industrial civilization' (xii). In his view, 'the preservation of the Western order and culture will be determined by the manner in which these peoples [the developing areas] find their way into the twentieth century' (xix). However, 'the pressures in the new states and the developing areas are so urgent, and their resources so thin, that they will inevitably turn to authoritarian and totalitarian methods in order to give coherence to the diffuse energies of their peoples, and in order to extract savings to invest in industrial development' (xx). Nevertheless, standing in the way of the United States effectively spreading its influence into the new nations, while countering Soviet expansionism, were the outlook and practices of the foreign-policy elites. Almond argued that foreign policy in the 1950s had 'hardened and narrowed [becoming] a primarily defensive policy, emphasizing military strength and security diplomacy' (xi). There had, moreover, been a 'return to the spirit of isolationism ... a withdrawal from creative contact [and] a real alienation of the political leadership ... from its own intellectual and moral resources.' Symptomatic of the latter was 'the rejection of the "egghead"' (xv). Almond argued that these disquieting trends in foreign policy resulted from its domination by 'the more parochial elements of the American political elite, elements drawn from or close to the American business elite.' In addition to not supporting a 'program of foreign aid ... without some direct tangible return *to us* ... the American business elite lacks an anthropological or sociological sense.' Almond maintained that 'the idea of growth in the non-Western world – economic, social, and political growth – as the central objective of American foreign policy cannot be fully grasped by an elite group which cannot think anthropologically and sociologically' (xxix–xxx).

If it is true that the survival of Western culture is dependent upon its assimilation in significant measure in the modernizing societies of Asia, Africa, and Latin America, our foreign policy must be informed by an anthropological appreciation of cultural differences and by a sound theory of social and cultural change. Our foreign policy must be based on a clearly understood conception of the interdependence of economic, social, political, and cultural factors in the processes of social change. Our diplomatic, military, propaganda, and foreign-aid programs must be based on such a theory and must operate the interdependent levers of change with virtuosity. Without this kind of social-science thinking, we will be unable to affect the course of change in the non-Western world in directions favorable to the preservation and spread of our own culture. And if we fail to achieve this, we shall find ourselves isolated, our security treaties mere scraps of paper, and our system of foreign bases a precarious house of cards. (xxx)

Almond's proposals for comparative politics represented an effort to help overcome the 'parochialism and ethnocentrism' that he saw as endemic among the foreign-policy elites. An infusion of social-scientific insights into American foreign policy, as he implied, would enable the United States to hold its 'lead over the Soviet Union,' and undergo 'cultural and psychological growth which will enable us to provide moral and political leadership over an expanding free world' (xxx). The comparative politics movement constituted an effort to develop a social science of relevance to American designs in the rapidly changing world order. Through its theoretical framework, which elaborated the social, psychological, and cultural conditions making for 'democratic politics,' more effective policy decisions could be implemented leading to the formation of 'moderate center' political systems.

Correspondingly, the political theory provided by empirical analysis within this schema could be promulgated to the elites of these foreign countries as an alternative to communism.

It was through adapting insights from Parsons's social theory that Almond was able to develop a theoretical framework for comparative politics, bearing the promise of generating cumulative data pertinent to stabilizing the world political order along the lines suggested by the Anglo-American prototype. That Almond's efforts were successful is indicated by the fact that in 1956 the Ford Foundation provided extensive support ($260,000) for research in comparative politics, allowing the committee to embark on 'a five year program of field research on political groups.' Given its priorities, the Ford Foundation had agreed to underwrite the committee's activities because its leading advocates had finally evolved an approach or 'theoretical framework' that bore the promise of underpinning the accretion of cumulative results over a prolonged period. Through such a program, knowledge of strategic relevance to the Ford Foundation's global concerns could potentially be forthcoming. This framework became consolidated among researchers in comparative politics, culminating in a series of full-scale and extensive political studies in which Almond's practical concerns were implicit.

The Consolidation of Comparative Politics

Almond's theoretical framework almost immediately influenced the course of research in comparative politics, for the ssrc Committee, which Almond chaired, was given responsibility for co-ordinating the Ford Foundation–sponsored program of research on political groups. The committee had the power not only to administer the funding and to select the recipients of the awards, but also to orient the research in a manner compatible with its theoretical and ideological preferences. That the committee immediately sought to impart a particular focus to research in comparative politics is evident in Almond's discussion of 'the first research planning seminar.'[6] Its main value, according to Almond, 'was to create among the younger political scientists, specializing in various parts of the world, the notion that they were members of a common discipline concerned with the same theoretical problems and having available to them the same research methodologies' (1970, 16). Guiding the 'discussion of the central problems confronting the committee in the development of plans for needed research' was an agenda paper (by Myron Wiener and Almond) that attempted 'to codify the views of the committee on research strategy' (Almond 1956b, 46). Reflecting the committee's debt to Parsons, the paper recommended that 'field work should stress *function* and the interrelationships between political, cultural, and social processes' (47). By the end of the seminar, as Almond reported, there appeared to be a consensus that 'the actual functioning of political parties and interest groups might distinguish more accurately the different types of political systems' (47). In conclusion, Almond noted that as a result of the seminar discussions, the committee would not only 'promote collaboration among recipients of grants for field studies' under its program, but prepare 'a series of theoretical memoranda under the committee's auspices' (48).

One can conclude from the report on the first of 'three research planning sessions ... held for the recipients of grants for field studies of political groups' (1970, 16–17)[7] that Almond's theoretical framework was beginning to gain acceptance. According to Almond, the report of the session 'contains some early formulation of the "functional approach" and a number of hypotheses regarding the consequences of different kinds of interest group systems for the performance of political parties, legislative bodies, and bureaucracies' (17). The participants in the session, as Almond reported, agreed that comparative analyses confined to 'formal governmental institutions, and to political party and electoral systems' ([1958] 1970, 52) were inadequate. It was agreed that 'a good research job on interest groups in a particular country ... must examine the interest group system in its relations with the social structure and culture on the one hand and the other parts of the political structure on the other. In identifying the interest group system in any particular country this broad functional approach will prevent us from identifying interest groups with any particular kind of structure' (54–5). That is, the new set of categories was to facilitate comparison by specifying how the same functions were performed by different interest groups, depending on the society in question. As Almond noted, one could state 'the theme of the comparative study in the form of a single question ... What form does the articulation of political interests take in various societies, and how are these interests transmitted to other parts of the political and governmental structure, and translated into choices of political personnel and public policy?' (55). While the United States, the United Kingdom, and the Commonwealth were characterized by functionally specific and bureaucratized interest groups, the politics of non-Western areas were dominated by the presence of kinship groups, status groups, and informal cliques. Moreover, 'Anglo-American politics' was based on a 'clearer distinction between the functions of parties and interest groups' than could be found 'on the European continent and [in] non-Western areas' (56). In all four thematic areas in which interest groups were examined – interest groups and public opinion, the legislative process, bureaucracies, and non-Western political systems – the influence of Almond's approach was noticeable (71–5). As Almond concluded: 'By setting common questions and discussing common approaches the Committee on Comparative Politics hopes to introduce greater coherence in the research efforts under way. More recently it has begun to plan a series of comparative analyses which will draw the findings of these and other research efforts together' (1958, 282).

The planning sessions and seminars co-ordinated by the committee served to initiate area specialists into the comparative politics movement and to impress upon them the interplay between their research and the theoretical development of comparative politics.

In the praise which has been heaped on the work of the Committee on Comparative Politics it is easy to forget that we were moving with a trend, and that all that we really did was to give this movement support, legitimacy, a feeling for framework, and a sense of direction. We understood our roles to be that of introducing a comparative perspective, and theoretical and methodological sophistication ... The early life of the Committee was spent in bringing these young area-specialists together encouraging them to be comparative in their approach and to view themselves as political theorists, using their specific geographic and cultural areas as laboratories. We urged upon them a conception of their role as that of contributing to a theory of political development, relevant both to political theory and public policy. (1970, 12–13; emphasis added)

While Almond confessed that the 'program as a whole did not immediately produce the comparative and theoretical studies combining the results of the individual field projects' (16), nevertheless, by the end of the 1950s the movement had consolidated to the point that 'the Committee's program on political development emerged.' At 'a conference on political modernization held at Gould house in Dobbs Ferry, June 8 to 11, 1959 ... it had become clear ... that one useful function which the Committee could perform was to draw on existing knowledge about the principal institutions of modernization and democratization and to examine them from the point of view of the problems and consequences of introducing these institutions into pre-modern societies' (19–20). Subsequently, noted Almond, 'during the years 1961 and 1963, five conferences were held with Committee members assuming the responsibility for the direction of these conferences and committed to the preparation of theoretical and summary papers. These five conferences eventuated in five of the seven volumes in the Committee's Studies in Political Development series' (1970, 20).[8]

Pye observed that this series of monographs owed their conceptual basis to Almond's theoretical efforts. During the early phase of the committee's history, notes Pye,

it soon became apparent ... that without a more solid theoretical basis comparative studies of groups and leadership would only produce a proliferation of ad hoc research that would not be cumulative. At this point Gabriel A. Almond, then chairman of the committee, gave critical direction by indicating the need for macrosystemic comparative studies. The concept of political development requires the conceptualization of the total political system, and not just the comparative study of isolated institutions or groups. As a basis for the necessary macro-analysis, Almond demonstrated the utility of a form of structural-functional analysis. The theoretical orientation of The Politics of the Developing Areas *(Almond and Coleman, 1960) profoundly shaped the subsequent work of the committee and set the stage for its series of 'Studies in Political Development.'* (Pye and Ryland 1971)

Pye's estimation of the impact of this work upon the comparative politics movement has been widely shared.[9] Of particular influence, as a cursory reading of the volumes in the Studies in Political Development series will testify, was Almond's introductory statement that culminated his early efforts to provide a theoretical framework for comparative politics ([1960] 1970, 79–151). This essay was notable for its thoroughgoing elaboration of functional categories, given form and substance by insights drawn from systems theory. 'The particular functional categories' that Almond employed in this statement 'were developed for the purpose of comparing political systems as whole systems; and particularly for comparing the modern Western one with the transitional and traditional.' These categories, as Almond attested, were derived from an analysis of Western political life: 'The problem ... was to ask a series of questions based on the distinctive political activities existing in Western complex systems. In other words, we derived our functional categories from the political systems in which structural specialization and functional differentiation have taken place to the greatest extent' (95). Almond distinguished between the 'input' and 'output' functions of the political system. On the input side, Almond specified the functions of interest articulation, aggregation, political communication, and recruitment/socialization. For the outputs, Almond made a case for 'three authoritative governmental functions, *rule-making, rule application,* and *rule adjudication'* (96).

On the face of it, the theoretical framework developed by Almond appears to be fully at odds with the stated intentions of the comparative politics movements, i.e., as Pye put it, 'to look beyond the formal institutions of government and to study the groups and interests that provide the dynamics of politics in different settings' (Pye and Ryland 1971, 2). If anything, the set of categories offered by Almond was *more* formal and *less* specific than the terms widely in use. For in his effort to develop a new 'conceptual vocabulary of political science,' permitting a comparison of the 'political systems of the "developing" areas ... according to a common set of categories' (Almond [1960] 1970, 79), Almond was almost obliged to proceed with a formal typology. And by assuming functionality as a criterion for categorizing political phenomena, he could hardly avoid abstractness and a sense of generality. Purely on descriptive terms, then, it is difficult to understand how Almond's new theoretical framework marked an analytical breakthrough. Even more puzzling was the enthusiasm with which this conceptual schema was greeted. Yet if one examines Almond's framework in terms of the underlying strategic assumptions of the Committee on Comparative Politics, its significance and impact become intelligible.

As noted, the committee members sought to develop an approach to the study of politics that could at once serve as a *normative* political theory, providing an alternative to communism, while generating data about the social, psychological, and cultural conditions making for 'moderate center' politics. This empirical knowledge was to be of *instrumental* use to the 'policy-elites.' Given their assumption that the Anglo-American political system represented a developmental prototype for the other countries of the world, the problem they faced was one of understanding more accurately how this system was able to generate sufficient consensus to permit the effective implementation of coercive force. This normative and instrumental wisdom could then be disseminated to the less-developed nation-states, with the hope that their developmental trajectories could be brought closer in line with that of the Anglo-American model, and deflected away from the totalitarian variant. To these ends, Almond's functionally conceived political system was thought to have considerable promise. First, it provided a framework for the cumulative generation of data, showing 'probabilistically' how particular 'structures' were performing the universal 'functions.' Indeed, claimed Almond, 'the statements about politics now to be found in the political science literature are codable into such functional-structural statements of probability' (145). He suggested, then, that 'great advantage would be gained if we were to make explicit the essentially statistical nature of our propositions about the structures, functions, and styles of the polity' (146).

Second, the empirically grounded political system offered the basis for a political theory capable of challenging communism. Thus, the key institutions of American politics – namely the three divisions of government (legislative, executive, and judiciary) and the four social phenomena of political consequence (parties, pressure groups, elite/education, public opinion) were relabelled as *functions*. As a symbolic depiction of political life, this implied that the various components of what was called the Anglo-American system were not only empirically necessary but morally correct. Other political systems were then evaluated in terms of their conformity with or their deviance from this implicit standard. For the 'modernizing elites' of transitional societies, the workings of the Anglo-American political system served to generate a political theory of how a particular set of structures functioned to produce the effective circulation of inputs and outputs. Moreover, because the non-Western political systems were viewed as mixtures of rational, traditional, and charismatic elements, the comparative approach could show to what degree these societies differed from the Anglo-American prototype.

The political system evolved by Almond represented an adaptation of the Parsonsian schema to the strategic problems faced by comparative politics. Almond's political system was both a model of the modern nation-state based on the Anglo-American prototype and a framework for undertaking research in comparative politics. Given that the research was underpinned by a commitment to this form of political organization, then the knowledge produced would be of practical relevance to its consolidation and spread. Thus, Almond's theoretical framework served the dual purpose of generating empirical knowledge of instrumental relevance, and affirming the virtues of the Anglo-American political system. Fully in keeping with Parsons's own theoretical efforts, then, Almond's schema combined a scientific orientation having value relevance, with a defined subject matter. The comparative-politics movement embodied the categories of practice that Parsons had originally derived from the medical profession, namely disinterestedness (relative autonomy from foreign policy), universalism (scientific orientation), affective neutrality (value relevance), and functional specificity (disciplinary concentration in comparative politics). Through social-scientific practice guided by these categores, comparative politics could thereby contribute to the global 'rationalization' of political systems. For 'the "modern" solution of the problems of cultural dualism,' argued Almond, was 'a penetration of the "traditional" styles of diffuseness, particularism, ascriptiveness and affectivity, by the "rational" styles of specificity, universalism, achievement, and affective neutrality' (150). This 'penetration,' however, was not in any sense foreordained. It was dependent upon the active growth and co-operation of new, professionalized social strata, including the social scientists. By espousing a theoretical framework grounded in the primary patterns, comparative politics was to help bring about 'modernization.' In the aftermath of McCarthyism, when Cold War consensus at last appeared to have become a reality, the theoreticians of comparative politics could confidently view the American political system as a developmental prototype and seek to encourage a comparable path of modernization in other parts of the world. To this end, their efforts converged with those of the 'sociology of politics' as developed by Seymour Martin Lipset.

11

Seymour Lipset and the Sociology of Politics

Lipset's Practical Concerns

Widely acknowledged as the main contributor to the development of the sociology of politics in the post-war period (Abrams 1974; Barry 1970), Seymour Lipset, like Parsons and Almond, was originally drawn to the social sciences for reasons of practical commitment. However, his interest in pursuing social-scientific research had its origin in concerns that were directly political rather than religious. This set of political concerns, he noted in an autobiographical statement, 'developed out of my experience with and interest in socialist politics. I belonged to the Young People's Socialist League while in high school and as a freshman at City College in New York' (1964a, 97). Lipset's commitment to socialism appears to have been tempered by his interpretation of 'the experience of the left and labor movements in various countries,' which indicated to him 'that the building of a large socialist or labor movement, or even its coming to power, was not sufficient to democratize a society' (97). Moreover, he came to believe that 'the various organized movements (Socialist and Communist) had been total failures either creating totalitarian oppressive states such as the Soviet Union, or failing to successfully resist Fascism or influence the structures of power in other countries' (1969, 144).

This sense of disillusionment with mainstream socialist movements affected Lipset's subsequent political concerns. Influenced by the analysis offered by Robert Michels in *Political Parties* (1969, 144–5; 1964a, 98), his vision of how socialism could be put into practice became much more circumscribed.[1] This revised political interest was evident in the research topics Lipset began to pursue as a graduate student: 'The political system of the ITU [International Typographical Union] and the emergence of a large socialist party, the Cooperative Commonwealth Federation (CCF) in Canada' (99). Implicit in this choice of research areas, as Lipset would later attest, was a concern with deviant-case analysis: 'I selected two major cases which contradicted what appeared to be general laws and desired to find out whether the general law was wrong or whether there were some new or special factors present in the deviant cases which permitted the unexpected to occur' (99). 'The CCF ... was the first mass socialist party in English-speaking North America. Its success seemingly challenged the assumptions of those who argued that elements inherent in the history of current social structure of America made an American socialism impossible' (99). The ITU was similarly chosen as a topic of research by Lipset because of its apparently exceptional features: 'The record of the ITU ... seemingly contradicted Michels. Here was a large trade-union which governed itself through an elaborate democratic political system ... If there was an answer to the "iron law of oligarchy," it might lie in the Typographical Union' (1964a, 98).

Lipset recalls that 'in large measure [his] interests as a prospective graduate student flowed from [his] political concerns.' Because he wanted 'to find out whether there was a realistic "socialist" alternative to Stalinism [and] to know why all efforts to build any kind of socialist party in the United States had failed miserably,' he decided to study the CCF. Since 'most of the explanations of "why no socialism in the United States" seemed to apply equally strongly to Canada,' he felt that 'an analysis of the CCF might shed light on the conditions under which a socialist movement could be built in this country' (98–9). Mirroring similar political convictions, he believed that 'a study of the Typographical Union might shed light on the ways in which one could inhibit or prevent authoritarian practices in the labor movement' (1969, 147). While he was at Columbia, however, his politically oriented concerns became tempered by the canons of empirical methodology.

Although my sociological interests remained tied very closely to my political values when I was a graduate student, there's little doubt that my years at Columbia led me to define research in a very different way from what I thought when I first entered graduate school. The commitment to an effort at objective scholarship, to learning the techniques to test hypotheses, to relating one's work to broader bodies of theory, all became meaningful, real objectives in this period. (148)

Upon entering graduate school, Lipset was faced with the dilemma of reconciling his political commitment with the objective standards of social-scientific research. If he were to pursue research based on his political interests – without appearing to be biased or partisan – it was necessary that he find a way of claiming objectivity for his work. This would permit him to carry on research of intended practical relevance, while still assuming the objective coloration necessary for academic life. It is instructive that Lipset – like Parsons and Almond – justified his commitment to morally and politically informed research by vesting a particular interpretation of Max Weber's views with authoritative status: 'Although I never then or since have accepted the idea that value-free, research or academic, concerns are possible, I did then learn largely through our discussions of Max Weber and his ideas that a scholar, if he was to be creative, had to try as consciously as he could to negate his political and other biases and prejudices insofar as they affected his work' (148–9).

Lipset maintained that one could undertake research that was both practically motivated and scientifically objective by keeping scientific conclusions separate from political biases. 'A scholar should try to do objective research in spite of his political commitments ... One chose one's study because of beliefs about what was important to find out, so that research could lead to action ... The commitment to action-relevant topics did not contradict agreeing with Weber that one should try to avoid letting one's values affect one's conclusions' (149–50). In practice, however, this would mean that the 'objectivity' of the results would none the less be circumscribed by one's initial value premises. Given that the answers ultimately reached are inherently linked to the questions initially posed, then the conclusions cannot be arbitrarily separated from one's original set of values. Early in his career, the standards of social reform and equality implicit in the notion of socialism provided the impetus for Lipset's published work on the CCF in Saskatchewan ([1950] 1971) and on the ITU (1952).

Lipset's subsequent research reveals a continuity in his commitment to produce knowledge of practical relevance. However, as he came to identify more closely with the principles of Cold War liberalism in the fifties, the values that guided his intellectual activity were no longer the abstract standards of a socialist society, but rather the prevailing mores of the American political and social order. For him, the United States represented – as it did also for Almond and Parsons – a 'Kingdom of God' on earth whose redemptive ideals were to guide the values and actions of those whose chosen calling was to serve it.[2] That Lipset shifted his commitments from building socialism to widening the vital centre of American politics is evident in his writings on McCarthyism.

The Impact of McCarthyism on Lipset's Thought

Lipset's involvement with the study of McCarthyism was itself part of a broader reorientation of research concerns attendant upon the Ford Foundation's increasing influence upon academic life. He recalls that 'The Fund for the Republic, a subsidiary of the Ford Foundation, became interested in the possibility of supporting a comprehensive study of the phenomenon of McCarthyism and asked the Columbia Bureau of Applied Social Research to undertake a preliminary investigation to see to what extent such an undertaking was feasible and to detail what substudies ought to be done. I took part in a Bureau committee which supervised this preliminary study' (1969, 157).

This investigation led to the publication of an article ([1955a] 1963), which according to Lipset 'was the first time that the term "radical right" was applied to extremist movements in the United States' (158). He maintained that McCarthyism represented an appeal to the resentments of individuals or groups 'who desire to maintain or improve their social status' ([1955a] 1963, 309). In Lipset's view, 'status politics' of this kind 'becomes ascendant in periods of prosperity, especially when ... many individuals are able to improve their economic position.' Since status conflict could not be resolved through a rational solution, one could then conclude that 'the political movements which have successfully appealed to status resentments have been irrational in character, and have sought scapegoats which conveniently serve to symbolize the status threat' (309). McCarthyism could be understood as the latest outbreak of status politics resulting from 'the continuing prosperity of the late nineteen forties and early fifties' (315) – an irrational reaction by an assortment of social groups experiencing anxieties as their relative statuses changed (336).

There was more, however, to Lipset's account of McCarthyism than simply an attribution of irrational concerns with status to particular strata in American society. Implied by the notion of a 'radical right' was an assumption that the core of American politics was rational and tolerant. From a moral standpoint affixed to the moderate centre of American politics, Lipset collapsed both right- and left-wing social movements into a common category of 'extremist politics,' which erupted periodically as American society underwent particular historical changes. While 'status' politics, as embodied in movements of the radical right, occurred during periods of prosperity, 'class politics' as practised by the 'traditional left ... have usually gained strength during times of unemployment and depression' (308–9).

Lipset offered a tentative diagnosis of America's susceptibility to the appeals of both radical right *and* left extremism. In his view, 'the most significant issue cutting across the left-right dimension today is political democracy versus totalitarianism' ([1960] 1963, 233). From this standpoint, Lipset no longer conceived of the lower classes as the bearers of progressive change.[3] The fact that the data indicated that the 'support for various extremist movements' came 'largely from the underprivileged and less educated elements in society ... sensitized [him] for the first time to the possibility that the less privileged groups in the society were not only potential bases of support for leftist movements advocating ... progressive social change, but that they also constituted a potential mass base for reactionary authoritarian movements' (1969, 158). From the 'various studies of attitudes toward civil liberties and McCarthy,' Lipset concluded that 'the lower a person is in socio-economic status or educational attainment, the more likely he is to support McCarthy, favor restriction on civil liberties, and back a "get tough" policy with the Communist states.' This propensity, Lipset thought, was quite understandable, particularly in comparison to the predispositions of the middle classes, whose tolerance was founded on 'both a high degree of material and psychic security, and considerable sophistication' ([1955a] 1963, 344–5).

Lipset's contentions about the social support for McCarthyism and working-class authoritarianism in general have been persuasively contested, on both ideological and empirical grounds (Peck 1962). Indeed, it is striking that he came to conclude that McCarthyism represented a *mass social movement* on the basis of so little tangible evidence.[4] Lipset's conception of McCarthyism perhaps tells us more about his own values and tensions than it does about American social history in the post-war period. If his commitment to the Cold War order were to be retained, then he was compelled to explain McCarthyism as an extremist movement – an irrational projection of status anxieties upon the rational mainstream of American democratic politics. His view of McCarthyism as a movement of the 'radical right' could thus be understood as an effort to defend 'democratic politics' against a potential threat. By explaining how irrational, extremist tendencies were translated into political movements, the social scientist could contribute to the defence of democratic institutions against disruptive intrusions.

Lipset's response to McCarthyism culminated an intellectual migration from New Deal progressivism to Cold War liberalism. As he understood the New Deal period and its aftermath, liberal and leftist views had predominated (because of 'the need for socio-economic reforms') during the depression and were followed by the wartime struggle against fascism. However, with the onset of the Cold War, in Lipset's view, 'fascism and the "right"' no longer posed a threat. Instead, there was 'a war against communism, identified with the "left." And while it is possible to validly argue that Fascism and Communism are much closer to each other in practice than either is to the democratic right or left, the fact remains that each is considered as an extreme version of conservatism or liberalism (leftism)' (1955, 184).

From Lipset's new vantage-point affixed firmly to 'the vital center' of Cold War liberalism, his former leftist sympathies could be explained and his shift to a more conservative stance sanctified. Because the 'political dynamic' had been 'in the hands of the left,' his previous socialist views were thereby legitimated and he could safely distance himself from 'the Communist left,' which made 'considerable headway in penetrating and manipulating the liberal or moderate left groups.' Correspondingly, in the changed political climate of the Cold War, he could identify with the conservative drift of 'democratic foreign policy' (184), yet distinguish his own position from that of 'the radical right,' whose 'agitation has facilitated the growth of practices which threaten to undermine the social fabric of democratic politics' (176). Thinly disguising his own changing position as a comment on intellectuals in general, he would later remark upon the 'shift toward the center' by American intellectuals, attendant upon 'the social consequences of prolonged postwar prosperity.' An equally important circumstance leading to greater intellectual conservatism, he argued, was

the reaction of liberal leftist intellectuals in America, as elsewhere, to the rise of Communism as the main threat to freedom. Faced with a society far worse than the one which now exists in the West but one which claims to be fulfilling the values of the American and French revolutions, such intellectuals, including many of the socialists among them, now have for the first time in history a conservative ideology which allows them to defend an existing or past society against those who argue for a future utopia. Like Burke, they have come to look for sources of stability rather than of change. The very social classes which the intellectual reformer saw as the carriers of the good society – the lower classes, especially the workers – back the

*new despotism, and not only the despotism of the left, but as
McCarthyism and Peronism showed, often of the 'radical right.'*
([1960] 1963, 368)

Self-serving as this conception of the intellectual might have been, it
was not without its basis in reality. It was very probably through his
increasingly close identification with the ideals and beliefs of the
militantly anti-Communist and internationally minded body known as
the Congress for Cultural Freedom[5] that Lipset came to look upon his
own intellectual identity as having universal validity and significance.

The Congress for Cultural Freedom

With the demise of McCarthyism in 1954, Lipset's treatment of the
nature and significance of American politics shifted accordingly. No
longer compelled to analyse internal extremist threats to American
society, he directed his attention to understanding how the United
States could lead the other capitalist democracies in the struggle against
world communism. To this end, he joined with a number of like-minded
Western scholars, scientists, and literary figures in an effort to combat
the spread of communism through intellectual means. The organizational centre of this movement was the Congress for Cultural Freedom,
which from its inception held the view 'that conventional political
distinctions had become irrelevant in the face of the need for a united
front against Bolshevism' (Lasch 1969, 64). The ideology of the 'end of
ideology' represented an effort to undermine and erode the appeal of
communist and left-wing movements. By defining the major struggle in
the world as one between totalitarianism and freedom, political
commitments based on the traditional left-right distinctions could be
treated as irrational if not disloyal. At the founding conference of the
Congress of Cultural Freedom, the 'end of ideology' was expressed as an
ideal (Hook 1950). However, by the time of the next major conference
under the auspices of the congress – 'The Future of Freedom,' held in
Milan in 1955 – the thesis had gained widespread acceptance among the
congress membership as both a moral position and a description of
politics in Western democracies.[6] As Edward Shils remarked (1955, 53),
'It was the intention of the conference's organizers to move thought
further around the turning point [the end of ideological enthusiasm] to
which we have come in the last years.' Lipset was among the participants at the conference, presenting a paper in a session on 'the impact of
extremist ideologies on the working of democratic institutions' (56).[7]

That the mood and spirit of the Milan meetings had a noticeable impact upon Lipset's outlook is evident from his comments in a letter to *The Canadian Forum*.[8] Taking exception to the criticisms put forth in a previous letter (Scott 1955) that the *Forum* was no longer 'a vigorous exponent of Canadian socialism,' Lipset drew attention to the fact that both Scott and the *Forum*'s editors had ignored 'the current content of democratic party controversy' as revealed in the conference at Milan. He noted that 'the sponsoring group, the Congress for Cultural Freedom, is an international organization of pro-democratic, which means vigorously anti-Communist, intellectuals, and has affiliates around the world. It unites in one political organization socialists and right-wing conservatives.' Despite the wide spectrum of political perspectives represented, Lipset was struck by the lack of 'intense political debate.' Indeed, as he reported, 'the only occasions in which debate grew warm were when the conference could make someone serve as a "surrogate Communist"' (1955b, 170). In view of the widespread agreement at the conference that the left-right distinction had become superfluous, Lipset chided Scott and the other leaders of the CCF for holding outdated views on the possibility of developing socialism in Canada. In his view, they were 'in the sorry position of being leaders of a minor socialist party which failed to achieve major party status before the traditional basis of the emotional cleavage between the left and right ended.' In holding to the view that 'a strong socialist party' would make a difference to Canada, they were out of step with 'the leaders of strong socialist parties in other countries [who] no longer believe that the differences between the left and right are profound.' Lipset contended that the CCF leadership's concern to arouse 'political passion' was misplaced, for the 'growing apoliticalization of intellectuals in Canada,' as evidenced in 'the changes in the political tone of *The Canadian Forum*, [is] just another symptom of the decline of political controversy within the democracies' (1955b, 170–1).

One can conclude from Lipset's comments that he stood in full agreement with the views about Western democracies put forth in Milan.[9] However, despite the general consensus at the conference about the 'end of ideology,' there was little cause for complacency on the part of Lipset and other Cultural Freedom intellectuals. It became evident to the Western delegates that the struggle for 'freedom' could not be confined to their own societies. As Michael Polanyi, one of the conference organizers, noted in his final remarks, 'I took it for granted ... that the decisive problems or our age were those raised in Europe by Europeans ... But the interventions made at this meeting by Asiatic,

African, and South American delegates have made me realize that this perspective was altogether distorted ... We shall not begin to understand them until we accept the fact that in these new nations ... we are facing our partners in the shaping of man's destiny on this planet' (in Shils 1955, 58). Concurring with this assessment, Shils drew the conclusion that 'we must no longer think only for European or American society. Our theories of liberty, of the relation between religion and progress, tradition and intellectual independence, must be thought out and formulated in such a way that they will do justice to the situations of the new countries of Asia and Africa and South America' (57).

The congress intellectuals were not alone in their concern with the fate of developing countries. As noted, the Ford Foundation, in the aftermath of the House investigations, began to direct its efforts more towards understanding the requisites of Western democracy with a view to influencing the course of political development in the new nations. This reorientation of research priorities by the Ford Foundation had a significant impact on Lipset's research concerns, intersecting with his own change of direction in the mid-fifties. As he noted, 'the study of McCarthyism' of which he was a part 'never came to fruition since the Fund for the Republic decided not to support it' (1969, 158). This decision was indicative of the shifting mood in the Ford Foundation after the House investigations. Under the duress of right-wing attack, it shifted its funding priorities away from civil liberties and towards the support of research that affirmed the virtues of American democracy. Reflecting the new set of priorities within the Ford Foundation, Lipset noted that his next research project after his study of McCarthyism, 'an effort at systematizing the bases of political cleavage on a comparative perspective, stemmed from a project which was also located at the Bureau. The Behavioral Sciences Division of the Ford Foundation, then under the direction of Dr. Bernard Berelson, decided to support a number of inventories of knowledge in different areas of social science. Berelson gave the Bureau a grant for an inventory in the general field of political behavior' (158).

Lipset took advantage of this opportunity 'to look into the literature bearing on the factors determining the political orientations of occupational classes in Europe and America.' The Ford Foundation supported Lipset for a year (1955–6) at the Center for Advanced Study in Behavioral Sciences, where along with Juan Linz he 'spent the year writing up and trying to systematize the materials bearing on the factors which differentiated support for different political tendencies among various strata' (1969, 158–9). Having participated extensively in the stock-taking ventures on the social bases of political behaviour sponsored by the Ford Foundation, Lipset increasingly came to assume the role of spokesman for the field of political sociology. Indeed, he not only was largely responsible for redefining the sub-discipline, but infused it with his own commitments and political designs.

The Field of Political Sociology

Lipset's first effort to impart a sense of direction and unity to political sociology took the form of a survey article commissioned by UNESCO for a volume on trends in American sociology (1956). After surveying the various directions the field had taken, he concluded that political sociology was still very much an inchoate area of study (55). Yet in his next assessment of the field, written with Reinhard Bendix ([1957] 1966), he was able to stipulate that 'the common denominator of studies in political sociology consists in a refined "interest-theory" of political behaviour and in a political commitment to the values of democratic institutions' (14–15). He held that political phenomena were to be considered as the *outcomes* of 'conflicts and strategies' in democratic societies (17). This definition of political sociology not only reflected the 'end of ideology' sentiments expressed at the meetings in Milan, but also corresponded to the methodological guide-lines developing within the Committee on Comparative Politics. At 'the first research planning session' of the committee (April 1957) in which Lipset participated, the guiding theme of the discussions was the question, 'what form does the articulation of political interests take in various societies, and how are these interests transmitted to other parts of the political and governmental structure, and translated into choices of political personnel and public policy?' (Almond 1970, 55). Revealing his debt to the goals and orientation of the committee, Lipset maintained that political sociology faced the task 'of analysing the tensions and cleavages which arise from the social and economic order of society; and it should do so on a comparative basis in order to show from what range of abstractly available alternatives given political choices have been made' ([1957] 1966, 25).[10]

It was on the basis of this comparative orientation, focusing on 'interest-groups' and guided by a commitment to democratic institutions, that Lipset was able to impart order to 'studies of voting behavior.' In his view, 'their ... impetus' stemmed from 'an "interest theory" of political behaviour,' and their 'chief concern ... has been to elucidate the social conditions of different types of electoral participation (or nonparticipation), in order to reveal the social processes underlying democratic institutions.' Voting studies have been concerned 'with the social bases of political diversity in democratic societies [and] special topics such as the extent and implications of non-voting.' These topics of research reveal 'that scientific knowledge is sought out of a concern with the survival of democracy' (11). In view of the widespread acceptance he perceived of the end-of-ideology thesis, and on the basis of the agreement by the planning session's members about the need to study politics in a comparative and sociological manner, Lipset could come to the conclusion that there was 'a tacit consensus among Western scholars interested in political sociology.' None the less, he still maintained that 'political sociology ... lacks a theoretical frame-work' (15). In his view, 'the studies grouped under the general title "political sociology" lack unity except for the basic assumptions' that were sketched in the 1957 survey article (25). Such a deficiency posed severe problems if political sociologists' 'concern with the survival of democracy' (11) were to be activated. If the empirical voting studies were to be communicated into the public realm, and were to have significance for values and beliefs, they required an integrative frame-work. As long as they remained nothing more than strictly empiricist descriptions of voting patterns, they could neither offer a normative defence of democratic politics nor prescribe political actions thought to be necessary for democracy's survival. A schema integrating the studies of voting would guide further research, giving the field both continuity and social-scientific credibility. Thus, political sociology would remain normatively irrelevant and scientifically backward unless its research could develop an overarching *theory*.

In view of the lack of theoretical integration in political sociology, Lipset felt that 'it will be necessary to work towards ... unity, and to relate the "interest theory" of social action to other theories of action in order to establish a theoretical framework for political sociology as an integral part of sociology *sans phrase*' (25–6). In Lipset's next venture into codifying the field (1959a), the beginnings of a unifying theoretical approach building on this set of assumptions were revealed.

Conflict within Consensus

Upon reappraising his political behaviour data in preparation for an edition of his collected essays (*Political Man*), it struck Lipset that 'looking at these materials solely from the point of view of cleavage was a mistake, and in some ways was even unsociological' for, in reality, 'one is looking essentially at the operation of a social system, namely the system of political conflict in democratic societies' (1969, 161). The 'social system,' then, borrowed directly from Parsons, provided Lipset with the framework necessary for the integration of political conflict, on the one hand, and cleavage data, on the other. Concurring with Parsons that the 'problem of order [is] the basic issue of much of contemporary sociological analysis' and that 'the stability of society is a central issue for sociology as a whole,' Lipset argued that political sociology should concern itself with 'the *social* conditions of democracy' ([1959a] 1965, 91–2).[11]

Lipset acknowledged that his conception of the sociology of politics was indebted to *Voting* and to Parsons's reformulation of that study's results and insights. Unlike other works in the field of voting behaviour, *Voting* made a contribution to the understanding of consensus, even though 'it was not a major concern in the initial design of the Berelson study, and hence the extent to which the authors could deal with the problem was limited' (97–8). This deficiency, however, as Lipset noted, was rectified by Talcott Parsons, whose paper on *Voting* 'is full of suggestive hypotheses and interpretations concerning the American electoral system' (95–6).

In adapting Parsons's social system to the sociology of politics, Lipset had found an approach of practical relevance to the consolidation and spread of democracy. The research framework for understanding the social basis of democracy embodied the same duality between empirical model and research exemplar as did the political systems elaborated by Parsons and Almond. Lipset assumed the standpoint of 'the democratic system,' dependent for its stability upon its 'effectiveness' and 'legitimacy.' Effectiveness referred to 'the capacity of a political system to satisfy the basic functions of government as defined by the *expectations* of most members of society, and of powerful minorities ... which might threaten the system. It is almost self-evident that basic to high effectiveness is an efficient bureaucracy which is receptive to the needs of its clients, and a complex decision-making system of which representative voluntary associations are a part' (108). Legitimacy, as Lipset defined it, 'involves the capacity of the system to engender and maintain the belief that the existing political institutions are the most appropriate ones for the society. The extent to which contemporary democratic political systems are legitimate depends in large measure upon the ways in which the key issues which have historically divided the society have been resolved' ([1960] 1963, 64).

Both legitimacy and effectiveness, Lipset suggests, are founded in particular dimensions of knowledge. 'The effectiveness aspect of the relationship,' according to Lipset, 'is primarily instrumental in character' ([1959a] 1965, 108). In other words, if the bureaucracies and decision-making bodies are to get things done, they require knowledge that permits them to fit means to ends. 'The legitimacy component,' in contrast, as described by Lipset, 'is much more affective and evaluative. Groups may regard a system as legitimate or illegitimate according to the way in which its values fit in with their *Weltanschauung*' (108–9). The very notion of legitimacy, then, implied the presence of symbolic knowledge, communicated into civil society and intersecting with the values and goals of social actors. From the standpoint of the political system, legitimacy and effectiveness constituted problems that required solutions if stability were to be ensured. Only if the public and the key social strata could be convinced that the political system was at once legitimate and effective could consensus be maintained. It was in periods of a transition to a new social structure, argued Lipset, that 'crises of legitimacy' could occur, 'following the rise of sharp cleavages among groups which are able, because of mass communication, to organize around different values than those previously considered to be the only acceptable ones' ([1960] 1963, 64–5). A crisis of legitimacy during a period of change was possible, in Lipset's view, if the major groups in society are denied access to its most significant institutions (65).

If the political system were to survive periods of change, the problems of legitimation and effectiveness had, therefore, to be solved. The solution to the problems implied an infusion of the appropriate symbolic and instrumental knowledge. Since 'the symbolic world of man, including art, science, and religion' (333), was the creation of intellectuals, a complementary shift in intellectual activity was suggested as well. For the social scientist, this shift implied an *isomorphism* between the orientation of his research and the dimensions of knowledge inherent in the solution to the legitimacy and effectiveness problems of the political system. One may suggest, therefore, that the 'sociology of politics' advocated by Lipset represented a response to 'a crisis of transition' experienced by the United States during its ascent to global hegemony in the post-war period. This is seen in the way his notion of a political system – with its duality between a socio-political order and a research exemplar – embodied the isomorphic relationship between the social sciences and society.

Orienting himself towards the problem of 'effectiveness' within the order, the researcher was to be concerned with problems of cleavage; by producing empirical knowledge of instrumental relevance to the nation's leaders, the political sociologist was to contribute to the *effectiveness* of the democratic system. In terms of the problem of 'legitimacy' – the ability of a political system to cultivate and sustain support for its institutions – the political sociologist would orient his research towards problems of *consensus*; by empirically examining the cleavages as they pertained to the generation of consensus, the researcher would be offering a legitimating depiction of the democratic system. By virtue of this political system, the researcher could simultaneously produce knowledge of relevance to the problems of legitimacy and effectiveness faced by the social order, thereby contributing to its stability. And through the production of knowledge within the framework of the research exemplar, political sociology would mediate between civil society and the state, providing the basis for sociopolitical cohesion. Because the empirical knowledge produced was consensually oriented, it would be of relevance to the instrumental problems faced by the state elites. Correspondingly, the objective character of this knowledge would invest its consensual definitions with authoritative status, thereby making it an effective basis for legitimation when projected to the public. The social order produced in this fashion would represent a transcendence of class and status politics, incorporating both into a higher synthesis. On the one hand, the presence of cleavages superseded 'class politics' based on traditional left-wing concerns with reform and social change.[12] On the other hand, consensus had taken the place of 'status politics' concerned with the conservation of traditional values. By assuming the standpoint of this social order, political sociology was to contribute to the internal containment of left- and right-wing extremism and to the international struggle against totalitarianism.

The sociology of politics, with its affirmation of consensual values, and its specification of the conditions making for 'democratic politics,' was thus the form of social-scientific activity 'functionally specific' to the problems of the American state in the Cold War order. This orientation, suggested Lipset (again following the lead of Parsons), proceeded from a particular *relation* to society and the state, namely one of *relative autonomy*. The political sociologist would not align with particular social interests, but rather would support in a disinterested manner the core values of American society and politics. As Lipset described the stance of the 'intellectual' in Cold War America:

Many American liberal intellectuals in the 1950s know that they should like and defend their society, but they still have the uneasy

feeling that they are betraying their obligation as intellectuals to
attack and criticize. Their solution to this dilemma is to continue to
feel allied with the left, but to vote Democratic; to think of them-
selves as liberals – and often even as socialists – but to withdraw
from active involvement or interest in politics and to concentrate
on their work, whether it be writing poetry or scholarly articles.
([1960] 1963, 369)

From a position akin to 'relative autonomy,' the intellectual was to
retain 'the inherent tendency to oppose the status quo,' yet by accepting
the basic value premises of the American political system, contribute to
its maintenance. Lipset outlined the range and consequences of intellectual 'dissent': 'Any *status quo* embodies rigidities and dogmatisms
which it is the inalienable right of intellectuals to attack, whether from
the standpoint of moving back to traditional values or forward toward
the achievement of the equalitarian dream. And in so doing the
intellectual helps to maintain the conflict which is the lifeblood of the
democratic system' (371). In other words, intellectuals could, with
impunity, criticize the *status quo* from *within* the system, without
abandoning their penchant for dissent. And since Lipset defined the
American system as 'leftist,' he could continue to identify himself as a
'man of the left,' while supporting the goals and values of the United
States. 'Now the fact is, I consider myself a man of the Left. But
confusing or not, I must add that I think of the United States as a nation
in which *Leftist values* predominate' ([1962] 1968, 153).

Lipset's conception of the Left not only defies the canons of normal
discourse, but is also patently self-serving. Rather than admitting to his
growing conservatism and support for a state whose progressive
credentials were questionable, Lipset characterized mainstream American values as *Leftist*, thereby legitimating his own orientation.[13] Its
biographical origins aside, Lipset's stance towards the Cold War order
was both faithful to the tenets of Cold War liberalism and consistent
with the 'relative autonomy' of professional practice set out by Parsons.
From a position 'relatively autonomous' from state and civil society, the
social-science professional was to produce expert 'functionally specific'
knowledge of symbolic relevance (affective neutrality) to the problem of
political legitimation and of instrumental relevance (universalism) to
the problem of state effectiveness. Lipset's sociology of politics, then,
carried out in 'relatively autonomous' universities, was to help overcome the 'strains' of 'status politics' attendant upon the progressive
rationalization of the political and social order.

This new orientation also served to establish the continuity between the new sub-discipline and a venerable tradition of political and social analysis. In his effort to establish the intellectual credentials of political sociology by invoking the founding fathers, however, Lipset succeeded only in revealing his own biases and shifting priorities. Although he acknowledged that Marx was 'the intellectual most responsible for the tendency to view conflict as the central interest in the study of politics and freedom,' Lipset was none the less troubled by Marx's view that 'conflict and consensus were alternatives rather than divergent tendencies that could be balanced within a society' ([1959a] 1965, 84). This meant in turn that 'he was unconcerned with society's need to maintain institutions and values which facilitate its stability and cohesion.' Marx was, moreover, 'uninterested in safeguards against state power, or the need for the division of powers, or the protections of juridicial guarantees, or a constitution, "bill of rights," and other democratic mechanisms' (86). It was with these considerations in mind that Lipset approvingly turned to Tocqueville, who 'unlike Marx, deliberately chose to emphasize the *positive* political aspects of social units which could maintain political cleavage and political consensus at the same time. He did not project his harmonious society into the future and did not separate in time and space the factors making for social integration from the sources of cleavage' (87). Through his 'interpretation of the central trends of modern society,' Tocqueville thus was able to specify the constituents of 'a pluralistic political system [and] the mechanisms for creating and maintaining the consensus necessary for a democratic society' (87).

Lipset's dismissal of Marx and his acceptance of Tocqueville were thus based more on normative than on analytical criteria. Marx was rejected not for his analysis of capitalism, but rather for his lack of concern with the integrative institutions that would make for capitalism's survival. It was Marx's *negativity* – his identification with a 'harmonious future society' set against the capitalist social orders of his day – that caused Lipset distress. Tocqueville, in contrast, both affirmed the basic health of the prevailing order and sought *positively* to understand how conflicts could be integrated within it, resulting in the maintenance of 'political cleavage and political consensus at the same time' (87). Lipset invoked the authority of Tocqueville to validate his own concern with contributing to the building of stable democratic systems. As he put it, political sociology should 'return to the problem posed by Tocqueville: the social requisites and consequences of democracy' (114). The implication was that the perspective on democracy derived from Tocqueville – buttressed by Parsons's conception of the political system – could be used to defuse and undermine contemporary variants of Marxist thought that emphasized cleavage and conflict to the exclusion of consensus. For such points of view, with their emphasis upon left-right distinctions and their partisanship on behalf of particular social strata, could potentially threaten the building of democracy if they gained currency. The concern to discredit and invalidate perspectives emphasizing cleavage is evident in the research agenda for political sociology that Lipset laid down.

A Research Agenda

'The prime concern of political sociology,' in Lipset's view, was 'the stability of a specific institutional structure or political regime' ([1959a] 1965, 91–2). Given that a stable democratic system requires both consensus and cleavage, one was obliged to study both these processes in order to understand 'the conditions encouraging democracy.' However, as Lipset observed, 'what is most striking about American political sociology has been its tendency to focus on cleavage and relatively to neglect the question of consensus.' The field had shown more interest 'in the questions posed by Marx than in those set by Tocqueville.' Consistent with his commitment to the end-of-ideology thesis and the overcoming of partisan conflict that it implied, Lipset sought to free political sociology from its left-wing legacy of emphasizing cleavage to the neglect of consensus. In doing so, he could contribute to the struggle against ideology and to the consolidation of democratic politics. This preoccupation affected Lipset's selection and treatment of the various research areas that he saw as constituting political sociology.

Of particular concern to Lipset was a reorientation of voting studies from 'political strife' to 'political consensus,' for 'the focus on cleavage ... tends to direct voting research away from sociological concerns toward social psychology, since the actual research is designed to find out how various structural cleavages affect the decision of the individual.' As a corrective to this practice, 'emphasis on the integrative aspects of electoral behavior would not only fill lacunae in our understanding of democracy as a system but would necessarily be more sociological in orientation than the study of cleavage' (92–3). Within a consensual framework, one's whole view of voting patterns would thereby change. 'Such phenomena as the Tory worker or the middle-class socialist,' according to Lipset, are for instance 'examples not only of deviation from class patterns, but also of a necessary condition for the maintenance of the political system.' This suggests the 'hypothesis that a stable democracy requires a situation in which all major political parties include supporters from many segments of the population.' If the parties relied too exclusively on particular social strata for their support, maintained Lipset, society would find itself troubled by 'a state of conflict among groups so intense and clear-cut as to rule out all possibility of compromise' (93).

The problem of political participation could be reinterpreted along the same lines. Rather than worrying about the degree of participation as opposed to apathy, one would try to determine 'under what conditions can a society have "sufficient" participation to maintain the democratic system without introducing sources of cleavage which will undermine the cohesion' (95). By undertaking research directed by the problem of how particular patterns of voting were related to political consensus, the political sociologist could thus help in the building of stable democracies. Lipset implied that research on voting emphasizing cleavages and political strife prevented political sociology from making a positive contribution to the consolidation of democratic systems. Presumably, by ignoring the implications of patterns of voting for consensus, research of this kind could neither deliver empirical relevance to the stable democracies nor provide the public with a consensual definition of the political order. Accordingly, through a research program oriented towards understanding how voting intersected with the presence or absence of stable democratic systems, political sociology could overcome its tendency to undermine political consensus.

Along similar lines, Lipset argued that 'most of the sociological studies of bureaucracy ... have concerned themselves with bureaucracy as a source of tension.' This 'provides further illustration that political sociology has been more concerned with cleavage than with integration' (101). As opposed to this perspective, Lipset held that the allegedly conservative 'bureaucratic political neutrality' actually was one of the important 'requisites of a democratic political system' (102). Lipset also suggested a re-examination of how voluntary associations contributed to the overall stability of the order (104). As an example of an alternative approach emphasizing the *consensual* role of voluntary associations within the political order, he referred to his own work, *Union Democracy* (with Trow and Coleman 1956), which 'is almost alone among studies of trade unions or other voluntary interest groups in suggesting that democracy and conflict ... contribute to cohesion and solidarity' (105). *Union Democracy* was viewed by Lipset as a prototype for future studies examining the relationship between the internal

arrangements of organizations and the workings of the overall democratic system. By specifying how the structure and dynamics of
organized groups affected the wider political process, the researcher
would thereby make a contribution to the cultivation and maintenance
of democracy.[14]

Lipset's dissatisfaction with the prevailing orientation of political
sociology was most evident in his discussions of research on 'social
movements' and 'power.' Repeating an earlier observation (1956), he
noted that 'American as well as European social scientists have been
much more interested in reform movements than in conventional and
conservative parties.'[15] In Lipset's view, 'these studies indicate the way
in which the left or liberal bias of American political sociologists has led
them to emphasize the aspects of change and conflict in their choice of
research subjects as well as in their conceptual schemes. Conservative
movements and forces, and the problems of integration and cohesion,
have been virtually neglected until fairly recently,' although Lipset
conceded that social scientists had studied right-wing extremism and
fascism at some length. These accounts, however, had focused on 'the
factors which create and sustain right-wing extremism ... rather than on
the factors which curtail it and cause its decline.' As a corrective, Lipset
suggested that more studies be done 'locating the sources of American
resistance to extremes of right and left during the Depression.' Similarly, he argued that research on McCarthyism should seek to explain its
decline rather than the basis for its support (98–9).

Thus, Lipset advocated that the study of social movements be
reoriented towards showing how they might be prevented, rather than
explaining their emergence and vitality. His concern was not so much
with social movements per se, but rather with how they were chosen for
study and what aspects of them were examined. By implication, he held
to the view that particular theoretical approaches, because of their
orientation and emphases, were inherently threatening to the building
of stable democratic systems. In particular, like Parsons, he was
concerned with the possible negative impact of ' "mass-society theory"
... a body of hypotheses ... about the vulnerability of social and political
systems to the yellow press, the hucksters, the commercialized mass
media, and totalitarian movements.' While he admitted that this
perspective has led to a better understanding of 'the sources of these
negative forces in society,' it has, all the same, 'developed fundamentally in the context of accounting for "evil" ' (100).

Mass-society theory, as 'another example of the political sociologist's
preoccupation with social disintegration,' was, according to Lipset,

unconcerned with the 'erection of a theory to explain why some societies are healthy and relatively invulnerable to such threats, or how new mechanisms are developed to fulfill the functions no longer satisfied by older, pre–mass-society institutions.' While they point out 'the threats carried in certain structural changes [they] do not see or look for possible resolutions of the problem' (100). By dwelling upon the presence and nature of mass-society tendencies, social scientists had failed to address questions related to how these developments could be prevented and overcome.

Lipset was also concerned about the way power had been studied. In particular, like Parsons, he took exception to the power-elite thesis developed by C. Wright Mills. This perspective in his view, mistakenly emphasizing the 'composition or social backgrounds of the decision-makers, is in part based on the assumption that actions flow logically and directly from the narrowly defined self-interests of those who hold power' (106). Such a view of power implies that 'the only way in which fundamental changes can be made in a society is by changing the incumbents of power positions.' Lipset concluded that this tendency to view power in terms of 'scarcity and composition ... provides another example of the preoccupation of political sociology with conflict alone rather than with conflict as part of the larger topic of social integration' (107). In terms of Parsons's concerns with the building of stable democratic systems, the conflict theory of power represented a potential threat. By viewing power 'as serving only the "interests" of power-holders,' such theories challenged the legitimacy of the political order and could potentially reinforce cleavages and conflict. Accordingly, Lipset favoured the view that 'the operation of a system of power ... serves basic needs of the entire society.' Lipset supported the adaptation of Parsons's conception of power as a 'facility or resource of the social system [which] implies a concern with consensus as well as with struggle.' 'The current ... efforts of Lynd and Parsons to free power-system analysis from its present almost total identification with the conflict of interests offers much promise for future research' (107). By implication, in pursuing research along these lines, the political sociologist would not only contribute to the definition of power as a functional necessity, but also produce empirical knowledge of relevance to its operation.

In general, to 'correct this bias' of political sociology's 'identification with the concerns of the political left' and its emphasis upon 'conflict and cleavage' to the neglect of 'consensus and cohesion,' Lipset suggested 'some important problems which should be investigated.'

What are the conditions of integration and legitimacy of a political system? How do multiple-group affiliations and deviations from normal cleavage patterns help to sustain the stability of political systems by reducing the strength of participation for unlimited goals? How can we measure and compare the relative cohesion of political structures? How do organizations handle conflict and create consensus? What is the role with respect to the political systems of the more integrated institutional spheres, such as the family, religion and secular culture? (113–14)

Complementing his proposed reorientation for the various subfields of political sociology, this list of areas was affected by the practical problem of how to build and sustain stable democratic systems. In Lipset's view, it was only through directing its attention towards how the system could reconcile consensus and cleavage that political sociology could overcome its former emphasis upon conflict and dissent. Lipset's own research was beginning to develop a coherence based on this unifying principle, as evidenced by *Political Man* ([1960] 1963). Although the chapters of this book had been previously published as separate articles elsewhere, they had been integrated into a common structure based on the overall problem of 'democracy as a characteristic of social systems.'[16] Guided by this concern, the book's major topics included 'the conditions necessary for democracy in societies and organizations; the factors which affect men's participation in politics, particularly their behavior as voters; and the sources of support for values and movements which sustain or threaten democratic institutions' (x).

Despite its programmatic format and proposals for further research, the conclusions reached in *Political Man* suggested that its practical aims were already near the point of realization. The set of collected essays served to vindicate Lipset's abiding intellectual commitments. With the apparent demise of McCarthyism and mass-society theory, and the apparent lack of widespread support for the power-elite thesis, he could proclaim in the concluding chapter the reality of the 'end of ideology,' and the victory of the intellectual orientation that accompanied it: 'If we limit our analysis to domestic threats to the system ... there is reason to expect that stable democratic institutions will continue to characterize the mature industrialized Western societies' ([1960] 1963, 453).

Inherent in this consolidation, he noted, was 'the shift away from ideology towards sociology.' That is, 'the very growth of sociology as an intellectual force outside the academy ... is a tribute ... to the loss of interest in political inquiry (453). According to Lipset, the apparent decline of interest in politics – as manifest in cleavage and conflict – signified that the goals of political sociology as a stabilizing force in Western democracies had already been accomplished. Nevertheless, in keeping with the sentiments at the Milan meetings, the newly emerged field had in no sense become superfluous. The challenge remained to help extend the democratic system to the rest of the world (454). Having overcome internal extremism, the Western states could be viewed as 'vital centers' faced with the task of expanding their forms of political organization to the new nations. Correspondingly, while the professional social scientist in advanced industrial societies no longer had to confront the strains of 'status politics' endemic to rationalization, his contributions to overcoming ideologies were urgently needed in lesser developed countries.

Ideology and passion may no longer be necessary to sustain the class struggle within stable and affluent democracies, but they are clearly needed in the international effort to develop free political and economic institutions in the rest of the world. It is only the ideological class struggle within the West which is ending. Ideological conflicts linked to levels and problems of economic development and of appropriate political institutions among different nations will last far beyond our lifetime, and men committed to democracy can abstain from them only at their peril. (456)

In this sense, 'the leftist intellectual, the trade-union leader, and the socialist politician in the West have an important role to play in this political struggle.' More particularly, 'Western leaders must communicate and work with non-Communist revolutionaries in the Orient and Africa at the same time that they accept the fact that serious ideological controversies have ended at home.' The consolidation of the sociology of politics, in Lipset's view, was a crucial aspect of this enterprise:

This book's [Political Man] concern with making explicit the conditions of the democratic order reflects my perhaps over-rationalistic belief that a fuller understanding of the various conditions under which democracy has existed may help men to develop it where it does not now exist ... Democracy has existed in a variety of circumstances, even if it is most commonly sustained by a limited set of conditions. It cannot be achieved by acts of will alone, of course, but men's wills expressed in action can shape institutions and events in directions that reduce or increase the chances for democracy's development and survival. (455–6)

As a self-confessed modern-day Tocqueville, Lipset viewed the development of the sociology of politics as inherently linked to the sociology of democratic development. In the same way that Tocqueville studied America in the 1830s in order to help the cause of democracy in absolutist Europe, Lipset believed that the clarification of 'the operation of Western democracy in the mid-twentieth century may contribute to the political battle in Asia and Africa' (456).

The apparent 'end of ideology' in the United States and Western Europe marked a new phase in the sociology of politics. As a capstone to his efforts, Lipset was designated president of the Committee on Political Sociology established at the Fourth World Congress of Sociology in Stresa, 1959. The themes considered by the committee in the following decade bear testimony to Lipset's general concerns.[17] Through the consolidation of the new sub-discipline on an international basis, the experience of the American nation in combining cleavage with consensus in a stable polity could serve as an implicit standard for how 'the new masses' could be assimilated into both advanced-industrial and 'modernizing' countries. Consistent with this view, his work now began to take an explicitly comparative focus as he sought to demonstrate the relevance of American democracy to other countries, while diagnosing the barriers to the spread and growth of democracy that existed in other parts of the world. In relation to developments in Europe, Lipset noted that the United States, as 'the most advanced society technologically,' with 'the most developed set of political and class relationships ... has presented the image of the European future' (1967a, 338).

As the 'First New Nation,' the United States, in Lipset's view, 'perhaps ... can contribute more than money to the latter-day ones; perhaps its development can show how revolutionary, equalitarian and populist values become incorporated into a stable nonauthoritarian polity.' He held the American experience to be of particular relevance to the developing countries, which faced many of the same problems solved by the United States after its break from colonial rule. The United States made a break with the past and 'like other new nations ... was unstable because this break was associated with a rejection of traditional institutions and values as means and standards for solving national problems. As a result it had to find new ways to meet these problems' (1964b, 308–9).

In addressing himself to the task of demonstrating the relevance of the American experience to the developing nations, Lipset adapted Parsons's pattern variables. In 'specifying the value system in the United States as contrasted with that in other countries,' he concluded that 'the Parsonian pattern-variables formed the most useful set of classifications for such comparative analysis' (1969, 163). Fully consistent with the Parsonsian project, the categories that had originally been derived by Parsons to offer guide-lines for professional contributions to rationalization were now implemented with global designs. In the same way that they had helped to 'modernize' advanced societies, practice oriented by the primary patterns would, it was hoped, lead to the same pattern of consolidation in the third world. This isomorphism between the sociology of politics and the political systems of pluralist democracies led to an intellectual crisis, when these societies were wracked by their own crises of legitimacy in the late 1960s. The comparative-politics movement also experienced a crisis, as its bias towards 'political modernization' was belied by the events in the third world during the same period. These interrelated crises had their origins in Parsons's legacy to comparative politics and the sociology of politics.

12

The Decay of Political Sociology

The Convergence between Political Science and Sociology

By the mid-1960s, it had become evident to its proponents that political sociology had established itself as a field of knowledge. Parsons remarked in the introduction to *Politics and Social Structure* that

'political sociology' ... was scarcely heard of before the middle of this century, but now has become a prominent conception giving a title to the interests and work of a considerable number of people on both sides of the disciplinary line. Indeed, this trend has gone far enough to suggest that, if political sciences has not shifted its principal partnership among related disciplines from economics to sociology, at least its allegiance has tended to become more nearly 'bigamous.' (1969, xiii)

Parsons observed that political sociology was 'an "interstitial" discipline in some ways comparable to social psychology.' Attesting to the prominence of the new approach, Parsons 'made a quick canvass of names' of those active in 'the field which sociologists call "political sociology" and political scientists do not yet have a stable term for – the nearest perhaps being the "behavioral" orientation in political science.' This list included, 'on the political science side,' Gabriel Almond, Lucian Pye, Sidney Verba, and Myron Wiener. 'On the sociological side,' he mentioned, among others, Reinhard Bendix, Bernard Berelson, Paul Lazarsfeld, Seymour Lipset, and Edward Shils (xiii–xiv).

Lipset was even more explicit in his observations that political science and sociology had converged towards a common perspective. At the request of the editor of the *American Journal of Sociology,* he was asked, as 'a sociologist of political life,' to comment on the following trends:

Particularly in the past decade the theoretical and methodological interplay between sociology and political science has intensified greatly. In sociology this interplay has involved the rapid development and consolidation of the subfield of political sociology; in political science it has seen the development of the 'behavioral approach' to politics and the analytic treatment of political systems. (1964, 730)

Lipset described the apposite changes within political science: 'From a predominant concern with the conditions sustaining the good society (political theory) – the nature of public administration, the operation of government, and the history of politics – political scientists have increasingly turned to the elaboration and testing of relevant aspects of social science theory' (730). He noted that

the increasingly close theoretical and methodological identity between political science and sociological orientations makes it difficult to generalize about social scientists who call themselves political scientists without also discussing those who describe themselves as political or comparative sociologists. Political scientists writing on the emerging polities of the 'third world' such as David Apter, Gabriel Almond, James S. Coleman ... Lucien Pye, Karl Deutsch, Myron Wiener, and many others, are as conversant with sociology and employ its principles and findings as much as any sociologist. (732)

'The interaction between the fields which has led to a common set of theoretical and methodological formulations,' in Lipset's view, 'has thus flowed from "behavioral" political scientists' efforts to analyze political systems and behavior within a social science framework and from the growing emphasis on comparative analysis in sociology which forces sociologists to pay considerable attention to the role of political institutions' (733). This in turn has meant that 'in various books dealing with macroscopic political problems and edited by political scientists, the writings of political scientists, sociologists, economists, and psychologists are brought together on the basis of their common social science approach, rather than the writer's academic discipline' (733–4).

Lipset suggested that 'the coincidence of interests, theoretical approaches, and methodology ... suggests the need for a more conscious collaboration than has hitherto occurred, particularly on the part of sociologists.' Political science had much to offer sociologists, according to Lipset, for 'perhaps more work analyzing the properties of complex systems is being done in political science than in sociology. The writings of Parsons, Levy, and Merton in this area are extremely influential, while a number of political scientists have endeavored to go beyond or to modify their conceptual approaches.' Lipset was to conclude that 'closing the conceptual and methodological gaps between the two disciplines may, perhaps, establish a common endeavor that accepts the basic premises of a general social science, asserting the primary concern of both disciplines to understand and account for human group behavior in terms of theory relevant to every society and to all forms of behavior at every level within society' (734).

The remarks of Parsons and Lipset attest to their conviction that political science and sociology had converged towards a common approach. Underlying the social-scientific theory that both fields shared was the conceptual apparatus developed by Parsons. It was through the production of knowledge based on Parsons's primary patterns (as discussed earlier) that political sociology was to contribute to the processes of instrumentation and legitimation carried out by the modern state in both first- and third-world settings. Given that political sociology derived its orientation from a commitment to the development and growth of the capitalist nation-state, the knowledge the field produced was intrinsically related to the institutions and practices within it. Accordingly, when countries in the Western sphere of influence began to experience crises in the mid sixties, political sociology found itself in a state of crisis as well.

During the halcyon days of the 'American celebration,' the adaptation of Parsons's thought to the nascent sub-discipline gave it both rigour and relevance. However, less than a decade later, when American fortunes had turned full circle, the Parsonsian premises of political sociology would betray themselves with a vengeance. The crises that developed in both the first and third world led not only to the abandonment of Parsons's practical categories, but to the decoupling of political science and sociology, signalling an end to their short-lived common venture into political sociology.

International Disorder and the Shift in Comparative Politics

By the late 1960s, comparative politics was in disarray. As Almond described the state of the field at that time,

the polemic was resounding all about us, and disillusionment was rife ... The contrast with the mood that characterized this field of interest at the time of its beginnings some fifteen years earlier was striking. The search for development theory had begun in the same era that produced the Peace Corps. Many naive hopes and expectations of the end of ideology and of revolution in the West, and the discovery of low-cost high-yield approaches to modernization in the new nations had been dashed in the interval. (Almond 1973, 22)

The original impetus to comparative politics had been a practical concern to contribute to the modernization of developing countries. However, when the desired pattern of change was not forthcoming, 'modernization theory' itself became discredited. The crisis within comparative politics was closely tied to the crisis of American foreign policy in relation to the new nations. As it became increasingly evident that the course of events in the third world did not conform to American designs, the premises underlying development policy were called into question as well. During the early 1960s, in the wake of the Cuban Revolution, American foreign policy in relation to developing countries came to be guided by a variant of modernization theory. It was believed that through economic development – as fuelled through increased levels of American assistance – political, social, and cultural development could be cultivated, and democratic rather than communist systems established.

The main vehicle for this assistance was the Agency for International Development (AID), which disbursed an average of over $4 billion per year between 1961 and 1963 (as compared to an annual average of $2.5 billion during the five-year period prior to 1961). Moreover, a much larger share was used for 'developmental' as opposed to 'security of military purposes' (Packenham 1973, 60). However, the increasing instability in the developing countries during the early years of the Alliance for Progress gave little reason to believe that AID was realizing its stated objectives. In 1962 and 1963 alone, Latin America was the scene of six military coups. After Lyndon Johnson acceded to the presidency, the premises of the Kennedy Doctrine as articulated through AID were called into question with 'the shift in practice back to a greater emphasis on security objectives for foreign aid,' marked by 'an explicit and fairly intense concern with *political* development' (87–8; emphasis added). Very possibly, the new stress upon *political develop-ment* was given impetus by revelations of the Project Camelot debacle.[1] Funded by the U.S. Army, Project Camelot was to explore, through social-scientific theory and research, the possibilities for conducting effective counter-insurgency in selected developing countries. The discovery by Chilean officials that such a study was being planned strained relations between the United States and developing countries, resulted in a cry of public outrage, and ultimately forced the cancella-tion of the project by the State Department. Nevertheless, that the Department of Defense felt it necessary to resort to 'manipulation of internal political forces as a means of moving political systems in particular directions' revealed, as Braibanti suggested, 'the absence of a doctrine of political reform' within the State Department (1969, 23–4).

In any case, largely through congressional initiative, the doctrine of political development became an important feature of American foreign policy through the Title IX amendment to the Foreign Assistance Act of 1966 (Braibanti 1969, 4–21; Packenham 1973, 155–60). Title IX broad-ened the goals of foreign assistance to include *political* criteria. 'AID's reports,' recommended the House Committee on Foreign Relations upon approving the amendment, '"should evaluate American assis-tance not only in economic terms, but also in terms of the extent to which our aid encourages democratic political processes"' (in Packen-ham 1973, 100).

The shift in government attitude indicated by Title IX, therefore, bore the promise that social-scientific research would become an essential part of formulating policy for a new program of political development. If this close working arrangement with the government were to be realized, however, social scientists faced the problem of demonstrating the relevance of the knowledge they produced to the problem of political development. The comparative-politics approach, based on the practi-cal guide-lines of Talcott Parsons (that through the infusion of the 'primary patterns' into developing countries, 'modernization' was to take place and democracy ensured), was deemed inadequate. A variant of this mode of thinking came to influence foreign policy under the Kennedy administration. The turbulent events of the early sixties, however, raised questions about both the policy and the theory underlying it. It was no longer taken for granted that economic and social development would automatically lead to political development and stability. Rather, in view of the increasing incidence of political instability in developing countries, the greatest concern of the American state managers was the construction of stable political orders in developing countries. Hence to be of relevance to this new concern, political science had to address the problem of how political stability could be ensured. However, as long as political scientists subscribed to modernization theory, in which political development was derived from economic and social development, they would be unable to orient themselves specifically to the task at hand. This meant that if political science were to take advantage of the new opportunities arising from 'political disorder,' it would have not only to separate itself from modernization theory, but also to generate an approach specific to questions surrounding 'political development.' In response to political turbulence in the third world, and to the shift in American foreign policy towards a concern with political development, a realignment of this kind could be detected within comparative politics.

The Decoupling of Sociology and Political Science

The close connection between the shortcomings of modernization theory and the failure of American foreign policy received particular attention in the writings of Samuel P. Huntington, one of the most strident and influential advocates of a reorientation in comparative politics. Huntington's criticisms of political development *theory* and political development *practice* were two sides of the same coin. 'The most striking gap in American foreign policy toward the third world,' he observed, 'has been its failure until recently to deal directly with the problems posed by this mounting violence and instability.' Mistakenly, 'the United States has actively attempted to reduce poverty and to promote development of the nations of the third world [and] devoted little attention to the problems of promoting political stability and political development in these countries.' America's failure rested upon the belief 'that instability is the result of poverty and hence that efforts to promote economic development will also promote political stability' (U.S. Congress 1967, 117).

Huntington took issue with the conventional theory of modernization because it could not offer a specific account of political development. Rather, it assumed that modernization *entailed* political development. This not only 'limited too drastically the applicability of the concept of political development, "in both time and space" ' but also 'tended to reduce its empirical relevance, and made it difficult if not impossible to conceive of its reversibility, *i.e.*, to talk about political decay' (1971, 301–2). Modernization theory assumed that economic and social development would inevitably lead to political development. However, according to Huntington, these changes in fact could lead to the disintegration of political institutions. What Huntington proposed was that political development proceeded – and by extension, could be studied – *autonomously* from social and economic development. More fundamentally, Huntington was concerned with the teleological nature of modernization theory. In assuming that the advanced countries 'had "arrived" ... their past was of interest not for what it would show about their future but for what it showed about the future of those other societies which still struggled through the transition between tradition and modernity.' 'The theory of modernization thus rationalized change abroad and the status quo at home. It left blank the future of modernity. Modernization theory combined an extraordinary faith in the efficacy of modernity's past with no image of the potentialities of modernity's future' (292–3).

According to Huntington, modernization mistakenly assumed that advanced societies could serve as models for countries in the process of development. By extension, it was similarly misguided to uncritically seek to replicate the characteristics of advanced societies in developing countries. In this view, he again deviated from the assumptions of conventional comparative politics. As Huntington saw it, 'the variations of the North American political system which North Americans would like to reproduce in Latin America are simply too weak, too diffuse, too dispersed to mobilize the political power necessary to bring about fundamental change' (1968, 136). Rather, 'the primary need' faced by developing countries was 'the accumulation and concentration of power, not its dispersion, and it is in Moscow and Peking and not in Washington that this lesson is to be learned' (137–8).

Huntington advanced the contentious thesis that 'political modernization in America has ... been strangely attenuated and incomplete' (98). This weakness of political institutions, in his view, made the United States vulnerable to the 'democratic distemper' that he felt was rampant in the 1960s: 'Democracy ... can very easily become a threat to itself in the United States. Political authority is never strong here, and it is peculiarly weak during a period of intense commitment to democratic and egalitarian ideals. In the United States, the strength of the democratic ideal poses a problem for the governability of democracy in a way which is not the case elsewhere' (1976, 37).

Huntington argued for a similar antidote to political instability at home and abroad, namely, a limitation to the extension of democracy and/or a strengthening of political institutions. Given America's archaic polity, it could scarcely serve as a prototype for developing countries. Nevertheless, political expertise could still be offered to developing countries. But rather than trying to impose the American model on foreign political systems, an effort should be made, he contended, to adapt advice to the situation of the country in question. As Huntington pointed out, this course of action was already in the process of realization in that the United States 'supported and attempted to promote the development of the most varied types of political systems around the world,' such as the 'essentially authoritarian monarchy' of Iran, 'one-party systems in Tunisia and Bolivia, a military led dominant party system in Korea, monarchial-bureaucratic regimes in Thailand and Nepal, and also, of course, a variety of competitive democratic systems in which the dominant groups have been socialist, Catholic, and liberal, as well as highly conservative' (1968a, 24–5). Agreeing with this tendency in foreign policy, Huntington maintained that the United States should support regimes in terms of their *effectiveness* rather than because of their political coloration or make-up.

Huntington not only took issue with the assumption of modernization theory that the Anglo-American system could be exported, but also called into question the methodology that such a standpoint implied. As he pointed out, the prototypical statement on modernization, authored by Almond and Coleman (1960), 'is concerned with the analysis of the political systems of societies which are presumed to be developing (or modernizing) and the comparison of those systems with the political systems presumed to exist in modern societies. Its key categories ... (system, role, culture, structure, function, socialization) ... are ... essential to the comparative analysis of political systems; they are not oriented to the change and development of political systems' (1971, 299). Most critically, it is unable to give an account of a dynamic process. Implicit in the conception of modernization offered by Almond and Coleman was not only a framework of 'comparative statics' but also a teleological emphasis. Traditional societies were thought to be becoming inexorably more modern; the typological approach was a way of diagnosing to what degree that path had been traversed. With its static emphasis, modernization theory, in Huntington's view, was of little value for indicating how the dynamic process of political development could be achieved. This meant that the political scientist subscribing to this point of view would be unable to offer knowledge of relevance to policy-makers.

Concern with the practical limitations inherent in the static nature of modernization theory became commonplace in comparative politics during the late 1960s. In a contribution to a symposium on political science and public policy in 1966, Lucian Pye essentially echoed Huntington's criticisms: 'our biased view of science, which has impeded our capacities for analyzing change, has also restricted our potential for either studying the dynamic processes of policy output or contributing effectively to policy-making. Just as we have tended to look to the past rather than to the future, so we have been more interested in analyzing sources and causes than in studying consequences and outcomes' (Pye 1966, 240). It was the 'typological' approach, drawing primarily upon Weber and Parsons, Pye argued, that led to a static mode of theorizing in which 'the dynamics of change' were neglected. While 'this classificatory approach ... has greatly enhanced our skills in "judging" societies in the same manner as skilled judges can appraise prize cattle,' at the same time it 'has taught us little about the kind of science necessary for the controlled breeding of cattle. And there is quite a difference between the art of judging cattle and the science of breeding them; a difference comparable to that between static and dynamic analysis' (249).

A further feature of the social sciences that 'may ... limit our capacity to help policy-makers with the problems of dynamic change,' Pye maintained, was 'our innocent faith in the ultimate utility of all pure science.' This led to the conception that 'time can ... ensure the utility of the most abstract speculations.' Pye suggested that 'the view of the spontaneous linkage between theory and practical knowledge,' favoured by social-scientific purists, 'rests upon a distorted and much too intellectualized view of the nature of the scientific enterprise.' Indeed, 'this faith in the ultimate utility of pure theory has been used to justify a posture of disinterest in the pressing public policy issues of the moment' (260).

From Static Analysis to Political Development

Implied by this critique of static analysis was the need to give more attention to the *process* of development, for by examining the way in which change had occurred, one could be in a position to make recommendations of relevance to public policy. This shift towards more historically grounded analyses was evident in the seventh volume of the Studies in Political Development series, which appeared in 1971 after a five-year hiatus (Binder et al. 1971).

Rather than continuing to elaborate the typological distinctions set out by Almond and Coleman, the participants, from a 'concern with the tensions in the developmental process ... moved on to the identification and analysis of those key problems or crises that appear to have arisen historically in the process of political development,' namely, '*identity, legitimacy, participation, penetration, and distribution.*' The new, shared perspective was hence a dynamic one, with an emphasis upon how various societies had addressed the '"problem areas" that either plague a society or regime or demand the attention of its leaders and aware citizens' (Pye 1971, viii).

Verba suggested in a summary statement to the volume that the most effective method for analysing patterns of political development was a 'sequential model.' He emphasized that 'such models do not have to be deterministic; they may allow predictions of probable paths of change and estimations of the consequences of alternative paths' (Verba 1971, 285). In fact, the 'causal model' approach assumed the standpoint of the planner concerned with how certain sequences of problems and their attempted solutions led to particular political outcomes. 'Such an approach,' Verba contended, 'might produce findings of great relevance to those interested in applying the findings of developmental studies to policy choice situations. It might not be in the power of developmental planners to schedule developmental problems or crises ... but the planner would be armed with important information if he knew something of the consequences of various orderings of the problems or crises' (316).

This shift of comparative politics towards analyses of 'sequences' and 'crises' was provoked by a dissatisfaction with the static and teleological characteristics of modernization theory. It was this sense of disillusionment, Almond suggested, that lay behind 'an impulse to "return to historical nature."' This 'search for a cure in history ... took a more modest, empirically grounded, form ... Since the development that we were seeking to explain occurred in history, why not select historical episodes, examine them in great detail, try out varieties of developmental explanation, and see how they fit?' (1973, 22). The reorientation by comparative politics towards a more historical approach, Almond attested, flowed from its theoretical and practical irrelevance to the course of events in the late sixties. Given the growing tide of disaffection in the West and the widely acknowledged failure of modernization in the developing countries, a theoretical framework based on a tacit progressive evolution from the 'lesser' to the 'more' modern nations could no longer be convincingly upheld. A theory that prescribed the 'modernization' of the social structure as antecedent to political stability was of little value to policy-makers concerned with the short-term problems of quelling political unrest. As the comments of Huntington, Pye, Verba, and Almond suggest, the 'return to historical nature' was consistent with these overriding practical concerns. The political unrest of the sixties, from the perspective of the leading figures in the Committee on Comparative Politics revealed the inefficacy of a strategy for inducing modernization based on a unilinear historical vision, with political development necessarily following from economic, social, and cultural change.

The inability of comparative politics to cope with the practical demands of the present flowed from its assumptions about the past. It was therefore essential for the committee members to reassess their view of history in light of the practical demands they now faced, namely, generating a theory of political development relevant to the amendments to the Foreign Assistance Act. The new conception of history that emerged embodied implicit policy concerns of the committee. The historical standpoint it assumed was that of the contemporary policy-maker, facing the task of choosing a course of action whose timing and sequence were appropriate to the crises and problems inherent in building political order. The dynamics of change were of importance because they permitted understanding of how a desired political transformation might be induced. By specifying which sets of conditions in the past, occurring in which sequences, had led to which political outcomes, the theorist could provide the policy-maker with knowledge of relevance to expediting political development. History, then, was to be mined for its insights into how strong, effective states had been built and stable political orders established. These new theoretical concerns were fuelled by growing prospects for the application of political development to policy formation through the various consulting and advisory bodies that sprang up with the demise of the Alliance for Progress and the escalation of the Vietnam War in 1965–6.

Political Science and Political Engineering

The political scientist was to assume the role of 'political engineer' whose task was to contribute to political development. For instance, it was through a specific concern with 'polity-building,' argued Giovanni Sartori, that political science could establish itself as an *applied* discipline. Just as economists were actively involved in the planning of growth, said Sartori, political scientists ought to be more explicitly concerned with the 'deliberate planning of political development,' even though this 'squarely amounts to a deliberate "manipulation of man." ' It is no more reasonable, Sartori argued, 'to resent the kind of political manipulation which is required to "plan democracy" any more than we resent the kind of economic manipulation which is required to "plan growth"' (1968, 271). He suggested that 'whatever is done by the economist should also be done by the political scientist ... To shun political engineering only leaves us as impotent as we are, to the advantage of the power of someone else. We cannot afford a unilateral growth, the growth of the *pure* science to the detriment of the *applied* science' (271–2).

The new emphasis upon political development was hence intrinsically of practical implication, for to address the 'frontal problems of political development' was to ask 'which are the means and the levers of polity-building?' This in turn raised 'the central question of political engineering,' which is, 'how can we intervene *politically* in steering and shaping a process of political development?' (272). A researcher had to seek a practical understanding of how 'political organizations and procedures' could be institutionalized and 'differentiated political structures, functions, and capabilities' created (263). According to Sartori, 'through a refined understanding of how particular configurations of electoral and party systems *channelled* political action and affected political order, the researcher could thereby acquire applied expertise in the field of *political* development' (273–4). This could provide a position from which to advise policy-makers on how stable political order could be created.

Lucien Pye maintained that to overcome the gap between theory and practice in the social sciences, a working arrangement similar to that obtaining between the '*theoretical scientist*' and the '*engineer*' ought to be established. He pointed out that in the natural sciences, 'the translation of theoretical developments into practical achievements depends upon the existence of large cadres of engineers and applied scientists whose skill and knowledge only imperceptibly shade off from those of the most advanced theoretical scientists. The great gap that exists between the social scientist and the policy-maker thus has no counterpart in the physical sciences, for it has been filled by the role of the engineer.' In Pye's view, the study of 'the relationship of the scientist to the engineer' could shed light on how the social sciences might 'help with the problem of change.' It was Pye's conviction that 'if we ever are to make sure that the results of our theoretical work will be relevant to policy-making, we will have to take it upon ourselves to train people who will have the skills necessary to translate such knowledge into the principles necessary for guiding public policy.' This entailed a 'more complicated division of labor' involving 'a high degree of specialized skill' overlapping with the disciplines' more theoretical concerns. For the process of contributing to policy-making could no longer depend solely upon 'the passage of time during which we can make more and more advances in theory' (Pye 1966, 260–1).

Whether fortuitous or not, Pye's reflections on a more efficacious division of labour within comparative politics were rapidly finding an approximation in reality. Huntington, as the leading exponent of the political-engineering approach, sought to show government officials how political development could best be achieved. In light of the American experience in Vietnam, Huntington suggested that the 'U.S. ought to encourage the development of more highly structured and broad-based party systems in modernizing countries (1968a, 22). He reasoned that 'modernization means increasing political participation. That participation has to be organized. The principal institutional means for organizing the participation is the political party. Why should it be thought immoral or inappropriate to help strengthen these essential institutions of modern society?' (23). Huntington maintained that a program of political development would have distinct advantages over programs based on social reform and military intervention.

Such a program of preventive political involvement would be less visible to both the American public and foreign publics. In an age of introversion and of hostility to massive expenditures overseas this has much to be said for it. Stimulating political organization, in particular, would get the U.S. out of the job of attempting to promote social and economic changes on its own. Instead of trying to pressure a reluctant government to introduce land reform as a substitute for peasant revolution, we would instead focus on the promotion of peasant organization which could then, if they wished to, put the pressure on the government. Political involvements of this nature could well be more discreet, less expensive, and more productive of political stability, than current reliance on economic development, social reform, and ultimately, military intervention. (27)

The United States could as part of its foreign-aid program, 'advise ... on the prerequisites and requirements of political organization, even as they do for economic development, and give them technical and material assistance in the development of political organizations' (U.S.

Congress 1967, 120). The 'new activities directed specifically toward political development ... might include assistance to political parties, programs to develop and train political leaders, assistance to more broadly based and public-oriented interest groups, and more widespread support for community development programs.' Huntington suggested that 'somewhere, either inside AID or outside AID, but preferably inside, we need an office for political development. We need diplomats and economic planners, but we also need to recruit and train personnel skilled in the techniques of analyzing political change and promoting political organization. What we need, perhaps, is a new-style CIA, more skilled in building governments than in subverting them.' Such a 'prescription for political stability,' Huntington stressed, was not 'highly adventurous,' but rather 'a highly conservative prescription for political stability.' 'The vacuum of power and authority which exists in so many modernizing countries may be filled temporarily by charismatic leaderhip or military force. But it can be filled permanently only by political organization' (121).

Huntington was not alone as a mediator between the social-scientific community and the federal government. In the wake of Title IX, a number of institutional linkages developed whose purpose was to provide close ties between the academic world and policy-makers. One link between academic research and AID, observed Braibanti, 'is the research advisory committee within AID but composed of both AID officials and academic scholars. That committee was consulted on Title IX implementation soon after the amendment appeared.' Another organization that could potentially mediate between the 'academic community and the Agency for International Development,' he maintained, was 'the Southeast Asia Development Advisory Group (SEADAG)' (1969, 26). Braibanti harboured the hope that 'under conditions of the best possible rapport between academic theorizing and AID field experience, the gradual codification of such doctrines might be the new gristmill into which the now elusive, unsystematized speculations and experiences relating to political development might be fed' (21–2). He speculated that 'the consequence might be, in a decade or so, the articulation of strategies of administrative reform to those of political growth, and of experience in transnationally induced change to academic theory construction' (21–2).

Through organizations mediating between the state and the academy (SEADAG, etc.), spokesmen such as Huntington, Pye, and Braibanti were able to present their views on how political order might be developed. These same applied consultants, correspondingly, were involved with the development of theory within their profession, and indeed played a mediating role between the applied and theoretical branches of the field. It is noteworthy that while comparative politics was gaining greater credibility and leverage as an applied discipline, the more theoretical concerns of the movement were undergoing a transformation as well. As Braibanti noted, 'the extensive operations of the Agency for International Development designed to induce administrative reform in developing states' had 'implications for theory' as well as for 'operational pertinence.' This led to 'several conferences on closely allied problems' (vii).

Possibly the most ambitious of these was held at Bellagio in 1967. Its purpose was to reorient 'political development thought' in view of the changes in the foreign-assistance acts that had given 'fresh cogency [to] the relationship of induced administrative change to the development of political systems' (4). Title IX, as Braibanti admitted, 'while providing no answer to the problem of political development, does serve to direct attention to some formulation for the engineering of political systems' (639–40). This leitmotif of 'political engineering' had an effect on the contributions to the symposium. Even though a 'model of dazzling complexity' did not develop from the discussions, there did emerge, in Braibanti's view, 'the glimmerings of a common perspective ... the configurative or ecological tissue in which administration is embedded, the indigenization of political institutions, and the insistence on typological schema' (638–9). And perhaps most significantly, the symposium served to orient the theoretical basis of the political development movement towards concerns raised by the practical problems of implementing Title IX.

The shift of comparative politics towards political engineering, augmented by a revised historical vision, thus flowed from a rejection of conventional modernization theory on *practical* grounds. The course of events during the 1960s discredited the view that the gradual 'rationalization' of developing countries would inevitably lead to stable political systems comparable to the Anglo-American prototype. This apparent failure lay behind the rejection of Parsonsian theory as well. The conventional approach to modernization was based on Parsons's view that the development of professionalized social-scientific knowledge was *constitutive* of the transition from tradition to modernity. That is, through a form of practice guided by the primary patterns of disinterestedness, universalism, affective neutrality, and functional specificity, the social sciences were to actively contribute to the process of modernization.

However, from the vantage-point of comparative politics in the late sixties, the Parsonsian framework began to appear increasingly irrelevant to the problems at hand. Pye noted that the 'disinterest' inherent in the 'scientific enterprise,' as favoured by Parsons, put its faith in 'the ultimate utility [of] pure science,' rather than in addressing 'pressing public policy issues of the moment' (Pye 1966, 260). The universalism inherent in Parsons's notion of 'general theory' did not easily lend itself to particular analyses and applications. Substantively, Huntington and Sartori challenged the lack of autonomy given to the political sphere within the schema derived from Parsons. If the theorist of political development was to contribute to the formation of public policy, they argued, a framework in which the sphere of politics received primacy would have to be provided. This meant that those working in comparative politics must demonstrate rigorously and in more detail how effective political order could best be constructed from the various components available. The problem they confronted was one of determining which set of political institutions would be appropriate for ensuring order in a given situation. The role of the academic social scientist was thus to become increasingly a technical one – helping determine which means (institutions, components) would be suitable for realizing the accepted end (political order).

If the solution to the problem of order was viewed in technical terms, then it was of less immediacy to consider the problems of building consensus through communicating values into the 'political culture.' If political order was thought to follow directly from the building of strong political institutions, then the 'political theory' inherent in the Parsonsian political system (intended to 'define the situation' for the 'modernizing elites' of developing countries) became unimportant. Indeed, in light of the increasing demands of rising groups for greater participation, which thereby destabilized political systems, attempts to inculcate foreign cultures with Western values were now regarded with suspicion. Following Huntington's analysis, the problem became one of dampening democracy and expanding political authority by creating stronger, more resilient institutions.

The crisis in political sociology was not, however, confined to its comparative-politics wing. During the same period, the sociology of politics was called into question for its irrelevance in the face of political turbulence in capitalist democracies.

Berlin 1968: Political Sociology in Crisis

Propitiously, the Third International Conference on Comparative Sociology was held in 1968 in Berlin – scene of one of the largest and most intense student movements in Western Europe. That the encounter with student activism had a profound and disturbing effect upon the course of the comparative sociology of politics was left undisguised in a joint statement issued by Stein Rokkan and Seymour Lipset prefatory to the collected conference proceedings. In their view, 'the year 1968' was at once 'a watershed in the history of democratic mass politics [and] a watershed in the history of the international discipline of political sociology.'

The quiet years of accommodation, integration, and domestication were finally over, new waves of mobilization and counter-mobilization brought a number of western democracies out of equilibrium, a new generation challenged the assumptions and the rhetoric of the old ... the violent eruption of new forces did not only challenge the models and the theories of the fifties and the early sixties, but also forced a revaluation of data-gathering techniques and analysis strategies. (Lipset and Rokkan 1968, ix)

In assessing the timing and the impact of the student movement in this manner, the authors made explicit the normative assumptions of political sociology. While the level of activism and dissent was cresting in 1968, to say that 'new forces suddenly erupted with violence' in that year was a gross misrepresentation of the decade, if not the entire post-war period.[2] The fact that political sociologists did not confront the full significance of developments like these until 1968 (when political dissent was literally under their noses) is indicative of the self-induced myopia of the field and its built-in resistance to the emergence of new political challenges in the sixties.[3] Their perception of the new political phenomena was mediated by the political commitments and values that permeated the overall explanatory framework that had been constructed. As Lipset and Rokkan revealed, the theoretical apparatus and methodological techniques of political sociology originated 'during the quiet years of consolidation and deideologization from 1945 to 1965.' The conceptual schema of political sociology, with its emphasis upon 'unhurried attempts at theoretical systematization,' *coincided* with a commitment to 'the slow pace of political development' that was perceived to have been characteristic of Western democracies (ix).

Indeed, political sociology, as originally conceived of by Lipset, was *practically* linked to the process of 'democratization' considered to be occurring around the globe. By virtue of a theoretical framework that affirmed the values of democratic politics (while providing empirical knowledge about the social, cultural, and psychological conditions making for democracy), political sociology was to contribute to the process of what came to be called nation-building. It was this close identification with the supposedly post-ideological process of political development in Western democracies that accounts for political sociology's inability to offer a satisfactory explanation for the upsurge of protest movements. The new set of phenomena in the form of 'the violent eruption of new forces' could not be explained in the prevailing conceptual framework, but rather posed a 'challenge to the models and theories of the fifties and early sixties [and] forced a revaluation of data gathering techniques and analysis strategies.' This statement suggests that political sociology had a self-image of objectivity, with value judgments clearly separated from methodological concerns. However, the fact that the student radicals were regarded as 'extremist activists' revealed the value-laden character of political sociology's scientific premises. For the meaning of this caricature of the protest movements was dependent on a normative vision of 'stable deideologized democracies.' The collective behaviour attributed to the extremist activists in the form of 'new waves of mobilization and countermobilization' could only be understood in so far as it 'brought a number of western democracies out of equilibrium.' In other words, the very conceptualization of the new activism belied political sociology's claims to objective 'theoretical systematization.' The new 'developments' could only be viewed as 'disturbing' if one was committed to political equilibrium and the processes of 'consolidation and deideologization' (ix).

For political sociology, the theoretical framework that had served to guide empirical research was conceptually inseparable from the value configuration embodied in a conception of stable democracies. The implicit standpoint assumed by political sociology was that of the abstract 'nation-builder,' faced with the task of constructing an effective state apparatus, cultivating its legitimation within territorial boundaries, and regularizing political processes. Given this equivalency between the theory and the desired reality, value preferences merged imperceptibly with empirical claims. Moreover, the problems confronting theory and the reality upon which it was based reflected one another. Just as Western democracies faced problems of instability and dysfunction, political sociology had to somehow integrate disruption into its theoretical framework.

Clearly the solution of the problems in one realm had active implications for the state of affairs in the other. If, for example, 'the waves of discontent and protest' abated, the original models of 'stable, deideologized democracies' could be reintroduced. Similarly, any cogent explanation that political sociology could offer as to the origins of extremism implied the possibility that steps could be taken to reduce this form of behaviour. In their desire to develop a form of social-scientific inquiry of relevance and instrumental consequence to problems of political integration, political sociologists had developed an approach that reduced politics to sociology.

Among the most outspoken critics of this tendency was Sartori, who called into question the sociology of politics in a paper presented at the International Sociological Association (ISA) conference on political sociology in West Berlin in 1968 (1969). Expressing his commitment to political engineering, Sartori maintained that 'much of what goes under the misnomer of "political sociology" is nothing more than a sociology of politics ignorant of political science; in substance, an exploration of the polity that sets as "givens" the variables of the political scientist.' 'The sociology of politics is ... a *sociological reduction* of politics' (69). In contrast, Sartori argued that 'a real *political sociology* is, then, a cross-disciplinary breakthrough seeking enlarged models which reintroduce as variables the "givens" of each component source' (92). He maintained that, 'if the demarcation between sociology and political science is sought – as it should be – at the level of their respective conceptual frameworks, it soon appears that the formal theory of the social system leaves off where the formal theory of the political system begins.' Hence, in his view, 'Parsonian-type models are of little use to political science,' for they assume that the sociological sphere is more fundamental than the sphere of politics (69). 'Political sociology,' Sartori suggested, 'is only born when the sociological and "politological" approaches are combined at their point of intersection' (92). Rather than treating the political as a *consequence* of social forces, the researcher could examine the *interplay* between the political and the sociological. For instance, on the question of how cleavages were translated into party systems, Sartori held that cleavages are not '*reflected in*' but, rather, '*produced by*' political systems (89).

It was Sartori's contention that political sociology, with its emphasis upon the primacy of socio-economic indicators for the explanation of politics, had failed to address the crucial question of how the political itself shaped and determined social processes, and how *power* operated as a factor independent of social forces (93). He advocated that political sociology must abandon its sociological reductionism and, instead, examine the interplay between political and sociological factors. There was more to Sartori's indictment of political sociology, however, than simply a concern to affirm the autonomy of politics from society. As indicated in his plea for political engineering, it was through the decoupling of the political sphere from social factors that political scientists could make a contribution to the strengthening of political institutions. Sartori's observations on political sociology were reflective of a growing preoccupation of political scientists in the late sixties with the conditions making for stable political orders (O'Brien 1972). By examining how states had historically overcome crises to establish their authority, knowledge of relevance to public policy was to be generated. This growing preoccupation with questions of political order was attendant upon political science's increasingly close contacts with government in the wake of the Title IX amendment to the Foreign Assistance Act.

This reorientation was evident within the sociology of politics as well. Mirroring the developments within comparative politics, the cumulative research program in the sociology of politics – based on the framework inspired by Parsons – could no longer be sustained. It is significant that with the increasing prominence of intellectual dissent in the sixties, Lipset abandoned his role as the driving force behind the international political-sociology movement and turned his attention almost exclusively to analyses of student radicalism and academic politics (Lipset and Altbach 1969; Lipset and Schaflander 1971). Parsons himself turned his attention away from the political sphere towards a greater concern with dissent in the universities (1968b). Reflecting their preoccupation with values and integration, both Lipset and Parsons responded to the turbulence of the sixties by shifting their attention from questions of national political integration to the more immediate issues surrounding intellectual dissent.

The vacuum left by the abandonment of the sociology of politics, however, was quickly filled by an approach to political sociology akin to the political-engineering model that had taken root in political science. Given impetus by the path-breaking historical studies of Bendix ([1964] 1977) and Moore (1966), the assumptions of this new perspective were given summary expression by Randall Collins in a contribution to a reader in comparative political sociology (in Bendix, 1968). Like his counterparts in comparative politics, Collins grounded the new departure in political sociology in a rejection of Parsons's thought. However, while the criticisms of Parsons within political science were based on practical considerations, Collins's dismissal of 'structural-functional analysis' as based on 'Talcott Parsons' contributions' was on analytical grounds. In his view, 'structural-functionalism is not a good theory of politics. It involves several conceptual difficulties, and its usefulness for empirical research has not yet been convincingly demonstrated' (42–3). As an alternative, Collins outlined an approach grounded in Max Weber's writings on politics. In contrast 'with Parsons' treatment of power as a "generalized symbolic medium" in the political system,' the view derived from Weber stresses that 'the polity is first of all ... an organization through which particular individuals or groups attempt to achieve their interests.' In this sense, 'the polity is ... an apparatus of domination.' Moreover, rather than stressing value-consensus and integration, the Weberian-inspired approach emphasizes the diversity of material and ideal interests (49–50). It is the 'struggle for political advantage ... made continual by the instabilities and dilemmas of legitimatizing principles and of arrangements of domination' (67).

The movement away from the sociology of politics signalled by the comments of Sartori and Collins marked the beginnings of an approach to historical political sociology that stressed state building and political conflicts in a comparative perspective.[4] Akin to the move towards political engineering within comparative politics, emphasis was placed on how strong and effective state structures had been historically established. In the same manner that comparative politics exorcised the Parsonsian demon by decoupling politics from sociology, historical political sociology laid structural functionalism to rest by severing states from their nations.

The Hobbesian Problem of Order Revisited

Ironically, with their rejection of Parsons's conception of social-scientific practice in favour of variants of political engineering, political sociologists returned to a utilitarian solution to the Hobbesian problem of order – the very line of thought that had moved Parsons to embark on a lifelong project of formulating an alternative. This trend was particularly evident in comparative politics, which, as O'Brien observed, was haunted by the spectre of Thomas Hobbes, 'the nightmare vision of a "war of all against all" unconstrained by shared social values or by political institutions' (1972, 363). Analogous to Hobbes' reaction to the *bellum omnium contra omnes* of seventeenth-century England, leading members of the comparative-politics movement viewed with dismay the civil unrest of the 1960s. The solution they prescribed for these 'excessive' and 'destabilizing' demands for participation was increased *political order*. It is evident that such a proposal had both empirical and normative components.

Political order was held, prima facie, to be desirable, and excessive political participation in politics was viewed as deleterious. 'The public interest,' in Huntington's view, 'is the interest of public institutions' (1968, 25). To make such a statement, Huntington must assume that the citizenry would willingly vest authority in public institutions in return for the guarantee of security and harmony. Having made the claim that the interest of the public is necessarily *realized* through the presence of public institutions, Huntington collapsed *legitimation* into these institutions as well. As he put it, 'the legitimacy of governmental actions can be sought in the extent to which they reflect the interests of governmental institutions' (27). Based on his assumption that governmental institutions are by definition legitimate, Huntington could now address the questions of which political components offer optimal effectiveness in reducing disorder. His line of reasoning paralleled Hobbes's.[5] As an artefact of human effort and will, the particular form and content Hobbes gave to leviathan was to reflect its role as a guarantor of public order. Similarly, Huntington was concerned with how political order could be ensured through strong and effective political institutions. Given this conception of politics, and its relation to political theory, it is not at all surprising that the leading thinkers in comparative politics, such as Huntington, Pye, and Sartori, were attracted to the 'political engineering' metaphor. Just as the ordinary engineer drew upon his experience and skills to design effective structures, the political engineer would use empirical knowledge, gleaned from both 'diachronic' and 'synchronic' analyses, to determine how political order might best be preserved in a particular situation.

Since the public was viewed as an aggregate of self-seeking individuals whose desires and demands posed a perpetual threat to political stability, the need for political engineering would be a continuous one. If a return to the Hobbesian 'state of nature' were to be avoided, the building and refinement of political order had to increase more rapidly than the rate of political participation.[6] Because the order was to be ensured through a strengthening of political institutions, the problem of gaining diffuse mass loyalty to political authority was of diminished significance. The process of legitimation, and the concern with symbolic meaning, intersubjectivity, and communication that it implied, was not essential to establishing and maintaining political stability. For the applied social scientist concerned with political development, this suggested little concern with how the values embodied in the production of knowledge affected the ideals, beliefs, and actions of the public at large. As evidenced in the writings of

Huntington, and judging from discussions on the implications of Title IX (MIT 1968), there was growing suspicion that the dissemination in developing countries of 'Western values,' such as those embodied in the social sciences, only served to increase demands for 'democratization' and 'participation,' thereby destabilizing the political system. With the new conviction that the political order was to be constituted less by cultural diffusion than by technical adjustments in political institutions, the practitioners of political development reasserted to some degree the objectivist, atomistic view of social life that Parsons detected in the positivistic-utilitarian tradition[7] a point of view that resonated with Hobbes's call for a strong sovereign state.

The increasing technical emphasis upon control (at the cost of attending to cultural factors that affect the stability of a political order) meant that comparative politics had moved away from the assumptions of Parsonsian social science. In the same manner that the approach of the political engineers could be likened to that of Hobbes, Parsons's perspective – with its emphasis upon the active role of the professionals in constituting the nation state – approximated the standpoint of Hegel. Avineri described Hegel's conception of the state and the manner by which it was to be constituted:

Hegel ... introduces the state as a system of integration aimed at overcoming the atomistic individualism of the economic sphere. A state that would merely express the dominant economic interests is to Hegel ... an abomination. Hegel's emerging political theory is an attempt to achieve a universality (a 'general will') that would not be, on the one hand, an aggregate of individual wills yet would appear, on the other, as a merely external, coercive antithesis to the individual wills. To achieve this, Hegel has to find a moment of meditation, and this he sets out to do. (1972, 99)

The 'moment of mediation' found by Hegel – the 'universal class' of the bureaucracy – had a close affinity with Parsons's conception of the 'professional strata.' Avineri wrote of Hegel's conception of 'the integrative functions of the state' that

this integration is carried out through the mediation of ... the universal class ... Universality becomes concrete only in the class of public servants who represent 'the intervention of the universal into all particularity'; ... The specific academic background of the German bureaucratic tradition is very much in evidence in this concept of the universal class as an educated estate, including not only civil servants in the narrow sense but also teachers, doctors, lawyers. (107–8)

Similarly, Parsons viewed the professional strata as the bearers of a fundamental cultural realignment. Through their orientation to action guided by the categories of disinterestedness, universalism, affective neutrality, and functional specificity, they would not only create a common bond among atomized individuals, but also propel society along the path of 'rationalization.' The movement towards modernity, then, was in no sense necessary or automatic. It was contingent upon the effort of the professionals to 'modernize' their own activities. The Hobbesian problem of order and the deficiencies in both market society and social theory that it signified were Parsons's points of departure for elaborating a theory of how professional development intersected with a wider process of rationalization. Through the production of knowledge that was at once impersonal, instrumental, symbolic, and specific to the problems of political integration, the social scientist was to contribute to the growth and consolidation of the capitalist nation-state.

The widespread acceptance of Parsons's thought can be understood on practical grounds. With the demise of McCarthyism in the mid fifties and the simultaneous growing concern with the fortunes of the developing countries, a social-scientific practice was called for that could produce knowledge relevant to extending the American prototype of modernization to the lesser developed countries. Parsonsian thought easily lent itself to long-term research programs because of its theoretical framework of both scientific rigour and normative relevance and its implicit emphasis upon the social basis of 'democratic politics.' Its systematized character and complexity helped to attract the funding support of foundations concerned with supporting cumulative research. In the relative lull between the storms of McCarthyism and the student movement during the Vietnam War a Parsonsian-inspired political sociology thrived, for it not only vindicated the end-of-ideology doctrine current at the time, but also provided a theoretical sophistication and rigour that was otherwise lacking in the social sciences.

However, with the turbulence of the sixties, and the growing incapacity of the American state to either achieve its aims abroad or legitimate its actions at home, the strategic and analytic virtues of Parsonsian political sociology were severely questioned, and new forms of practice oriented towards state building became characteristic of both wings of the political-sociology movement. Within comparative politics, this took the form of political engineering. The turn away from

Parsonsian theory within comparative politics was given impetus both by the difficulties of the American state and by the increasing involvement by American social scientists in the affairs of state. A manifest failure of American foreign policy and the growing civil unrest undercut Parsons's assumptions of the United States as a prototype for development. And the tighter working relationship between social scientists and policy-makers concerned with the short-run problems of counter-insurgency and political order forced academics to view their research increasingly in technical, applied, and relevant terms. Within sociology, the 'sociology of politics,' as derived from Parsons's schema, was rejected – not for practical reasons but on analytical grounds – in favour of an approach that stressed comparative state building in a historical perspective. Nevertheless, with its emphasis upon analysis of objective structures and material interests, a form of practice in the spirit of the political engineer was in evidence. Eschewing values, culture, and the problem of legitimation, the shift towards historical political sociology based on objective comparisons across time implied both a denial of one's own historicity and a lack of relevance to immediate questions of ideology and public consciousness.[8] The rejection of Parsons's orientation to values in favour of 'objective' and 'structural' analyses had come at the expense of sacrificing intellectual engagement in the public sphere of values and ideologies.[9]

In view of their shifting practical and professional concerns, it was understandable that social scientists became impatient with the intricacies of Parsonsian theory; instead they returned full circle to more directly instrumental solutions to the problem of order. To invoke a Hegelian dictum, 'Parsonsian theory was its time apprehended in thought.' But when times changed, thought turned to other modes of apprehension, captured pithily by the words of Hobbes: 'when nothing else is turned up, clubs are trumps' (Hobbes in Rustow 1967, 170).

13

Troubling Paradigms

Thomas Kuhn and the Social Sciences

During the turbulence of the 1960s, Parsonsian theory (and the political sociology it inspired) was not only abandoned by its mainstream proponents, but came under attack for its alleged conservatism and irrelevance by a new wave of detractors. In the confusion of the times, it became commonplace for critical and orthodox social scientists alike to reorient themselves by adapting insights from Thomas Kuhn's *Structure of Scientific Revolutions* ([1962] 1970). Supporters of the conventional social sciences used Kuhn's notion of a paradigm as a theoretical rallying-point (Almond [1966] 1970; Truman 1965; Easton 1969). Kuhn's critics, however, contended that particular disciplines were already dominated by paradigms (Surkin and Wolfe 1970; Wolin [1968] 1980), a state of affairs thought to be detrimental to the vitality and the advancement of the field in question. Kuhn's notion of the paradigm figured prominently in explanations of both regeneration and degeneration of social-scientific inquiry (Urry 1973) and continues to exert a powerful hold on those seeking to clarify patterns of change in the social sciences and other fields (Gutting 1980).

I would like to show how my analysis of Parsonian theory and political sociology has a direct bearing on the status of *The Structure of Scientific Revolutions* (hereafter SSR) as a model for research into the history of the social sciences. While numerous efforts have been made to examine the history of a particular social-scientific field or discipline using SSR as a prototype, few of these accounts have questioned the validity of doing so. In unquestioningly transposing Kuhn's insights from the history of the natural sciences to their own concerns, writers of

social-scientific history have ignored his admonition that the application of the paradigm was confined to the natural sciences ([1962] 1970,
ix–x). As a consequence, the historical accounts of the social sciences
modelled on ssr rest on the assumption that the natural and the social
sciences are fundamentally alike, thereby obscuring the problems that
may be unique to understanding the historical development of social-
scientific thought. Despite the plethora of historical studies of the social
sciences inspired by ssr, therefore, little headway has been made in
assessing its historiographical merits for the tasks at hand. By attempting to apply Kuhn's thought rigorously to the case study of political
sociology's history, it is hoped that insights into the wider significance
of ssr for social-scientific historiography can be developed.

The Nature of Paradigms

As the conceptual backbone of ssr, Kuhn's notion of paradigm has borne
the brunt of commentators' criticisms (Lakatos and Musgrave 1970)
and, correspondingly, has been the focal point for Kuhn's clarification in
his rejoinders to his critics ([1962] 1970, 174–210, 1970a, 1974).
Responding to charges that his discussion of the paradigm in ssr was
both imprecise and misleading (Masterman 1970), Kuhn defined the
meaning of paradigm much more precisely in his subsequent writings.[1]

The most fundamental meaning of the paradigm, Kuhn argues, is the
exemplar: 'the concrete problem-solutions that students encounter
from the start of their scientific education, whether in laboratories, or
examinations, or at the end of chapters in science texts' ([1962] 1970,
187). Masterman refers to this as an 'artifact' or 'construct' paradigm,
'the concrete accomplishments of a scientific community' (Eckberg and
Hill 1980, 119). The paradigm is defined not so much by what it is, but
rather by what it does, namely, to provide the basis for the solution of
puzzles. As Eckberg and Hill note (120), 'the function ... of an exemplar
is to permit a way of seeing one's subject-matter *on a concrete level*,
thereby allowing *puzzle solving* to take place ... For a discipline to be a
science it must engage in puzzle-solving activity.' A secondary aspect
of paradigm Kuhn calls the 'disciplinary matrix,' which represents
'the shared commitments of any disciplinary community, including
symbolic generalizations, beliefs, values, and a host of other elements'
(118). This corresponds to what Masterman calls the 'sociological
paradigm,' the belief system of a scientific community's subculture,
which shares a common approach to puzzle-solving activity. Masterman distinguishes a third type of paradigm in ssr – the 'metaphysical

paradigms' or 'metaparadigms' (Masterman 1970, 65) referring to unstated and unquestioned assumptions of a broader nature. In his rejoinders to his critics, Kuhn does not distinguish the metaphysical as a particular sense of what he means by a paradigm, preferring instead to consider the metaphysical paradigm as a component of the disciplinary matrix. On the basis of Masterman's close analysis, however, it must be concluded that the metaphysical paradigm, with its emphasis upon general orienting assumptions, cannot be easily included in the disciplinary matrix, but should be viewed as a distinct entity.

As both Masterman, and Eckberg and Hill, suggest, the interdependence of the three levels of paradigm is fundamental to Kuhn's model of scientific progress. A community of scientists not only shares a set of broad metaphysical assumptions, but is bounded by a disciplinary matrix characterized by a unifying belief system and subscribes to a common exemplar that guides their puzzle-solving activities. 'Normal science' can only proceed, then, if the three paradigmatic dimensions are in place.

Most efforts to apply insights from SSR to sociology, as Eckberg and Hill point out, pay little heed to the specifications of the paradigm offered by Kuhn. Characteristically, they fail to distinguish between Kuhn's notions of a disciplinary matrix and an exemplar, and mistakenly apply the paradigm to a discipline as a whole rather than to particular substantive areas. These authors conclude that 'if paradigms (exemplars) exist in the discipline of sociology, they are difficult to find. Moreover, if they do exist, they (1) must not be discipline-wide, (2) must be found within substantive areas of research, (3) must have communities of practitioners which coalesce around them, and (4) must be used to both generate and solve puzzles and thus generate a visible research tradition' (132).

Paradigms and Political Sociology

Political sociology, as it emerged in the late 1950s and early 1960s, would appear to have the features, as specified by Eckberg and Hill, for paradigmatic status. Above all, it was restricted to a particular substantive area[2] and developed a set of concrete problem-solutions that enabled its practitioners to 'solve' puzzles. The problem-solutions had slightly different expressions in the two wings of political sociology. Within comparative politics, the exemplar took the form of applying functional categories to political systems on a comparative basis. Using the Anglo-American political system as a prototype, the researcher faced the task of determining to what degree various institutions and practices 'functionally' served to maintain different variants of political systems. The sociology of politics shared this general functional concern, but addressed itself more narrowly to the social basis of democracy in the developed countries. Despite their various substantive and conceptual differences, both wings shared a concern specifying the requisites for the development of political systems modelled on those of the Western democracies. This exemplar was cultivated and refined through workshops, seminars, and collaborative efforts, as co-ordinated by the Committee on Political Sociology of the International Sociological Association, and by the Committee on Comparative Politics. Concrete instances of appropriate 'puzzle-solutions' were available in the form of *Political Man* (Lipset [1960] 1963) and *The Politics of the Developing Areas* (Almond and Coleman 1960). Interdependent with the research exemplar held in common was a 'disciplinary matrix' consisting of social scientists who shared a commitment to do research in the substantive area of political sociology. This interdependence between exemplar and disciplinary matrix permitted the practice of 'normal science' which sought to show how the cumulative generation of knowledge is related to the social bases of political systems.[3]

The rise of political sociology constituted a 'scientific revolution' in the Kuhnian sense of the term. Previously, in its pre-paradigmatic state, research in comparative politics and the sociology of politics was uncoordinated and non-cumulative and had no central puzzle-solving tendency. However, once political sociology had become a distinct subdiscipline, research proceeded in a cumulative, puzzle-solving manner.[4]

However, if we examine the kind of metaphysical assumptions underlying political sociology, a different picture emerges. According to Kuhn, metaphysical paradigms referred to the 'shared commitment [as] beliefs in particular models [which] supply the group with preferred or permissable analogies and metaphors. By doing so they help to determine what will be accepted as an explanation and as a puzzle solution' ([1962] 1970, 184). In political sociology, it may be argued, the metaphysical paradigm took the form of a commitment to help in the consolidation of liberal democratic political systems on a global basis. The set of assumptions implicit in the adaptation of Parsons's pattern variables to political sociology provided puzzle-solving activities with meaning and direction. This commitment corresponded to the concerns of the Ford Foundation and enabled political sociology to receive material support sufficient to allow it to undertake research of an intentionally cumulative nature. During the period of 'normal science,' these metaphysical beliefs became tacit and unquestioned premises. One could engage in puzzle-solving activities without explicit reference to them. Puzzles were defined purely in an objective manner, within the guide-lines provided by the research exemplar. As long as the phenomena and events under investigation conformed to the metaphysical premises as encoded in the exemplar, normal science, in the form of puzzle-solving activity, could proceed. The apparent ideological lull and the seeming trend towards consensual politics and modernization in the late 1950s and early 1960s lent credence to the puzzle-solutions that were proposed. Because Western democracies and third-world nations appeared to be moving in a direction consonant with the commitments underlying its research program, political sociology – at least from the standpoint of its practitioners – seemed to be accumulating social-scientific knowledge and building a solid foundation for future work.

As long as the use of the paradigm is confined to making generalizations about the coherence and consensus of political sociology, the Kuhnian account suggests possibilities. However, if one attempts to press the analysis further – to explain the process of social-scientific change through the appearance of anomalies and the onset of crises – the limitations of Kuhn's model become readily apparent. According to Kuhn, 'the awareness of anomaly [represents] the recognition that nature has somehow violated the paradigm-induced expectations' ([1962] 1970, 52–3). The paradigm, then, provides the background necessary for the detection of an anomaly. For example, the phlogiston theory of air presupposed the 'anomalous' occurrences that ultimately led to the discovery of oxygen (52–6). It is the persistent inability of the prevailing paradigm to solve the puzzle posed by the anomaly, argues Kuhn, that sets the stage for the emergence of a new paradigm, which by enabling one to apprehend reality in an entirely different manner renders the anomaly intelligible.

Its merits for explaining scientific change aside, the Kuhnian model breaks down when it is uncritically transposed to the developments in political sociology I have examined. Unlike the anomalies discussed by Kuhn, the upsurge of the New Left and movements of national liberation did not represent merely unexpected violations of scientific expectations. It was only because political sociology was premised upon the hegemonic view of stable, de-ideologized political orders in the West, mirrored by benign 'modernization' in the third world, that widespread dissent was at all 'anomalous.' In other words, the anomalies confronting political sociology were as much political as they were scientific. They were not so much violations of scientific expectations as they were contraventions of metaphysical commitments. Their appearance ushered in a period of extraordinary scientific development (similar to the phase in scientific development discussed by Kuhn) in which the old paradigm was called into question (Easton 1969; Lipset and Rokkan 1968; Almond 1973). Although political sociology was disbanded as an exemplar and disciplinary matrix, it was not replaced by a unified paradigmatic approach capable of accounting for what was previously an anomaly, as stated in the Kuhnian model. Rather, the former proponents of political sociology embarked on new paths reflecting their value orientations and practical concerns. Many political scientists abandoned faith in the integrating possibilities of the primary patterns, and shifted their activities towards more directly instrumental pursuits.

Comparative politics regrouped as a disciplinary matrix guided by the exemplar of political engineering. The puzzles it sought to solve were related to how strong political orders could be built. This led to greater use of historical case studies, for by examining historically how political order had been successfully attained, it was hoped that knowledge of relevance to policy formation could be generated. Meanwhile, within the sociology of politics, Lipset abandoned his role as the driving force behind developing the field as a programmatic venture. Turning away from a direct concern with the operation of the political system, he began to examine more closely the value dispositions of those involved in different aspects of higher education (Lipset and Altbach 1969). Paralleling Lipset's shift of direction, Parsons also began to examine more closely the nature of cultural life within the universities (Parsons and Platt 1973). The vacuum that was left by the collapse of the sociology of politics was filled by a form of comparative historical sociology (Collins 1969; Tilly 1975). This approach, with its emphasis upon structure, change, and conflict and its downplaying of values, shared much in common with political engineering. In effect, the breakdown of the exemplar of political sociology, accompanied by the decoupling of the disciplinary matrices of comparative politics and the sociology of politics, could be attributed to their respective responses to the violations of their metaphysical commitments occasioned by the outbreak of political turbulence in the late 1950s and early 1960s. Those in comparative politics saw the crisis as a breakdown of state effectiveness. Thus, they abandoned the normative orientation of Parsons, replacing this set of assumptions with a more direct and instrumental view of political knowledge. Meanwhile, Lipset and Parsons, in retaining their original metaphysical orientation, perceived the crisis as one of legitimation and, accordingly, began to concern themselves with the value orientations of students and intellectuals, while ignoring issues more directly related to the exercise of state power.

This pattern of development indicates that one can neither discuss the 'crisis of explanation' in political sociology, nor its resolution, apart from the overall crises of authority experienced by 'advanced' and 'modernizing' societies in the late sixties. However, for Thomas Kuhn, the whole process of crises, revolution, and scientific change turns on the *autonomy* of the scientific community from wider social influences. As Alan Dawe describes the Kuhnian perspective, 'despite the language of crisis and revolution, there are still distinctly scientific values which define science and the scientific community ... a Kuhnian anomaly [is] a technical puzzle which persists to the point of causing a purely cognitive crisis' (1971, 143).

If Kuhn's notions are to be rigorously applied to social-scientific change, one must accept his ontology of science as well. In Kuhn's view, scientific reality consists of a world entirely separate from the scientific community. Through the artifice of theory, Kuhn maintains, the scientific practitioner seeks to apprehend and explain particular aspects of this externalized reality. Given his assumption of the inherently objective quality of the phenomena in the natural world, and his views on the correspondingly value-free nature of scientific activity, a crisis for Kuhn results from a lack of 'fit' between theory and reality, and change comes about through the development of a closer correspondence between the two. Even though he stresses the role of the scientific community in maintaining and enforcing the paradigm, the relationship of this collectivity and its theoretical frameworks to the world it seeks to explain is avowedly a positivistic one.

Science progresses, in Kuhn's view, fully autonomously from the world in which the scientific community is embedded. This implies that the truth claims made by social-scientific inquiry can be treated separately from considerations of what political and social order scientific practitioners believe to be good, desirable, and legitimate. Kuhn not only abstracts the scientific community from overall political and social values, but effectively 'brackets' the preferences of the scientific investigators themselves.

My analysis of Parsonsian theory and political sociology, however, reveals a much different relationship between theory, scientific community, and social reality. The orientation of Parsons, Lipset, and Almond to the external world bore little resemblance to that of the detached observer implicit in Kuhn's conception of scientific investigation. This is not merely to say that each of these thinkers was influenced by the social and political context in which he found himself, as a historicist account would suggest (see chapter 1). Rather, all three theorists sought actively to help *constitute* social and political reality through their contributions to social-scientific theory and practice. Such activity, in each case, flowed from an acute awareness of the strategic importance of social-scientific knowledge for the wider historical process. As discussed earlier, the empirical research programs of the two wings of political sociology rested upon Parsons's practically conceived 'theory.' Embodied in the categories of action derived from a study of medical practice, Parsons's theoretical approach provided the guide-line for effective and relevant social-scientific action. In view of the inherently engaged and committed theory that underpinned political sociology, we are forced to reassess the hiatus between the 'context of discovery' and the 'context of validation' that is implicit in Kuhn's analysis of scientific activity, thereby casting into serious doubt its applicability to the social sciences.

This analysis of Parsonsian theory and political sociology – undertaken in Kuhnian terms – calls into question the efforts of both mainstream social scientists and their critics to seek conceptual and practical solace in SSR. Given that the paradigmatic consolidation desired by mainstream thinkers was premised on a vision of a stable, equilibrating political system, the conceptual unity they called for in the late 1960s (Almond 1966; Easton 1969; Lipset and Rokkan 1968; Truman 1965) was possible only in so far as the wider crises of state effectiveness and legitimation could be overcome. Similarly, the replacement of the prevailing paradigm, called for by a number of critics (Friedrichs 1970; Surkin and Wolfe 1970; Wolin [1968] 1980), was hardly conceivable in the absence of a radical realignment of the social order in general. The notion of the paradigm, while metaphorically suggestive, would appear to be an inappropriate vehicle for reconstituting social-scientific thought, for the Kuhnian model cannot be rigorously and consistently applied to the social sciences without arbitrarily assuming a separation between the 'context of discovery' and the 'context of validation.'

Yet as my analysis of political sociology indicates, its validation was inherently related to the ability of the capitalist nation-state to solve its problems of instrumentation and legitimation. The affinity between this form of social-scientific thought and the society it studied was in no sense accidental. It rested upon the awareness by Talcott Parsons that the emergence and consolidation of the capitalist nation-state was contingent upon particular patterns of knowledge, produced in part by social scientists. As I have argued, an understanding of how the social sciences and society have been mutually implicated rests on an 'activist' historiography of past social-scientific thought. However, there is more at issue here than demonstrating how social-scientific thought has been practically conceived. It is my contention that an analysis of this kind has implications for how the social sciences could be of consequence for radical social transformation. In order to begin making changes in the categories, practices, and alignments so critical to any radical agenda, one must have a more precise idea of how knowledge in the prevailing order is structured in oppressive and inegalitarian ways. The present work, though by no means exhaustive, can best be viewed as an attempt to take such an inventory. Thus, the relation between political sociology and the capitalist nation-state, as discussed here, can serve a useful heuristic purpose. Given that political sociology was practically linked with and committed to the fortunes of the capitalist nation-state and to the ascendancy of the economic and political elites within it, one can use this body of knowledge as a convenient point of departure for elaborating a much more radically disposed social science, equally grounded in political and social life. This alignment would proceed from a shift in practical commitment from the state and the elites to the interests of the subordinate strata, i.e. those who are structurally excluded from access to political and economic power. In effecting a realignment of this kind, the categories and content of political sociology could serve as a helpful guide-line because they reflect the perceived needs of the state and the dominant strata. An inversion of political sociology's implicit orientation, while retaining its substance, could redirect the social sciences towards the production of knowledge that would be at once radically conceived and yet firmly situated in the reality of advanced capitalist society.

Knowledge and the Nation-State

States function through a monopoly of coercive force by state authorities and assume the right to intervene internally in matters of perceived national interest and externally on behalf of the national collectivity in foreign arenas. States vary enormously, of course, in their capacity to act – both historically and comparatively. The strength, composition, and political organization of classes and strata, the degree of political institutional development, and the degree of public acceptance of state institutions, for instance, all affect the state's ability to intervene in domestic and international spheres. Inherent in the very notion of the state, then, is a degree of active intervention. This action ranges from coercion and repression to more indirect forms of control such as fiscal and monetary policy. Characteristic of the various forms of state action is the conception of the natural and social orders as consisting of objective conditions or phenomena. If the interventions of the state into these orders are to be effective, then objective, empirical knowledge about them would seem to be an essential requisite. To pursue such objectives as controlling dissent and ensuring high productivity, as well as a satisfactory rate of growth and politically acceptable levels of unemployment, scientific knowledge of technical use must be forthcoming. Consequently, the capacity of a state to act domestically and externally is predicated upon the objective, instrumental knowledge at its disposal.

This capacity to act, however, is not simply a question of the organizational unity and the level of scientific development at the disposal of the state. The manner and extent of the state's activities are limited and constrained by the degree of public acceptance of its policies. If they are to intervene in the social order, the political managers of the state apparatus must establish the credibility of their policies through a process of legitimation. To be sure, state managers have authority to act by virtue of procedures and statutes specified in the state's legal codes. However, *how and to what degree* they are able to act depends upon their ability to generate public support for the particular policies they wish to implement. This implies a distinction between primary and secondary aspects of legitimation. Primary legitimation involves an appeal to rational legality and is exclusively concerned with one's claim to rule. Secondary legitimation, however, is concerned with how specific policies or lines of action are made acceptable to the public. If the process of secondary legitimation is successful, members of the public give their approval to the actions that the state managers have sought to legitimate. This is not to say that citizens are completely free to evaluate the legitimating definitions and the lines of action state managers seek to justify. Because the accounts of reality given in the legitimation process originate in a state that has primary legitimacy by virtue of rational legality, then a citizen is bound to accept these definitions, and to act upon them to avoid charges of disloyalty.[5] Projected into the public realm, legitimating definitions impart 'correctness' to the policies pursued by state managers by portraying these lines of action as factually based, morally conceived, and contributing to the 'national interest.' Inherent in the process of legitimation, then, is symbolic knowledge communicated into the sphere of public life and affecting the knowledge, beliefs, values, and actions of the citizenry. The process of legitimation, if successfully carried out, results in a widespread *internalization* by members of the public of a particular definition of reality. The public judges the depiction of reality as empirically valid, accords it value, and is motivated to act upon it through appropriate responses, such as paying higher taxes, accepting a pay settlement, or going to war. In the same way that instrumental knowledge is constitutive of the *state's* actions, symbolic knowledge is inherently related to the process by which support of the *nation*, comprising the members of the political community, is sustained.

State actions and the legitimation process are closely related. The operations of the state require some measure of legitimation if they are to be carried out. Similarly, the process of legitimation calls for the presence of a set of institutions claiming sovereignty in a particular territory. The types of knowledge upon which state intervention and legitimation rest, though analytically separable, like the state and nation, are interrelated in reality. Instrumental knowledge, concerned with the technical manipulation of objectified phenomena, is imbued with values. The range of phenomena to be considered, the choice of some particular phenomena as the objects of action, and the nature and extent of action to be taken all involve moral decisions. Moreover, the empirical knowledge upon which action is based owes its usefulness to how well it reflects the set of values defined by the national interest. Correspondingly, the symbolic knowledge legitimating state actions makes claims of cognitive validity because the justification given to a course of action depends upon its appearance of detached objectivity for its persuasiveness. By subjecting members of the national society to symbolically based processes of legitimation, state managers are able to pursue lines of action guided by their empirical knowledge of domestic and external conditions.

This suggests that both the coercive and legitimating activities of the state can only be understood in relation to social strata. In particular, state intervention and legitimation are in turn contingent upon the instrumental and symbolic actions of the dominant and subordinate social strata, as they seek to realize their respective interests. Given the predominance of capitalists and the means of sabotaging economic well-being and political stability at their disposal, state managers are generally compelled to act at the behest of this group rather than in the interests of the working class and the subordinate strata.[6] The latter groups, nevertheless, under particular circumstances, are able to realize their collective interests through instrumental and expressive collective action (Piven and Cloward 1977). However, neither state managers nor subordinate and dominant strata have as their primary vocation the creation and spread of knowledge. This is undertaken by a social group, the intelligentsia, which is defined neither by its ownership or non-ownership of capital, nor by its possession of political power, but by its production and dissemination of ideas and symbols. Like the dominant and subordinate strata, members of the intelligentsia are linked both institutionally and more informally with the state apparatus. Nevertheless, whatever their alignment with the state might be, their activities are of consequence to the success or failure of the processes of intervention and legitimation.

Political sociology rested on an awareness of how the social sciences could contribute to the processes of intervention and legitimation, and from what standpoint in society this contribution could best take place. Accordingly, its categories were isomorphic with the dimensions of knowledge inherent in the American variant of the capitalist nation-state. In concentrating its efforts on elaborating the social and cultural requisites to 'democratic' development, political sociology was to produce knowledge 'functionally specific' to this area of expertise. By virtue of specializing in the set of empirical and normative concerns defined by the field, it was the intention of political sociologists to both influence the educated public and gain credibility in the eyes of the funding elites. Its stress upon the development of 'general theory' was to provide the sociology of politics with the ability to produce, in cumulative fashion, knowledge of instrumental relevance to the activities of the state apparatus. Of particular concern was the extraction of data on voting, for such material was thought to offer insights into how potentially disruptive social cleavages could be integrated by the political system. In 'comparative politics,' researchers took a particular interest in the set of social/psychological dispositions held by the public that would provide the basis for the development of political systems approximating the Anglo-American prototype. In carrying out empirical research programs guided by such questions, both wings of political sociology assumed the viewpoint of the political manager in the state apparatus who faced the problem of building and maintaining a stable political order.

Complementing this concern with general scientific theory, political sociology was imbued with cultural commitment, as it sought to provide a normative depiction of reality consonant with the political culture of the American nation-state during the Cold War. Within the 'sociology of politics,' this took the form of an abiding commitment to the 'consensual' virtues of democracy. Similarly, in comparative politics, the cultural commitment was realized through the affirmation of a new 'political theory,' which embodied the values of a 'secular' and 'rational' political system. In both instances, by defining political reality in this manner, modernization was to be expedited and ideology was to be defused throughout the American sphere of influence. Finally, reflecting an overall orientation of disinterestedness, political sociology was to align itself directly neither with the elites of civil society nor with the state bureaucracy. Rather, centred as it was within institutions of higher education, it was to be practised in a manner relatively autonomous from both the government and the dominant social strata. Thus, through the production of instrumentally and culturally oriented knowledge that was both focused on the social requisites for 'democratic' politics and pursued relatively autonomously from the state and civil society, political sociology was to help consolidate this form of political system at home and contribute to its adaptation abroad.

Social Sciences and Radical Rejuvenation

The content, categories, and orientation of political sociology were derived from reflection on the actual processes and priorities of the capitalist nation-state. If one is to make radically democratic inroads into the manipulation and oppression that characterize modern political, social, and economic life, this suggests an *inversion* of political sociology as the basis for developing more popular forms of control. In this sense, rather than generating technical data for the manipulation of voters, consumers, and workers, an effort could be made to produce empirical information relevant to the actions, decisions, and organizational strategies of the subordinate strata. As guided by this priority, research could feed into an expanding corpus of knowledge about how popular control over political processes and economic life might be implemented.

Along the same lines, a radical inversion of political sociology would involve a shift in the production of symbolic knowledge. Rather than justifying the political order through a supportive 'definition of reality,' one could seek to *demystify* power relations, by revealing the domination and inequality masked by the notion of 'the national interest.' Correspondingly, efforts could be made to help members of the subordinate strata become aware that their disadvantages are not due to individual inadequacy, but are rooted in socially structured inequalities of economic and political power.

Instrumental and symbolic knowledge of this orientation might still be produced in 'relatively autonomous' institutions of higher education. However, with a commitment to the interests of the subordinate strata rather than to those of the political and economic elites, social scientific activity would shift its priorities and concerns accordingly. Such a reorientation could not obviously be effected without a redefinition of how knowledge is validated and what qualifies as academic currency. An essential requisite for a redirection of social-scientific activity along more radically relevant lines would be more recognition and support given to activity undertaken on behalf of the disadvantaged.

This is not to say that an orientation more attuned to the struggles of subordinate groups is sufficient to effect radical transformation. Mirroring the organization of knowledge that has long characterized the mainstream social sciences, what is needed are 'progressive' versions of such bodies as the Social Science Research Council and the Ford Foundation. Such organizations would mediate between popular forces and critically disposed intellectuals, providing the guidance and the material support so important to rigorous and relevant social research. Within such a configuration, a new division of labour among the 'critical' social sciences could be elaborated. While all of the subfields would subscribe to the overall project of carrying out radically relevant research, each would produce knowledge 'functionally specific' to particular realms of society in which inequality and powerlessness occur. This would mean going beyond what is passed off as 'interdisciplinary' work. Indeed, implied by a new realignment would be a breakdown of the whole notion of discipline itself and a redefinition of knowledge in terms of its bearing upon urgent social issues.

As part of an overall realignment of this kind, an understanding of how social-scientific knowledge has come to support prevailing patterns of domination is of critical importance. This task can qnly be undertaken if we acknowledge the dialectical unity between social-scientific ideas and the institutions and practices of the capitalist nation-states that many of us live in. The two realms of 'knowledge' and 'society,' of course, can be conceived of independently of each other. Indeed, their separation has become an implicit feature of our identity as social scientists and a pre-condition for our analyses of social life. Yet, in maintaining this division, and by acting as if it were genuine, we both deny our complicity in the shaping of wider political and social arrangements and fail to visualize how our lines of action could be more liberating in their consequences. If we are to understand how our current forms of practice are constrained, yet potentially emancipatory, we must come to terms with how social-scientific knowledge and society have been mutually implicated. And if we are to comprehend more specifically how our fields of study reflect and complement variants of the capitalist nation-state, we must acknowledge that the founding figures of social science may well have interpreted the world in order to change it. A project of social renovation can hardly be undertaken without a grasp of how the categories, constructs, and empirical insights left to us by our predecessors are imbued with unstated ideological assumptions and tacit practical commitments. If we claim that, as social scientists, we stand on the shoulders of giants, we should at least be aware of the directions in which they have pointed us.

Notes

1 Alvin Gouldner's (1971, 14) plea for a 'reflexive sociology' emerges from a 'close critique of ... what is by far the dominant system of American social theory, namely that created by Talcott Parsons.' As 'the discipline's foremost theorist,' Robert Friedrichs argues, Parsons imbued sociology with his 'equilibrating predilection' ([1970] 1972, 295). More recently, as Jonathan Turner notes in his textbook on sociological theory (1982, 38), 'rarely has anyone quarreled with the assertion that he [Parsons] has been the dominant sociological figure of this century.'

2 'The Parsonian enterprise,' concludes Bierstedt (1981, 441) after a lengthy and nuanced treatment of its constituent features, 'is for the most part a sad picture of misdirected industry.'

3 'Although we do not object to being called Parsonians,' writes Jan Loubser (1976, 2), 'we strongly prefer to be seen as collaborators of Parsons or simply workers on the theory of action.'

4 Loubser (ibid.) notes further that 'we are working with the theory of action because we share Parsons' conviction that the development of general social science theory is a task to which some people must pay special attention. We share his conviction that the theory of action provides a framework for the development of such a theory.' See also Muench 1981; Bourricaud 1981; Alexander 1978, 1979, 1983; Adriaansens 1979, 1980; for a comprehensive account of recent developments in action theory, see Gerstein 1982.

5 Alexander (1978, 177), in response to both the 'antagonistic tradition' and the followers of Parsons 'unable to present an objective critical evaluation of his intellectual contributions,' calls for 'a perspective which is both critical and appreciative.'

6 This has been my experience on a number of occasions. American

reviewers, in particular, assume that to write about Parsons is to support his position.

7 The detached and abstracted nature of Parsons's theorizing has become a commonplace (yet completely unwarranted) assumption of commentaries on his work. Among those who view Parsons in this manner are Moore ([1958] 1968) and Bottomore ([1969] 1975).

8 This distinction was first given expression by Butterfield (1931). More recent commentaries on the presentist/historicist controversy include Stocking (1965), Kuklick (1980), and Jones (1983).

9 Bottomore ([1969] 1975, 33) remarks that 'Parsons's sociology accorded well with' the era of 'the 1950's ... a conservative and uncreative period, dominated, especially in the United States, by the rigid attitudes and relationships of the Cold War, and by naive ideologies of economic growth and affluence.'

10 Scott (1963) gave this distinction currency. It can also be found in Giddens 1976, 16; Gouldner 1971, 142–4; and Friedrichs [1970] 1972, 231. See also Scott (1962).

11 Foss (1963, 123) characterizes 'Parsons's views on industrialization as a political ideology,' which can best be expressed as 'modernizing corporationism.'

12 Bottomore notes that 'Parsons ... excludes from the domain of theory ... two elements which have usually been regarded ... as vital in all theoretical sociology ... the attempt to formulate empirical generalizations and to establish systematic connections between them' ([1969] 1975, 37).

13 Bottomore (ibid., 42) describes the ideological significance of Parsons: 'Parsons's general ideas convey a profoundly conservative outlook in which belief in stability, integration, order, and the determining influence of religious values, plays a large part. But even this is not an active conservatism such as might lead to a distinctive interpretation of the dangers and opportunities which confront men, individually and collectively, in the modern world. It is a detached, diffuse, unexamined, and undeclared conservative predisposition which reveals itself more in Parsons's whole approach to the subject than in any empirical statements about actual societies.'

14 As Foss (1963, 125–6) notes, Parsons's 'sociology of complacency is a failure in dealing with the experiential reality of industrial society. It fails to touch upon an entire vast realm of the industrial experience, horror.' What may be needed is a 'sociology of horror' in which social science tries to be honest with the industrial world and with itself. In Bottomore's view, 'what is most obviously lacking [in Parsons's thought] is a focus, a constellation of problems, around which sociological theory might be constructed, as it has been constructed by others who have directed their thought to the problems of class and inequality, science and industrialism, rationalism and bureaucracy.'

15 This is particularly noticeable in the field of sociology. It became evident at the American Sociology Meetings held in Boston in 1968 that the discipline was polarized along ideological and practical grounds (Roach 1970). Voicing the sentiments of 'The Sociology Liberation Movement,' Martin Nicolaus noted that 'the professional eyes of the sociologist are on the down people, and the professional palm of the sociologist is stretched toward the up people ... he is an Uncle Tom not only for this government and ruling class but for any' (in Gouldner 1971, 10). The eventual response of the American Sociological Association was to allow the formation of a variety of sections representing a range of 'critical' perspectives (e.g. Political Economy of World Systems, Marxism). Today, these approaches have been authorized as reasonably legitimate standpoints, capable of minting negotiable academic currency. However, given their minimal impact upon changing the way in which social scientists relate to society, it is questionable whether they are any more radical than their mainstream counterparts.

CHAPTER 2

1 In his prefatory remarks to the 'Symposium on the Culture of Unbelief' ([1971] 1978, 233), however, he admitted that he was 'not a Roman Catholic, but a somewhat backsliding Protestant of Congregationalist background.' To be sure, Parsons repeatedly acknowledged an *intellectual interest* in religion. As he notes in his autobiographical statement (1970a, 872), 'In a variety of ways, problems of religion have been prominent for me almost from the beginning. It was Weber's Protestant Ethic essay which set off a major development for me, and the *common* concern of Weber, Pareto, Durkheim, and later Freud with the intellectual problems posed by religion as a human phenomenon became a major reference point in the earlier phases of my career.'

2 As Robertson (1982, 308) observantly attests, 'there can be little doubt that Parsons' "religious" identity was sustained and nourished by his *scientific* work, rather than the latter being an outcome or a projection of his personal convictions (although there probably was an element of that).' Parsons appears to corroborate this assessment in his autobiographical statement; 'The concern with religion – in the role not of a *dis-* but more of an *un*believer, in the terminology of a recent Vatican conference – has been a major orientation point in my intellectual career. It was already a major aspect of my early rejection of "positivism," but at the same time has been a focus of a continuing attempt to understand the balance of the roles of rational and nonrational components in human action. Clearly, however, such a focus of intellectual concern leads one beyond the more purely cognitive problems of religion into those of moral commitment,

affective engagement, and practical action' (1970a, 873).

Given the paucity of documentation on Parsons's personal views on religion, one can only infer the linkage between his religious commitments and his intellectual activities. Nevertheless, some evidence can be found in a letter from Parsons to Graham Morgan (1970c), responding to an article the latter had written on the relation between sociology and the social gospel movement in the United States. Parsons noted that the Social Gospel was an important part of his background. His father, Edward S. Parsons, though coming from a business-oriented family, decided not to take over the family firm when his elder brother died prematurely, but rather went to Yale Divinity School. Upon graduating, he accepted a posting as a home missionary in Colorado. Parsons commented that this choice of activity reflected the social-service orientation of the Social Gospel, and influenced his own shift of career plans from biology or medicine toward social science.

3 In elaborating this notion, he drew extensively on the work of his former student, Robert Bellah (1967).

4 As Robertson (1982, 309) describes it, according to Parsons, 'The constitutive significance of human societies was manifested particularly in the struggle to deal with – to frame and infuse with meaning – the economic *and the erotic* appetites in relation to the "reality" *beyond* society. Religion was the core of the "struggle." '

5 The metaphysical nature of Parsons's postulates has been a consistent strand of criticism of his position (Black 1961a; Dahrendorf 1958). It is quite correctly pointed out that Parsons offers neither explanation nor justification for the presence of consensual values, but simply asserts their existence. However, by assuming that Parsons's concerns were purely descriptive ones, such critics fail to grasp the link between this idealized conception of society and Parsons's practical designs, as rooted in his Calvinist-based commitments to help ensure the gradual approximation of an otherworldly utopia in secular society.

6 See also Parsons [1937] 1968, 43.

7 By isomorphism is meant more than congruence or elective affinity. Because the theory was based on an extraction of reality – reformulated so as to provide the basis for its consolidation along certain lines – it would have the same basic shape and distinctions as the social order.

8 This preoccupation with social control is evident in his 'Varran Speech,' given in 1934. Noting the increasing public questioning of 'the unqualified benefits of freedom,' and 'the possibility that it may mean freedom to abuse, to exploit ... to gain at the expense of the rest,' he maintains that 'this shift of emphasis in the public mind has been accompanied by a parallel development in the quieter recesses of sociological thought. Always sensitive to the great changes of the surrounding social milieu the same changes which have altered public opinion have been one main factor in prompting a very thorough

reconsideration of the basis of our social life in the last generation or so. It is some of the outstanding results of this reconsideration in their bearing on the problem of control of the individual that I wish to bring before you this evening ... My own preoccupation has been with some of the broadest and most general questions of sociological theory, not with the details of practical problems or programs. What I can offer is only a view as to how the broadest lines of the situation lie, and what kind of problem of control a society like ours is faced with. What kind of methods lie at our disposal and what the general range of their probable adequacy is. The answers of general sociology to these questions, though far from being detailed and specific are not without their concrete and even practical relevance' (1934d).

9 Parsons 1928, 1929, 1931, 1932, 1934b, 1934c, 1935a, 1935b.

10 See also Parsons (1976) for an account of how the views on 'institutional economics' of Clarence Ayres affected his developing perspective.

11 As Parsons notes in the introduction to the paperback edition (1968) of *The Structure of Social Action*, 'I have always maintained that *The Structure of Social Action* was an empirical work in a double sense. First, it is very much oriented to problems of the macroscopic developments in Western Society, especially as seen through the eyes of the four principal authors discussed in the study. Secondly, it was an empirical study in the analysis of social thought.'

12 By assuming that Parsons's concerns were exclusively interpretive ones, these commentators, however, have not recognized that the biases were of a piece, and reflected Parsons's intent to engage classical social theory with practical designs in mind. Rather than taking issue with Parsons's rendering of the various thinkers and approaches per se, the purpose of the present work is to link Parsons's selective interpretations of the theorists he examines to his practical concerns.

CHAPTER 3

1 See Wearne (1981) for an account of Marshall's ambiguous and shifting status within Parsons's analysis of classical social theory.

2 Parsons describes his reasons for examining Marshall in letters to Frank Knight: 'For me the study of Marshall had served the purpose of defining my own attitude to "orthodox economics," finding a place for it but at the same time setting limits to its place in social science (1934e). The latter [the Marshall study] was undertaken mainly as a means of clarifying in my own mind a number of "relatively" fundamental questions which had been worrying me for a very long time, which might be summed up in the query: What was wrong with the orthodox "neo-classical" economics?' (1932b).

3 Parsons notes that 'in his [Robbins's] anxiety to make economics a "positive" science free from "metaphysics," he is continually being pressed into a radically positivistic position which really eliminates ends altogether' (1934c, 514).

4 'Can anyone,' Parsons writes, 'who has lived through the era of the great war, of communist and fascist revolutions, of oil scandals and Kruger debacles doubt the importance of force and fraud?' (1932a, 34).

5 This corresponds to the Calvinist social order, in which a strong state sought to establish a 'Kingdom of God on Earth' by overcoming the worldly appetites and desires of its members.

6 In a Hegelian sense, the system of ultimate values represented a stage of history that preserved the essential features of the ages of faith and scepticism, while transforming them into a historically unique form of society.

7 As Parsons concludes his discussion of Pareto's contribution in *Social Action*, 'all this in turn has empirical consequences of the first magnitude. It leads to a conception of the contemporary social situation, and of the nature and trend of the main processes of social change, which is in the most striking contrast with the views on the same subjects of Marshall and his utilitarian predecessors' ([1937] 1968, 460).

8 Parsons notes that 'Durkheim ... brought into clear relief the role of the institutional element in relation to the intrinsic means-end chain and carried out a much further differentiation of the structure and modes of manifestation of the ultimate-value system, which for Pareto had remained residual' (ibid., 713–14).

9 See Giddens (1974, 1–4); Kolokowski ([1968] 1972, 9–19).

10 The 'lack of social integration' revealed by this set of phenomena, Parsons comments, is 'approaching as a polar type the state Durkheim called *anomie*' ([1937] 1968, 291).

CHAPTER 4

1 In one of his early articles (1928, 641), he contrasts the historically attuned German thinking with 'Anglo-American economic thought.' While the former is concerned with 'the working out of the differences between, and the specific characteristics of, the different cultural epochs,' the latter was characterized by 'its rather abstract generality [and] its formulation in terms implying ... universal applicability wherever human economic life is lived.'

2 Parsons defends his exclusion of Marx from direct consideration in his discussion of approaches to capitalism in Germany: 'I have only failed to deal with him [Marx] separately because the most important elements of this aspect of Marx's thought have been taken up by Sombart and incorporated into his work' (ibid., 661).

3 As Parsons noted shortly after the outbreak of the Second World War, 'It is not our great tradition for the individual simply to "mind his own business" but rather to take an active and responsible part in the affairs of the community. There is great historic precedent for this in the old puritan conception of the "Kingdom of God on Earth" ' (1940, 36).

4 That Parsons was sympathetic to this orientation at an early age is evident in an article in a student newspaper he co-authored as a senior at Amherst. Commenting on two of his teachers – Walton H. Hamilton in economics and Clarence Ayres in philosophy – he noted that 'what these two men in particular gave us in the way of solid ground on which to build our social, ethical and economic ideas was not only very satisfying but also exceedingly stimulating for further thought and investigation. From them we got the point of view that the economic and social order was a matter of human arrangements, not one of inevitable natural law, and hence that it was subject to human control' (Parsons and Cutler, 1924).

5 There are interesting parallels between Parsons's voluntarism and that of Puritan culture. Creelan (1978, 184) summarizes the teachings of the 'Congregationalists' and the 'Separatists': 'The covenant that the Puritan believer joined is not seen as something he has chosen out of his own sovereign will, deciding between good and evil. Puritan voluntarism rather implied that human wills were thoroughly disposed by divine grace and revelation toward that which is God's higher purpose for them, which is to join with others who manifest the Spirit for mutual edification.'

According to the Congregationalist covenant, 'a church is formed when believers are joined together by a special bond of grace among themselves, a pregiven communal bond that is the body of Christ.' By the same token, 'men have no power *of themselves* to form churches' (183). Indeed, any act originating in the will of man, rather than in the word of God, was viewed as idolatrous. Puritan voluntarism, then, was based on the belief that religious agency was only possible through divine intervention in conjunction with human action. Creelan goes on to argue that Parsons, by celebrating human agency, deviated from the Puritan view of voluntarism (184–5). Yet if we examine Parsons's conception of ultimate values closely, it was completely consistent with the voluntarism of the Congregationalist covenant. In the same manner that people could not create a Church without divine intervention, the actors in the order could not act on their wants without the intervention of the system of ultimate values. Within Parsons's schema, action was only voluntaristic in so far as it was informed by this divinely inspired normative system. And the 'immanent' or 'emergent' basis of voluntarism as grounded in accepting ultimate values corresponded to the human potential to achieve a state of grace through faith in the divine.

6 As Schutz ([1940] 1978, 43) pointed out as part of a penetrating analysis of Parsons's theory of action, 'Professor Parsons does not really analyze the subjective categories of action, but rather the objective categories for scientifically describing the actor's subjective points of view.'

7 Parsons notes that 'there is implied in the relations of these elements [end, means, conditions, and norms], a normative orientation of action, a teleological character. Action must always be thought of as involving a state of tension between two different orders of elements, the normative and the conditional. As process, action is, in fact, the process of alteration of the conditional elements in the direction of the conformity with norms' ([1937] 1968, 732).

8 This concern to develop a division of labour among the social sciences has been a consistent, yet overlooked tendency in Parsons's thought (for an exception see Burger 1977). Wearne (1983) suggests that this concern had its origins in the 'federation approach' to the social sciences and society propounded by Carl Friedrich at Harvard during the 1930s. Friedrich, in turn, drew extensively on the thought of the post-Calvinist philosopher Johannes Althusius to develop his conception of how the study of politics related to the political aspect of society. Althusius advocated not only that society ideally should consist of a federation, but also that the disciplines studying it should have distinct concerns. As Frederick Carney (1965) notes, Althusius 'insists that each discipline must limit itself to that aspect of the common material that is essential to its own purpose, and to reject what is not.' Parsons acknowledges his indebtedness to Friedrich's conception of specialized disciplines as applied to politics in *The Structure of Social Action* (769).

9 Brinton (1939) was critical of sociology, above all, for its lack of scientific development. In his view, 'Sociology was committed ... to bringing forth the kind of cumulative and systematic knowledge achieved by sciences like zoology and geology. This it has certainly not yet done.' Along the same lines, he noted that 'sociologists can't agree on anything' and 'there just isn't any such central core as yet in sociology.' He also held a low opinion of 'its practitioners [who] are to an overwhelming extent partisans, improvers, preachers.' Parsons not only read this article, but also underlined and expressed his disagreement – through 'Xs' and '?s' in the margin. His extreme displeasure with the article was revealed in a letter he wrote to Brinton (1939a). Objecting to the article and its 'rather superior,' and 'contemptuous' tone, Parsons stressed that 'the relatively amateur fringe' of sociology (e.g. Robert Lynd, Stewart [sic] Chase, Harry Barnes, and Thurman Arnold) emphasized by Brinton 'are pretty far away from the central professional core,' and hence were not deserving of the attention they were given. According to Parsons, Brinton 'give[s] the impression that the field as a whole is completely dominated by people

of the Lynd type or a different category but perhaps an equally objectionable one, the Sorokin type. I am willing to grant that the people who have done and are doing a really high level of scientific work are a minority. But they are an extremely significant minority who are coming to set the tone more and more, rather than as one might infer from your discussion are merely off in a corner completely ignored.'

Parsons also took exception with Brinton's contention that sociology was lacking in scientific development. In Parsons's view, 'sociology has now reached a level of theoretical maturity which makes it the equal of general physiology.' Parsons noted that 'we are living in an epoch of extraordinarily rapid theoretical development in the social field which will turn out perhaps to be comparable to that of mechanics in the 17th century. And precisely the most significant aspect of this development is the rapid emergence of just such a central core, a common conceptual scheme [Brinton] flat-footedly state does not exist.'

Parsons sent a copy of the letter to Lawrence Henderson, who in his reply (1939), reiterated Brinton's point of view. According to Henderson, sociologists were on the whole doing harm rather than good. Not only did they mislead their students and the general public, but their teaching failed to provide the discipline essential to a well-grounded scientific education. He attributed the inadequacies of sociology, in part, to the inferiority of those recruited to the field in comparison to those who had entered the natural sciences. Henderson, then, like Brinton, was impressed neither by the scientific standards of sociology, nor by the calibre of its practitioners. All the same, in a response to Parsons's letter (1939b), Brinton admitted that he had been mistaken in giving the impression that the work of people such as Robert Lynd and Pitirim Sorokin dominated the field of sociology. Conceding that *The Structure of Social Action* was a pioneering work, Brinton none the less expressed his doubts about its influence upon sociologists and social commentators.

10 Commenting on the program of the nascent Department of Sociology, Parsons argued in favour of a sophomore rather than a freshman introductory course, because it was 'very important on the whole to emphasize the difficulty of the field and to avoid laying oneself open to the charge of superficiality and dilettantism.' A freshman introductory course was 'especially undesirable since economics has its introductory course in sophomore year. Sociology should not let itself be compared unfavorably with economics in point of difficulty, plenty of its ill-wishers would be only too glad of a chance' (1930).

Indicating a concern to effectively supplant social ethics, Parsons maintained in a memorandum that 'sociology is pre-eminently concerned with understanding the role of ethical elements in social life, and the limitations on this role ... "social ethics" may be considered a proper part of sociology, and hence part of the field of a department of sociology ... It may be of great influence on students' attitudes in the sense that it gives them a deeper understanding of the nature of society in which they live and hence of the issues involved in matters of policy' (1935). The manner in which Parsons sought to establish a sociological perspective combining the analytical rigour of economics with the moral relevance of social ethics very likely was affected by his immediate situation at Harvard.

CHAPTER 5

1 Parsons noted in a fellowship application, written shortly after the completion of *Social Action*: 'I am entering in the second year of a study concerned with the workings of institutional controls in the medical profession. It is a study in the mechanisms by which a certain type of order is maintained in the relations of the physicians, with others of the community, especially with his patients and with his professional colleagues' (1923–40c).
2 A fifth pair, achievement/ascription (quality/performance), derived from the work of Ralph Linton and was added later.
3 'Collectivity-orientation' replaced 'disinterestedness' in Parsons's later writings.
4 Parsons notes that 'the sciences of action ... are distinguished ... by the indispensability of the subject aspect, hence of the method of *Verstehen* ([1937] 1968, 764–5).

CHAPTER 6

1 'When Mr. [Edward] Hartshorne and I were asked to undertake the organization of the defense group's work on national morale in the role of chairman and vice-chairman respectively ... we decided that for the present we would not set up a regular committee. It was understood ... that our mandate would be interpreted as doing intellectual work which might be useful for clarification of thinking and policy on problems in the field of national morale, interpreted broadly as the morale of any country involved in the present crisis' (1930–59).
2 This organization, directed by Carl Friedrich, and located in New York, concerned itself with building support for American involvement in the war effort.
3 The draft of this MS in the Parsons Papers bears the tentative title 'The Development of Groups and Organizations Amenable to Use against American Institutions and Foreign Policy and Possible Measures of Prevention' (1940).
4 In all probability, this claim of Parsons was based on findings of researchers in the Harvard Business School, who had carried out exhaustive studies on how the morale and productive efficiency of

workers were affected by their working conditions (Roethlisberger and Dickson [1939] 1961; Mayo [1933] 1960). As Cohen (1983) points out, there are strong affinities between the action theory of Parsons and the 'nonlogical social code' of factory work, proposed by his fellow member of the Pareto circle Elton Mayo.

5 Parsons's analysis of the degree to which the three religious orientations made for loyalty was foreshadowed in his discussion of Weber's views on 'religion and modern capitalism' in *The Structure of Social Action*. Here he maintained that ascetic protestantism with its disinterested orientation made for activity that was at once 'thisworldy' and oriented towards ultimate values. This in turn made for 'rational, systematic labour' in the service of impersonal ends. The political implication was obedience to the rules of bureaucratic rational legality. Lutheranism and Catholicism, however, predisposed people towards 'traditionalism' and 'authoritarianism' – fully at odds with loyalty to a bureaucratic order.

6 As Parsons noted in a letter to Robert MacIver (1929–67b, 6), 'The organ of the community [the state] seems to me to have a very particularly close relation to the cultural aspect of the community. Being the only all-inclusive association and the only one exercising the sanction of force, 'legitimately' at least, it is natural that it should become the main organ of enforcement and promotion of the cultural aims the community sets itself as a whole.'

7 The origins of this orientation, as we saw, came from Parsons's reading of Weber's *Protestant Ethic*, and the emphasis he placed upon the impersonal and disinterested commitment to 'ultimate ends' as the basis for the rationalization of capitalism.

8 He noted in a report of the Committee on National Morale that 'feeling that German national socialism was the storm center of the present disturbance, we first initiated a group in Germany which is well under way. We secondly initiated a group on the problems of Japan since this is so important and so little understood' (1930–59). In addition to his discussion of national socialism in the memorandum to the Council for Democracy, Parsons wrote three articles on Germany ([1942] 1964; 1942a; and [1945a] 1964), and one on Japan ([1946] 1964).

9 Parsons commented on the origins of his concerns about fascism: 'For all observers of social and political processes in the Western world of the time, the Nazi movement presented not only intellectual, but also profoundly moral, problems. Perhaps I can say that these were somewhat more poignant for me than for most other American intellectuals, not only because of my German experience, owing to the fact that I had come to love and respect that aspect of Germany which I had known. The critical question was, Why and how could this happen in what from so many points of view should be evaluated as a "good society"'?

'It is obvious that there are at least two ways of reacting to such disturbing phenomena: to try to "do" something about them, and to try to understand them. As an academic man, in a situation heading toward the danger and eventual outbreak of a new world war, I became relatively active as an anti-Nazi, but as a sociologist, particularly in view of the limited opportunities for action, I came under very strong "internal" pressure to try to contribute both to my own and to other's understanding of what had gone on' (1969, 60–1).

10 Parsons encountered this position at a conference on Germany after the war, where the 'psychoanalytically oriented psychiatrists' in attendance suggested that if 'psychiatrically oriented "teams"' would 'educate German parents to change their ways, so as to produce nonauthoritarian personalities in their children,' German society would be transformed (1969, 63).

11 Parsons's discussion of the two extremist ideologies appears to be a restatement of his earlier analysis of the Paretan 'residues.' From the standpoint developed by Pareto, it was possible, in Parsons's view, to defuse both the non-scientific, irrational 'persistent aggregates' and the pseudo-scientific 'combinations.' In his wartime writings, similarly, he sought to demonstrate how 'rationalistic utopianism' and the equally irrational 'romanticism' could be superseded by an integrative and consensual set of values.

CHAPTER 7

1 The final National Science Foundation bill, however, was not approved until 1950. For an account of the reasons for the delay, see Lyons (1969, ch. 7) and Greenberg (1967, ch. 6).

2 This committee was formed by leading members of the SSRC, particularly Robert M. Yerkes and Donald Young at the annual meeting of the American Association for the Advancement of Science (AAAS), held in December 1946. It represented a broadening of the Committee for a National Science Foundation formed by Harold C. Urey and Harlow Shapley in 1945. With its support for a single administrator appointed by the president, and the inclusion of the social sciences in the foundation, it stood in opposition to another group of natural scientists, under the leadership of Isaiah Bowman, who had formed the Committee Supporting the Bush Position. Accepting the proposals for the National Science Foundation as outlined by Vannevar Bush in his report to the president (1945), this latter group favoured an administration run by scientists, and the exclusion of the social sciences from the foundation. In view of congressional suspicion of the social sciences, this group maintained, their inclusion in the foundation would jeopardize the bill's passage. For accounts of the post-war deliberations on the National Science Foundation see Lyons 1969, 126–36; Greenberg 1967, 106–23; and Miller 1982.

3 This endeavour was guided by the prophecy that 'within another century we shall have achieved a totally different level of knowledge and potentiality of practical control from what any of us knows at present. It seems likely that the difference will be something akin to those between the state of medical science a century ago and now' (1947a, 502).

4 In his view, 'interaction between anthropology and psychology, particularly in the "culture and personality" field, has been the center of one of the most active growing points of theoretical analysis of behavior [and] has already done much to articulate psychology with the analysis of social systems' (1948, 17).

5 This concern to find common ground among sociology, psychology, and anthropology was both a major raison d'être for the formation of the Department of Social Relations at Harvard and the focal point for an elaboration of the 'action frame of reference' undertaken by Parsons in conjunction with others during 1949–50 (Parsons and Shils [1951] 1962, v–vi).

6 Drawing out the implications of the conclusions reached in *The Structure of Social Action*, Parsons noted that 'after a period of considerable groping and division into "schools" there are signs of crystallization of the theoretical interests of sociology about the analysis of the institutionalized patterns of the structure of social systems and their relation to behavior. This theoretical focus, which has received important impetus from European thought, especially in the work of Pareto, Durkheim and Max Weber, has great integrating potentialities for the whole field of social science ... It [this theoretical focus] makes it possible for sociology directly to assimilate the results of the integration of anthropology and psychology' (1948, 18).

7 As he noted in his report to the SSRC on the state of the social sciences, 'by making the more general analysis of culture patterns and institutional structure relatively systematic, explicit, and (a) technical, these two disciplines [social anthropology and sociology] have in a sense sent a keystone into the arch of our systematic knowledge of social phenomena and made a great advance toward treating them in terms of a single systematic conceptual scheme' (ibid., 16–17).

8 Creelan ingeniously suggests that 'if one in fact revises the A-G-I-L sequence of letters – and reads them from right to left as in the ancient Hebrew – one is left with the Latin word L-I-G-A, meaning "bond" or "tie." The actors in the Parsonian world thus are united in a bond that is symbolized by a box, bound to a common law, as were the Old Testament Israelites to whom Congregationalists looked for the forms that would guide their own communities ... Parsons emphasizes a voluntary religion as the nature of the social system, a way of life that tends to substitute specific human works or acts for a receptivity to and expression of divine revelation and the Holy Spirit' (1978, 186).

CHAPTER 8

1 Evidently Parsons's considerations of McCarthyism were galvanized by his contact with the climate of intellectual opinion in the United Kingdom during 1953–4, when he held a visiting professorship at Cambridge University (1969, 158).

2 Indeed, by affirming the authoritative nature of his professional viewpoint, Parsons implied that *The Power Elite* lacked sociological validity: 'Undertaking as a professional sociologist to review Mills' book, I am motivated largely by the opportunity to test some of his main conclusions against expectations derived from a type of technical theory that is at best only partially shared by the author of the book' ([1957] 1969, 186).

3 This referred to an inchoate group whose members criticized the United States for the banality of its culture and its tendency towards massification. Mills (1956, ch. 13) was singled out by the Bauers as an exponent of 'mass society,' while the collection edited by Rosenberg and White ([1957] 1964) was considered by them to be representative of 'mass culture' criticism.

4 Adriaansens (1979, 20) notes that 'the general character of the new theory of action, and especially of the four function paradigm, is most vigorously expressed by Parsons' claim that this paradigm and the axes on which it is built function to integrate the formerly disconnected disciplines in the area of human action. He conceived of his action frame of reference as being a newly developed charter for the unification of, at least, the social sciences.'

5 'As relatively autonomous institutions,' Parsons noted, 'colleges and universities undertake a large share of self-government' (1968b, 182).

CHAPTER 9

1 In the 1952 annual report of the Ford Foundation, it was noted that 'the trustees, after three years of operating experience and after thorough reexamination, remain convinced that the basic objectives originally determined should stand unchanged' (Ford Foundation 1952, 12). That the Ford Foundation had come to follow the practical guide-lines recommended by the study committee was evident in the assessment of its activities given by Dwight Macdonald: 'The Ford Foundation is "problem oriented," as were the Carnegie and Rockefeller Foundations in the golden age; it first decides on a problem that it thinks needs attention – the inroads of civil liberties within this country, say, or the gains of the Soviet Bloc outside it – and then finances projects in the 'disciplines' relevant to that problem' (1956, 49).

2 According to Merton and Lazarsfeld (1950, 9), this work represented 'a body of empirical findings that push forward on several frontiers of

social psychology and sociology.' Underlying the welter of empirical observations, none the less, noted Robert S. Lynd, was the concern to 'sort out and to control men for purposes not of their own willing' and to better grasp 'how to turn frightened draftees into tough soldiers who will fight a war whose purposes they do not understand' (in Merton and Lazarsfeld 1950, 221). Alfred M. Lee, in a similar vein, commented on this trend towards 'social engineering': 'If managerial problems for industry and the military are to continue to dominate the research of leading social psychologists and sociologists, the value orientation of the managerial technician rather than the value orientation of the social science educator will dominate what evolves and is called social science' (in Merton and Lazarsfeld 1950, 221–2).

3 For an assessment of American sociology as it stood following the Second World War, see Shils (1947).

4 While the Ford Foundation brought the term behavioural sciences into popular currency with its area-five program, the post-war incarnation of the concept originated in an effort not only to make the social sciences more scientifically rigorous but also to enhance their possibility of gaining financial support by avoiding the socialist stigma attached to the social sciences. James Miller described the genesis of the term behavioural sciences: 'About 1949 a group of scientists at the University of Chicago ... began to consider whether a sufficient body of facts exists to justify developing an empirically testable general theory of behavior. To refer to the biological and social fields involved, we coined the term 'behavioral sciences.' We adopted this phrase, first, because its neutral character made it acceptable to both social and biological scientists, and, second, because we foresaw a possibility of someday seeking to obtain financial support from persons who might confound social science with socialism' (1955, 513).

5 Their main vehicles for the cultivation of behavioural methodology were conferences and training seminars such as the conference on political behaviour held at the University of Michigan in 1949 (Heard 1949) and the interuniversity seminar on the same topic held at the University of Chicago in the summer of 1951 (Leiserson 1951).

CHAPTER 10

1 Almond notes that Simon bar Giora, 'a Zealot extremist, became the leader in Jerusalem in those last bloody days, killing off the less resolute and pressing the city to destruction in order in some sense to save it. He survived the fall of Jerusalem, was one of the prize captives in the triumph of Titus, and was thrown from the Tarpeian Rock as a sacrifice to the victory' (Almond 1970, 7).

2 Almond describes him as 'a princely aristocrat, influenced by Hellenic culture, and aware of the great power of Rome [who] first counseled

against the rebellion, and then led it in Galilee. When further resistance appeared hopeless he surrendered and went over to the Romans' (ibid.).

3 'I have a scholarly style,' Almond notes, 'which moves restlessly back and forth from theorizing to empirical research. To remain too long at the theoretical level has always filled me with mixed feelings of anxiety and futility. At the same time to remain in the field too long, to get lost in detail, to lose a sense of context and of purpose, similarly is intolerable' (ibid., 4).

4 'The professional and business classes,' Almond maintained, form the foundation of a decentralized elite and an attentive public which 'small as they are, affect the political tone of the society at large in most significant ways' (1955, 104–5).

5 Almond's conviction that the Anglo-American political system could serve as a model for others stemmed from his revised assessment of the American public in the decade after 1950. Almond sensed that there had been 'a real stabilization in foreign policy awareness and attention, a broad plateau of appreciation of the continued gravity and salience of international and security problems.' Such a 'high level of perception of foreign policy problems' suggested to him 'a real moderation in the fluctuation of American moods' ([1950] 1960, xxii). 'As the American mass public has matured in the last decade, displaying both greater stability and responsibility, so also has the depth of the segment of the public attentive to foreign policy increased.' This has been coupled with 'a trend towards greater homogeneity in American foreign policy opinion' (xxiv).

6 The seminar was conducted over three weeks in June 1956 at Dobbs Ferry, New York.

7 The planning session was held 5–10 April 1957 at the Center for Advanced Study in the Behavioral Sciences at Stanford University.

8 The five conferences were Communication and Political Development, September 1961; Bureaucracy and Political Development, December 1961; Education and Political Development, June 1962; Political Development in Turkey and Japan, September 1962; Political Parties and Political Development, September 1963.

9 Robert Packenham (1973, 260) judged that 'probably no book in the field of comparative politics over the last ten or fifteen years has had a greater impact than *The Politics of the Developing Areas.*' For a similar assessment, see Dahl (1963, 112).

CHAPTER 11

1 According to Michels ([1915] 1968), inherent in any large-scale organization – including socialist parties – were tendencies towards oligarchy and the loss of control by the rank and file membership.

2 As 'The First New Nation,' the United States, in Lipset's view, with its

institutionalization of egalitarianism and democracy, was to serve as a prototype for other, less advanced, countries of the world. Concurring with Parsons, Lipset maintained that the value orientations derived from Calvinistic puritanism 'made possible the legitimation of equalitarian values and democratic government' in the United States (1964b, 360).

3 This marked a departure from his epilogue to *Agrarian Socialism* in which he maintained that 'an answer to stagnation lies in the bold actions of such men as the "agitators" of Saskatchewan, who are not satisfied with anything but utopia. These men ... may ... be destined to help form mighty social movements to advance human welfare ... As long as there are social organizations that produce men who do not accept the *status quo*, who see "the inhumanity of man to man" as a crime, there will be hope in the human race' ([1950] 1971, 342).

4 As Michael Rogin (1967) convincingly demonstrates, McCarthyism was less a popular rebellion than it was a bid for greater power by certain elites within the Republican party. Along similar lines, revisionist historians (Griffith 1970; Theoharis 1971; Griffith and Theoharis 1974) show how the emergence of the McCarthyist movement was inherently related to the forces set in motion by the Truman administration.

5 Founded in 1950, this organization sought to develop a unified, international front against communism by attempting to influence intellectuals and writers. To this end, it sponsored meetings, conferences, and the magazine *Encounter*. Its core membership included prominent anti-Communists, many of whom were also ex-Communists. Among the sources of its funding were the Ford Foundation and the Central Intelligence Agency. For a brief but extremely insightful account of the history and significance of the Congress for Cultural Freedom, see Lasch (1969).

6 Macdonald (1955, 68) commented that participants generally agreed with Raymond Aron's statement in a paper delivered at the conference that ' "the political categories of the last century – Left and Right, liberal and socialist, traditionalist and revolutionary – have lost their relevance." But it was hardly necessary to bring together so many thinkers from the ends of the earth to establish these truths – which, in fact, were already sketched out in the call to the conference itself.' It can be argued that the conference represented an effort to consolidate the doctrine of the 'vital center' as articulated by the Americans for Democratic Action (Schlesinger [1949] 1962).

7 According to Shils, Lipset's paper, which 'touched in an imaginative way on the dangers of lower-class fundamentalism and authoritarianism, and ... raised the question of "McCarthyism" without the usual stereotypes, aroused not a word of comment' (1955, 56).

8 Lipset's previous association with the journal undoubtedly accounts for his concern with its editorial policy. As Romalis (1972, 227) notes, 'while writing up his Ph.D. dissertation and holding his first teaching position at the University of Toronto, [Lipset] was associated with the socialist circle controlling the magazine *Canadian Forum*.'

9 Despite his agreement with the views that dominated discussion at the meeting of the Congress for Cultural Freedom in Milan, Lipset denied that the conference was a source of new ideas for him. As he stated in a 1972 interview, 'It [the Milan conference] was a visible demonstration of what I thought was true, but it wasn't important in the sense of giving me new ideas on the subject' (in Dittberner 1979, 340).

10 Lipset's debt to the Committee on Comparative Politics was not only a theoretical one. The committee, along with the Behavioral Sciences Division of the Ford Foundation, provided the funds for a 'project analyzing research on comparative political behavior,' of which a later inventory of political sociology ([1959a] 1965) was a part. Moreover, as Lipset noted in the forward to *Political Man*, 'much of the work reported in Chapters 1, 6, 7, 8 and 9 was done ... with the support of a grant from the Behavioral Sciences Division of the Ford Foundation for an inventory of research in the field of political behavior.' He added, 'Much of the work underlying the original form of publication of the remaining chapters was done with its [The Berkeley Institute of Industrial Relations] sponsorship, and with the support of additional grants from the Behavioral Sciences Division of the Ford Foundation, and the Committee on Comparative Politics of the Social Science Research Council. The year which I spent as a Fellow of the Center for Advanced Study in the Behavioral Sciences in 1955–56, free from all responsibilities except my own concerns, must also be gratefully acknowledged' ([1960] 1963, xiii, xiv).

11 Lipset elaborated his debt to Talcott Parsons, 'perhaps the major contemporary sociological theorist,' in *Political Man*: 'The study of politics cannot be "treated in terms of a specifically specialized conceptual scheme ... precisely for the reason that the political problem of the social system is a focus for the integration of all its analytically distinguished components, not of a specially differentiated class of these components"' (in ibid., 3–4).

12 In a reply to an article critical of his work (Scheglof and Kruytbosch 1961), Lipset advanced the view that '"the political struggle should be regarded as an extension of the class struggle"' (in Peck 1962, 155).

13 Responding to Lipset's contentious view of the left, Irving L. Horowitz ([1963] 1968, 170) rightly asks, 'Is it possible that Lipset, in his anxiety to identify the going course of American history with the strange course of one man's strange Leftism, has simply attributed to the nation qualities which he possesses as an individual?'

14 The evolution of *Union Democracy* is itself indicative of how Lipset's point of reference evolved over time. Originally, taking the standpoint of the unionized worker, he was concerned with how authoritarian practices in the union could be prevented through mechanisms of participatory democracy (1952). However, in the final published version of *Union Democracy* (1956), Lipset's standpoint had shifted to the interests of the system itself and how it could maintain its stability. Accordingly, he now stressed the mechanisms of the union that permitted it to contain conflict and possible challenges from dissenting members.

15 In effect admitting his own ideological shift, Lipset noted that 'this comment applies to my own work as much as to that of any other social scientist' ([1959a] 1965, 99).

16 He noted in the foreword that 'these studies in the sociology of politics are not intended primarily as a collection of essays which happen to be written by the same person. Rather, I tried to select from my various articles those which best illustrate the contribution the sociologist can make to an understanding of democratic political systems' ([1960] 1963, x).

17 Rokkan (1970) gives an overview of the committee's concerns and activities from 1959 to 1968.

CHAPTER 12

1 On Project Camelot and its aftermath, see Irving L. Horowitz, ed. (1967).

2 Since 1960 the United States alone had already witnessed numerous stirrings of new protest movements. Teodori chronicled the upsurge of radical movements in the United States during the first half of the decade: 'In May 1960, 8,000 people picketed against HUAC in San Francisco; 5,000 demonstrated against nuclear testing in Washington in February 1962; 200,000 participated in the civil-rights march on Washington of April 1963; 80,000 blacks voted on the Mississippi Freedom Ballot in 1963; over 6,000 students were involved in some way in the Berkeley Free Speech Movement of 1964; 25,000 people answered the SDS call and went to Washington to protest against the Vietnam War in April 1965' (1970, 35).

3 Lipset, however, had been concerned with the student movement from its outset (Lipset and Wolin 1965).

4 This orientation received full expression in Tilly (1975) and Skocpol (1979).

5 As Peters described it, 'Hobbes ... pictured the state as an artificial machine based on a social contract and controlled by an absolute monarch with unlimited, perpetual, and indivisible sovereignty' ([1956] 1967, 181).

6 This closely corresponded to Hobbes's proposition, as described by Hannah Arendt, that 'a never-ending accumulation of property must be based on a never-ending accumulation of power ... The limitless process of capital accumulation needs the political structure of so "unlimited a Power," that it can protect growing property by constantly growing more powerful' ([1951] 1958, 143).

7 As Camic (1979) points out, Parsons's generalizations about utilitarian thought can be called into question because they impart a spurious unity to diverse theorists and ignore the moral and practical thrust of many so-called 'utilitarian' thinkers.

8 This trend is particularly evident in *States and Social Revolutions* by Theda Skocpol (1979). While she convincingly demonstrates the interplay between the emergence and consolidation of state structures in relation to class forces, she all but ignores the role of ideas, culture, and the sustaining forms of legitimation. Since the three revolutions she examines are described exclusively in objective structural terms, it is implied that radical ideas and intellectual engagement are of little relevance to social and political transformations.

9 This tendency is most noticeable in the academicization of Marxism in American sociology as a whole. Rather than affecting the practice of sociology in any significant way, it has simply been incorporated into the reward structure as another line of inquiry. In adapting to the canons of a profession dominated by quantification, it has itself become predominantly positivistic in its outlook.

CHAPTER 13

1 The following discussion draws heavily on the analysis of the paradigm given by Masterman (1970) and by Eckberg and Hill (1980).

2 Political sociology is a much more appropriate object of analysis than structural functionalism, which Robert Friedrichs (1970) argued had become the main paradigm for sociological analysis in the 1950s and early 1960s. As Alan Dawe commented in an extended review of Friedrichs, 'The real test of the applicability of Kuhn to sociology can be made only at the point where research actually proceeds; that is, in the sub-discipline or research specialization.' Moreover, political sociology, unlike structural-functional systems theory, was marked by 'fully-developed experimental research models and procedures which convey them as concrete exemplars in Kuhn's "puzzle-solving normal science.' (Dawe 1970, 143).

3 Holt and Turner (1975) question whether any cumulation of knowledge actually occurred in comparative politics, pointing out that the general conceptual looseness of the field made the claim of cumulative development by its proponents unwarranted.

4 Almond, in fact, maintained that the political system constituted

a new paradigm that had considerable promise for theoretical development (1966). Similarly, Lipset spoke of the sociology of politics in paradigmatic terms in his efforts to establish a research agenda for the field ([1959a] 1965, [1960] 1963).

5 This relation between primary and secondary legitimation as it pertained to members of the public is well illustrated by events in the United States during the early years of the Cold War. To legitimate its increased level of domestic and foreign intervention, the Truman administration defined the world as beset by a global struggle between freedom and totalitarianism, accompanied by a high degree of internal communist infiltration. Those who questioned this definition of reality were subject to charges of disloyalty and were subject to reprisals. Freeland (1974) offers a compelling explanation of how the Truman administration sought to legitimate its desired involvement in the European Recovery Program through a domestic loyalty drive.

6 This account has been very much influenced by the analysis of state and class given by Block (1977).

Bibliography

This bibliography consists of two sections. The first contains all works of Talcott Parsons cited in the body of the text. These have been listed chronologically in their order of publication, followed by those works of Parsons that he co-authored with others. Parsons's unpublished manuscripts are included in this first section. Those manuscripts that are undated are referred to by the date of the section of the Parsons Papers in which they appear. If items that appeared in a re-published form were used, the original publication date is given in square brackets, followed by the date of the edition used as a reference in this book. When the version of an essay from a collected edition has been used the same format has been adopted. The second section contains all other cited works and lists items alphabetically by author, with works of each author listed chronologically.

Abbreviations

ATHC (1978) *Action Theory and the Human Condition* (Parsons)
ESS (1930–5) *Encyclopaedia of the Social Sciences* (New York: Macmillan)
EST (1964) *Essays in Sociological Theory* (Parsons)
IESS (1968) *International Encyclopaedia of the Social Sciences* (New York: Macmillan Co. and the Free Press)
PSS (1969) *Politics and Social Structure* (Parsons)
SSP (1970) *Social Structure and Personality* (Parsons)
PP Parsons Papers, Harvard University Archives
CRP 1923–40 Correspondence and related papers (PP)
CRP 1930–59 Correspondence and related papers (PP)
UM 1929–67 Unpublished manuscripts (PP)

Works by Talcott Parsons

1923–40a 'SSRC Project.' Undated manuscript. PP, CRP 1923–40, box 2

1923–40b 'The Professions.' Undated manuscript. PP, CRP 1923–40, box 2

1923–40c 'Fellowship Application.' Untitled and undated manuscript. PP, CRP 1923–40, box 2

1928 ' "Capitalism" in Recent German Literature: Sombart and Weber I.' *Journal of Political Economy* 36:641–61

1929–67 'Conference.' PP, UM 1929–67, box 1

1929–67a 'Sociological Reflections on the United States in Relation to the European War.' PP, UM 1929–67

1929–67b Letter to Robert MacIver, undated, PP, UM 1929–67

1929 ' "Capitalism" in Recent German Literature: Sombart and Weber II.' *Journal of Political Economy* 37:31–51

1930–59 'Report of the Committee on National Morale.' PP, CRP 1930–59, box 3

1930 'Sociology Department – Comments by T. Parsons.' PP, CRP 1923–40, box 2

1930a 'Jean Calvin.' ESS, vol. 3, 151–2

1931 'Wants and Activities in Marshall.' *Quarterly Journal of Economics* 46: 101–40

1932 'Economics and Sociology: Marshall in Relation to the Thought of his Time.' *Quarterly Journal of Sociology* 46:316–47

1932a 'Pareto and the Problems of Positivistic Sociology: An Essay in Sociological Theory.' PP, UM 1929–67

1932b Letter to Frank Knight, 13 October. PP, UM 1929–67, box 1

1933 'Pareto.' ESS vol. 11, 576–8

1934 'Service.' ESS, vol. 13, 672–4

1934a 'Society,' ESS, vol. 14, 225–31

1934b 'Sociological Elements in Economic Thought, I.' *Quarterly Journal of Economics* 49:414–53

1934c 'Some Reflections on "The Nature and Significance of Economics." ' *Quarterly Journal of Economics* 48 (May):511–45

1934d 'Varran Speech-Social Control.' PP, CRP 1923–40, box 1, box 2

1934e Letter to Frank Knight, 25 November. PP, UM 1929–67, box 1

1935 'Memorandum on Department of Sociology.' PP, CRP 1923–40, box 2

1935a 'H.M. Robertson on Max Weber and His School.' *Journal of Political Economy* 43:688–96

1935b 'The Place of Ultimate Values in Sociological Theory.' *Ethics* 45 (April):282–316

1935c 'Prolegemena to a Theory of Social Institutions.' PP, UM 1929–67

1936 Review of *Max Weber's Wissenschaftslehre*, by Alexander von Schelting. *American Sociological Review* 1 (August):675–81

[1937] *The Structure of Social Action.* New York: Macmillan, Free Press,
1968 paperback edition. Originally published in New York: McGraw-Hill

[1939] 'The Professions and Social Structure.' *Social Forces* 17:457–67.
1964 Reprinted in EST, 34–49

1939a Letter to Crane Brinton, 11 July. PP, CRP 1923–40

1940 'Memorandum for Council for Democracy.' PP, UM 1929–67, box 2

1940a 'Reply to Professor Knight.' *Canadian Journal of Economics and Political Science* 6 (August):466–72

[1940b] 'The Motivation of Economic Activities.' *Canadian Journal of*
1964 *Economics and Political Science* 6:187–203. Reprinted in EST, 50–68

1940c Letter to Robert K. Merton, 23 October. PP, CRP 1923–40, box 2

1940d Letter to Mr A.J.R. Fraser-Taylor, 11 December. PP, CRP 1923–40, box 3

1941 Letter to the editor of the *New York Herald Tribune*, 19 January. PP, CRP 1930–59, box 3

1941a Letter to Edith Nourse Rogers, 23 January. PP, CRP 1930–59, box 3

1941b Letter to the editor of the *Boston Post*, April. PP, CRP 1930–59, box 3

1941c Letter to Edward Hartshorne, 29 August. PP, CRP 1930–59, box 3

[1942] 'Democracy and Social Structure in Pre-Nazi Germany.' *Journal of*
1964 *Legal and Political Sociology* 1:96–114. Reprinted in EST, 104–23

1942a 'Max Weber and the Contemporary Political Crisis.' *The Review of Politics* 4:155–72

[1942b] 'Propaganda and Social Control.' *Psychiatry* 5, 4:551–72. Reprinted
1964 in EST, 142–76

[1942c] 'Some Sociological Aspects of the Fascist Movements.' *Social*
1964 *Forces* 21, 2:96–114. Reprinted in EST, 124–41

[1945] 'The Present Position and Prospects of Systematic Theory in
1964 Sociology.' In *Twentieth Century Sociology*, edited by Georges Gurvitch and Wilbert A. Moore. New York: Philosophical Library. Reprinted in EST, 212–37

[1945a] 'The Problem of Controlled Institutional Change: An Essay in
1964 Applied Social Science.' *Psychiatry* 8:79–101. Reprinted as 'The Problem of Controlled Institutional Change' in EST, 238–74

[1946] 'Population and Social Structure.' In *Japan's Prospect*, edited by
1964 Douglas G. Haring. Cambridge, Mass.: Harvard University Press, 87–114. Reprinted as 'Population and Social Structure in Japan' in EST, 275–97

1946a 'The Science Legislation and the Role of the Social Sciences.' *American Sociological Review* XI, 6 (December):653–66

[1947] 'Certain Primary Sources and Patterns of Aggression in the Social
1964 Structure of the Western World.' *Psychiatry* 10:167–81. Reprinted in EST, 298–322

1947a 'Intercultural Understanding and Academic Social Science.' In *Science, Philosophy and Religion in Their Relation to the Democratic Way of Life*, edited by Lymon Bryson, et al. New York: Harper and Bros, 498–502.

1947b 'Note on the Science Foundation Bill in the 80th Congress.'

	American Sociological Review 12, no. 5:601–3
1947c	'Some Aspects of the Relations between Social Science and Ethics.' *Social Science* 22 (July):213–17
[1947d] 1964	Introduction to *Max Weber: The Theory of Social and Economic Organization.* Co-edited and translated with A.M. Henderson. New York: Oxford University Press. Republished in paper in New York: The Free Press.
1948	*Social Science: A Basic National Resource. A Report Prepared for Social Science Research Council* (July). Preliminary draft. Confidential for review and criticism by Cora Dubois. PP, UM 1929–67, box 3
1949	'The Rise and Decline of Economic Man.' *Journal of General Education* IV, 1:47–53
[1950] 1964	'Psychoanalysis and the Social Structure.' *Psychoanalytic Quarterly* 19:371–84. Reprinted in EST, 336–47
1950a	'The Institutionalization of Social Science and the Problem of the Conference.' Chapter 14 in *Perspectives on a Troubled Decade,* edited by Lymon Bryson. Science, Philosophy, and Religion, 1939–49, Tenth Symposium. New York: Harper's, 221–44
[1950b] 1964	'The Prospects of Sociological Theory.' *American Sociological Review* 15, 1:3–16. Reprinted in EST, 348–69
[1951] 1964	*The Social System.* New York: Free Press. Republished, paperback edition
[1952] 1964	'A Sociologist Looks at the Legal Profession.' Conference on the Profession of Law and Legal Education, Conference Series Number II. Chicago: Law School, University of Chicago, 49–63. Reprinted in EST, 370–85
[1953] 1964	'A Revised Analytical Approach to the Theory of Social Stratification.' In *Class, Status, and Power: A Reader in Social Stratification,* edited by Reinhard Bendix and Seymour M. Lipset. New York: Free Press, 92–129. Reprinted in EST, 386–439
1953a	'Some Comments on the State of the General Theory of Action.' *American Sociological Review* 18, 6 (December):618–31
[1954] 1963	'"McCarthyism" and American Social Tension: A Sociologist's View.' *Yale Review* 44, no. 2 (December):226–45. Reprinted as 'Social Strains in America' in Bell [1955] 1963, 209–29
[1957] 1969	'The Distribution of Power in American Society.' *World Politics* 10:123–43. Reprinted in PSS, 185–203
1958	'Some Highlights of the General Theory of Action.' In *Approaches to the Study of Politics,* edited by Roland Young. Evanston: Northwestern University Press, 282–301
[1959] 1969	'"Voting" and the Equilibrium of the American Political System.' In *American Voting Behavior,* edited by Eugene Burdick and Arthur Brodbeck. New York: Free Press. Reprinted in PSS, 204–40
1959a	'Some Problems Confronting Sociology as a Profession.' *American Sociological Review* 24:547–59

1959b   'An Approach to the Sociology of Knowledge.' *Proceedings*, vol. 4, 25–49. Fourth World Congress of Sociology, Milan

1962   'The Cultural Background of American Religious Organization.' In *Ethics and Bigness; Scientific, Academic, Religious, Political and Military*, edited by Harlan Cleveland and Harold Lasswell. New York: The Conference on Science, Philosophy and Religion in Their Relation to the Democratic Way of Life, Inc., 141–67

1964   *Essays in Sociological Theory* [EST]. New York: Free Press, paperback edition. Originally published in 1949; revised edition in 1954

[1964a]   'Some Theoretical Considerations Bearing on the Field of Medical
1970   Sociology.' SSP, 325–59

1968   'Christianity.' IESS 2, 425–47

1968a   'Professions.' IESS 12, 536–47

1968b   'The Academic System: A Sociologist's View.' *The Public Interest* 13 (Fall):173–97

1969   *Politics and Social Structure* [PSS]. New York: Free Press

1970   *Social Structure and Personality* [SSP]. New York: Free Press, paperback edition. Originally published in 1964

1970a   'On Building Social Systems Theory: A Personal History.' *Daedalus* 99, 4:826–81

1970b   'The Intellectual: A Social Role Category.' In *On Intellectuals: Theoretical Studies/Case Studies*, edited by Phillip Reiff. Garden City, NY: Doubleday, Anchor, 3–26

1970c   Letter to Graham Morgan, 30 November. Recipient's collected letters

[1971]   'Belief, Unbelief, and Disbelief.' In *The Culture of Unbelief:*
1978   *Studies and Proceedings*, the First International Symposium on Belief, edited by Rocco Caporale and Antonio Grumelli. Berkeley: University of California Press, 207–45. Reprinted in ATHC, 233–63

1972   'Higher Education as a Theoretical Focus.' In *Institutions and Social Exchange: The Sociologies of Talcott Parsons and George Homans*, edited by Richard Simpson and Herman Turk. Indianapolis: Bobbs-Merrill, 233–52

1974   'Religion in Postindustrial America: The Problem of Secularization.' *Social Research* 41 (Summer):193–225

1976   'Clarence Ayres's Economics and Sociology.' In *Science and Ceremony: The Institutional Economics of C.E. Ayres*, edited by William Breit and William Patton Culbertson, Jr. Austin: University of Texas Press, 175–9

1978   *Action Theory and the Human Condition* [ATHC]. New York: Free Press

Joint Publications with Others

Parsons, Talcott, and Cutler, Addison T. 1924. 'A Word from Amherst Students.' *The New Student* 3 (October 20):6–7

Parsons, Talcott, and Barber, Bernard. 1948. 'Sociology 1941–46.' *American Journal of Sociology* 53 (January):245–57

Parsons, Talcott, and Shils, Edward, eds. [1951] 1962. *Toward a General Theory of Action.* New York: Harper & Row. Originally published in Cambridge, Mass.: Harvard University Press

Parsons, Talcott, and Kroeber, A.L. 1958. 'The Concepts of Culture and of Social System.' *American Sociological Review* 23, no. 5 (October):582–3

Parsons, Talcott, and White, Winston. [1960] 1969. 'The Mass Media and the Structure of American Society.' *Journal of Social Issues* XVI:67–77. Reprinted in PSS, 241–51

– [1961] 1970. 'The Link between Character and Society.' In *Culture and Social Character: The Work of David Riesman Reviewed,* edited by Seymour M. Lipset and Leo Lowenthal. New York: Free Press, 89–135. Reprinted in SSP, 183–235

Parsons, Talcott; Pitts, Jesse; Naegele, Kaspar; and Shils, Edward, eds. 1961. *Theories of Society.* 2 vols. New York: Free Press

Parsons, Talcott, and Platt, Gerald. 1973. *The American University.* Cambridge, Mass.: Harvard University Press

Other Works

Abrams, Philip. 1974. 'On Political Sociology.' Paper presented to SSRC (UK)-sponsored conference on political sociology held at the University of Exeter, 15–16 March

Adriaansens, Hans P.M. 1979. 'The Conceptual Dilemma: Towards a Better Understanding of the Development of Parsonian Action-Theory.' *British Journal of Sociology* 30, 5–24

– 1980. *Talcott Parsons and the Conceptual Dilemma.* London: Routledge and Kegan Paul

Alexander, Jeffrey C. 1978. 'Formal and Substantive Voluntarism in the Work of Talcott Parsons: A Theoretical and Ideological Reinterpretation.' *American Sociological Review* 43 (April):177–98

– 1979. 'Once Again: The Case for Parsons's Voluntarism.' *American Sociological Review* 44 (1):175–7

– 1983. *Theoretical Logic in Sociology.* Volume 4: *The Modern Reconstruction of Classical Thought: Talcott Parsons.* Berkeley: University of California Press

Allardt, Erik, and Rokkan, Stein, eds. 1970. *Mass Politics.* New York: Free Press

Almond, Gabriel. 1946. 'Politics, Science and Ethics.' *American Political Science Review* 40 (April):283–93

– 1948. *Western European Politics and American Policy.* Memorandum twenty-six in Yale Institute of International Studies Series. New Haven, Conn.: Yale Institute

– [1950] 1960. *The American People and Foreign Policy.* New York: Frederick

A. Praeger, Inc. Originally published in New York: Harcourt, Brace and Co.
- 1950a. 'Anthropology, Political Behavior, and International Relations.' A
  Review of Clyde Kluckhohn, *Mirror for Man* and Alexander Leighton,
  Human Relations in a Changing World. *World Politics* 2 (January):277–84
- 1954. *The Appeals of Communism*. Princeton, NJ: Princeton University
  Press
- 1955. *The Politics of German Business*. Santa Monica, Cal.: The RAND
  Corporation
- [1956] 1970. 'Comparative Political Systems.' *Journal of Politics*
  18:391–409. Reprinted in Almond 1970, 29–49
- 1956a. 'Public Opinion and National Security Policy.' *Public Opinion
  Quarterly* 20 (Summer):371–8
- 1956b. 'The Seminar on Comparative Politics,' June 1956. *Items*
  (December): 45–8
- 1958. 'A Comparative Study of Interest Groups and the Political Process.'
  American Political Science Review 52 (March):270–82
- [1958a] 1970. 'A Comparative Study of Interest Groups and the Political
  Process. Ibid. Revised and reprinted in Almond 1970, 51–76
- [1960] 1970. 'A Functional Approach to Comparative Politics.' In Almond
  and Coleman (eds) 1960. Reprinted in Almond 1970, 79–151
- [1966] 1970. 'Political Systems and Political Change.' *American Political
  Science Review* 60 (December):869–79. Also in Almond 1970, 235–71
- 1970. *Political Development: Essays in Heuristic Theory*. Boston: Little,
  Brown and Co.
- 1973. 'Approaches to Developmental Causation.' Chapter 1 in *Crisis,
  Choice and Change*, edited by Gabriel Almond, Scott C. Flanagan, and
  Robert Mundt. Boston: Little, Brown and Co.
Almond, Gabriel; Cole, Taylor; and Macridis, Roy C. 1955. 'A Suggested
  Research Strategy in Western European Government and Politics.'
  American Political Science Review 49 (December):1042–9
Almond, Gabriel, and Coleman, James S. 1960. *The Politics of the Developing
  Areas*. Princeton, NJ: Princeton University Press
Arendt, Hannah. [1951] 1958. *The Origins of Totalitarianism*. Cleveland:
  World Publishing Co., A Meridian Book. Originally published in New York:
  Harcourt, Brace, and Co.
Avineri, Shlomo. 1972. *Hegel's Theory of the Modern State*. Cambridge,
  England: Cambridge University Press
Barry, Brian. 1970. *Sociologists, Economists, and Democracy*. London:
  Collier-Macmillan
Bauer, Raymond A., and Bauer, Alice H. 1960. 'America, "Mass Society" and
  Mass Media.' *Journal of Social Issues* 16, 2:3–66
Bell, Daniel, ed., [1955] 1963. *The Radical Right*. New York: Doubleday,
  Anchor Books. Originally published as *The New American right*, New York:
  Criterion Books
Bellah, Robert. 1967. 'Civil Religion in America.' *Daedalus* 96, 1 (Winter): 1–21

Bendix, Reinhard. [1964] 1977. *Nation Building and Citizenship*. Berkeley: University of California Press. Originally published in New York: John Wiley and Sons, Ltd

Bendix, Reinhard, ed. 1968. *State and Society*. Boston: Little, Brown and Company

Berelson, Bernard: Lazarsfeld, Paul F.: and McPhee, William N. [1954] 1968. *Voting: A Study of Opinion Formation in a Presidential Campaign*. Chicago: University of Chicago Press. Sixth impression 1968

Berelson, Bernard. 1956. 'The Study of Public Opinion.' In White (ed.) 1956, 219–318

Bierstedt, Robert. 1981. *American Sociological Theory: A Critical History*. New York: Academic Press

Binder, Leonard, et al., contributors. 1971. *Crises and Sequences in Political Development*. Princeton, NJ: Princeton University Press

Black, Max, ed. 1961. *The Social Theories of Talcott Parsons: A Critical Examination*. Englewood Cliffs, NJ: Prentice-Hall

Black, Max. 1961a. 'Some Questions about Parsons' Theories.' In Black (1961):268–88.

Block, Fred. 1977. 'The Ruling Class Does Not Rule: Notes on a Marxist Theory of the State.' *Socialist Revolution* 33 (May–June):6–28

Bottomore, Tom. [1969] 1975. 'Out of this World: The Sociological Theory of Talcott Parsons.' *New York Review of Books* XIII, 8 (6 November 1969). Reprinted in Bottomore, *Sociology as Social Criticism*. London: George Allen and Unwin, 29–43

Bourricauld, Francois. [1977] 1981. *The Sociology of Talcott Parsons*. Chicago: The University of Chicago Press. Originally published as *L'Individualisme Institutionel* by Presses Universitaires de France (trans. A. Goldhammer)

Braibanti, Ralph. 1969. *Political and Administrative Development*. Durham, NC: Duke University Press

Brinton, Crane. 1939. 'What's the Matter with Sociology.' *Saturday Review of Literature*, 6 May, 1–4 and 14

– 1939a. Letter to Talcott Parsons, 19 July, PP, CRP 1923–40

Burger, Thomas. 1977. 'Talcott Parsons, the Problem of Order, and the Program of Analytic Sociology.' *American Journal of Sociology* 83:320–54

Bush, Vannevar. 1945. *Science, the Endless Frontier*. Washington, DC: U.S. Government Printing Office

Butterfield, Herbert. 1931. *The Whig Interpretation of History*. Harmondsworth: Penguin

Camic, Charles. 1979. 'The Utilitarians Revisited.' *American Journal of Sociology* 85 (November):516–50

Carney, Frederick. 1965. Introduction to *The Politics of Johannes Althusius*. Translated by Carney, preface by Carl J. Friedrich. London: Eyre and Spottiswoode

Cartwright, Dorwin. 1947. 'Social Psychology in the United States during the Second World War.' *Human Relations* 1 (November):333–52

Chase, Stuart. [1948] 1956. *The Proper Study of Mankind*. New York: Harper and Row. Second revised edition

Cohen, Jere; Hazelrigg, Lawrence E.; and Pope, Whitney. 1975. 'De-Parsonizing Weber: A Critique of Parsons's Interpretation of Weber's Sociology.' *American Sociological Review* 40 (April):229–41

Cohen, Steven R. 1983. 'From Industrial Democracy to Professional Adjustment: The Development of Industrial Democracy in the United States, 1900–1955.' *Theory and Society* 12, 1:47–67

Collins, Randall. 1968. 'A Comparative Approach to Political Sociology.' In *State and Society*, in Bendix 1980, 42–67

Creelan, Paul G. 1978. 'Social Theory as Confession: Parsonsian Sociology and the Symbolism of Evil.' In *Structure, Consciousness, and History*, edited by Richard Harvey Brown and Stanford M. Lyman. Cambridge: Cambridge University Press, 173–96

Dahl, Robert. 1961. 'The Behavioral Approach in Political Science: Epitaph for a Monument to a Successful Protest.' *American Political Science Review* 55 (December):763–72

– 1963. *Modern Political Analysis*. Englewood Cliffs, NJ: Prentice-Hall

Dahrendorf, Ralf. 1958. 'Out of Utopia: Towards a Reorientation of Sociological Analysis.' *American Journal of Sociology* 64 (September):115–27

Dawe, Alan. 1971. 'Extended Review of Robert W. Friedrichs, *A Sociology of Sociology*.' *Sociological Review* 19 (February):140–7

Dittberner, Job L. 1979. *The End of Ideology and American Social Thought: 1930–1960*. UMI Research Press

Easton, David. 1951. 'The Decline of Modern Political Theory.' *The Journal of Politics* 13 (February):36–58

– 1953. *The Political System*. New York: Alfred A. Knopf

– 1969. 'The New Revolution in Political Science.' *American Political Science Review* 63, 4:1051–61

Eckberg, Douglas Lee, and Hill, Lester, Jr. 1980. 'The Paradigm Concept and Sociology: A Critical Review.' In Gutting 1980, 117–36

Ford Foundation. 1949. *Report of the Study for the Ford Foundation on Policy and Program*. Detroit: Ford Foundation

– 1952. *Annual Report*. Detroit: Ford Foundation

– 1953. *Annual Report*. Detroit: Ford Foundation

Foss, Daniel. 1963. 'The World of Talcott Parsons.' In *Sociology on Trial*, edited by Maurice Stein and Arthur Vidich. Englewood Cliffs, NJ: Prentice-Hall, 96–126

Freeland, Richard M. 1974. *The Truman Doctrine and the Origins of McCarthyism*. New York: Schocken

Friedrich, Carl. 1947. 'Political Science in the United States in Wartime.' *American Political Science Review* 41 (October):978–89

Friedrichs, Robert W. [1970] 1972. *Sociology of Sociology*. New York: Free Press, paperback edition. Republished

Garceau, Oliver. 1951. 'Research in the Political Process.' *American Political Science Review* 45 (March):69–85

Gerstein, Dean. 1982. 'The Coming Renaissance.' *Perspectives.* The American Sociological Association, The Theory Section Newsletter, 5 (1).

Giddens, Anthony, ed. 1974. *Positivism and Sociology* (with an introduction by Giddens). London: Heinemann Educational Books, Ltd

Giddens, Anthony. 1976. *New Rules of Sociological Method: A Positive Critique of Interpretive Sociologies.* London: Hutchinson and Co. Ltd

– 1976a. 'Classical Social Theory and the Origins of Modern Sociology.' *American Journal of Sociology* 81, 4:703–29

Gouldner, Alvin. 1971. *The Coming Crisis in Western Sociology.* London: Heinemann. Originally published in New York: Basic Books 1970

Greenberg, Daniel S. 1967. *The Politics of Pure Science.* New York: New American Library, a Plume Book

Griffith, Ernest G. 1948. *Research in Political Science.* Chapel Hill: University of North Carolina Press

Griffith, Robert 1970. *The Politics of Fear.* Lexington: University Press of Kentucky

Griffith, Robert, and Theoharis, Athan, eds. 1974. *The Specter: Original Essays on the Cold War and the Origins of McCarthyism.* New York: New Viewpoints, a Division of Franklin Watts, Inc.

Gutting, Gary, ed. 1980. *Paradigms and Revolutions: Applications and Appraisals of Thomas Kuhn's Philosophy of Science.* Notre Dame: University of Notre Dame Press

Hacker, Andrew. 1961. 'Sociology and Ideology.' In Black 1961, 289–310

Hallowell, John. 1944. 'Politics and Ethics.' *American Political Science Review* 38, 639–55

Hamilton, Peter. 1983. *Talcott Parsons.* Chichester and London: Ellis Horwood Ltd and Tavistock Publications Ltd

Hawley, Claude, and Dexter, Lewis A. 1952. 'Recent Political Science Research in American Universities.' *American Political Science Review* 46 (June):470–85

Heard, Alexander. 1949. 'Research on Political Behavior: Report of a Conference.' SSRC *Items* 3 (December):41–3

Henderson, L.J. 1939. Letter to Talcott Parsons, 17 July, PP, CRP 1923–40

Herring, Pendleton. 1950. 'Basic Social Science Development: The Role of the Council in a New Program of Support.' SSRC *Items* 4 (September):25–6

– 1953. 'On the Study of Government.' *American Political Science Review* 47 (December):961–74

Holt, Robert, and Turner, John. 1975. 'Crises and Sequences in Collective Theory Development.' *American Political Science Review* 69:979–94

Hook, Sydney. 1950. 'The Berlin Congress for Cultural Freedom.' *Partisan Review* 17:715–22

Horowitz, Irving. [1963] 1968. 'Another View from Our Left.' *New Politics* 2, no. 2 (Winter):77–88. (1963) In Waxman 1968, 166–81

Horowitz, Irving L., ed. 1967. *The Rise and Fall of Project Camelot: Studies in the Relationship between Social Science and Practical Politics.* Cambridge, Mass.: MIT Press

Huntington, Samuel P. 1968. *Political Order in Changing Societies.* New Haven, Conn.: Yale University Press

– 1968a. *Military Intervention, Political Involvement and the Unlessons of Vietnam.* Chicago: Adlai Stevenson Institute of International Affairs

– 1971. 'The Change to Change.' *Comparative Politics* 3 (April):283–322

– 1976. 'The Democratic Distemper.' In *The American Commonwealth – 1976*, edited by Nathan Glazer and Irving Kristol. New York: Basic Books, 9–38

Jones, Robert Alun. 1974. 'Durkheim's Response to Spencer: An Essay Toward Historicism in the Historiography of Sociology.' *Sociological Quarterly* 15, 3:341–58

– 1977. 'On Understanding a Sociological Classic.' *American Journal of Sociology* 83, 2:279–319

– 1983. 'New History of Sociology.' *Annual Review of Sociology*, vol. 9. Edited by Ralph H. Turner. Palo Alto: Annual Reviews Inc.

Kahin, George McT.; Pauker, Guy J.; and Pye, Lucian W. 1955. 'Comparative Politics of Non-Western Countries.' *American Political Science Review* 49 (December): 1022–41

Kolakowski, Leszek. [1968] 1972. *Positivist Philosophy: From Hume to the Vienna Circle.* Harmondsworth, UK: Penguin Books. Originally published in New York: Doubleday and Co. Inc.

Kuhn, Thomas. [1962] 1970. In *The Structure of Scientific Revolutions.* Chicago: University of Chicago Press. Second edition, enlarged

– 1970a. 'Reflections on My Critics.' In Lakatos and Musgrave (eds), 1970, 231–78

– 1974. 'Second Thoughts on Paradigms.' *The Structure of Scientific Theories*, edited by Frederick Suppe. Urbana: University of Illinois Press, 459–82

Kuklick, Henrika. 1980. 'Restructuring the Past: Toward an Appreciation of the Social Context of Social Science.' *Sociological Quarterly* 21:5–21

Lakatos, Imre, and Alan Musgrave, eds. 1970. *Criticism and the Growth of Knowledge.* Cambridge, England: Cambridge University Press

Lasch, Christopher. 1969. *The Agony of the American Left.* New York: Alfred A. Knopf

Lasswell, Harold. [1936] 1958. *Politics: Who Gets What, When, How.* Cleveland: World Publishing Company, Meridian edition. Originally published in New York: McGraw-Hill

Lazarsfeld, Paul F.; Berelson, Bernard; and Gaudet, Hazel. [1944] 1968. *The People's Choice: How the Voter Makes Up His Mind in a Presidential Campaign.* New York: Columbia University Press. Republished, paperback edition. Originally published in New York: Duell, Sloan, and Pierce

Lazarsfeld, Paul F., and Stanton, Frank N., eds. 1949. *Communications Research 1948–49.* New York: Harper

Leiserson, Avery. 1951. 'Systematic Research in Political Behavior: A Preliminary Report.' SSRC *Items* 5 (September):29–32

Lerner, Daniel, and Lasswell, Harold, eds. 1951. *The Policy Sciences: Recent Developments in Scope and Method.* Palo Alto, Cal.: Stanford University Press

Lipset, Seymour M. [1950] 1971. *Agrarian Socialism: The Cooperative Commonwealth Federation in Saskatchewan.* Berkeley: University of California Press. Republished, paperback edition

– 1952. 'Democracy in Private Government: A Case Study of the International Typographical Union.' *British Journal of Sociology* 3 (March):47–63

– 1955. 'The Radical Right: A Problem for American Democracy.' *British Journal of Sociology* 6 (June):172–209

– [1955a] 1963. 'The Sources of the Radical Right.' In Bell (ed.) [1955] 1963, 307–71

– 1955b. 'The State of Democratic Politics.' *The Canadian Forum* 35:170–1

– 1956. 'Political Sociology, 1945–55.' In *Sociology in the United States of America*, edited by Hans Zetterberg. Paris: UNESCO, 43–55

– [1959a] 1965. 'Political Sociology.' In *Sociology Today* I, edited by Robert K. Merton, et al. New York: Harper and Row. 81–114. Originally published in one volume in New York: Basic Books

– [1960] 1963. *Political Man.* Garden City, NY: Doubleday. Republished, Anchor Books edition

– 1961. 'Reply [to Scheglof and Kruytbosch].' *Berkeley Journal of Sociology* 6 (1).

– [1962] 1968. 'My View from Our Left.' In Waxman (ed.) 1968, 152–65

– [1963] 1967. *The First New Nation.* New York: Doubleday Anchor Books. Originally published in New York: Basic Books

– 1964. 'Sociology and Political Science: A Bibliographical Note.' *American Journal of Sociology* 49 (October):730–4

– 1964a. 'The Biography of a Research Project: Union Democracy.' In *Sociologists at Work: Essays on the Craft of Social Research*, edited by Phillip E. Hammond. New York: Basic Books, 96–120

– 1964b. 'The United States – The First New Nation.' In *Transactions of the Fifth World Congress of Sociology*, vol. III. International Sociological Association, 307–61

– 1967a. 'The Changing Class Structure and Contemporary European Politics.' In *A New Europe*, edited by Stephen R. Graubard. Boston: Beacon Press, 337–69

– 1969. 'Socialism and Sociology.' In *Sociological Self-Images: A Collective Portrait*, edited by Irving L. Horowitz. Beverly Hills: Sage, 143–75

Lipset, Seymour M., ed. 1967. *Student Politics.* New York: Basic Books

Lipset, Seymour M., with Martin Trow and James Coleman. 1956. *Union Democracy.* New York: Doubleday, Anchor Books

Lipset, Seymour M., and Bendix, Reinhard. [1957] 1966. 'Political Sociology.'

Current Sociology VI, 2:79–98. Reprinted as 'The Field of Political Sociology.' In *Political Sociology*, edited by Lewis A. Coser. New York: Harper and Row, Harper Torchbooks

Lipset, Seymour M., and Wolin, Sheldon, eds. 1965. *The Berkeley Student Revolt: Facts and Interpretations*. Garden City, NY: Doubleday

Lipset, Seymour M. and Rokkan, Stein. 1968. Forward to Stammer (ed.) 1968

Lipset, Seymour M., and Altbach, Philip G., eds. 1969. *Students in Revolt*. Boston: Houghton Mifflin

Lipset, Seymour M., and Schaflander, Gerald M. 1971. *Passion and Politics: Student Activism in America*. Boston: Little, Brown and Company

Loewenstein, Karl. 1944. 'Report on the Research Panel on Comparative Government.' *American Political Science Review* 28:540–8

Loubser, Jan J. 1976. General introduction to *Explorations in General Theory in Social Science: Essays in Honor of Talcott Parsons*, edited by Jan. J. Loubser; Rainer C. Baum; Andrew Effrat; and Victor Lidz. 2 vols. New York: Free Press, 1–23

Lyons, Gene M. 1969. *The Uneasy Partnership: Social Science and the Federal Government in the Twentieth Century*. New York: Russell Sage

Macdonald, Dwight. 1955. 'No Miracle in Milan.' *Encounter*, vol. 5, no. 6 (December):68–74

– 1956. *The Ford Foundation: The Men and the Millions*. New York: Reynal

Mannheim, Karl. [1936] 1960. *Ideology and Utopia*. London: Routledge and Kegan Paul. Republished, Routledge paperback

Massachusetts Institute of Technology, Center for International Affairs. 1969. *The Role of Popular Participation in Development: Report of a Conference on the Implementation of the Foreign Assistance Act, June 24 to August 2, 1968*. Report no. 17. Cambridge, Mass.: MIT Press

Masterman, Margaret. 1970. 'The Nature of a Paradigm.' In Lakatos and Musgrave (eds) 1970, 59–89

Mayo, Elton. [1933] 1960. *The Human Problems of an Industrial Civilization*. New York: Viking Press, Compass Books edition. Originally published in New York: Macmillan Press

Menzies, Ken. 1975. *Talcott Parsons and the Social Image of Man*. London: Routledge and Kegan Paul

Merriam, Charles. [1925] 1970. *New Aspect of Politics*. Chicago: University of Chicago Press. Republished.

Merton, Robert K. [1949] 1968. *Social Theory and Social Structure*. New York: Free Press. Republished, enlarged edition

Merton, Robert K., and Lazarsfeld, Paul F., eds. 1950. *Continuities in Social Research: Studies in the Scope and Method of 'The American Soldier.'* Glencoe, Ill.: Free Press

Michels, Robert. [1915] 1968. *Political Parties: A Sociological Study of the Oligarchical Tendencies of Modern Democracy*. Introduction by Seymour Martin Lipset. Second Free Press, paperback edition. Originally published in New York: Hearst's International Library

Miller, James G. 1955. 'Toward a General Theory for the Behavioral Sciences.' *American Psychologist* 10 (September):513–31

Miller, Roberta B. 1982. 'The Social Sciences and the Politics of Science: The 1940's.' *American Sociologist* 17:205–9

Mills, C. Wright. [1956] 1959. *The Power Elite.* New York: Oxford University Press. Republished, paperback edition

Moore, Barrington, Jr. [1958] 1968. *Political Power and Social Theory.* New York: Harper Torchbooks. Originally published in Cambridge, Mass.: Harvard University Press.

– 1966. *The Social Origins of Dictatorship and Democracy: Lord and Peasant in the Making of the Modern World.* Boston: Beacon Press

Muench, Richard. 1981. 'Talcott Parsons and the Theory of Action, I: The Structure of the Kantian Core.' *American Journal of Sociology* 86, 4:709–39

– 1982. 'Talcott Parsons and the Theory of Action, II: The Continuity of the Development.' *American Journal of Sociology* 87, 4:771–821

O'Brien, Donal Cruise. 1972. 'Modernization, Order, and the Erosion of a Democratic Ideal.' *Journal of Development Studies* 8 (July):351–73

Packenham, Robert. 1973. *Liberal America and the Third World.* Princeton, NJ: Princeton University Press

Peck, Sidney M. 1962. 'Ideology and "Political Sociology": The Conservative Bias of Lipset's "Political Man." ' *American Catholic Sociology Review* 23 (Summer):128–55

Peters, Richard [1956] 1967. *Hobbes.* Harmondsworth, UK: Peregrine Books. Originally published as a Pelican Book

Piven, Frances Fox, and Cloward, Richard A. 1977. *Poor Peoples' Movements: Why They Succeed, Why They Fail.* New York: Pantheon Books

Pollak, Michael. 1979. 'Paul F. Lazarsfeld: Fondateur d'une Multi-nationale Scientifique.' *Actes de la Recherche en Sciences Sociales* (Paris): 45–59

Pope, Whitney. 1973. 'Classic on Classic: Parsons' Interpretation of Durkheim.' *American Sociological Review* 38 (August):399–415

Pope, Whitney; Cohen, Jere; and Hazelrigg, L.E. 1975. 'On the Divergence of Weber and Durkheim: A Critique of Parsons's Convergence Thesis.' *American Sociological Review* 40 (August):417–27

Pye, Lucian. 1956. *Guerilla Communism in Malaya: Its Social and Political Meaning.* Princeton, NJ: Princeton University Press

– 1966. 'Description, Analysis and Sensitivity to Change.' In *Political Science and Public Policy*, edited by Austin Ranney. Chicago: Markham, 239–61

– 1968. 'Political Cuture.' IESS 12, 218–24

– 1971. Forward to L. Binder et al. 1971

– 1972. 'Culture and Political Science.' *Science Quarterly* 52 (September):285–96

Pye, Lucian, and Verba, Sydney, eds. 1965. *Political Culture and Political Development.* Princeton, NJ: Princeton University Press

Pye, Lucian, and Ryland, Kay K. 1971. *Committee on Comparative Politics: A Report on the Activities of the Committee, 1954–1970.* New York: SSRC

Reeves, Thomas C. 1969. *Freedom and the Foundations: The Fund for the Republic in the Era of McCarthyism.* New York: Alfred Knopf

Riesman, David. 1956. 'Observations on the "Older" and the "Newer" Social Sciences.' In White (ed.) 1956, 319–39

Roach, Jack L. 1970. 'The Radical Sociology Movement: A Short History and Commentary.' *American Sociologist* 5 (August): 224–33

Robertson, Roland. 1982. 'Parsons on the Evolutionary Significance of American Religion.' *Sociological Analysis* 43, 4:307–25

Roethlisberger, F.J. and Dickson, William J. [1939] 1961. *Management and the Worker.* Cambridge, Mass.: Harvard University Press

Rogin, Michael. 1967. *The Intellectuals and McCarthy: The Radical Specter.* Cambridge, Mass.: MIT Press

Rokkan, Stein. 1970. 'Introduction: International Cooperation in Political Sociology.' In Allardt and Rokkan (eds) 1970

Romalis, Coleman. 1972. 'A Man of His Time and Place: A Selective Appraisal of Seymour M. Lipset's Comparative Sociology.' *Sociological Inquiry* 42 (3–4):211–31

Rosenberg, Bernard, and White, David Manning, eds. [1957] 1964. *Mass Culture: The Popular Arts in America.* New York: Free Press. Republished, paperback edition

Rustow, Dankwart A. 1967. *A World of Nations.* Washington: The Brookings Institution

Sartori, Giovanni. 1968. 'Political Development and Political Engineering.' *Public Policy* 17. Cambridge: Harvard University Press, 261–98

– 1969. 'From the Sociology of Politics to Political Sociology.' In *Politics and Social Science*, edited by Seymour M. Lipset. New York: Oxford University Press, 65–100

Scheglof, E.A., and Kruytbosch, C. 1961. 'Some Comments on "Working-Class Authoritarianism."' *Berkeley Journal of Sociology* 6, 1:99–108

Schlesinger, Arthur M., Jr. [1949] 1962. *The Vital Center.* Boston: Houghton Mifflin.

Schutz, Alfred. [1940] 1978. Letter to Talcott Parsons, 15 November. In *The Theory of Social Action: The Correspondence of Alfred Schutz and Talcott Parsons*, edited by Richard Grathof. Bloomington: Indiana University Press

Scott, Frank. 1955. Letter to *The Canadian Forum* 35 (October):160–1

Scott, John F. 1962. 'The Impossible Theory of Action: Some Questions on Parsons' Prewar Classification of Action Theories.' *Berkeley Journal of Sociology* 7 (Spring):51–62

– 1963. 'The Changing Foundations of the Parsonian Action Schema.' *American Sociological Review* 28 (October):716–35

Senn, Peter R. 1966. 'What is Behavioral Science – Notes Toward a History.' *Journal of the History of the Behavioral Sciences* 2 (April):107–14

Shils, Edward. 1947. 'The Present State of American Sociology.' In *Pilot Papers*, London (June):8–37
– 1955. 'The End of Ideology?' *Encounter*, vol. 5, no. 4 (November):52–8
Skocpol, Theda. 1979. *States and Social Revolutions*. New York: Cambridge University Press
Somit, Albert, and Tanenhaus, Joseph. [1967] 1982. *The Development of American Political Science: From Burgess to Behavioralism*. New York: Irvington Publishers. Originally published in Boston: Allyn and Bacon, Inc.
Stammer, Otto, ed. 1968. *Party Systems, Party Organizations, and the Politics of the New Masses: Contributions to the Third International Conference on Comparative Political Sociology, Berlin 15–20 January, 1968*. Committee on Political Sociology of the International Sociological Association. Berlin: Institute for Political Science at the Free University of Berlin
Stocking, George. 1965. 'On the Limits of "Presentism" and "Historicism" in the Historiography of the Behavioral Sciences.' *Journal of the History of the Behavioral Sciences* 1:211–17
Stouffer, Samuel, and associates. 1949. *The American Soldier*. 4 vols. Princeton, NJ: Princeton University Press
Surkin, Marvin, and Wolfe, Alan. 1970. *Sense and Nonsense in Politics: An End to Political Science*. New York: Basic Books
Teodori, Massimo, ed. 1970. *The New Left: A Documentary History*. London: Jonathan Cape
Theoharis, Athan. 1971. *The Seeds of Repression*. Chicago: Quadrangle Books
Tilly, Charles, ed. 1975. *The Formation of National States in Western Europe*. Princeton: Princeton University Press
Truman, David. 1965. 'Disillusion and Regeneration: The Quest for a Discipline.' *American Political Science Review* 59 (December):865–73
Turner, Jonathan. 1982. *The Structure of Sociological Theory*. 3rd edition. Homewood, Illinois: The Dorsey Press
Urry, John. 1973. 'Thomas Kuhn as a Sociologist of Knowledge.' *British Journal of Sociology* 24 (December):462–74
U.S. Congress. House. 1953. *Tax Exempt Foundations*. Hearings before the select (Cox) committee to investigate tax-exempt foundations. House of Representatives, on H.R. 516, 82d Cong., 2nd sess.
– 1954. *Tax Exempt Foundations*. Report of the special (Reece) committee to investigate tax-exempt foundations and comparable organizations. House of Representatives on H.R. 217, 83rd Cong., 2nd sess.
– 1967. *Rural Development in Asia*. Hearings before the subcommittee on Asia and Pacific affairs. 90th Cong., 1st sess.
U.S. Congress. Senate. 1945. *Hearings on Science Legislation*, before a subcommittee of the committee on military affairs. Senate on S. 1297 and related bills. 79th Cong., 1st sess.
– 1946. *The Congressional Record*, 3 July
Verba, Sidney. 1967. 'Some Dilemmas in Comparative Research.' *World Politics* 20 (October):111–27

– 1971. 'Sequences and Development.' In Binder (ed.) 1971, 283–316

Waxman, Chaim, ed. 1968. *The End of Ideology*. New York: Simon and Schuster; Clarion Edition 1969.

Wearne, Bruce. 1981. 'Talcott Parsons's Appraisal and Critique of Alfred Marshall.' *Social Research* 48, 4:816–51

– 1983. 'Parsons' Theory as a Secularized Post-Calvinist Humanism: A Bibliographical Essay.' SAANZ Conference, Melbourne CAE, August

White, Leonard, ed. 1956. *The State of the Social Sciences*. Chicago: University of Chicago Press

Whyte, William F. 1943. 'A Challenge to Political Scientists.' *American Political Science Review* 37 (August):692–7

Wolin, Sheldon. [1968] 1980. 'Paradigms and Political Theories.' In *Politics and Experience*, edited by P. King and B.C. Parekh. Cambridge: Cambridge University Press, 125–68. Reprinted Gutting (ed.) 1980, 160–91

Index